THE DANEBURY ENVIRONS PROGRAMME

THE PREHISTORY OF A WESSEX LANDSCAPE

Volume 2 – Part 3

Suddern Farm, Middle Wallop, Hants, 1991 and 1996

by
Barry Cunliffe and Cynthia Poole

with contributions from

Ian Brooks, Lisa Brown, Gill Campbell, Emma Durham,
Helena Hamerow, Julie Hamilton, Martin Henig, Bari Hooper,
Cathy King, Andy Payne and David Williams

and line illustrations by
Simon Pressey and Alison Wilkins

English Heritage
and
Oxford University Committee for Archaeology
Monograph No. 49
2000

Published by the
Institute of Archaeology
36 Beaumont Street
Oxford

ISBN 0-947816-49-6

The publication of this volume was made possible by a grant from English Heritage

Designed and produced by Production Line
Printed in Great Britain by Bookcraft (Bath) Ltd

Contents

Contents of Fiche

List of Figures

List of Plates

1 Introduction

The site

The ditched enclosure at Suddern Farm was discovered from the air in 1976 (NMR 925/365 and 967/320) and was first published in the survey of the Danebury region (Palmer 1984, 44 and 113). The settlement is sited on a low spur of chalk at about 85 m OD. The relief hereabouts is slight and offers little defensive advantage (Fig. 3.1).

The aerial photographs taken in 1976 show a double or treble ditched enclosure, roughly circular in plan, measuring *c*.210 m in diameter and enclosing an area of 2.2 ha (Fig. 3.3). For most of the circuit three concentric features can be traced. Two are evidently substantial ditches 4–5 m wide at the top and roughly 10 m apart. Between them a narrower feature is discernible which, on the evidence then available, was interpreted as a wide palisade trench. An entrance was apparent at the north-west corner with the possibility of another in the southern side. The interior of the enclosure appeared to be scattered with pits and other features.

In its broader context the Suddern Farm enclosure is only one element in an ancient landscape dominated by extensive systems of linear ditches (Fig. 3.2). Two have a potential relationship with the settlement. One, which swings down from Suddern Hill, runs towards the north-west side of the enclosure but its course could not be fully traced on the photographs. The other, in plan a triple ditch system,

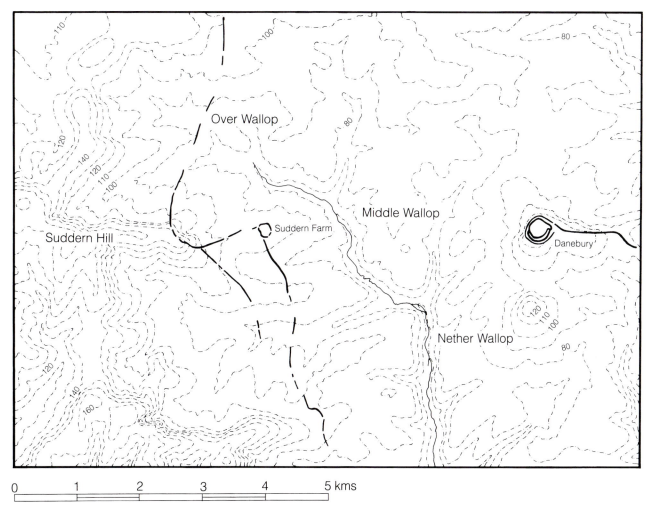

Fig. 3.1 The location of Suddern Farm

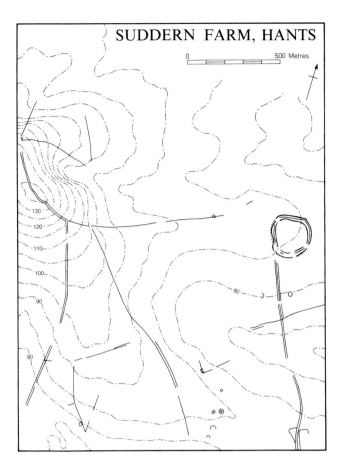

SUDDERN FARM, HANTS

0   500 Metres

runs southwards from the south-western corner and can be traced, albeit discontinuously, for many kilometres associated at intervals with settlements of Iron Age appearance.

The particular interest of the site is twofold:

- it represents a type of medium-sized, strongly defended enclosure of which several have been recognized throughout Wessex. They are thought to be of Late Iron Age date (Cunliffe 1974, fig. 7.6) but little is known about them or their position in the settlement hierarchy;
- it appears to lie at a focal point on a complex system of linear boundary ditches of a kind generally thought to have been first laid out in the Late Bronze Age.

Thus, based on the air photographic evidence, one possible interpretation of the site was that it may have originated as a palisaded or ditched enclosure contemporary with the ditch system in the Late Bronze Age and remained a focal location into the Late Iron Age. Its substantial enclosure ditches, probably of Late Iron Age date, suggested that by then it may have acquired a high status. Several similar sites are known from elsewhere in Wessex (Cunliffe 1990).

Fig. 3.2 (left) Features visible in the immediate environment of Suddern Farm

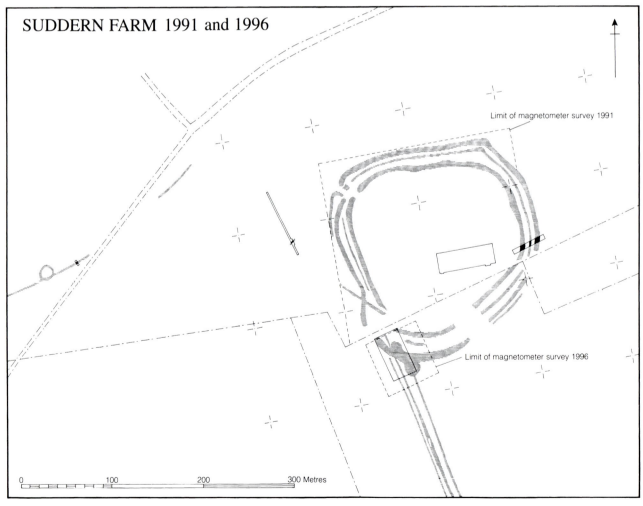

SUDDERN FARM 1991 and 1996

Limit of magnetometer survey 1991

Limit of magnetometer survey 1996

0   100   200   300 Metres

Fig. 3.3

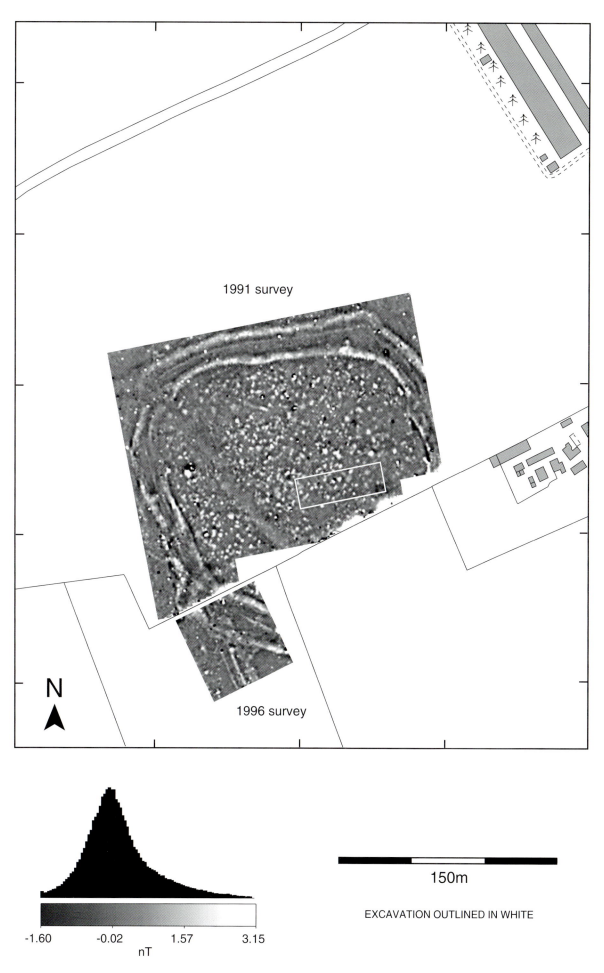

1991 survey

1996 survey

N

-1.60   -0.02   1.57   3.15
nT

150m

EXCAVATION OUTLINED IN WHITE

Fig. 3.4 Greyscale plot of survey on location plan

The history of excavation

Suddern Farm was chosen as the focus for the third season of excavations in the Danebury Environs Programme in 1991 at which time efforts were concentrated on sampling the main enclosure. In the eighth year of the programme, 1996, the site was revisited and the relationships of the triple linear ditches to the main enclosure ditches were examined.

Pre-excavation surveys (Figs. 3.3 and 3.4)

The site of Suddern Farm is presently divided unevenly by a field boundary of some antiquity. The land to the north of the boundary, owned by Messrs. William and Graham Carr of Suddern Farm Ltd., was the subject of investigation in 1991 while that to the south of the boundary, farmed by Mr. Gordon Barnard, was examined in 1996. Separate pre-excavation surveys were undertaken of the two fields.

We are particularly grateful to the farmers for the willingness with which they allowed the archaeological work to proceed and their practical help and support throughout the programme.

In preparation for the field season of 1991 a 100 m grid was established over the site and a magnetometer survey of the northern three-quarters of the enclosed area was carried out by the Ancient Monuments Laboratory of English Heritage. The results provided a remarkably detailed picture (Fig. 3.4) adding much to the air photographic evidence and allowing a new plan combining both to be offered (Fig. 3.5). A detailed commentary on the magnetometer survey is given below, pp. 203–5. As a result it is now clear that the enclosing ditches enjoyed a complex history. The two major ditches seen on the air photographs stand out as dominant features. The 'middle' palisade or ditch is also evident between them for much of the circuit but details apparent along the west side indicate something of the greater complexities of the site. Here an 'outermost' ditch can be traced which appears to be consumed by the massive outer ditch at

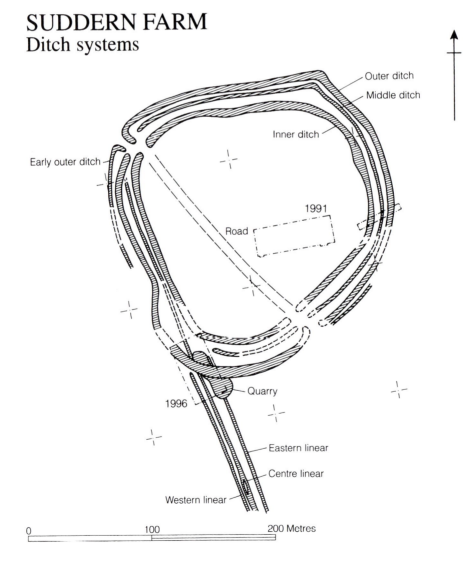

SUDDERN FARM
Ditch systems

Fig. 3.5

the south-western side. At the north-western entrance this outermost ditch turns into the enclosure to form one side of a corridor approach. The inturn of its northern counterpart can be seen but it shows signs of having been partly recut by the massive outer ditch. The south-eastern side of the enclosure also seems, from the air photographs, to have been delimited by four ditches.

The simplest explanation of these traces would be to suppose that two main phases were represented, the earlier comprising the outermost and middle ditches, the later, the more substantial outer and inner ditches. The true situation could, however, have been far more complex with frequent recuttings and replacements.

The magnetometer survey also confirmed that the interior was densely packed with pits and that a wide roadway ran across the site to the north-west entrance.

Random field-walking carried out at the time of the survey, when a young crop of wheat was already growing, produced a few sherds of pottery spanning the Middle Iron Age to Roman period, together with quantities of burnt flints.

On the basis of this survey the 1991 excavation was planned and carried out. In 1996 the team from the Ancient Monuments Laboratory returned to the site and surveyed an area of 60 m by 60 m immediately south of the field boundary to define the relationship of the triple linear ditch system to the ditches of the enclosure. The survey identified the main structural elements but showed that a complex of additional features existed in the area partially obscuring the relationships of the ditches (below, pp. 203–5).

Research designs

The principal questions raised by the site in the context of the Danebury Environs Project were:

- What was the date of the earliest enclosure, did it relate to the linear ditch system and what was the nature of the contemporary occupation if any?
- What were the date and nature of the double-ditched enclosure. What are the characteristics of this type of site and the nature of the internal occupation?
- Was the site continuously occupied and if so over what period?
- What can be deduced of the economic and social systems focusing on the enclosure and how did they change with time?
- What was the environmental setting of the site?

Pl. 3.1 General view of the 1991 excavation

Pl. 3.2 General view of the enclosure ditches excavated in 1991

– How well preserved are the buried features and to what extent is the present agricultural regime damaging them?

To approach these questions it was decided, in 1991, to excavate two separate areas. Area 1, measuring 5 by 38 m, was set out to straddle the defensive ditches where they appeared, from the survey, to be at their most typical (Pl. 3.2). Area 2, some 20 m by 60 m, was placed in the interior of the enclosure, oriented on the site grid for ease of recording, and placed so as to include part of a slight rise observable in the modern field surface (Pl. 3.1).

The ploughsoil was stripped mechanically, under archaeological supervision. Thereafter excavation was by hand.

The original intention had been to take wide sections through the ditches and this was done. Within the interior it was envisaged that the excavation would be selective: all small features, such as post-holes and gullies, were to be excavated but pits would be sampled, using a random number system to choose the preferred percentage for excavation. In the event the considerable variety of form represented by these larger features called for total excavation, and the favourable digging conditions allowed this to be accomplished within the scheduled time.

A sampling strategy was adopted for flotation. Ten per cent of the features were chosen on a random number basis and samples of all layers within them were taken. Molluscan samples were selected by Dr. John Evans after site inspection.

The linear ditch approaching the site from the west was tested in a single trial trench just west of the modern track. Between the track and the enclosure another line of ditch which appeared on the air photographs was also examined having been identified in a machine-dug trench 73 m long. No other features were encountered.

In 1996 the principal aim of the work was to define the relationships of the enclosure ditches to the triple linear ditches. The complexity of the detail revealed by the magnetometer survey suggested that the most efficient way to proceed was to strip the entire area of the intersections of topsoil and ploughsoil and to begin by examining, in plan, the intercutting of individual features. To include all the significant relationships an area of 45 by 24 m was stripped mechanically and cleared by hand to expose the natural chalk and the tops of features and stratified layers (Pl. 3.8). The spoil was scanned with a metal detector to recover unstratified metallic objects.

Many relationships were visible at this stage but to clarify points and to obtain more detailed structural information and dating evidence thirteen cuttings were made. The overall strategy from the outset was one of minimum intervention. In general this was adhered to but two exceptions were made: a discrete layer of Roman occupation material was removed in total to clarify underlying structural features (F409 layers 1 and 2); and in the south-east corner of the area a trial cutting, dug to test the existence of a linear ditch beneath an area of later quarrying, was extended to provide a larger sample after a number of Iron Age burials were discovered in the quarry fill.

2 The Excavation

Area 1 (1991): the enclosing ditches and related features (Figs. 3.6–3.8)

The Inner, Middle and Outer Ditches

The three boundary features visible on the air photographs and magnetometer survey were identified and sectioned. The inner and outer ditches (F64 and F66) were both massive while the middle feature (F65), which proved to be a ditch and not a palisade trench, was less substantial. Not all were in use at the same time and there are reasons for arguing that the middle ditch was the earliest of the features now surviving.

The *Middle Ditch* varied in profile along the 3.8 m that was totally excavated (Fig. 3.7 and Pl. 3.3). In the northern section it was 2.5 m wide at the top and 1.4 m in depth but it widened out and in the southern section was 3.4 m wide and 1.7 m deep. This variation in profile hints that the ditch may have been cleaned out and recut during its life. In its final form it was allowed to silt naturally until an angle of rest had been achieved. The silt comprised fine chalky rubble derived from the eroding ditch sides intermixed with brownish clayey soil (layers 3 and 2). The surface had stabilized sufficiently to allow a soil to begin to form.

A few sherds of pottery were recovered from the top of the natural silt. The forms were undiagnostic but the sandy fabrics suggest an Early Iron Age date.

Pl. 3.3 Section of the middle enclosure ditch, F65

SUDDERN FARM 1991
Section across defences (Trench 2)

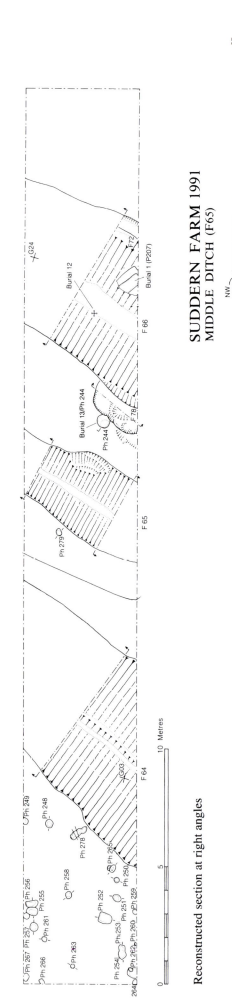

Reconstructed section at right angles

Fig. 3.6 (above)

SUDDERN FARM 1991
MIDDLE DITCH (F65)

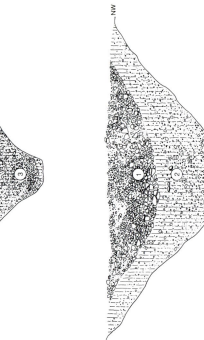

Fig. 3.7 (right) Ditch sections

By the time the silt had formed the ditch was still a recognizable feature. At some subsequent period, however, it was filled to the top with freshly quarried chalk rubble (layer 1).

The *Inner Ditch* measured some 6.3 m wide at the top by 2.75 m deep (Fig. 3.8 and Pl. 3.4). It was dug to a sharp V-shaped profile. There is some evidence of recutting on the eastern side where part of the original profile, sealed by a thin layer of chalky silt (layer 14), is still preserved. The lowest fill of the final recut of the ditch consisted of shattered chalk in a grey silt (layers 6 and 7) which merged up gradually to a less chalky grey silt (layers 10 and 4). Above this, in the upper part of the ditch, were a series of deliberate tips, thrown in from the west, containing a considerable amount of occupation debris especially pottery and animal bone. The lowest of these, layer 5, was most prolific. Above this came a thickness of grey silt with some finely eroded chalk and much occupation debris (layers 2 and 12). In the hollow formed by the surface of this deposit a layer of ash and charcoal had been thrown (layer 11). Then followed tips of chalky silt (layers 3 and 13), a grey ashy silt (layer 9), a deliberate dump of grey silt and charcoal (layer 15), a tip of angular chalk lumps (layer 1) and finally a localized dump of burnt clay (layer 8). That so much occupation rubbish, incorporated in a constantly developing grey silt with a high organic content, flowed and was thrown into the ditch from the west strongly suggests that no bank existed on this side, an observation supported (but not proved) by the scatter of small post-holes which extended right up to the inner ditch lip.

The large amount of pottery found in the ditch fill suggests that the entire process of silting and filling took place from the middle of the first century BC to the middle of the first century AD. The lowest layers (layers 6 and 7) produced sherds the form and fabric of which suggest a mid first century BC date. The occupation accumulation in the upper fill yielded an assemblage of local wares, including copies of Gallo-Belgic platters, together with imported wares comprising a sherd of an Italic amphora, Gallo-Belgic butt and girth beakers and a sherd with red painted decoration probably of north-eastern French origin. Taken together the evidence would indicate that the rubbish was being discarded in the first decades of the first century AD.

The *Outer Ditch* measured 5.7 m wide at the top and 3.1 m deep (Fig. 3.8 and Pl. 3.5). Its profile was steep-sided with a flat bottom nearly a metre wide. The silting profile was entirely natural with chalk shatter in the base becoming more silty as the ditch filled but with interleavings of more chalky material caused by the weathering of the ditch sides. Towards the top of this natural silting, quantities of occupa-tion rubbish, principally pottery and animal bone, had been thrown in (layer 5). Then followed a grey silt rich with occupation rubbish (layer 4) and a rather more grey-brown silt also with pottery and animal bone (layer 2). The final layer (layer 1) was a brown chalky soil.

The pottery from the lowest fill (layers 10 and 9) is of Late Iron Age type. Layer 8 produced an assemblage of the mid first century AD. By the time layer 5 was accumulating Roman pottery of the third century AD was being incorporated.

The development of the system of enclosure is, clearly, a complex process. The simplest interpreta-tion would be to see the Middle Ditch as the earliest, which, after some possible recutting, was allowed to silt naturally before being levelled with chalk. The Inner and Outer Ditches were dug later either together or, more likely, successively the Inner Ditch being the earlier. When however the possibility of recutting is considered in the light of the plan produced by the magnetometer survey a variety of more complex possibilities are opened up which will be considered in detail below (pp. 199–201).

Human burials

Three human burials were found in the region of the Outer Ditch two of which could be shown to post-date the ditch silt:

Burial 1 (F207): an extended inhumation of an adult cut largely into the soft ditch silt from the surface of layer 4.

Burial 2: a cremation placed in a small jar of late first or second century type dug, probably, from the surface of layer 5.

Burial 3 (ph 244): an inhumation of an infant in a small hole cut into the natural chalk.

The burials are considered in detail below (p. 171).

Post-holes

Immediately to the east of the eastern lip of the Inner Ditch 22 post-holes of various sizes and shapes were identified and excavated. They are entirely undated. Their close proximity to the Inner Ditch might suggest that they pre-date the ditch and could, therefore, be associated with the early settle-ment enclosed by the Middle Ditch. If the Middle Ditch had been backed by a bank the post-holes could well have belonged to occupation in the shelter of the bank.

Two other 'post-holes' were found, both undated, one close to the lip of the Middle Ditch, the other between the Middle and Outer Ditches. The latter contained the burial of an infant (burial 3) and is best considered as a small grave pit.

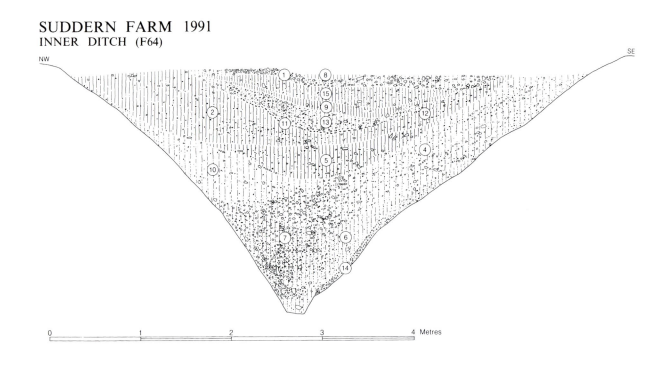

SUDDERN FARM 1991
INNER DITCH (F64)

NW

SE

0   1   2   3   4 Metres

Fig. 3.8a Ditch section

Pl. 3.4 Section of the inner enclosure ditch, F64

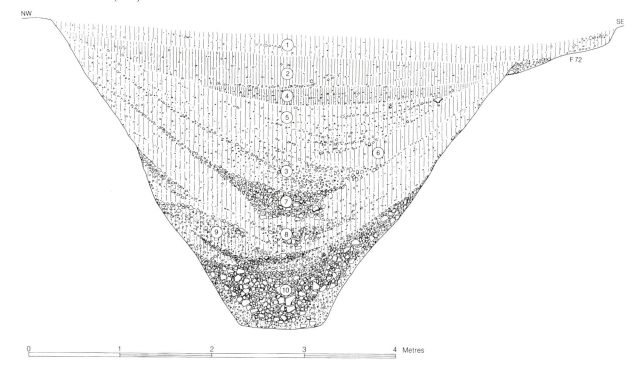

SUDDERN FARM 1991
OUTER DITCH (F66)

NW

SE

F 72

0   1   2   3   4   Metres

Fig. 3.8b Ditch section

Pl. 3.5 Section of the outer enclosure ditch, F66

Area 2 (1991): the interior area excavation

Introduction

Within the 1200 sq m examined in the excavation a large number of features were discovered cut into the chalk bedrock (Fig. 3.9 and Pl. 3.1). These consisted of post-holes, pits, quarries, working hollows and other scooped features spanning the period from the seventh century BC to the fourth century AD. Thereafter, in the early medieval period, the area appears to have been ploughed leading to the formation of a build-up of ploughsoil over the eastern part of the site.

In the absence of superficial stratigraphy the only way in which the individual features can be dated is by reference to the latest artefacts found in them supported by relative sequences established in those cases where features intercut. Bearing in mind the usual provisos, that a feature may contain only residual material, thus making it appear to be earlier than it really is it is possible to produce a series of provisional phase plans (Figs. 3.29 and 3.30) covering the period from the Early Iron Age to the late Roman period (c.700 BC–AD 400). In the text to follow the individual features will be considered according to their type. This will be followed by a summary of the chronological development of the settlement as sampled in the area excavation.

Fences, post structures and post-holes

A total of 118 post-holes were found in trench 1. Of these 42 could be assigned to fences and 36 to other post structures (PS9–25) leaving 40 unassigned. The greater number of the isolated post-holes was concentrated in the south-eastern corner of the trench with the remainder more sparsely scattered over the western and north-eastern areas.

Fences

There were five well-defined fences running diagonally across the trench. Fences 1, 3, 4 and 5 were aligned NE–SW with fence 2 at right angles joining fences 1 and 3. Along most of the fence lines the individual post-holes were placed at intervals of about 2 m except for fence 1 where the spacing averaged 3 m. Most of the post-holes were of similar size measuring 0.3–0.4 m in diameter and 0.1–0.2 m deep. Fence 2 had deeper post-holes averaging 0.2–0.3 m. The post voids, where they survived, were 0.20–0.23 m across. No evidence survived to suggest that the posts were other than circular in cross section. Flint packing, either *in situ* or collapsed into the void, was a common feature.

Fences 1–4, with their widely spaced verticals, were probably of post and rail type though it is possible

that the horizontal rails supported vertical boarding. Fence 5 differed in that it was defined by a continuous slot comparable in width and depth to the fence posts. It was not clear from the filling whether the slots held posts or planks but the filling was deliberate and not the result of natural silting.

Dating evidence is not plentiful. Only four posts contained pottery – nine sherds in all – all belonging to the Roman period. The same broad range is suggested by the sherds in the slot of gully 5. The absence of distinctive late sherds may be thought to indicate an early Roman date.

In addition to the major fences three other linear structures (fences 6–8) were identified in the southeast corner of the trench. Fences 6 and 7 were on the same E–W alignment and both were composed of a combination of slots and post-holes forming an irregular trench. These slots held stakes and stakeholes also occurred just beyond the limits of the slots. Fence 8 ran N–S at right angles to fence 7. Its slot was more regular than those of the other two but it too presumably held a stake-built/wattle wall of some kind. Taken together these three features are best interpreted as representing a light structure, either an insubstantial building or a fenced paddock. That fences 6–8 have a different alignment to the other fences suggests that they may be of different dates. The only direct dating evidence were a few sherds of third to fourth century AD date from the slot of fence 6.

Details of the fences are given in Fiche 4:A3–8.

Post structures

The 17 post structures (PS9–25) were all two-post structures with two possible exceptions which may have been elements of four-post structures. The pairing of the posts is suggested either by the close similarity of the holes (e.g. PS9 and PS10) or by the isolation of the pairs (e.g. PS13–PS15). The two possible four-post structures (PS16 and PS17) both lack a fourth post (one beyond the excavated area and one cut away by a pit) but in neither case is the argument for a four-post structure entirely convincing.

The post-holes were all shallow, less than 0.15 m deep, and tend to fall into two groups, narrow (c.0.2 m in diameter) and wide (0.4–0.6 m in diameter). The fills consisted largely of brown silty soil with small pieces of chalk and occasional flints: flint packing was uncommon.

It was noticeable that the distinctive large and deep post-holes with packing and post void, characteristic of the typical Iron Age four- and six-post structures, were absent. Nor did any of the pairs conform to the characteristic doorposts of typical circular Iron Age houses. A few of the post-holes belonging to two-post structures produced pottery which in each case was Roman.

Details of the post structures are given in Fiche 4:A9–13.

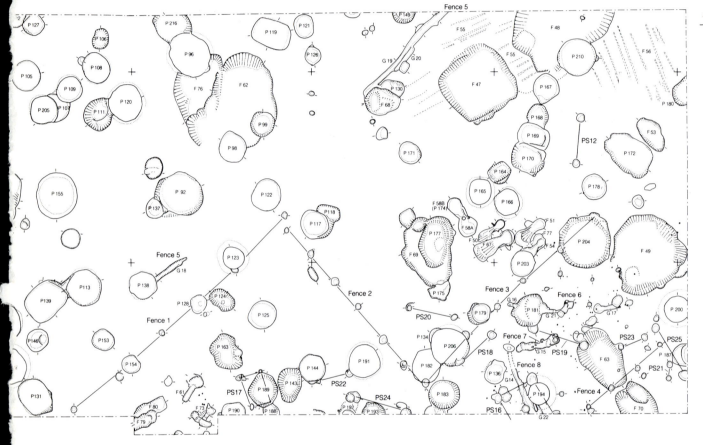

SUDDERN FARM 1991
TRENCH 1

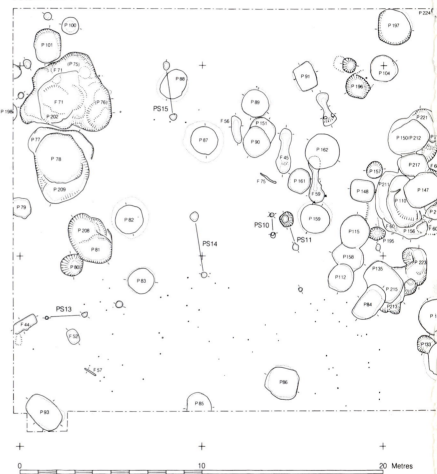

Fig. 3.9 Trench 1: plan of all features

Pits

A total of 78 pits were excavated and may be classified as beehive, cylindrical, subrectangular and barrel shaped. They range in date from cp 3 to Roman (first to second century AD). For the most part the date accepted is that suggested by the pottery assemblage recovered from the fill but in a few cases, where distinctive stratigraphical relationships demand it, cp dates have been modified accordingly. As the table (Table 3.1) shows dominant pit types vary significantly with period.

Table 3.1.
Quantities of pit forms by phase

Pit form	BH	BAR	CYL	S–R	Total
EIA cp 3–5	13	2	4	6	25
MIA cp 6	13	1	1	–	15
LIA cp 8–9	2	2	7	2	13
First cent.					
BC/AD	–	–	12	5	17
Roman	2	–	3	2	7
Undated	–	–	1	–	1
Total	30	5	28	15	78

Beehive pits were frequent in E–MIA and formed 38% of the total, whilst cylindrical pits, almost as common at 36%, are the main form in the later phases from LIA to Roman and is the only form to be present in all phases. The subrectangular pits (19% of the total pits) reflect the pattern of the cylindrical pits, but are absent in the MIA. Barrel pits (possibly a subset of beehives) were the smallest group (6.5%) and appear to mirror the beehive pattern. Though beehive/barrel pits appear to be absent in the first century BC/AD phase, one of the first century BC/AD cylindrical pits is rather borderline in form and in terms of size would fit better with the beehive/barrel category, thus allowing this combined group to be present in all phases.

Pit structure

Structural data and fill descriptions for each pit are given in Fiche 4:B1–9. Pit files have been prepared for all pits and form part of the site archive. Some of the information is summarized in Figs. 3.10–3.15, which characterize the pit types using base diameter, depth, volume, etc.

Of the 78 excavated pits only twelve had any evidence of a careful finish. Three beehive, one barrel and one subrectangular pit exhibited some toolmarks, both adze and bar type, on sides or base but never in any profusion. A further five beehive and two cylindrical pits were well finished with smooth sides. All the other pits were left in a roughly finished condition, which contrasts with the pits at Danebury, but not with the other Environs sites where toolmarks were equally uncommon.

No blocking walls were found. This is probably because few (only seven pairs) were intercut. The density of pits was never very great and where earlier pits were cut into by later pits their fill was already well consolidated.

No evidence of the primary use has been preserved, though one beehive and one subrectangular pit each had a burnt layer with carbonized grain on the base, which might imply grain storage. This is the likely function of beehive, barrel and cylindrical pits, but not for subrectangular pits which would be more difficult to seal effectively. The circular pits have mouths between 0.78 and 2.0 m diameter (up to 3.14 sq m in area) but with the majority 1.0–1.5 m diameter (0.79–1.77 sq m). The subrectangular pits included four with a surface area of 1.79 sq m or less, the remainder measuring from 1.9 to 3.7 sq m. However taking a pit with a surface area of 1.8 cu m, the circumference of a circular pit to be sealed would be 4.76 m long compared to a perimeter of 5.37 m for a subrectangular pit. Additionally, and perhaps a more important consideration, is that the quantity of stored grain lost around the walls of a circular pit would also be proportionately less. At Danebury there was evidence that the subrectangular pits were specifically related to circular structures, but at Suddern Farm though they were grouped fairly close together along the east side of the track/road no evidence of any buildings survived.

The diagrams (Figs. 3.10–3.13) show the groupings of the pits based on various combinations of their dimensions. The different pit forms can be seen to conform to distinct groups, which can be divided, on the basis of size, into small (mostly cylindrical) pits and medium and large (beehive and barrel) pits. The subrectangular pits were of the same areas as the cylindrical and the large beehive pits. The pits falling in the zone of overlap between cylindrical and beehive pits frequently exhibit characteristics of both pit forms.

Beehive pits (Table 3.2)

Two-thirds of these pits were uneroded, with the remainder having suffered some degree of erosion. It was only in the MIA that any pits were heavily eroded.

Pit sizes appeared to vary little from EIA to LIA, though there is a slight indication of an increase in size in the MIA, most pronounced in the eroded pits which had an average depth of 1.09 m compared to 0.95 m overall and an average base of 2.06 m compared to 1.95 m generally in cp 6/7 and 1.78 m in cp 3–5.

Table 3.2.
Fill and average values of pit dimensions of beehive pits by phase

	EIA (13)	MIA (13)	LIA–Ro (4)	ALL
Depth	0.96 m	0.94 m	0.91 m	0.94 m
Base	1.78 m	1.95 m	1.83 m	1.86 m
Top – unerod.	1.38 m	1.65 m	1.63 m	1.51 m
Volume	2.11 cu m	1.84 cu m	2.03 cu m	2.0 cu m
Fill cycle	2 x3, 2a, 2b, 2c x6, 1a	2 x5, 2c x2, 1a x2, 1b, 1c, 1d x2	2x2, 2c x2	

For the whole group depths ranged from 0.48–1.5 m, base diameters from 1.3–2.6 m, uneroded mouths from 1.1–1.8 m and volumes from 1.04–4.03 cu m.

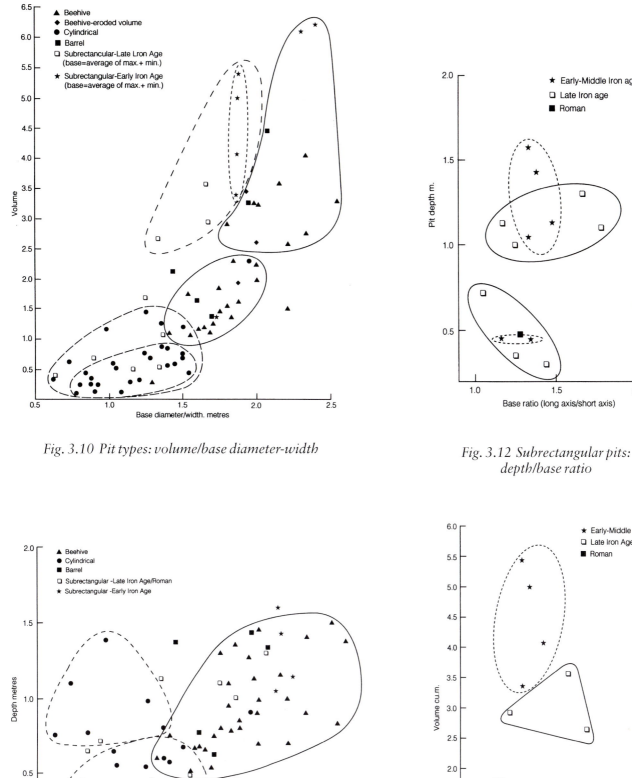

Fig. 3.10 Pit types: volume/base diameter-width

Fig. 3.11 Pit types: depth/base

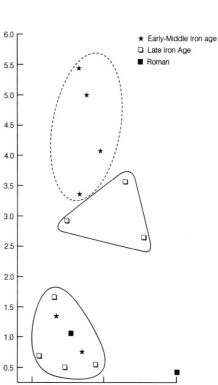

Fig. 3.12 Subrectangular pits: depth/base ratio

Fig. 3.13 Subrectangular pits: volume/base ratio

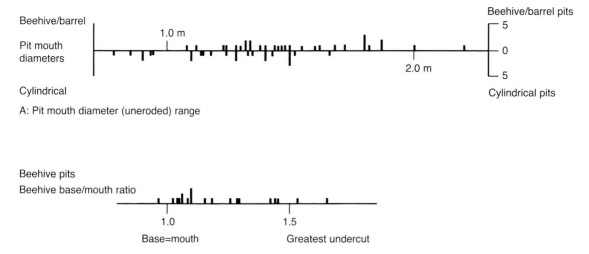

A: Pit mouth diameter (uneroded) range

Beehive/barrel

Pit mouth diameters

1.0 m

2.0 m

Cylindrical

Beehive/barrel pits

5

0

5

Cylindrical pits

Beehive pits
Beehive base/mouth ratio

1.0

1.5

Base=mouth

Greatest undercut

Base: Mouth ration in beehive pits illustrating extent of overhang

Fig. 3.14 Pit measurements

The main concentration of uneroded mouth diameters was between 1.1 and 1.5 m. They showed a distinct increase from 1.1–1.5 m in the EIA to 1.32–1.8 m in the MIA/LIA. Volumes however showed a slight decrease with the EIA average of 2.12 cu m being reduced to 1.95 cu m in the MIA.

The pit form had all the typical characteristics of beehive pits, though they appear to be somewhat squatter than at other sites being greater in width in proportion to the depth and having a wider mouth so the overhang is less pronounced. Though the mouth diameters were within the same range as Danebury and other Environs sites the distribution indicates a larger mouth size in general. The profiles were generally slightly concave forming a curving undercutting wall more often than a straight one. Where there was little overhang, the result was something closer to a barrel shape and is discussed further in relation to the barrel pits.

On Figs. 3.11 and 3.12 it is apparent that the beehive pits are tightly grouped both in the plot of base diameter v. depth and depth v. volume, though in the latter the groupings are closer with a more obvious subdivision into large and small sized pits. The small sized beehives overlap slightly with cylindrical pits and the barrel-shaped pits occupy the same range as the beehive pits. The subdivision into large and small size groups has been noted at other sites, in particular Bury Hill.

Barrel pits (Table 3.3)

Five pits were allocated to this category and one (P210) that appeared intermediate in form with the beehives was eventually designated a beehive. The pits are evenly spread from E–LIA and all but one were uneroded.

Their depths ranged from 0.62–1.42 m with a clear increase occurring from early to late. Base diameters ranged from 1.44–2.08 m with an average of 1.72 m, but with no comparable increase with time as in depth. The pit mouth ranged from 1.7–2.4 m with an

average of 1.9 m. However the maximum diameter of the pit was about halfway down the profile, but was not measured in most cases. Uneroded volumes ranged from 1.37–4.46 cu m with an average of 2.68 cu m. The greatest capacity appears to have been in the MIA pit.

Table 3.3.
Fills and average values of dimensions of all barrel pits

Depth	Base	Mouth	Volume uneroded	Fill cycle
1.1 m	1.72 m	1.9 m	2.68 cu m	1d x2, 2c, 2 x3

P210, though having a distinctly barrel-shaped profile was allocated to the beehive group on the grounds of its fill, which included a high proportion of erosion products indicating that the original profile must have had an overhang and was therefore beehive in form. This provides some indication of how the barrel shape formed: it is probable that they developed from typical beehive pits that had eroded and been cleaned out and reused at least once. The scatter diagrams show that the barrel pits are clearly grouped with the beehives in terms of structural characteristics implying a close relationship in terms of use and function. It was also suggested at Nettlebank Copse that the few barrel-shaped pits derived from reuse of beehive pits. If this is the case the small number of barrel pits implies a low rate of reuse.

Cylindrical pits (Table 3.4)

All but one of the 28 cylindrical pits were uneroded and the eroded example had only suffered very light erosion. This pit form was commonest in the later phases: 54% of the LIA pits rising to 70% in the first century BC/AD group compared to forming just 16% of EIA pits.

Pit sizes remained very similar throughout all phases. Depths ranged from 0.15–0.98 m with only a few deeper late ones up to 1.37 m; average depths for all periods were similar but showed a gradual increase from 0.45 m in the EIA to 0.61 m in the Roman period. Base diameters had a range of 0.6–1.82 m with the size decreasing from 1.44 m in the EIA to 0.89 m in the Roman phase. The pit mouth was generally slightly wider than the base with a range of 0.78–1.88 m with the average values showing the same tendency to decrease from 1.46 m in the EIA to 1.12 m in the Roman period. Uneroded volumes ranged from 0.12–2.28 cu m, though over two-thirds were less than 1 cu m. The average volumes for each phase were similar, though the lowest was in the LIA at 0.58 cu m, the same in the EIA and first century BC/AD at 0.71 cu m rising to 0.83 cu m, the highest value, in the Roman period.

Table 3.4.
Fills and average pit dimensions of cylindrical pits by phase

	EIA (4)	LIA (8)	First cent. BC/AD (12)	Roman (3)	All (28)
Depth	0.45 m	0.48 m	0.58 m	0.61 m	0.54 m
Base	1.41 m	1.1 m	1.13 m	0.89 m	1.11 m
Mouth	1.49 m	1.25 m	1.29 m	1.12 m	1.26 m
Volume	0.72 cu m	0.58 cu m	0.72 cu m	1.12 cu m	0.64 cu m
Fill cycle	2 x2, 2c x2	2 x3, 2c x5	1a, 2 x8, 2c x3	2c x3	

The scatter diagrams (Figs. 3.10 and 3.11) show that the cylindrical pits formed a tight group in terms of size and capacity with a small number having a somewhat deeper and narrower profile. A single example, P86, which on the diagrams falls well outside the cylindrical core within the beehive group, has been re-examined: it was found to have part of the base undercutting and was described in the site notes as cylindrical or barrel shaped in profile, which was also apparent in the section drawing. It appears to have mixed characteristics and would perhaps be better regarded as a barrel pit or reused beehive.

If P86 is excluded from LIA average values, then the average base top and volume measurements show a consistent decrease from EIA to Roman, whilst the average depth values are the reverse.

Subrectangular pits (Table 3.5)

The subrectangular pits can be divided into two distinct groups on the basis of phasing: an EIA group of six and a LIA–Roman group of nine.

The EIA pits had a depth range of 0.44–1.59 m, bases of 1.06–1.62 m (short axis) by 1.42–2.24 m (long axis), with tops generally 0.1–0.14 m longer than the bases. Pit capacity covered a considerable range from 0.73 to 5.46 cu m. The later phase group was on average smaller, but with a considerable overlap in size with the earlier group. The late pits had a depth range of 0.3–1.3 m and bases of 0.88–1.5 m by 0.92–2.06 m with the tops splaying out by 0.05–0.6 m. Volumes were 0.5–3.56 cu m.

The average values in Table 3.5 indicate a gradual decrease in size for this pit type from EIA to Roman. However the scatter diagrams indicate that the different phase pits do not fall into discrete groups, but appear to form two size groups, which comprise both early and late pits. In Figs. 3.12 and 3.13 a base ratio of long axis/short axis has been used, but in Fig.

3.11 the long axis value has been used and in Fig. 3.10 the average of long and short axes. Where the subrectangular pits appear in Fig. 3.11 using the base long axis value with the other forms the larger ones are mixed with the large beehives and the smaller ones mostly with the cylindrical pits. In Fig. 3.10 where the average of the two base values has been used the larger size group is separated from the beehive pits, but the smaller sized pits remain undifferentiated from the cylindrical pits. Certain criteria separate the pits on the basis of size, but when plotted with other pit forms the subrectangular pits cannot be differentiated on size, the plan shape being the defining characteristic. None of the plots separate the early and late phase pits. This may imply that subrectangular pits had the same function in both phases.

Table 3.5.
Fills and average dimension values for subrectangular pits by phase

	E–MIA (6)	LIA/FIRST CENT. BC–AD (7)	ROMAN (2)	ALL
Depth	1.02 m	0.84 m	0.57 m	0.87 m
Base – max.	1.99 m	1.54 m	1.19 m	1.67 m
Base – min.	1.49 m	1.13 m	0.81 m	1.23 m
Top – max.	2.08 m	1.69 m	1.34 m	1.8 m
Top – min.	1.55 m	1.24 m	1.15 m	1.35 m
Volume	3.33 cu m	1.79 cu m	0.71 cu m	2.26 cu m
Fill cycle	2 x4, 2c x2	2 x3, 2c x4	2, 2c	

The only observable, but rather subjective, characteristic that appears to differentiate EIA from LIA–Roman subrectangular pits is that the later pits tend to be much more angular with sharper corners and straighter sides. On this basis pit P91 might be regarded as late in spite of the fact that it has produced only a few sherds of cp 1–2.

The spatial distribution of pits

The spatial arrangement of the pits (Fig. 3.9) appears to be random, apart from the increased density of pits alongside the east edge of the road which runs diagonally across the west end of the trench. However this clustering is barely apparent when the pits are viewed by phase (Figs. 3.29 and 3.30) except in cp 3–4, when most of the pits were dug in this area apart from a few on the west side of the road and a lone one at the extreme east end of the excavation. The cp 4–5 pits are thinly scattered across the site, while in cp 6–7 the wide scatter is more dense. In cp 8–9 there was a concentration of nine pits in a rectangular area alongside the east side of the road possibly at the junction with a path/lane along the north side of the pits. In addition to this group there was a thin scatter of pits over the rest of the trench. In the first century BC/AD the pits formed an even scatter mostly over the eastern and southern areas of the trench, whilst the few second to fourth century AD pits were widely dispersed over the trench though still avoiding the road. No obvious rows of pits could be discerned in any of the phases.

The spatial arrangement of the different pit forms is equally lacking in any pattern, apart from the closer grouping of subrectangular pits already mentioned.

Pit fills (Table 3.6 and Figs. 3.15–3.20)

The fill of each pit has been assigned to one of the fill cycles as described for Danebury pits and is summarized in Table 3.6.

Table 3.6.
Quantification of pit fill cycles according to pit form

Fill	BH	BA	CYL	S-R	Total
1a	3	–	1	–	4 (5%)
1b	1	–	–	–	1 (1.3%)
1c	1	–	1	–	2 (2.5%)
1d	2	1	–	–	3 (4%)
All Slow	7	1	2	–	10 (13%)
2a	1	–	–	–	1 (1.3%)
2b	1	–	–	–	1 (1.3%)
2c	10	1	14	7	32 (41%)
2d	–	–	–	–	–
2	11	3	12	8	34 (44%)
All Fast	23	4	26	15	68 (87%)
Total	30 (38%)	5 (7%)	28 (36%)	15 (19%)	78

The immediately striking feature is that 87% of the fills are all fast cycle or deliberate fill. This is in contrast to Danebury and the other Environs sites, where slow and fast cycles occur more equally and to New Buildings where slow cycles predominate. Though Nettlebank Copse and Houghton Down are more comparable even here the numbers of eroded pits with slow fill cycle are a third or more of the total. Generally on non-hillfort sites pits with deliberate fills are the norm, a pattern into which Suddern Farm fits.

Of the fast fill pits nearly half were thought to represent very rapid infill – perhaps taking place in a single operation. Two of these had later pottery in their tertiary/top fill suggesting that compaction and settling of the layers had taken place before the upper layers were deposited. However in P123 Roman pottery and tile occurred in small quantities throughout its fill. In the case of P120 there was similar fill throughout with two pottery vessels and similar oven daub distributed from base to tertiary fill implying a rapid fill. Roman material was trampled into the surface of the infilled pit.

The slow/eroded fill cycles were largely confined to the beehive pits and to cp 6/7, though a small number occurred earlier and later up to the first century AD.

A total of 366 layers were identified, averaging five per pit, though the numbers could vary from one to fourteen. The greatest number of layers occurred in EIA pits with a maximum of 14 in a single pit, followed by a gradual decrease – up to 13 layers in MIA, 10 in LIA and only 1–4 layers in Roman pits. The same pattern is reflected by the total layers for all pits in each phase, though the slight increase in pits in the first century BC/AD is not reflected in any increase in numbers of layers.

The individual layers in the pits have been characterized resulting in 25 different types, of which seven were naturally formed and the rest were deliberate. Their distribution within the fill cycle is shown in Fiche 4:B10–C5, where they have been grouped according to characteristics in common. The natural layers are divided into natural soil/silt and eroded chalky layers. The deliberate deposits are grouped into soil and occupation/midden, burnt occupation debris (burnt flints, charcoal, daub, ash, grain), chalk tips, other rock (flint, clay) and mixed tips of chalk/stone and soil combined in varying ways.

Table 3.7.
Numbers of layers in pits by phase

Phase	Nos. Pits	Delib. layers	Nat. layers	Layers total	Average layers p.p.
EIA	25	136	3	139	6
MIA	15	84	16	100	7
LIA First cent.	13	56	4	60	5
BC/AD	17	48	4	52	3
Roman	7	19	1	20	3
Total	77	343	28	371	5

The naturally formed layers (8% of all layers) occurred in the slow fill cycle pits and the majority of these were formed of material eroded from the upper edge of the pit mostly chalk shatter, more rarely weathered chalk fragments and naturally silted/accumulated soils. Most of the shatter occurs at primary level, whilst a lesser quantity, but more varied selection of layers, occurred at secondary–tertiary level. Primary silt was observed on the base of only four pits, though it may have been masked if immediately succeeded by tips of soil. Higher in the fill there was only one layer of natural silt, though lenses occurred within a number of shatter layers. Only one pit was assigned to cycle 1d with very clear cut phases of erosion alternating with deliberate fill/activity. All the classes of deliberate layers occur throughout the fill process apart from the top position where they are very limited.

The initial breakdown appears to show the layers were distributed fairly evenly throughout the pits with roughly equal numbers in B – 1°, 2°, and 3° – T, representing roughly three equal divisions of the pit fill. However in beehive pits there are four equal divisions from B to 3° indicating that half the layers occurred in the lower third of the pit, when compared to other pit forms. This suggests that considerably more activity was taking place at the stage of initial infill in beehive pits, which is also reflected in the greater number and variety of special deposits in the basal especially and primary positions of beehive compared to other pit forms.

The most common group (32%) comprises the soil and occupation layers, divided between finds-dominated and burnt debris-dominated soils/midden. Following these in frequency were the layers of more concentrated burnt debris (21%) with burnt flints dominating the spectrum, followed by charcoal, daub, ash and finally the least common, burnt grain.

Chalk tips were frequent (19%) and consisted of equal numbers of tips of rounded and angular chalk, whilst puddled chalk, large rubble and pure chalk grit were infrequent or rare. Tips of chalk and soil mixes accounted for 14% of layers and included various combinations: a homogeneous mix of soil and chalk, alternating lenses of soil and chalk, mostly flat, or a

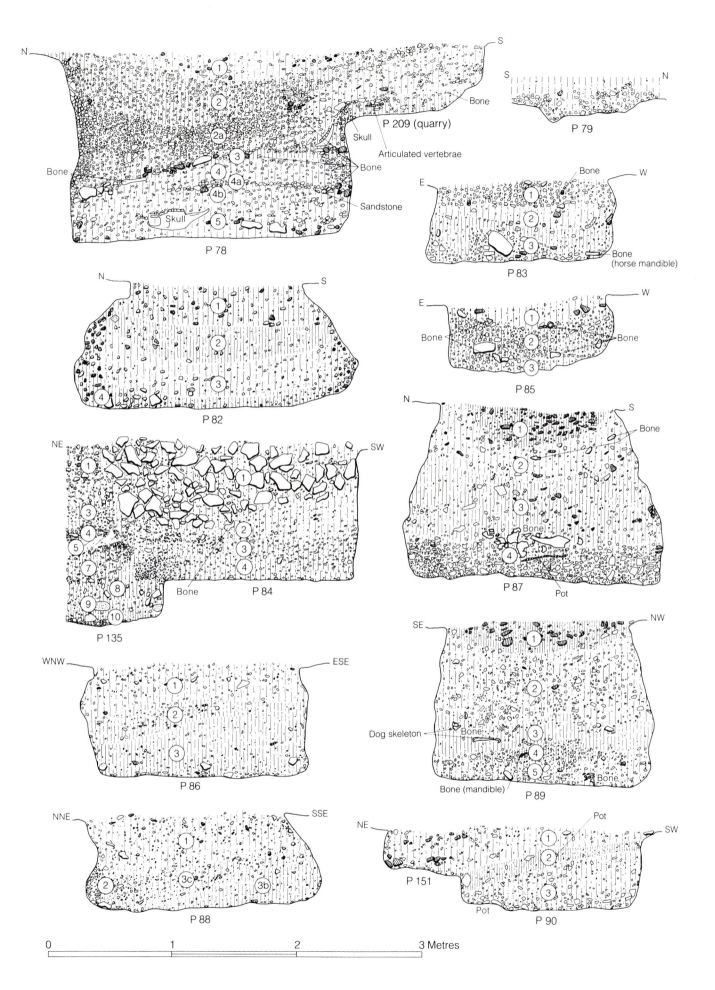

Fig. 3.15 Pit sections

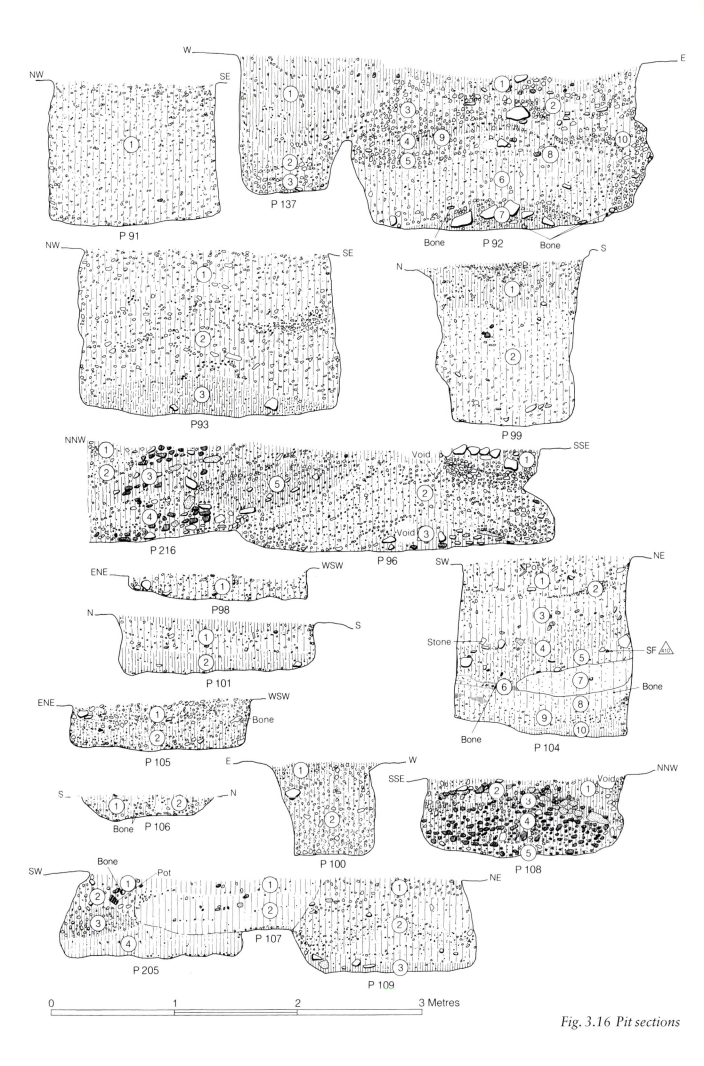

Fig. 3.16 Pit sections

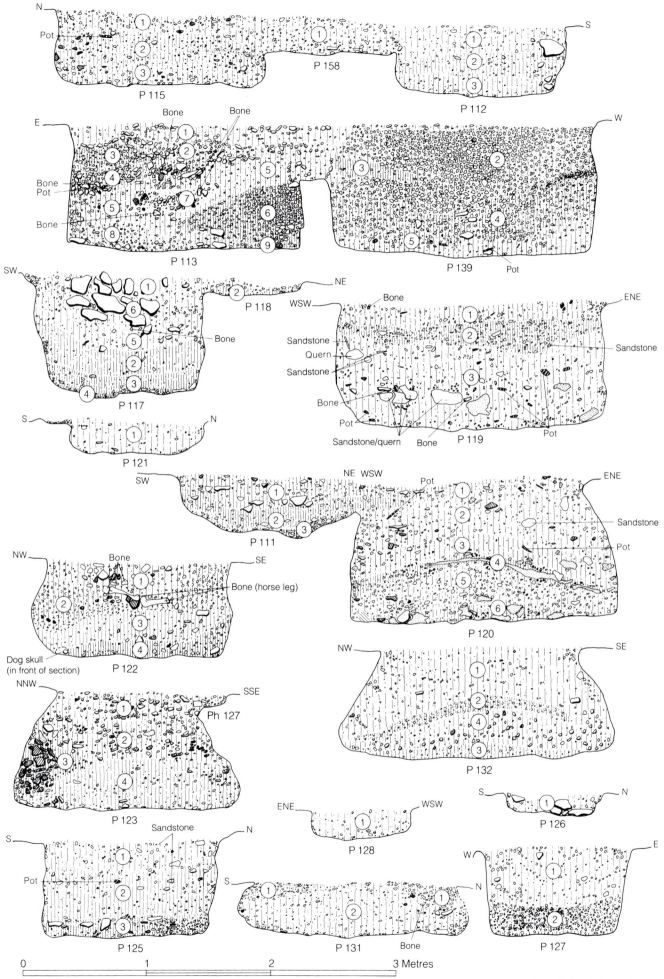

Fig. 3.17 Pit sections

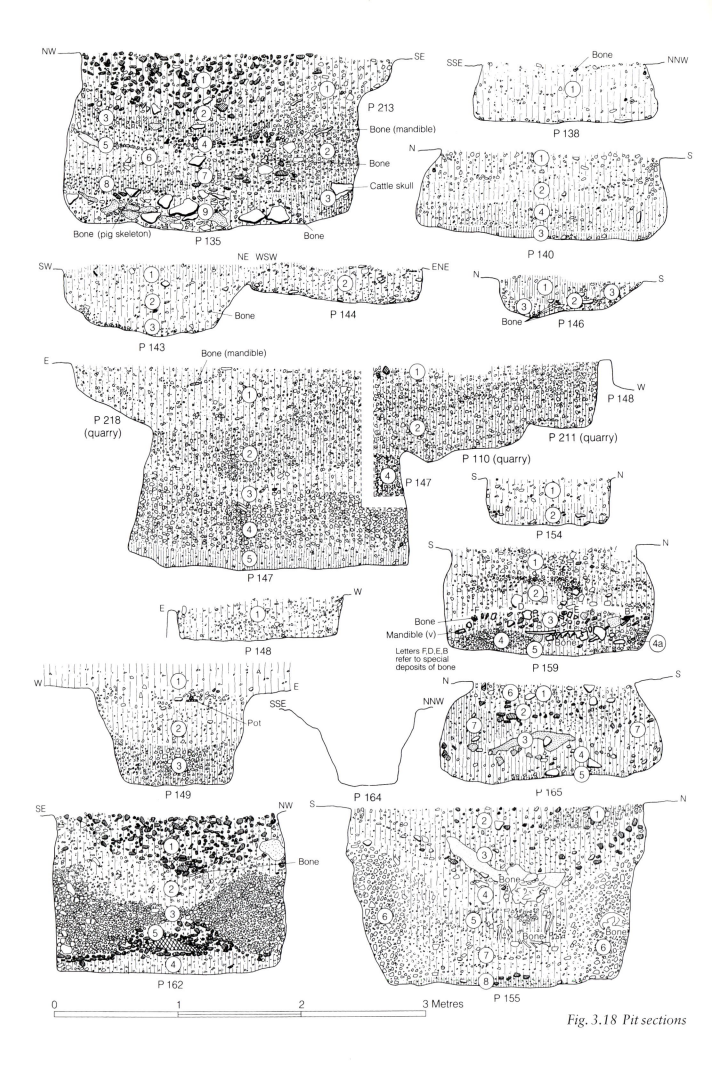

Fig. 3.18 Pit sections

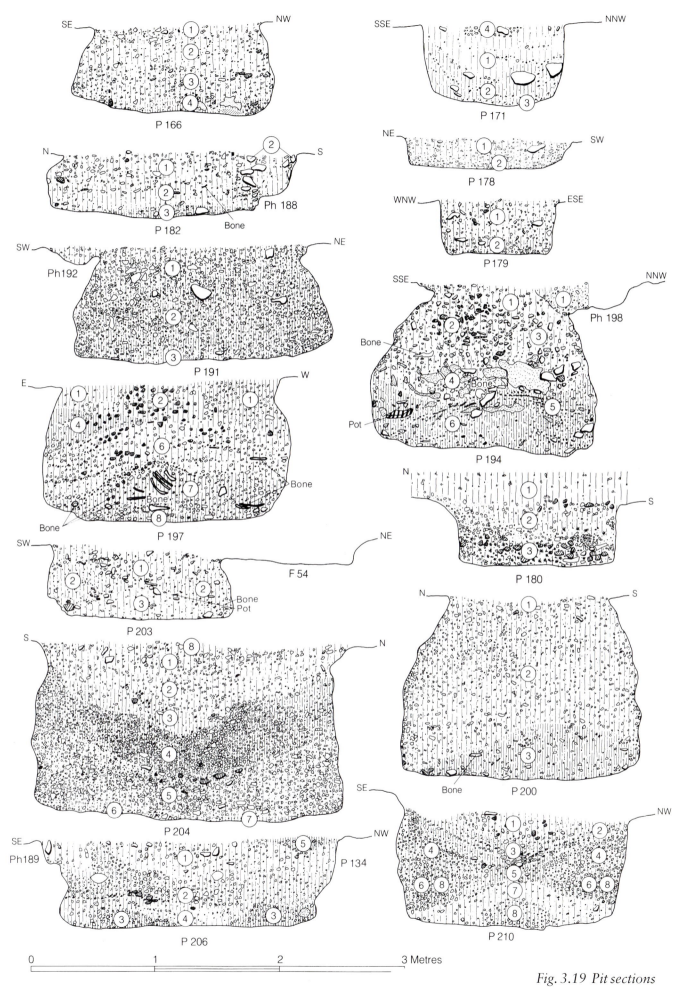

SE ... NW
P 166

① ② ③ ④

SSE ... NNW
P 171

④ ① ② ③

N ... S
P 182

② ① ② ③
Bone
Ph 188

NE ... SW
P 178

① ②

Ph192
SW ... NE
P 191

① ② ③

WNW ... ESE
P 179

① ②

E ... W
P 197

① ④ ② ⑥ ⑦ ⑧ ①
Bone
Bone
Bone

SSE ... NNW
Ph 198
P 194

① ② ③ ④ ⑤ ⑥ ①
Bone
Bone
Pot

SW ... NE
F 54
P 203

② ① ③ ②
Bone
Pot

N ... S
P 180

① ② ③

S ... N
P 204

⑧ ① ② ③ ④ ⑤ ⑥ ⑦

N ... S
P 200

① ② ③
Bone

SE ... NW
Ph189
P 134
P 206

① ⑤ ② ④ ③ ③

SE ... NW
P 210

① ② ④ ③ ④ ⑤ ⑥ ⑦ ⑧ ⑥ ⑧ ⑧

0   1   2   3 Metres

Fig. 3.19 Pit sections

35

heterogeneous layer made up of patches and tips of soil, chalk and other materials in variable proportions representing individual basket/shovel loads of sediment.

The distribution of layer types within all pits remained fairly constant through time without significant change. Soil and occupation layers occur throughout the fill cycle in E–MIA with a slight preference for the upper half (2°–3°) in LIA–Roman phases. Burnt debris occurred throughout in all phases except the first century BC/AD, when it concentrates in the lower half (B–2°). Tips of chalk or chalk and soil occurred throughout the pit fills in all phases.

Beehive pits contained the greatest variety of layers at all levels of the fill cycle from base to tertiary with no apparent preferences for any part of the fill cycle for particular layers. They accounted for 50% of the layers and contained an average of six layers per pit. Though almost equal in number the cylindrical pits contained only 21% of layers with an average of three layers per pit. This contrast can probably be largely accounted for by the basic size difference of the two pit forms. However it is clear differences are not entirely related to pit size as the barrel pits, comparable to beehives but forming only 6% of the pits, contained 12% of the layers with an average of nine layers per pit. Although as suggested above barrel pits may only be reused beehive pits, it appears there may have been some subtle difference in the patterns of backfilling.

The beehive pits contained 70% of the basal deposits, whereas at all other levels they contained a fairly consistent 40–50% of layers. The other pit forms did not have a high proportion of layers at basal level, but at secondary level for barrel and subrectangular pits and at primary level for cylindrical pits.

In cylindrical and subrectangular pits the greatest variety of layers occurred in the lower half (B–2°) with a more limited range in tertiary confined to soil, occupation, flints and mixed chalk and soil tips. The barrel pits are rather too few to reflect a clear pattern, but the greatest variety of layers occurred at secondary level and in general soil, occupation and burnt debris were the dominant layers. Layers of burnt debris were notably lacking from the upper fill of subrectangular and cylindrical pits. The subrectangular pits contained

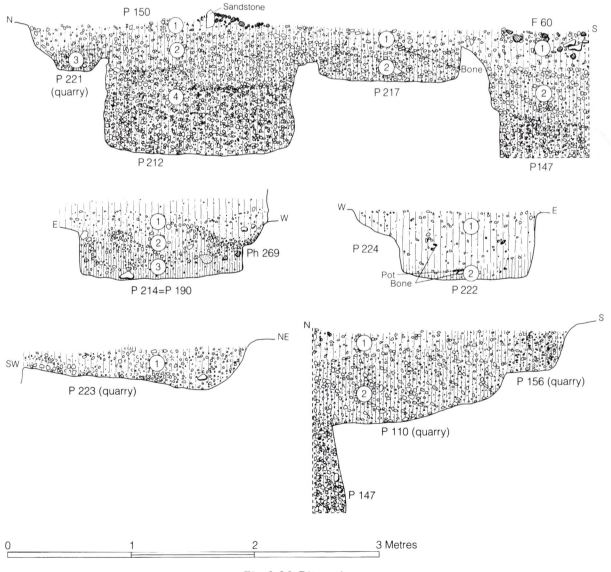

Fig. 3.20 Pit sections

as wide a range of layer types as the beehive pits, but the chalk and chalk/soil tips were slightly more common than the soil and occupation layers, in contrast to the beehive and cylindrical pits.

The shape of the layers at Suddern Farm was noticeably flat. This suggests the deliberate levelling of the layers, since such a pattern was unlikely to result from casual tipping. It is apparent in all pit types and phases and was a frequent feature of part or all of the pit fills. In a smaller number of cases mounds of sediment on the pit base, and reflected by overlying layers in the lower part of the pit, probably resulted from material being tipped through the narrower mouth of the beehive pits. This sometimes resulted in an asymmetrically placed mound. In a few cases layers were basin-shaped or wedge-shaped, the latter particularly applying to eroded layers thickest against the pit wall and thinning to the centre.

Suddern Farm is of particular interest in providing evidence of a long period of pit-use from the Early Iron Age to the early Roman period. This continuity is in marked contrast to other sites such as Houghton Down and might suggest that the inhabitants of Suddern Farm continued their traditional practices little affected by new techniques and behaviour introduced in the wake of the Roman invasion.

Quarries (Figs. 3.20 and 3.21)

Two areas of quarrying were found in trench 1 and have been designated as the *eastern quarry complex* and the *western quarry complex*.

The *eastern quarry complex* is composed of three discrete areas of quarrying, a northern lobe (P220 and P221) which developed around the top of the EIA pit P212, a middle lobe (F60, P110, P156, P211, P218 and ph 143) which grew out of the top of the EIA pit P147, and a southern lobe (P213 and P223) which developed in a similar way from the EIA pit P135/P215. The quarries can be shown to be later than the pits and have produced no pottery later than cp 8–9.

The form of the quarries and their relationship to the pits suggest that the quarrying of chalk began where a convenient exposure was visible around the upper edge of an old, largely silted-up, pit. From such a face fresh chalk could be won, superficial soil being thrown back into the pit hollow. In this way a series of individual shallow delves developed.

The *western quarry complex* is composed of two discrete areas, a northern lobe (F71, F75, F76 and P202) and a southern lobe (P77, P209). The southern lobe had developed from the sides of the MIA pit P78 but the northern lobe appears to have developed without the benefit of an early nucleus.

The quarry fills were all similar consisting of tips of chalk rubble, mostly in the smaller size range, puddled chalk, mixtures of chalk and soil and extensive dumps of chalk. In some (e.g. F71) the layers were sloping but usually they were horizontal. There is no definite evidence of progressive dumping, of the kind noted at New Buildings, and it may therefore be suggested that the quarries here were worked as part of a single operation.

Occupation debris and artefacts were few, though two special deposits, both of partial articulated

Quarries

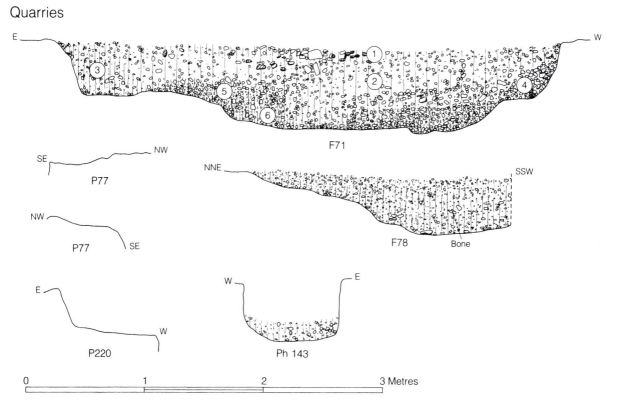

Fig. 3.21 Quarry sections

animals, occurred, one in each quarry complex. Such pottery as there is suggests a Mid–Late Iron Age date.

Detailed descriptions are given in Fiche 4:D12–E2.

Working hollows

Nine features of broadly similar type can be grouped together and classed as working hollows. All are Roman but may be divided into an early and a late group. The four early hollows lie close together at the east end of the trench, while the later hollows extend from the SE corner across the NE third of the trench. The more regular subrectangular hollows are aligned NW–SE and probably relate to the alignment of the fences.

The hollows fall into two main forms which relate to size. The smaller group is generally narrow and subrectangular or elongated oval in shape while the larger group is squarer or subcircular (Pl. 3.6). Of these only F47 is a distinct square with sharp corners and straight sides. Most have sloping sides which merge with flat or slightly dished floors. Four have evidence of a deeper oval hollow in the base close to one end or corner suggesting heavier wear in this area possibly related to an 'entrance'. F69 had shallow irregular hollows immediately outside at either end

that are more likely to have resulted from wear than any structural activity.

The working hollows range in size with lengths varying from 2.8–5.6 m, widths from 1.86 to 4.0 m and depths from 0.16 to 0.33 m. When length and depth are plotted as coordinates (Fig. 3.24) together with other scoops, hollows and bowl pits, the working hollows form a separate group approaching the larger scoops and hollows in size. The smaller working hollows are not distinguishable from the larger on this plot.

Associated structural features are few. F63 has a number of post-holes at its margins some of which may have taken related structures. A number have groups of large flint nodules close to the edge or over the base but no clear pattern emerges. The floors were subject to trampling or disturbance. The floor of F47 was smooth but others were more irregular. The nature of any superstructure which may have existed is unclear. The post-holes near F63 could have supported some form of covering. If, however, they were roofed it is more likely that the superstructure was taken on horizontal sill beams of which no trace survives. The possibility of timberwork may be reflected in the discovery of six iron nails in F47 and five each in F48 and F62.

Some evidence of function is provided by their fills which were usually of grey soil containing a quantity

Pl. 3.6 Feature F47 during excavation

of occupation debris. In three cases (F47, F48 and F62) a large number of metal artefacts were discovered. The absence of smithing products precludes ironworking but the items may have been fittings for composite wooden objects which could point to woodworking. Large numbers of cattle skulls were found in F47 and to a lesser extent in F48. While these *may* be special deposits (Fiche 5:C9–10) they could equally well reflect butchery or possibly even the initial stages of leather production. Another possibility which deserves to be borne in mind is that they were standings for midden deposits, used to accumulate organic rubbish to spread on the fields. The question is best left open allowing the possibility that the working hollows may have been used for a variety of activities.

Details of the individual structures are given in Fiche 4:E3–6.

Bowl pits, scoops and other hollows (Figs. 3.22 and 3.23)

Some 15 bowl-shaped pits and 20 scoops or hollows were found dating to the LIA or Roman period. Of the bowl pits five were assigned to cp 8–9, eight to the early Roman period, one to late Roman and one was undated. Of the scoops and hollows five were assigned to cp 8–9, seven to the early Roman period, three to the late Roman and four were undated. As Fig. 3.24 shows there is some overlap in size between these features and it is therefore simpler to describe them together.

The bowl pits (equivalent to hemispherical, type 7.0) range in size from 0.9–2.6 m long, though most are less than 1.9 m, and between 0.16 and 0.65 m deep. In form they are circular or oval with steeply sloping or vertical sides curving in at the base angle to merge with the concave floor. In several cases the pits appear to be composed of several cuts giving a somewhat irregular appearance.

The scoops/hollows ranged from 0.6 by 0.8 m to 2.0 by 2.45 m wide and 0.1–0.3 m deep. Most were roughly circular in plan, but some were oval, subrectangular or of more complex shapes. The sides were generally sloping and continuous with the curved bases. Overall they were irregular.

The fills of both types consisted of soily layers with a high proportion of occupation debris but the bowl pits contained more chalky layers. Layers of flint nodules were found in some of the scoops/hollows. Overall the fills seem to have been the result of deliberate tipping though some silting and erosion layers were noted.

The quantity of finds ranged from none (P153 and P193) to moderately prolific (P80, P167, F68). In general occupation debris was more commonly found in the shallow hollows than in bowl pits though only the latter contained special deposits: a human pelvis in F68 and a near complete pot in P196. Both features were dated to cp 8–9.

There is little to suggest function and in all probability the features were created by a range of activities. The recurrence of bowl pits on Roman sites does, however, suggest a recurring activity, possibly the small-scale extraction of chalk.

Details of these features are given in Fiche 4:F2–4.

Ovens (Figs. 3.25–3.28)

A total of 16 ovens were identified and in addition two other features may also have been ovens. These clearly divided up into four groups, ranging in number from 3 or 4 up to 7 or 8. The single oven assigned to a group 4 occurred at the edge of the excavation and is assumed to be part of a larger grouping extending beyond the area excavated. In each group the ovens are in fairly close proximity and tend to exhibit similar characteristics of form, alignment and size. Groups 2 and 3 appear to have been set within fenced enclosures, but there was no sign of any fencing defining the areas of the other two groups.

The ovens are all dated to the Roman period, but within that phasing is imprecise. However the majority of group 2 all appear to be early perhaps belonging to the first or second century AD, whilst all in group 3 probably date to the late third century or later, as does the single oven of group 4. Of group 1, one is dated to the mid third century or later and one to the first century AD or later, whilst the others provided no dating evidence, except for there being a Roman tile in one.

The ovens can be divided into four types: (1) a figure-of-eight shape, (2) dumb-bell or hourglass shape (Pl. 3.7), (3) keyhole shape, and (4) rectangular. Sizes vary from 1.1 m to 2.7 m in length, though types 3 and 4 are the smallest being under 1.6 m in length, whereas the others are greater than 1.4 m. The widths vary in proportion to the length and depths vary in any single oven, on average ranging from 0.1–0.3 m.

Each oven can be subdivided into three parts: a furnace chamber, a fire tunnel and a stokehole. The stokehole is always the widest and shallowest part of the oven taking the form of a gently shelving bowl. From this a narrow steep-sided slot led down to the furnace chamber, which was normally circular or oval with steep sides and a flat or slightly rounded base. Only in types 3 and 4 was the furnace chamber straight-sided and continuous with the fire tunnel, though a slight widening could sometimes be detected at the furnace end. In most cases the floor sloped continuously down from the stokehole to the furnace chamber, though in a few it was stepped. In nine ovens burning of the base and sides in the furnace chamber and fire tunnel was observed. The fire appears to have been placed in both fire tunnel and furnace chamber.

In some ovens additional small features were present. Some took the form of small hollows or stakeholes in the floor at the entrance to the fire tunnel, whilst others were small slots or shallow hollows in the surface of the chalk on either side of the fire tunnel or furnace chamber, often close to the junction of the two.

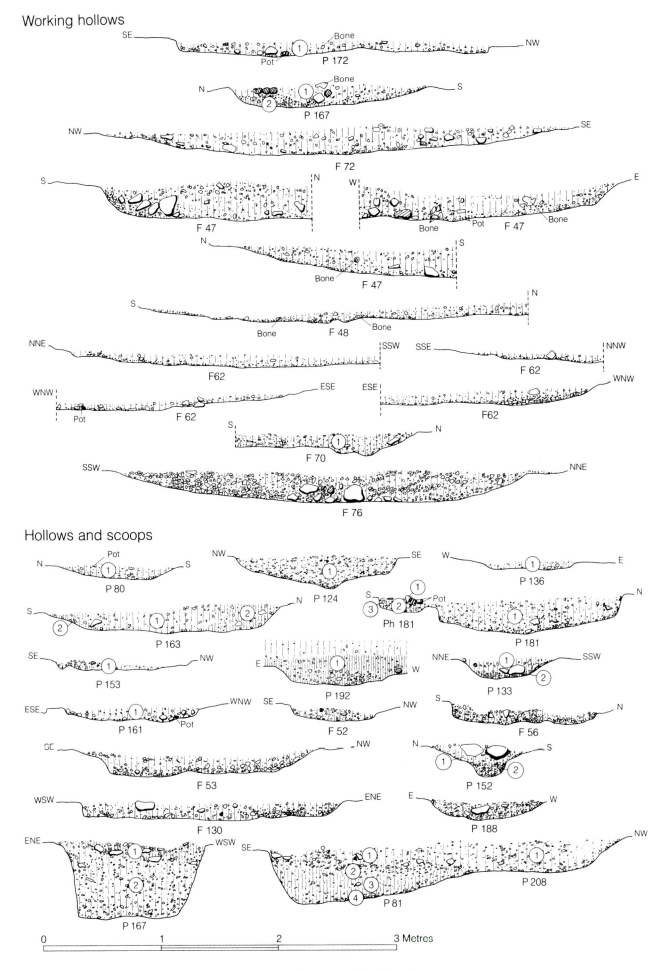

Working hollows

Bone
Pot
P 172

Bone
P 167

F 72

F 47
F 47
Bone
Pot
Bone

F 47
Bone

F 48
Bone
Bone

F62
F 62

F 62
Pot
F62

F 70

F 76

Hollows and scoops

Pot
P 80
P 124
P 136

P 163
Ph 181
Pot
P 181

P 153
P 192
P 133

P 161
Pot
F 52
F 56

F 53
P 152

F 130
P 188

P 167
P 81
P 208

0   1   2   3 Metres

Fig. 3.22 Sections of shallow features

Roman bowl shaped pits

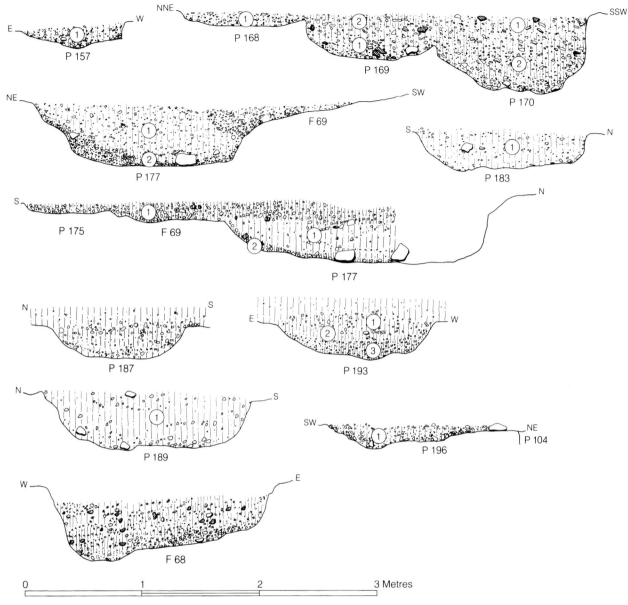

E ─ W
P 157

NNE
P 168

2
P 169

SSW
1
2
P 170

NE ─ SW
F 69
1
2
P 177

S ─ N
1
P 183

S
1
P 175   F 69
2   1
P 177
N

N ─ S
P 187

E ─ W
2   1
3
P 193

N ─ S
1
P 189

SW
1
P 196
NE
P 104

W ─ E
F 68

0   1   2   3 Metres

Fig. 3.23 Sections of shallow features

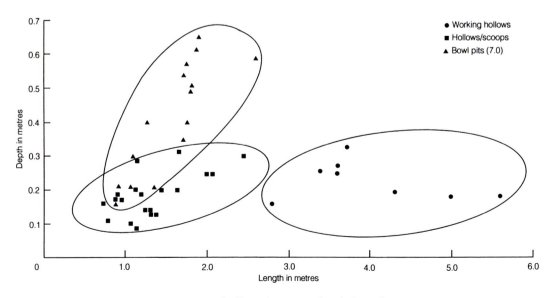

- Working hollows
- Hollows/scoops
- Bowl pits (7.0)

Depth in metres

Length in metres

Fig. 3.24 Shallow features: depth/length ratios

41

Group 1 Ovens

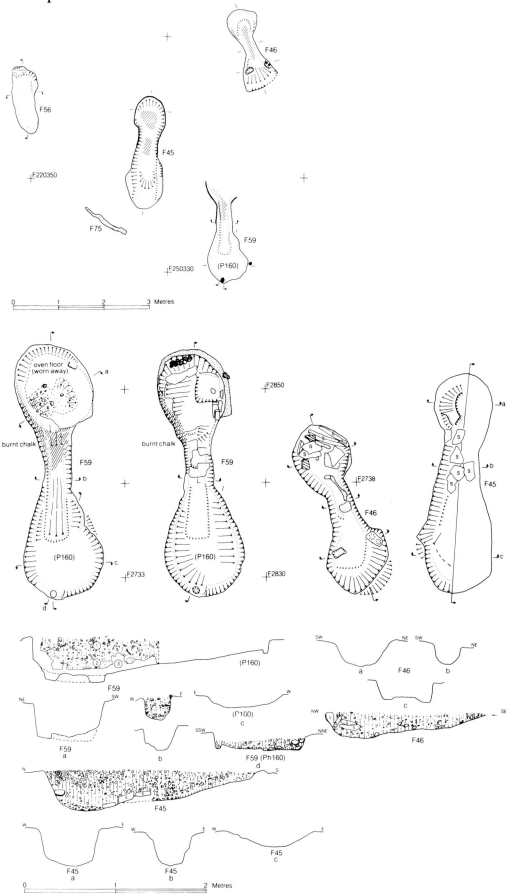

Fig. 3.25 Details of oven group 1

Group 2 Ovens

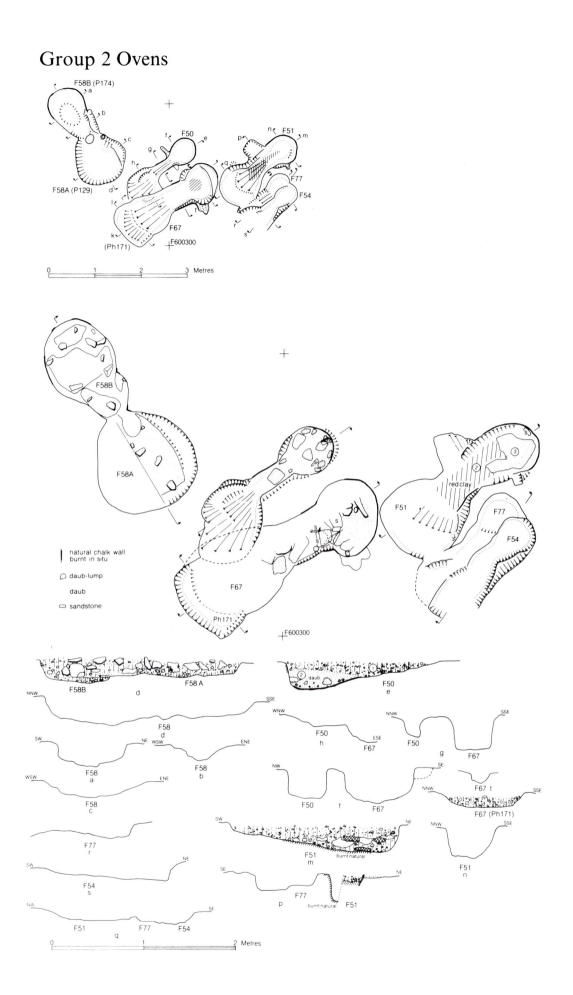

Fig. 3.26 Details of oven group 2

Group 4 Ovens

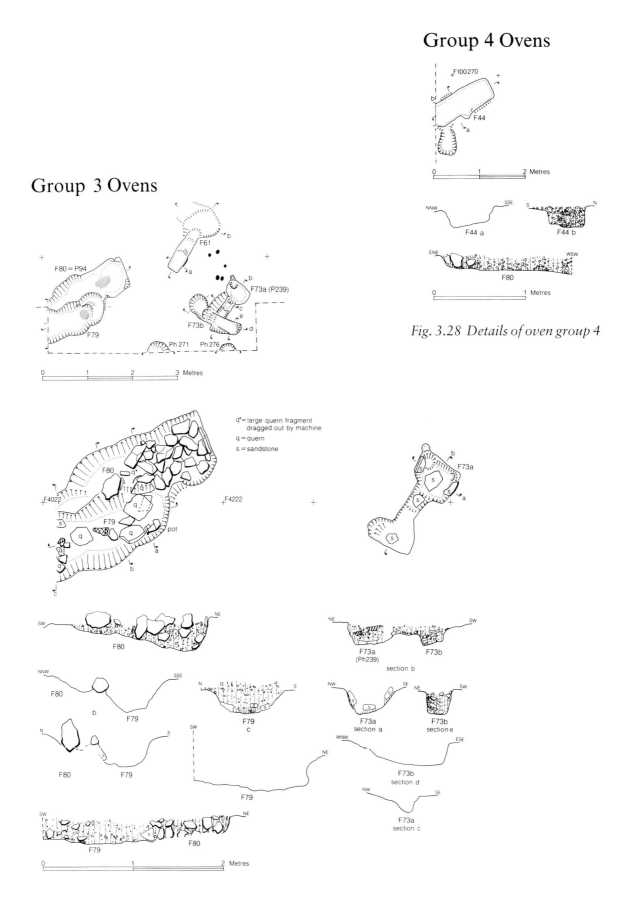

Group 3 Ovens

Fig. 3.28 Details of oven group 4

Fig. 3.27 Details of oven group 3

These features may have related to control of air flow, the former being perhaps structures for holding baffles at the entrance to the fire tunnel and the latter some sort of vent possibly to allow access for a bellows or escape of gases and smoke.

The form of the superstructure is uncertain, but in some there is limited evidence from the fill. The furnace chamber of F59 was lined with daub where it cut through a pit fill, and in a further six substantial quantities of daub were found. This was always fabric C or E, pink or light reddish-yellow, fairly soft and powdery, forming an amorphous, compressed mass. No shaping or distinctive features were noted on any of it and it is best interpreted as the weathered and collapsed upper walls of the ovens. The occurrence of flints and blocks of sandstone in close proximity with much of the daub may indicate that these were built into the upper walls. Whether there was a continuous dome or not over the top is impossible to say. However, it is likely that in at least some cases there was a separate oven chamber above the furnace chamber. Associated with eight ovens were large flat slabs of sandstone, apparently reused pieces of quern or roofing slab. Superficially these appeared to line the sides or base of fire tunnel or furnace chamber, but there was usually a layer of soil between them and the chalk natural and a likely interpretation is that the slabs had originally been built into the edge of the oven wall to form a floor to an upper oven chamber. It is possible that some sort of portable oven plate may also have been used but no evidence was found for these, or other types of oven furniture, either in the ovens or in any other Roman context.

Pl. 3.7 Oven F45

In several of the ovens a thin layer of fine charcoal and soot was found on the floor of the furnace chamber and fire tunnel, presumably representing the remnants of the last firing of the oven and indicating a fairly good combustion rate since most of the surviving charcoal was very small. Other than collapsed superstructure, which was also generally confined to fire tunnels and furnace chambers, the upper fill was generally the same throughout the oven, usually consisting of a deliberate infill of chalk or chalk and soil.

The alignments of the ovens were variable, though often within a group there was a preferred alignment, north–south in group 1 or north-east–south-west in groups 2 and 3, though not all conformed to this.

There is little evidence for the function of the ovens. In one, F61, a thin lens of carbonized grain was found which may hint at corn drying, but apart from this there was no further indication in the fills. Nothing suggested industrial activity nor do they appear to have been inside or close to any buildings. From their size they are most likely to be domestic in nature, probably being used for cooking or baking of bread.

Details of each oven are given in Fiche 4:F5–14.

Ploughing

The eastern part of the site was covered by an early ploughsoil reaching a maximum of 0.4 m in thickness. Beneath this in the north-east part of the excavated area it was possible to trace two areas of shallow plough marks scoring the surface of the chalk (Fig. 3.9). One zone of plough marks (F56) ran in a SW–NE direction while the adjacent series (F56) were at right angles. The individual furrows are discontinuous, cutting into the surface of the chalk to a depth of only about 10–30 mm and varying in width up to about 40 mm. The plough marks appear to be the latest features in the area.

The simplest explanation is that the soil build-up took place at a headland in a system of fields. Similar headlands can still be made out as low banks running N–S across the present field between the excavations and Salisbury Lane to the east. The plough marks were probably created at the beginning of this phase of ploughing towards the edge of the field where the rapid accumulation of ploughsoil prevented subsequent ploughings from further destroying the chalk surface.

The plough ruts post-date third–fourth century features and are therefore likely to be Saxon or medieval.

Chronological development (Figs. 3.29–3.30)

It is convenient, for ease of description, to divide the site into two phases: *Early to early Middle Iron Age* (cp 1/2–cp 6) and *Late Iron Age and Roman* (cp 8 to fourth century AD).

Early to early Middle Iron Age (cp 1/2–cp 6)

The only features which can definitely be assigned to this period are some 42 pits of storage pit type but it is possible that the western quarry hollows may belong to a late phase in this period. It is also likely that some of the undated post-holes are also of this date.

Taken together the pits tend to cluster in a zone along the east side of the road which would appear to run diagonally across the trench but apart from this concentration the pits are otherwise fairly evenly scattered. No evidence of circular buildings was noted but some of the two-post structures probably belong to this phase.

The majority of the pits date to cp 3–cp 6 (*c.*470–270 BC) but there is one small assemblage of pottery of cp 1–2 from P91 – some 24 sherds representing 23 different vessels. While, as has been pointed out above, the form of the pit is similar to Roman pits and it could be argued that the sherds were residual, it is simpler to assume them to be contemporary with the pit thus implying the structural activity dates back to the eighth–sixth centuries. The question of how long the occupation lasted after the end of cp 6 depends upon the dating of the latest groups of MIA pottery. The matter is considered below (p. 68) where it is suggested that occupation ended before the characteristic types of decorated cp 7 pottery came into use.

Late Iron Age and Roman occupation (first century BC to fourth century AD)

The late phases of occupation, spanning the 500 years or so from the beginning of cp 8 to the end of the Roman period, are most conveniently dealt with together because it is sometimes difficult to offer precise dating for some of the constituent features especially when they contain only a few sherds of nondescript grey sandy ware. It is, however, possible to distinguish groups of features containing reasonable quantities of pottery of cp 8–9, others with pottery broadly assignable to the first century AD and others producing distinctive Roman sherds of the second to fourth centuries AD. The three separate groups are shown on Fig. 3.30.

The question which immediately arises is does this represent continuous occupation following without a break from cp 8 or can chronological gaps be discerned? Given the comparatively small size of the total assemblage there can be no firm answer but since there are no readily apparent gaps in the ceramic sequence it is reasonable to suggest that occupation may have been continuous. Nor should we forget that trench 1 represents only a small fraction of the total occupied site. There may well have been periods when parts of the settlement area were left derelict as the focus of occupation shifted a little.

The features constituting the Late Period can be divided into three broad chronological groups on the basis of their associated finds – a Late Iron Age group characterized by pottery of cp 8–9 types; a first

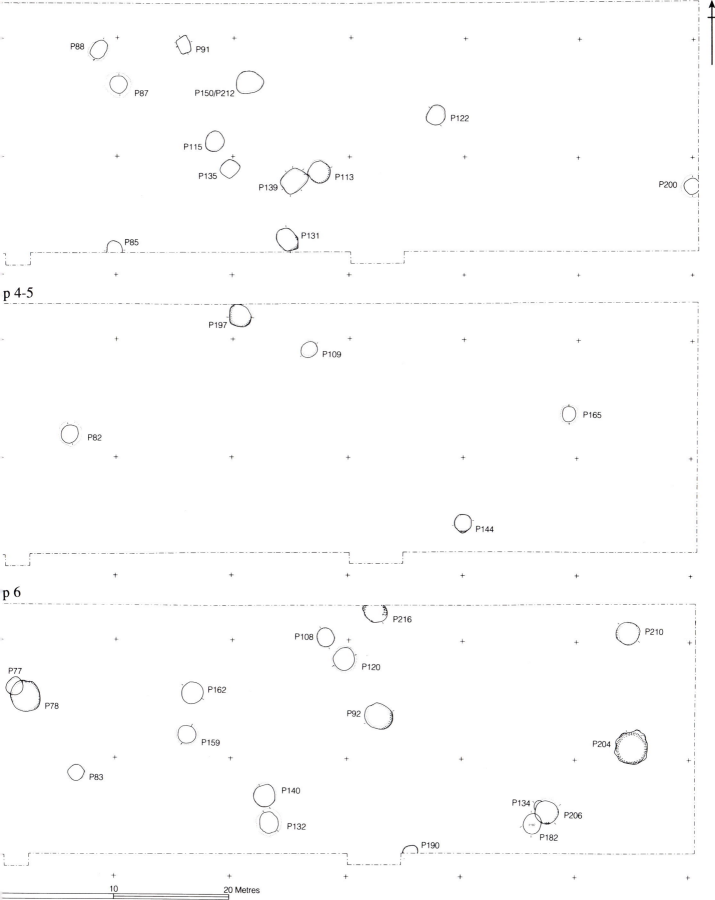

cp 1/2 and cp 3-4

P88
P91
P87
P150/P212
P122
P115
P135
P139   P113
P200
P85   P131

cp 4-5

P197
P109
P165
P82
P144

cp 6

P216
P108   P210
P120
P77
P162
P78
P92
P159
P204
P83
P140
P134   P206
P132   P182
P190

10   20 Metres

Fig. 3.29 Phase plans of trench 1

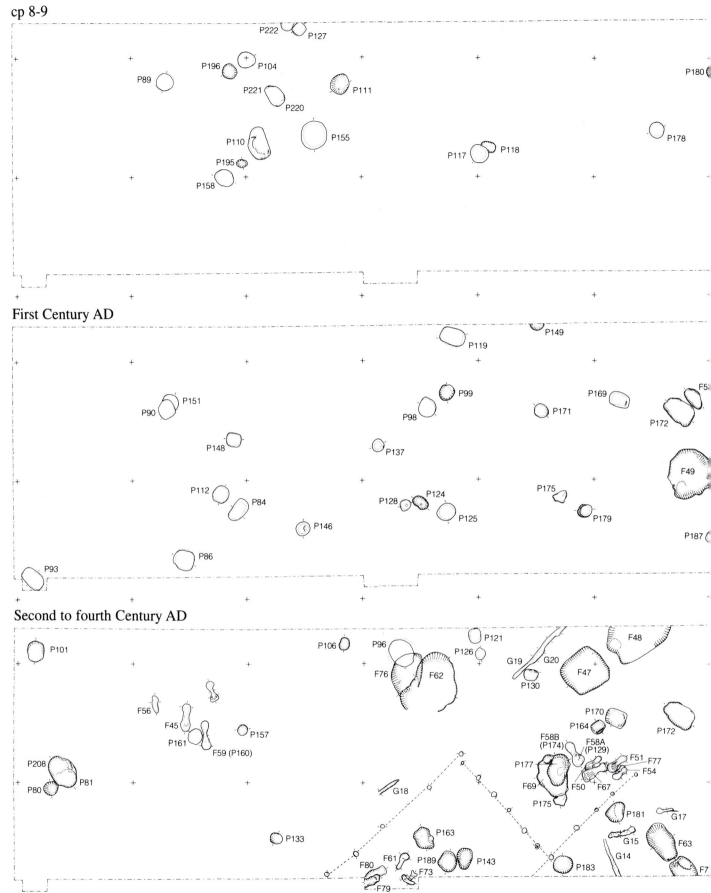

Fig. 3.30 Phase plans of trench 1

century AD group spanning the date of the Roman invasion and represented by a local coarseware assemblage incorporating a few scraps of imported Gallo-Belgic and samian sherds; and a third–fourth century group distinguished by New Forest and Oxfordshire colour-coated vessels together with contemporary Black Burnished wares. The absence of distinctive mid–late second century wares is probably fortuitous in such a comparatively small sample.

The Late Iron Age phase is represented by a number of standard storage pits together with at least one area of shallow quarrying. In the first century AD pits continued to be dug over much of the area with several large shallow 'working hollows' appearing at the east end of the trench. Thereafter occupation continues with a greater variety of features. A series of fences were erected dividing much of the eastern part of the site into small activity areas containing working hollows and groups of small ovens. Another cluster of ovens was found by the side of the road which presumably continued in use throughout the Roman period. Among the latest features to be identified were three large subrectangular working hollows and a light timber structure built of wattle and small posts which dates to the fourth century. It is interesting to note that the alignment of the Roman activity areas and structures seems to have been determined by the pre-Roman road the existence of which can be traced back to the Early Iron Age. The continuity of

boundary over so long a period is impressive.

The nature of the late Roman settlement cannot be characterized on so small a sample but it is probably best seen as the working yard of a larger establishment sited nearby. The discovery of stone roofing slabs, reused in oven bases, suggests that a substantial building, possibly of masonry, remains to be discovered somewhere in the vicinity.

Finally, some time after the abandonment of the Roman settlement, the area was ploughed sufficiently intensively to create a positive lynchet at the headland. In all probability the ploughing was associated with the development of the village of Middle Wallop in the nearby valley in the Saxon and early medieval period.

Area 3 (1996): the triple-ditched linear earthwork and the enclosure

Introduction

The magnetometer survey carried out in the southern field, to provide an indication of the way in which the three parallel linear ditches articulated with boundary ditches of the enclosure, demonstrated something of the potential complexity of the area. As we have explained (above, p. 17) it was decided that the only viable strategy was to strip the area of intersection

Pl. 3.8 General view of the 1996 excavation

totally and to test the relationship of the features exposed in small trial trenches only insofar as it was necessary to elucidate the sequence of the major structural elements. An area excavation of 45 by 24 m resulted within which 13, mainly small, trial trenches were cut (Pl. 3.8).

The overall plan which emerged when the surface below the ploughsoil was cleared showed a complex of intercutting features, some dug into the chalk bedrock, others cut into the fillings of earlier features (Fig. 3.31). It was comparatively easy, by surface observation, to define the relationships of the major features to each other. The results are shown on Fig. 3.32, the dates of the Roman features being assigned from an assessment of surface pottery as well as from pottery derived from the trial excavation.

The trial trenches

Having established the nature of the site and its potential 13 trial trenches were cut and a few isolated features were examined. The rationale behind these interventions and the results obtained may be briefly outlined.

Trench 1: to test the relationship of the Eastern linear (F411) to the Outer enclosure ditch (F400) and the area of quarrying (F410).

The trench showed that the enclosure ditch had cut the quarry and that the quarrying would have removed all trace of F411. It also demonstrated that the late Roman occupation material (F409 layers 1 and 2) represented an accumulation on the floor of a

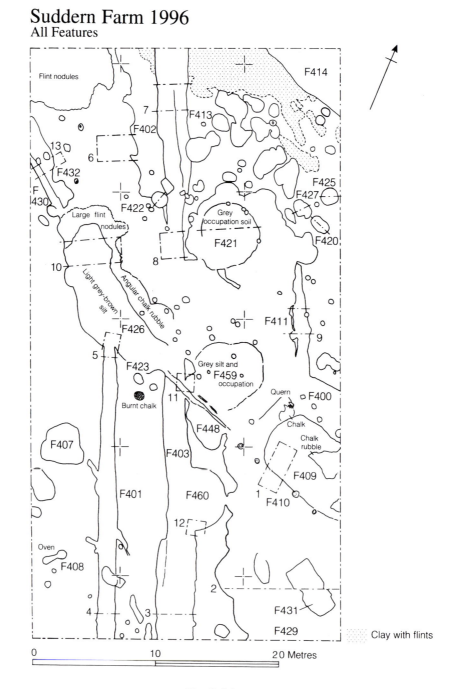

Suddern Farm 1996
All Features

Fig. 3.31

building. The entire floor was subsequently excavated (below, pp. 61–3).

Trench 2: to test the relationship of the quarry to the Eastern linear ditch (F411) given the possibility that the truncated remains of the ditch bottom might have survived the quarrying.

The trench demonstrated that the quarrying had destroyed all trace of the linear ditch but showed that the quarry had been used to dispose of bodies in the Early or early Middle Iron Age. To obtain a larger sample the original 2 m wide trench was extended to 4 m and a Roman corn-drying oven (F431), which had been cut into the quarry fill, was fully excavated. The cemetery and corn drier are described in detail below (pp. 58–61 and 152–170).

Trench 3: to provide a section of the Centre linear ditch (F403).

Trench 4: to provide a section of the Western linear ditch (F401).

Trench 5: to examine the relationship of the Western linear ditch (F401) to the Roman feature (F426) and the Outer enclosure ditch (F400) assumed to be obscured by the Roman feature.

The linear ditch ended some distance in advance of the lip of the ditch. The filling of the Roman feature lapped over the fill of the linear ditch.

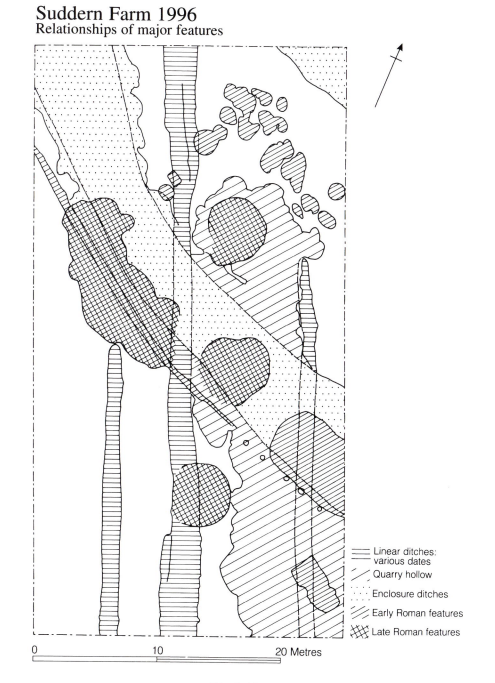

Suddern Farm 1996
Relationships of major features

Linear ditches: various dates
Quarry hollow
Enclosure ditches
Early Roman features
Late Roman features

0   10   20 Metres

Fig. 3.32

Trench 6: to explore the irregular inner lip of the Outer enclosure ditch (F400) in such a position that had the Western linear ditch continued some trace might have survived.

No sign of the linear ditch was seen. The upper silts of the enclosure ditch (F400) were partly sectioned together with the quarry which had developed from the ditch lip.

Trench 7: to obtain a section of the Centre linear ditch where two phases of silting were evident.

The profiles of the two different ditch cuts (F402 and F413) were obtained. The deeper (F402) was the later.

Trench 8: to examine the relationship of the Centre linear ditch (F402) to the Inner enclosure ditch (F400).

The fill of the linear could be shown to pre-date a phase of quarrying (F416) associated with the ditch (F400) and its later silting.

Trench 9: to obtain a section of the Eastern linear ditch (F411) and to examine it in relation to the quarry hollow.

The ditch was shown to pre-date the quarry.

Trench 10: to examine the Roman feature (F426).

The feature was sectioned and proved to be a hollow, caused by wheeled traffic, which had subsequently been metalled with flints. A shallow slot (F430) pre-dated the track.

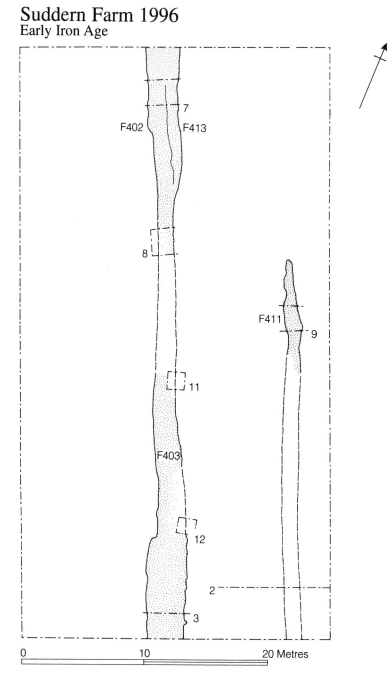

Suddern Farm 1996
Early Iron Age

Fig. 3.33

Trench 11: to examine the relationship of the quarry to the Centre linear ditch (F403) and of the slot F430, here renumbered F448, to both.

The slot cut both features and provided Roman material. The quarry respected the edge of the ditch.

Trench 12: to test the relationship of a large feature (F460), possibly part of the quarry, to the Centre linear ditch (F403).

The feature proved to be late Roman and cut the linear ditch fill.

Trench 13: to section the slot (F430) and the adjacent feature (F432) which proved to be a Roman track.

In addition to the trial trenches several features were half sectioned to obtain dating evidence:
F421 – a hollow of late Roman date
F420, F422, F425, F427 – isolated pits between the Inner and Outer enclosure ditches. All were Roman.
The sections obtained are presented in Figs. 3.37 and 3.38.

The results of these small interventions enabled the development of the site to be defined in some detail and sufficient material was recovered for broad dates to be assigned to the sequence. It is convenient to consider the features in broad chronological order.

The development of the site

The Early Iron Age (Fig. 3.33)

The earliest features to be defined are two linear ditches, the Centre ditch (F402/F403/F413) and the Eastern ditch (F411). It should, however, be stressed that there is no direct evidence to show that the two are contemporary or even broadly so.

The Centre ditch at its northern end shows clear evidence of having been recut on at least one occasion and there is some suggestion of limited recutting at the southern end seen in plan. The ditch profiles exposed in trenches 3 and 7 (Fig. 3.38) show that the ditch had silted naturally. Very little material was found but the few sherds recovered were characteristically Early Iron Age in type.

The Eastern ditch (F411) was traced only at its northern end (in trench 9) where its profile was slight (Fig. 3.38). The filling suggested natural silting.

The relationships of the two linear ditches to each other and to the first phase of the enclosure of the main settlement area remain undefined. In the 1991 excavation it was possible to show that the Inner and Outer enclosure ditches took their final form in the Late Iron Age though the latest profiles may have represented the final recuttings of earlier ditches. The Middle enclosure ditch, on the other hand, was significantly earlier and had been deliberately refilled after a period of silting. The Middle ditch does not exist within the area excavated in 1996 but on the air photographs and on the magnetometer survey it

appears to begin just beyond the eastern limit of the excavation. One possible arrangement, therefore, would be to suppose that the Middle linear ditch joined with the Middle enclosure ditch to the north of the excavation and that the Middle enclosure ditch, having encircled the settlement area, terminated just short of the eastern limit of the excavation leaving a gap between it and the northern end of the Eastern linear ditch. In this model all three structural elements could be broadly contemporary but it would allow for a number of chronological variations; for example, the Eastern linear ditch could have been added later (perhaps at the time that the Central linear ditch was redug). Alternatively the Eastern linear could have been the earlier, later replaced by the Middle linear. The exact chronology is beyond recovery but the fact that an Early–Middle Iron Age quarry almost obliterated the Eastern linear while apparently respecting the Middle linear is a reasonable pointer to the later survival of the Middle linear.

The early Middle Iron Age (Fig. 3.34)

The excavation of 1991 suggested that the Inner enclosure ditch may have functionally replaced the Middle enclosure ditch and remained in use into the Late Iron Age (but see pp. 199–201). In the area excavated in 1996 the Inner enclosure ditch occurred (F414) but was not examined.

Within this period an extensive area of the natural chalk was quarried to the depth of a metre or so in a somewhat irregular strip about 10 m wide immediately to the east of the Middle linear ditch (F429). The Middle linear may have continued to function as a boundary at this time and, indeed, it is possible that it was not dug (or redug) until this period. The quarry could be shown to post-date the Eastern linear ditch and to pre-date the Outer enclosure ditch, at least in its final form. The limited quantity of pottery found in the quarry fill was consistent with an Early or early Middle Iron Age date.

One wide section was cut across the quarry (trench 2) and the quarry was also encountered in trenches 1, 9 and 11 (Fig. 3.37). In trenches 1, 2 and 9 human remains were discovered. The extent and nature of the burials are particularly evident in trench 2 where in an area of some 34 sq m 18 adult, 2 child and 8 neonatal inhumations were recovered. The stratigraphy shows clearly that burial started after silting of the quarry had already begun and continued for some time, some burials disturbing others. For the most part the interments were complete and the mode was tightly flexed. There are, however, hints that bones may have been missing or dislocated at the time of burial and some of the interments were so tightly flexed and placed in such small grave pits that it is highly likely that bundled bodies had already lost much of their flesh before burial. Details of the cemetery are given below (pp. 152–170) and the human remains are described in detail (Fiche 6:C8–E6).

The Late Iron Age (Fig. 3.35)

In the Late Iron Age the Outer enclosure ditch was dug or redug, cutting through the quarry with its burials, and it is probable that the Inner enclosure ditch was cut either at the same time or a little earlier. No trace of a bank was found between the two ditches but a bank in this position could well have existed and been totally removed in later phases of activity. Before the ditch had completely silted some quarrying of the ditch lip took place. This was noted in the section cut in trenches 6 and 8 and suggests that the irregular inner edge of the ditch noted on the plan is the result of quarrying at this time. It is equally possible that the irregularities of the Outer ditch lip in the vicinity of trench 13 were also due to quarrying.

No attempt was made to section the ditch but partial sections were obtained in trenches 1, 6 and 8 and the top of the silt was encountered in trench 10. Trenches 1 and 6 produced quantities of Late Iron Age pottery and in both cases it was possible to show that, after a long period of silting, the upper hollow of the ditch had been deliberately filled with chalk rubble possibly shovelled back from the bank (Fig. 3.37).

It is probable that the Western linear ditch (F401) was dug at about this time. It terminated close to the ditch lip and was of a flat-bottomed profile which differed from the earlier linear ditches (Fig. 3.38). The lower silt also contained Late Iron Age or early Roman pottery.

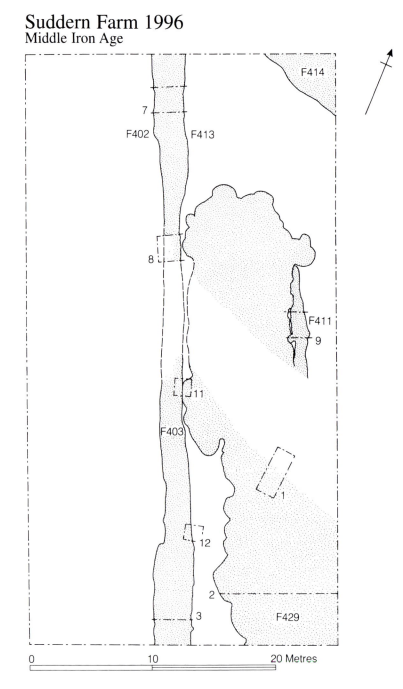

Suddern Farm 1996
Middle Iron Age

Fig. 3.34

The Roman period (Fig. 3.36)

By the beginning of the Roman period both of the enclosure ditches had silted up and been levelled. One of the earliest Roman features to be defined was a fence slot (F430 and F448) which was partially visible in plan and was sectioned in trenches 10, 11 and 13. The line of the fence followed reasonably closely the outer lip of the, now-filled, Outer enclosure ditch. It appears that the trench line was continued in a south-easterly direction by a setting of individual post-holes but the possibility remains that the posts were a later replacement of the fence the slot for which is no longer visible.

In the second century a worn hollow (F409) developed just north of the post row, over the fill of the earlier ditch (Fig. 3.37). Nearby post-holes would allow that a structure may have been built against the fence and that activity within created the hollow. The floor was covered by a layer of soil into which was trampled charcoal and a reasonable quantity of pottery, principally coarseware, of second century date. The structure is described in detail below (pp. 61–3).

To the south of the fence was a well-preserved corn-drying oven (F431) the details of which are described below (pp. 58–61). The few sherds of pottery found in the stokehole would suggest a third or fourth century date. At least one small bread oven (F408) was noted to the west of the corn drier but was not excavated. Other possible ovens were noted nearby.

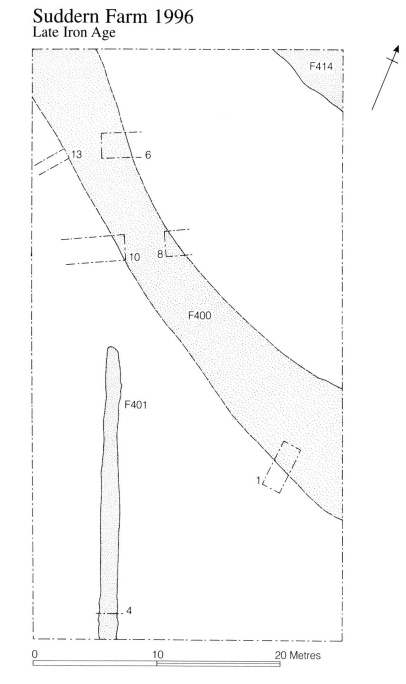

Suddern Farm 1996
Late Iron Age

F414

F400

F401

0   10   20 Metres

Fig. 3.35

In the fourth century several large roughly circular hollows 3–4 m in diameter and up to 0.3 m deep were created (F421, F459 and F460). One (F421) was half excavated in trench 8 (Fig. 3.37) and produced an assemblage of distinctive pottery of late third or fourth century date. A small cutting into F460 (trench 12) produced a few sherds of the same period. F459 was not excavated but surface sherds of the late Roman period were noted.

To the west of the site, and extending across the earlier Roman fence, a large elongated hollow occurred (F426). One cutting across the feature (trench 10) and others cut into its edge (trenches 5 and 13), showed it to be the surviving sector of a trackway which had worn deeply as a hollow way over the soft fill of the earlier ditch. The lower part of the hollow contained a layer of grey silt scored by wheel ruts. Later tips of chalk and flint nodules were thrown in to consolidate the ground and another layer of grey silt developed on the surface (Fig. 3.37). An expanse of flint nodules occurring in the north-western corner of the excavation is probably a continuation of the road line. Pottery from the silt layers is of fourth century date.

In the north-east corner of the excavation a number of pits were noted and planned. Four were chosen for sampling and were half excavated: all were of Roman date but produced very little occupation material (Fig. 3.38).

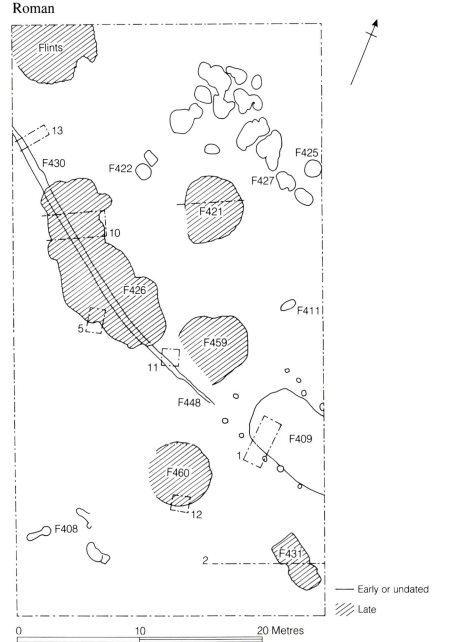

Suddern Farm 1996
Roman

Flints

13
F430
F422
F425
F427
F421

10
F426

5
F459
11
F448
F411

F409
1

F460
12

F408
2
F431

—— Early or undated
////// Late

0   10   20 Metres

Fig. 3.36

SW

906

F410

F400
(Outer enclosure ditch)

Burrow

F402

F416 (Quarry)

E

W

906

F453

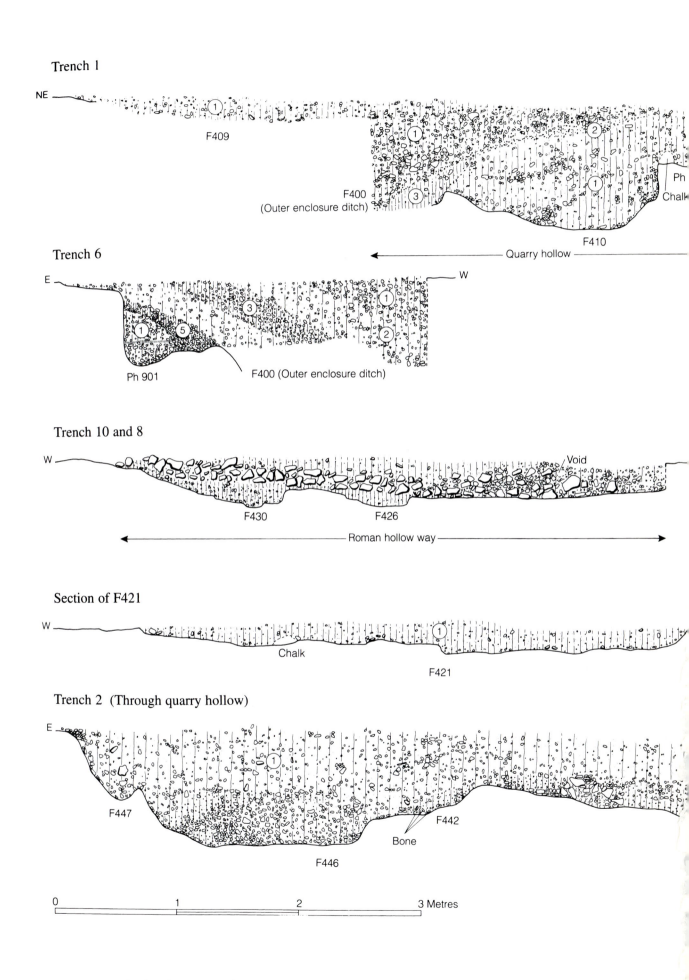

Trench 1

NE

①
F409

①

②

F400
(Outer enclosure ditch)

③

①

Ph

Chalk

F410

← Quarry hollow —

Trench 6

E

W

①

⑤

③

①

②

Ph 901

F400 (Outer enclosure ditch)

Trench 10 and 8

W

Void

F430

F426

← Roman hollow way →

Section of F421

W

①

Chalk

F421

Trench 2 (Through quarry hollow)

E

①

F447

F442

Bone

F446

0   1   2   3 Metres

Fig. 3.37 Quarries and other features in the 1996 excavation

Descriptions of selected features

As we have explained above the 1996 excavation was designed simply to define relationships between the triple linear ditches and the enclosure ditches and to do so with the minimum of excavation. It was intended to characterize the three linear ditches by cutting complete sections across them but otherwise no attempt was to be made to examine features on a large scale. However, as the excavation progressed the approach was modified to include the complete examination of the Roman corn-drying oven and of the possible Roman timber building while the surprise discovery of the Early–Middle Iron Age cemetery was followed up by extending the area of the sample.

The preceding section, describing the development of the site, gives sufficient account of the majority of the features sampled but the three elements explored on a larger scale require a more extended treatment. The Iron Age cemetery is considered in detail below (pp. 152–168). Here we give account of the Roman corn-drying oven and the Roman building.

The corn-drying kiln, F431 (Fig. 3.39 and Pls. 3.9 and 3.10)

The flue of the corn-drying kiln was discovered in cutting 2 and the excavation was subsequently extended to include the rest of the structure. The filling of the stokehole and flue was removed except for a narrow baulk of deposit in the flue, left to prevent the structure from collapsing.

The structure was built in a pit cut to a depth of 0.9–1.0 m through the filling of the Early–Mid Iron Age quarry hollow (and its cemetery) into the natural chalk beneath the quarry floor.

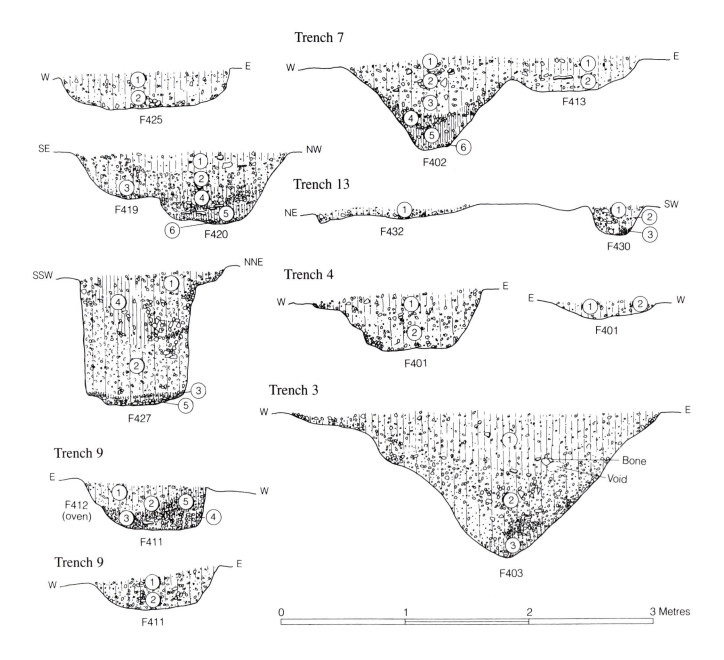

Fig. 3.38 Sections of features in the 1996 excavation

Suddern Farm 1996
Roman corn drying kiln, F431

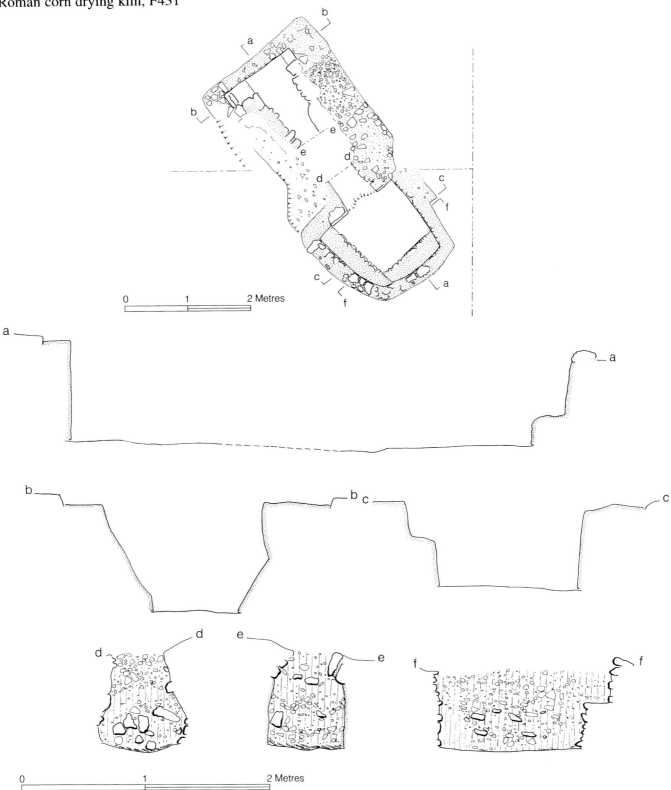

Fig. 3.39

Pl. 3.9 Stoking pit of the Roman corn-drying oven F431

Pl. 3.10 General view of the Roman corn-drying oven and the cemetery after excavation

At the south-east end was the roughly-square stoking chamber. The floor was the natural chalk, worn smooth. The walls, built directly on the floor, stood to a height of 0.64–0.76 m, incorporating six to eight courses of flint, and are up to 0.2 m thick revetting the side of the pit. The flints were roughly shaped and laid in a herringbone style set in a daub/cob matrix of pink brown silty clay tempered with rounded chalk grit. The lower part of the south-west wall was thickened, for the lowest four courses, to form a ledge 0.2 m wide and 0.42 m high. A similar ledge was created against the end (i.e. south-east) wall, 0.25–0.28 m wide and 0.21–0.25 m high. The stoking chamber, thus defined, measures 1.0 by 1.1 m at base level and c.1.35 m square at the contemporary ground level.

The flue opened from the north-west side. It measured 0.59 m wide at the base, narrowing to 0.5 m at the top. It was constructed of squared flint nodules 0.2–0.3 m long. The flue wall was built five courses high with the uppermost course jutting out over the others to form the seating for the arched roofing of the flue. One large flint of the arch remained in position and is shown in section e–e (Fig. 3.39) but the others had fallen into the flue where they remained comprising much of the lower filling of the flue. The flints of the flue walls were set in a daub/cob matrix of reddish-brown clay with chalk tempering. On top of the flints of the flue a compacted layer of chalk lumps in a chalky matrix had been laid to create the floor of the drying structure above.

At the north end the flue widened to 0.7 m and sloping vertical flues, 0.2 m wide, were provided. One sloped evenly while the other was angled. As the plan and section b–b will show the overall effect was to create a slot 0.2 m wide and 1.3 m long along the end wall of the structure. Unlike the main flue this slot was open to the floor above, no doubt to create the draught necessary to maintain combustion. Within the filling of the slot were found two complete tegulae and a complete hexagonal roof slab. In all probability these would have been used to cover the slot in such a way as to control the draught. The system, though simple, allowed the operator complete flexibility in adjusting the heat.

The main fire had been lit in the south half of the flue – the part which could be fed most simply from the stokehole. The intensity of the fire hereabouts had heavily calcined the chalk floor of the flue and had shattered the surfaces of the flints of the wall, reddening the daub in which they had been set. The intense heat which had been produced together with the lack of much soot on the walls and the fine ash produced, show that combustion was thorough. While it is possible that charcoal was used, the same result could have been obtained from wood so long as the draught was carefully controlled.

The filling of the stokehole consisted of two layers. In the bottom was a dark grey chalky soil containing finely comminuted charcoal. Above was a filling of angular and subangular chalk in a matrix of dark yellowish-brown chalky silt. The layer contains occasional charcoal flecks and some occupation debris. It has the appearance of being a deliberate fill (Fig. 3.39, section f–f).

In the flue the floor was overlain by a layer of fine charcoal c.100 mm thick sealed by a layer of grey ash of equivalent thickness but thickening in the angles. Above was the collapsed superstructure, first large flint nodules from the arch and the broken daub/cob in which they were set and then rather more chalky rubble deriving from the floor above the flue.

Nothing survives of any superstructure which may once have existed. Indeed it is quite possible that no permanent walls or roof were ever built, the structure consisting simply of a rectangular chalk floor upon which the grain (or other commodity) to be dried was laid.

Dating evidence is restricted to a brooch of the Flavian type (Fig. 3.77, no. 1.3), found protruding from the daub of the south-east wall of the stokehole, and a small quantity of pottery of the third or fourth century found in the filling of the stokehole.

The possible Roman timber building, F409
(Fig. 3.40)

It remains a possibility that a timber building was erected largely over the filling of the Outer enclosure ditch (F400).

The principal structural evidence consists of a line of large post-holes set roughly 0.7 m apart. The holes averaged 0.3 m across and the space between the upright timber and the edge had been packed with chalk and flint nodules. The post in ph 905 was 0.17 m in diameter. Other post-holes of similar type appear to have delimited the east end and north side of the structure. In total some 11 post-holes were identified of which four were excavated to provide a sample.

Within the area thus defined the soil had been worn away to a maximum depth of 0.2 m over a roughly rectangular area and the exposed surface heavily trampled. The hollow was filled with a layer of dark greyish-brown fine clayey soil containing small subangular chalk fragments and occupation debris including potsherds, animal bone, quern fragments, charcoal and ash (F409 layer 1). The overall quality of the layer suggests that it may have been created by the churning of the muddy surface of the soil, presumably by feet, at a time when occupation debris was being deposited. The way in which the potsherds were lying horizontally and were frequently crushed supports such an interpretation. At some later stage a chalk spread up to 0.15 m thick (F409 layer 2) was laid over the occupation material no doubt to consolidate the surface. The layer was limited in extent but the more superficial parts of it had probably been removed by more recent ploughing.

The nature of the structure is in some doubt, but the way in which the posts fairly precisely define the worn 'floor' suggests that the two were contemporary and the size of the posts would have allowed them to act as roof supports. A number of iron nails were recovered

Suddern Farm
Detail of Roman timber building F409

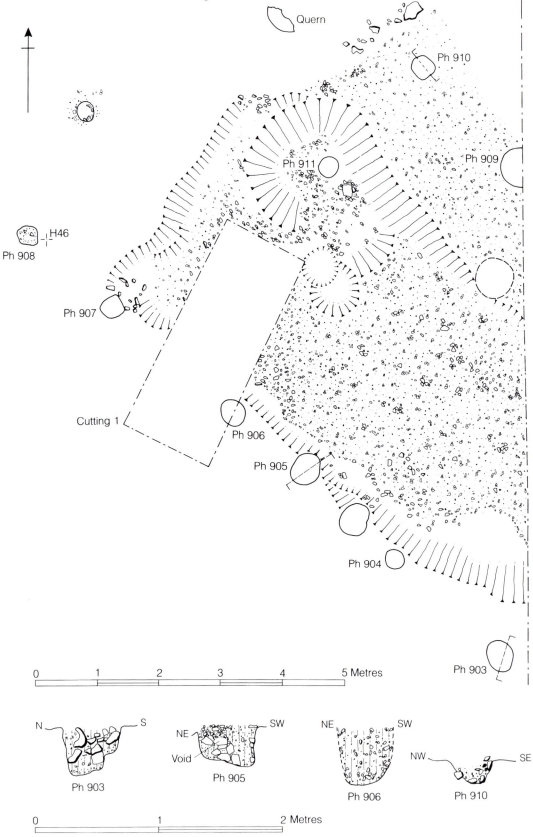

Quern

Ph 910

Ph 911

Ph 909

Ph 908

H46

Ph 907

Cutting 1

Ph 906

Ph 905

Ph 904

Ph 903

0   1   2   3   4   5 Metres

N   S   NE   SW   NE   SW   NW   SE

Void

Ph 903   Ph 905   Ph 906   Ph 910

0   1   2 Metres

Fig. 3.40

(Fiche 5:E10) which might have come from a roof structure but the few fragments of abraded tile found in the layer beneath the chalk spread cannot be regarded as indicative of a tiled roof. If the structure were roofed it is more likely to have been in shingles or thatch. There is no direct evidence to suggest function but use as a shed or a byre are possibilities.

It will be observed from the plan (Fig. 3.36) that the south wall was aligned with a fence slot (F448/F430) suggesting that the two features were part of a broadly contemporary layout.

The pottery recovered from the occupation level indicated a date spanning the second and early third centuries.

Area 4 (1991): the linear earthworks north-west of the enclosure

The linear earthworks visible on the air photographs to the west of the enclosure were investigated by trial trenching in 1991 (Fig. 3.2). The main question to be addressed was whether the earthwork which showed so clearly descending Suddern Hill, and is traceable on the air photographs as far as the trackway to the north-west of the site, approached the north-west corner of the enclosure and was the same as the vague cropmark noted closer to the enclosure (Palmer 1984, 113).

Suddern Farm 1991
Linear earthworks

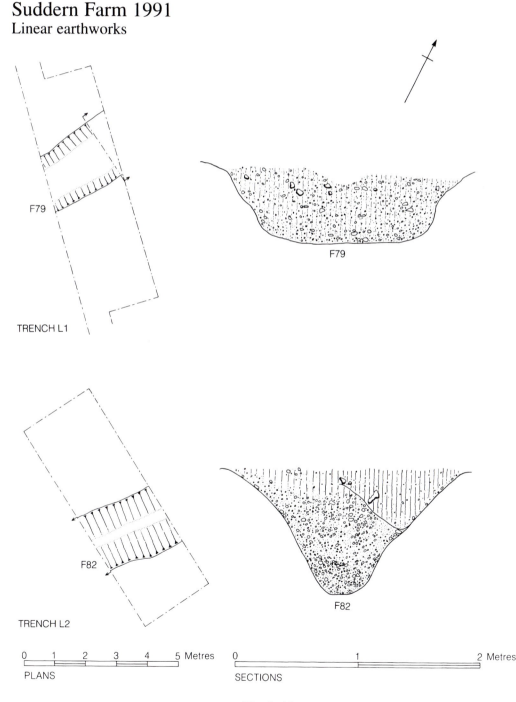

Fig. 3.41

63

Details of the sections

A machine-dug trench was cut across the field some 30 m west of the enclosure to test the nearer cropmark (Fig. 3.3). The ditch (F79) was located and the trench was extended to a width of 2 m and the ditch excavated (Fig. 3.41). The feature proved to be 2 m wide and had been dug to a depth of 0.6 m with steep sides and a flat bottom. The filling was uniform, consisting of a chalky silt which seems to have accumulated quite quickly. No dating evidence was recovered.

The main linear was located just to the west of the trackway and examined in a 2 m wide trench (Fig. 3.41). As originally cut the ditch (F82) was V-shaped in profile, 1.9 m wide and 1.0 m deep. It had silted naturally with a chalky silt in the lower part grading to a soil as the ditch filled. At a later date it was partially recut as a much smaller V-profiled ditch 1.1 m wide and 0.5 m deep. The filling of the later ditch was largely of chalky soil which had washed in from the sides. No dating evidence was found in either ditch.

The profiles and fills of the ditches sectioned in the two trial trenches were sufficiently different to suggest that they were not part of the same system. This observation together with the precise location of the ditches led to a reassessment of the air photographic coverage suggesting that the main linear, after crossing the line of the track, veered slightly northwards away from the enclosure and ran roughly parallel to the south side of the track (Fig. 3.3). The profile of the nearer ditch is so different from those of classic linears that it may well be totally unrelated and of an entirely different date. The profile of the ditch resembles the Western linear (F401) examined in Area 3 for which a Late Iron Age date is likely.

3 Material Culture

The pottery by Lisa Brown

Introduction

The total recorded ceramic assemblage from the two excavations at Suddern Farm consists of 14,257 sherds weighing 262.54 kg. Since the excavations were undertaken with different research objectives and sampling methods, it was decided that separate ceramic reports should be produced, suitably cross-referenced, and with a combined overview.

The ceramic assemblage from Suddern Farm is exclusively of Iron Age and Roman date and appears to lack the small Bronze Age component present at Danebury, New Buildings and Nettlebank Copse. In common with the Woolbury and Houghton Down groups, the Roman component is sizeable. The ceramics from these three sites have provided the basis of the recording format for sherds of specifically Roman type which is, essentially, an expansion and modification of the format originally devised for the largely Iron Age Danebury assemblage. Details of the integrated recording system are set out in the form of an updated type series in Volume 1, 79–126 and is listed for convenience in Fiche 5:C12–13.

The 1991 assemblage

The 1991 excavation at Suddern Farm produced 12,096 sherds weighing 243.78 kg, recovered from a total of 168 features: 107 pits, 30 post-holes and 31 other features including gullies and hollows. All sherds were retained, washed, marked and stored according to context. The record is stored on a Microsoft Access database.

Method

The pottery assemblage spans the period from the earliest Iron Age to the late Roman era. Consequently, a uniform recording procedure was not suitable and, in common with other Environs sites, separate *pro formae* were employed for pottery of characteristic Roman type. The Suddern Farm assemblage includes pottery types which substantially enhance the type series relevant to the latest Iron Age and the early Romano-British periods. There is, therefore, inevitably, a degree of chronological and typological overlap which cannot always be separated logically. For the purposes of this report, pottery attributable to a point within the first century AD and not demonstrably a product of an identified early Roman production centre has been recorded as a Late Iron Age type, and the recording system expanded to accommodate it. The fact that the site seems to have received very little in the way of fineware imports and much in the way of coarseware copies, hence demonstrating a high degree of cultural integrity until a point in the second century or thereabouts, justifies the treatment of the assemblage as a valid entity until the point at which it begins to receive products of the established Roman industries.

The result of this method is that the Iron Age and the Roman recording systems contain elements of overlap. For example, a butt-beaker produced as a coarseware copy in a fabric originating from a source which had previously manufactured Iron Age forms found at Suddern Farm, will appear in the record as form BkA, and the fabric recorded as the appropriate Iron Age type. A fineware butt-beaker produced at a site such as Colchester will be recorded as BE4 and the appropriate Roman fabric type entered.

A small proportion of the pottery was recovered from subsidence hollows within pit tops. In some cases, these sherds clearly post-dated the filling of the pit proper. These 930 sherds (weighing 13.12 kg) were, therefore, regarded as unstratified and were not recorded in detail. The vast majority of this group consisted of heavily abraded Roman sherds.

The remainder of the assemblage, all of which was recorded to the same level of detail, was divided as follows for purposes of accessing:

Iron Age and first century AD: 9366 sherds weighing 201.55 kg.

Roman: 1800 sherds weighing 29.11 kg.

Forms and fabrics: production and sources (Table 3.8 and Fig. 3.42)

Detailed descriptions of vessel forms and fabrics are provided in the integrated type series (Vol. 1, 81–91) and need not be summarized here. This section provides a general assessment and discussion of the nature of the assemblage.

The Iron Age pottery

The Early Iron Age assemblage is small, deriving from fewer than half a dozen pits. Pit P91 produced furrowed bowl sherds and fragments with fingertip decoration which correspond well with early types from Danebury (designated cp 1–2) and other sites in the region. Fabrics include fine untempered clay and fine sand or flint-tempered wares. Sources have not been securely established for these wares, but some of the sandy wares derive from glauconitic clays, and the fine smooth clay fabrics may be related to those used in the production of cordoned bowls, for which a Wiltshire source has been suggested (Cunliffe 1984, 245). Red-finished cordoned bowls were found in association with shouldered jars and tripartite bowls in coarsewares in three pits (P113, P135, P212) in common with numerous pit assemblages assigned to cp 3 and 4 at Danebury. EIA finewares are, however, rare at Suddern Farm with a mere nine vessels of forms BB1–3 represented by recovered sherds.

The Middle Iron Age assemblages from Suddern Farm and Danebury exhibit some significant discrepancies. At Danebury the proportions of flint-tempered wares (Fabric B) steadily increase at the expense of sandy wares until, by the late Middle Iron Age (cp 7) they predominate by a large margin. Sandy fabrics re-emerge as the dominant type in the mid first century (Cunliffe 1984, 237). At Suddern Farm, flint-tempered wares (Fabric B) represent only 3% of the total of Iron Age fabrics. This is not particularly surprising in view of the predominantly late nature of the assemblage, but even within the MIA pit deposits, flint-tempered wares are uncommon. This point is illustrated particularly well by the example of four pits (P78, P92, P120 and P140) which, on typological

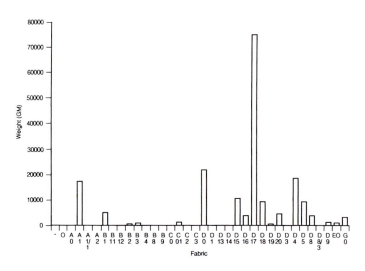

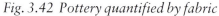

Fig. 3.42 Pottery quantified by fabric

grounds, have been assigned to cp 7. In these four pits the range of proportions of B fabrics is 0.5–23.0% whilst that of D fabrics (sandy wares) is 54.8–97.0%. In contrast, during this phase at Danebury Fabric B achieved its peak in relation to Fabric D.

It is necessary to look beyond the fabric proportions in order to attempt to explain this discrepancy. The occurrence of decorated sherds is very low at Suddern Farm but, within the MIA assemblage, the most common motif is the shallow-tooled arc (code 5.1h or 5.1f). The line and dot 'stitching' motif (5.1/3b), so common at Danebury in this phase, occurs extremely rarely within the Suddern Farm group. Furthermore, pit P140 produced a complete vessel (Fig. 3.46, no. 33) bearing a decorative motif which is represented by only a single uncertain

\multicolumn{24}{c}{Table 3.8. Iron Age pottery: form/fabric correlation}
Form											Fabric												
	A0	A1	B1	B3	B9	C01	C2	D0	D4	D5	D8	D9	D15	D16	D17	D18	D20	E0	G0	G1	G2	G3	VESSELS
BA						1	2								1			2					6
BB															1	1		7					9
BC2							1						1			1							3
BC3								3	1						47		2			3	2		58
BD2								4	1						3								8
BD4								13			1				20		3			2	1		39
BD5															2	1					1		
BE1		2									3												5
BK								9							5	1						1	16
C								3							1	5							9
DA1–2							1				1	2											4
F								4															4
JA		2						3								1							6
JB1–3	1	3				1		7	9			1	2	3	4		1						32
JB4		6		2				1						1	1								11
JC1		3						3		1		1	1										9
JC2		2	6			1		12			2		5			7							35
JC3			1					9			3		2	1	48		6		1	5	3	1	80
JD1–4			1	1				4	2			1	3		17	2	6		1	1			39
JD5															2				1	5	4		
JE1								2							1					1			4
JE4							1	4							30	5				3	1		44
PA1–3		15						10		2	1	6			4		1						39
PB1			15	1				9	1			6	2			10							44
PL1–3															18	28							46
LID															26	4		1			1	1	33

example from amongst the 158,000 sherd assemblage from Danebury (Cunliffe 1984, fig. 6.80, 716). This infilled arc and dot may be a variation of the simple arc described above. As was the case at Danebury, the arc motif occurred most commonly on vessels produced in a glauconitic sandy fabric which would have derived from Upper Greensand beds, probably to the west of Danebury in Wiltshire. Although the source has not been proven the fabric will henceforth, in this report, be referred to as 'Wiltshire type.' This fabric, D15, is amongst the most prolific of wares occurring in MIA contexts at Suddern Farm and represents 4.5% of all Iron Age fabrics. Vessel no. 33 was produced in fabric D15, suggesting a clear link between the simple and the dot-infilled arc motifs.

It appears that the settlement's ceramic intake range for the Middle Iron Age had a focus which was different to that of Danebury. Certainly there are areas of overlap, particularly with regard to vessel form, with saucepan pots and bipartite jars predominating at both sites. But whether for reasons of location or of site status, the occurrence at Suddern Farm of only four sherds of flint-tempered stitch-decorated sherds, so common at Danebury, represents an obvious disparity between the two assemblages.

If there are chronological implications to this anomaly, the sample of MIA pottery is too small to allow clarification of the point, but with regard to Fabric D15, one further point should be made. Most of the Suddern Farm deposits of cp 7 date have been so assigned on the basis of a very few sherds bearing shallow-tooled decoration. Most of these decorated sherds are of the 'Wiltshire' variety described above and were recovered in association with undecorated vessels in other fabrics which would, in the absence of the Wiltshire types, have been assigned a cp 6 date. It is worth considering the possibility that decorated vessels of the Wiltshire variety pre-date by a small margin the decorated types more commonly found at Danebury and that the Suddern Farm assemblage reflects not simply a difference in the import sources, but a chronological difference. If it can be argued that contexts containing only the Wiltshire-style decorated vessels amongst a preponderance of plain vessels should correspond to cp 6 at Danebury, then the evidence for the existence of cp 7 at Suddern Farm is slight.

Two salient points emerge from a consideration of the Late Iron Age assemblage. The first is that there is a virtual absence of true finewares of the type which commonly occur in central southern England in the first century BC–AD. No certain examples of Gallo-Belgic wares or fineware copies have been identified. A painted vessel of uncertain type from the top of the fill of the inner ditch may prove to be an exception (Fig. 3.63, no. 592). This sherd is unique to the site and its source, though unproven, may be France. Otherwise, there is a wide range of coarse 'native' copies of fineware forms in association with the common range of utilitarian vessels. Amongst the 'native' copies are platters, butt-beakers and girth

beakers. The copies were produced in a variety of sand-tempered fabrics, particularly D4, D17, D20 and, less frequently, a variety of grog-tempered wares (Fabric G). In the period following AD 180, some of these same vessel forms were also produced at the Alice Holt kilns. Fabric D4, which is discussed in detail elsewhere in this report, is an ill-defined sandy ware which may be a product of several production centres. Fabric D20, however, is distinctive and clearly derives from a single source, possibly related to D17, the tourmaline-rich Wareham–Poole Harbour ware (David Williams, pers. comm.). The majority of platter copies were manufactured either in fabric D20 or D17.

The second feature of the Late Iron Age assemblage is the high incidence of Wareham–Poole Harbour wares (D17). From the mid first century BC the proportion of sherds in this fabric is very high. It constitutes 25% of the total assemblage and if Fabric D20 is included in the statistics, the figure rises to just over 26%. If the Roman Black Burnished I Ware element is included, the total proportion of wares with a Wareham–Poole Harbour region source is over 30%. By contrast, the second most common Late Iron Age fabric, D4, comprises only 14% of the Iron Age total and grog-tempered wares just under 9%. Clearly, the Late Durotrigian production centres had achieved a certain significance if their products were supplying this relatively distant site with such a large proportion of their wares. The intriguing element in this scenario of movement of goods, however, is seen not so much in the importation of the standard range of Late Durotrigian pottery, but in the presence of a large number of non-standard Durotrigian vessels – platters, butt-beakers and girth beakers. Even the Hengistbury Head excavations did not produce such a wide range of exotic forms from Poole Harbour. The 'specialized' forms within that assemblage are copies of Armorican cordoned bowls. At Suddern Farm, the emphasis seems to have been on copying the Gallo-Belgic ceramic tradition. If the Suddern Farm settlement was of such low status, however, that it was not receiving true Gallo-Belgic wares or British finewares at least, it seems odd that coarse copies were obtained from so distant a source.

The Roman pottery

The paucity of finewares is a feature of the Suddern Farm assemblage which continued into the Roman period until the point at which New Forest and Oxfordshire colour-coated wares were introduced to the site. Only 24 sherds of samian ware (representing 13 or fewer vessels) were recovered. Of the small number of early style beaker and flagon sherds in fine white and orange fabrics, none has been clearly identified as a product of a particular production site, and all may be of relatively local production. The bulk of the early Roman assemblage is composed of reduced wares, most of which resemble fabrics produced at the Alice Holt kilns (Jane Timby, pers. comm.). Grog-tempered wares account for just over

15% of the total of Roman sherds and, although notoriously difficult to date, most can be assigned to first and second century date on the basis of associated material. Much of this group probably originated from production centres fairly local to the site, although there are several examples of a Savernake type (Fig. 3.61, no. 437) which should date to 180+.

In the third century the settlement was receiving products of the New Forest and, to a lesser extent, the Oxfordshire kilns. Most sherds of these wares are heavily abraded and fragmentary, but several well documented types have been identified including New Forest indented beakers (Fulford type 33) and a painted flask (type 1/10) (Fulford 1975, 44 and 52). A complete indented beaker (Fig. 3.67, no. 655) was recovered with an inhumation burial in the fill of enclosure ditch F66. In spite of the influx of New Forest fine and coarsewares, the Alice Holt kilns appear to have continued to be a major source of coarse reduced wares, although common grey wares of the two production sites can be difficult to distinguish from each other.

Black Burnished Ware I occurs in most of the Roman deposits. In some cases, body sherds with no distinguishing features may be mis-assigned Late Durotrigian wares, but BBI can usually be distinguished by its texture, wall thickness and other features such as slips. Intake from the Poole Harbour production centres continued at a significant level, BBI (Fabric 1.1) representing 10% of the Roman assemblage. The common assortment of straight-sided dishes, flanged bowls and cooking pots occur in association with a variety of reduced wares from other sources.

Oxidized wares (Fabrics 3, 4 and 5) represent only 9% of the Roman assemblage. Most examples are unfeatured body sherds and the majority are of a coarse or medium grade fabric. Most of the fine lightwares resemble the Oxfordshire varieties, but in the absence of diagnostic sherds, identification is tenuous.

The Roman assemblage as a whole does not suggest a site of particularly high status, even for the third century onwards. No evidence of substantial structures was produced and the utilitarian nature of those features which were excavated – ovens, small pits and 'working hollows' – reflect, on the whole, the essential character of the ceramics.

Chronology

The ceramic evidence indicates occupation of varying degrees of intensity beginning in the seventh century BC or marginally earlier and continuing, *possibly* with a break in cp 7, until some point in the fourth century AD. Pit P91 produced an assemblage including furrowed bowl fragments (form BE1) and body sherds bearing fingertipped decoration. Similar assemblages from Houghton Down are assigned to an 'Earliest Iron Age' phase, probably dating to c.800 BC. The small quantity of pottery dating to the seventh–fifth centuries was recovered from a few pits which, as they contained no later material (except

occasionally in the subsidence hollows) appear to have been filled during the period in which the pottery was being used. The fact that very little residual EIA material occurred in later pits suggests that this phase of occupation may not have been intense. Typical assemblages relating to this period are illustrated below (P135, P212) and in fiche (P113).

Fifth century style pottery was also recovered, although only two pits appear to date to that period. Both contain a sufficient quantity of pottery to indicate typological coherence but the combined evidence for occupation during the fifth century is scant. Similar ceramic forms, which would have been assigned a cp 4–5 date at Danebury, were found in a number of other pits in association with apparently later types. The circumstances of deposition of these vessels are puzzling in that they clearly do not occur as residual artefacts. P92, for example, contained a number of complete and near complete vessels, some of which were deliberately placed around the pit edge half way up the fill (layers 4/6). This group included vessels of Danebury cp 4–5 style (JB4, PA1) deposited in unmistakable association with decorated saucepan pots, heretofore dated to cp 7. In this case all decorated sherds were of the so-called Wiltshire type discussed above. There are several possible explanations for this apparent anomaly. Since it is unlikely that these cp 4–5 type vessels were curated in complete condition for 200–400 years, it may be necessary to accept that these simple utilitarian forms were produced over a long period and into the late Middle Iron Age (Brown in Cunliffe 1995, 246). There is also reason to believe that the Wiltshire-style decorated saucepan pots may pre-date, in their inception, their flint-tempered counterparts, as has been discussed above (and also elsewhere in this volume).

A relatively small collection of saucepan pots (PB1.1) and bipartite jars (JC2.1–3), mostly undecorated, attest to a MIA presence contemporary with the cp 6 occupation at Danebury. Sherds representing approximately 85 vessels of these types were identified. Most examples of both forms occur in a variety of sand-tempered wares including D15, the distinctive glauconitic ware discussed earlier above, and D18, another glauconite-rich fabric of quite a different character. The evidence for occupation correlating to Danebury's cp 7 is, however, less clear. It has already been argued that the arc/wave motif decorated glauconitic saucepan pots may pre-date cp 7 at Danebury. Decorated flint-tempered wares which dominate the cp 7 collection are virtually absent at Suddern Farm and suggest either a chronological gap at this point or a significant difference in ceramic tradition or status between the two sites.

Occupation of some form in the first century BC–AD is clearly demonstrated by the enclosure ditch sequences. The fills of both of the larger ditches produced substantial quantities of pottery of this date. The assemblage from the inner ditch (F64)

continues on page 102

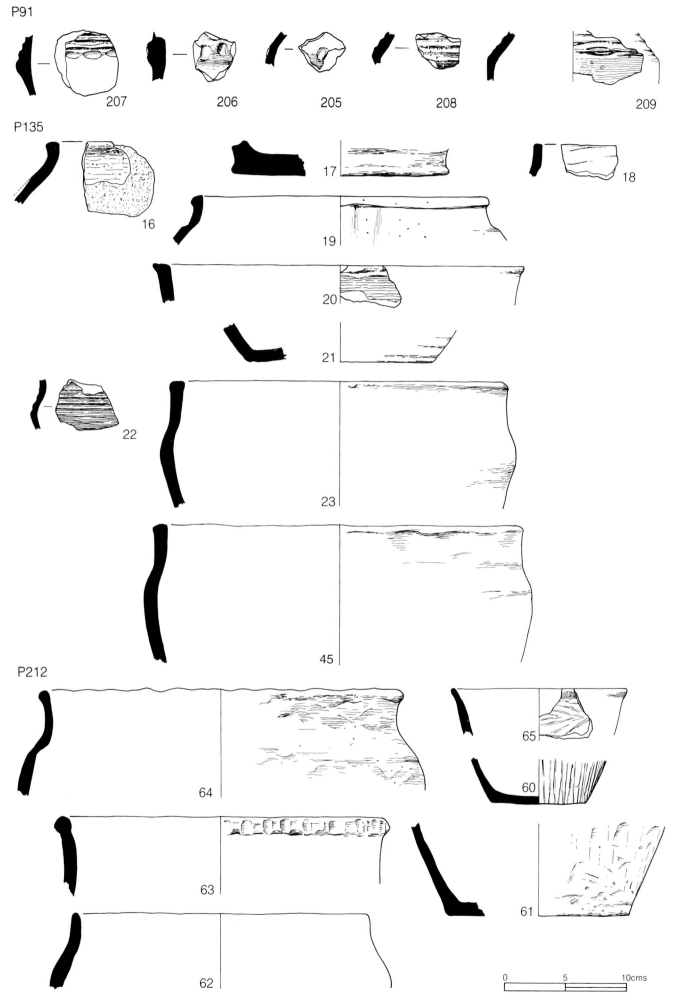

P91

207 206 205 208 209

P135

16 17 18 19 20 21 22 23 45

P212

64 65 60 63 61 62

0 5 10cms

Fig. 3.43 Pottery

P194

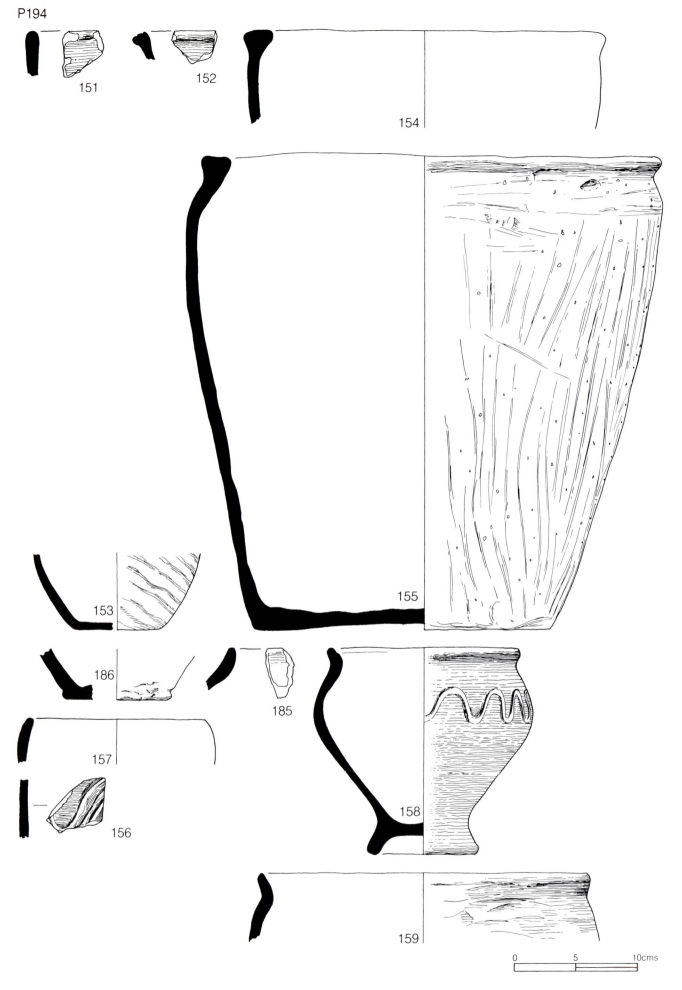

151

152

154

153

155

186

185

157

158

156

159

0   5   10cms

Fig. 3.44 (above) Pottery

Fig. 3.45 (right) Pottery

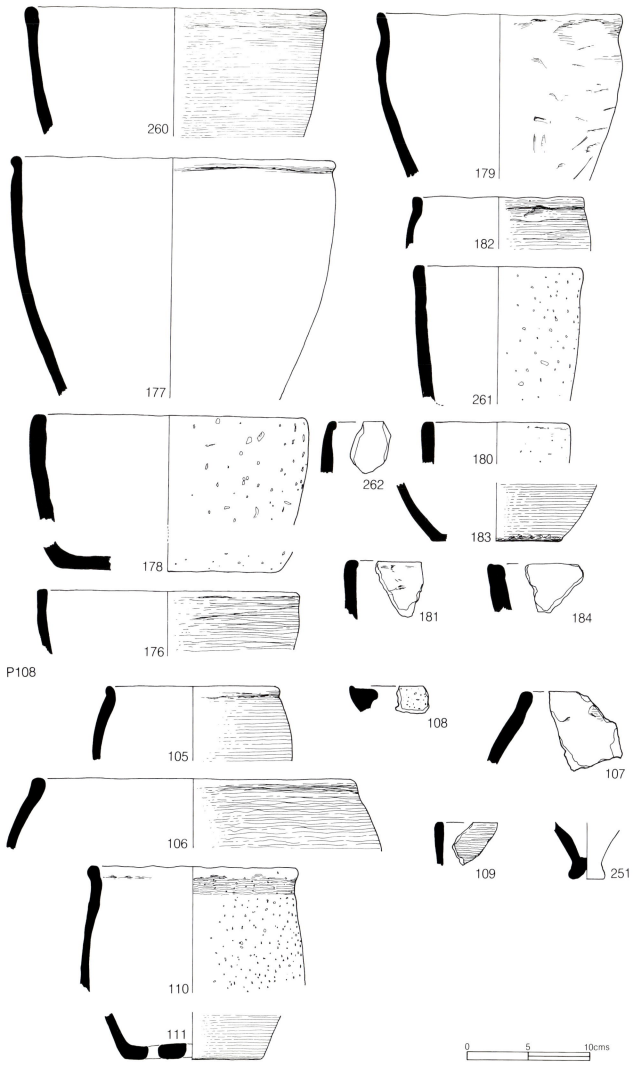

P197

260

177

178

176

179

182

261

262

180

183

181

184

P108

105

106

110

111

108

107

109

251

0   5   10cms

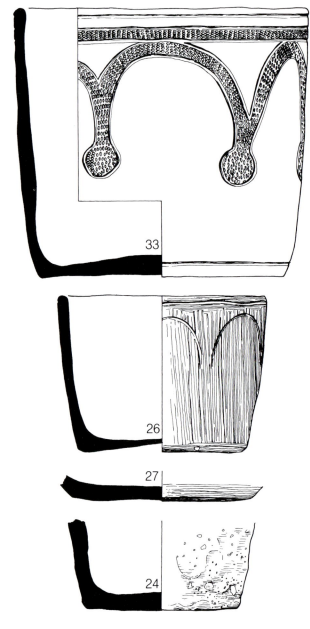

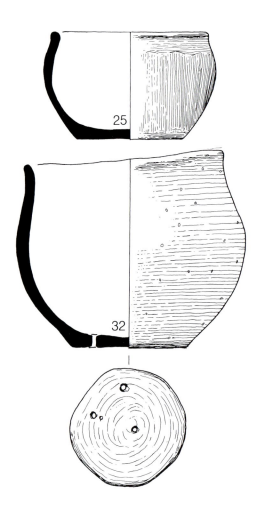

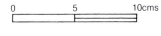

Fig. 3.46 Pottery

Fig. 3.47 (right) Pottery

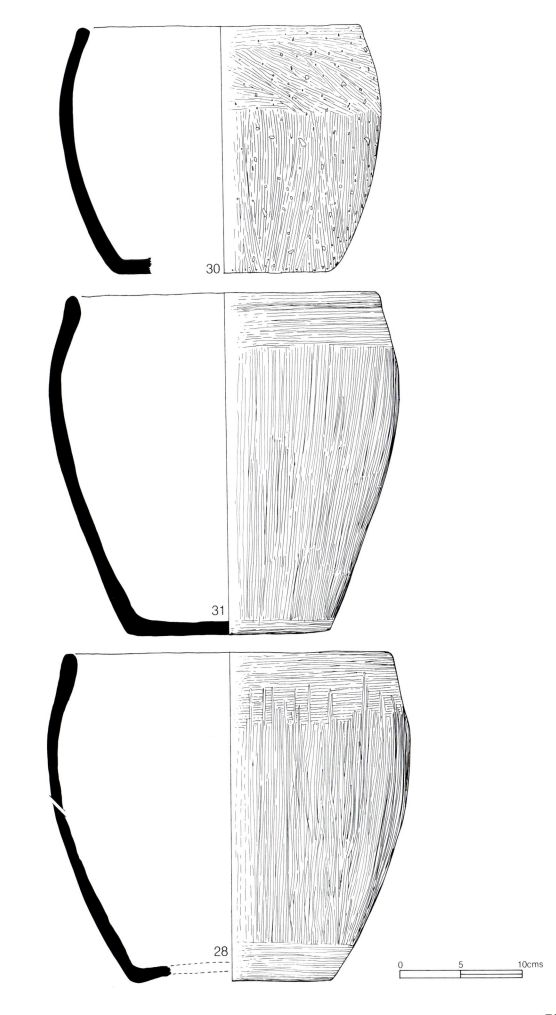

30

31

28

0   5   10cms

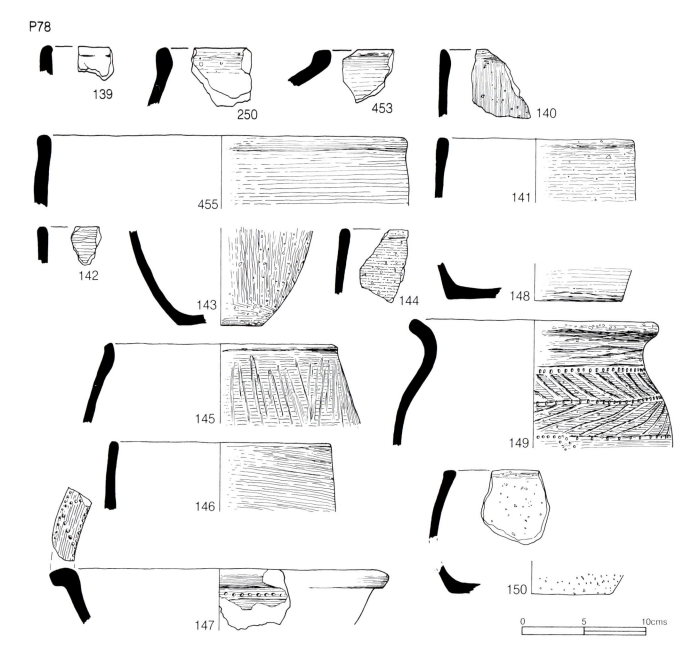

Fig. 3.48 Pottery

Fig. 3.49 (right) Pottery

P92

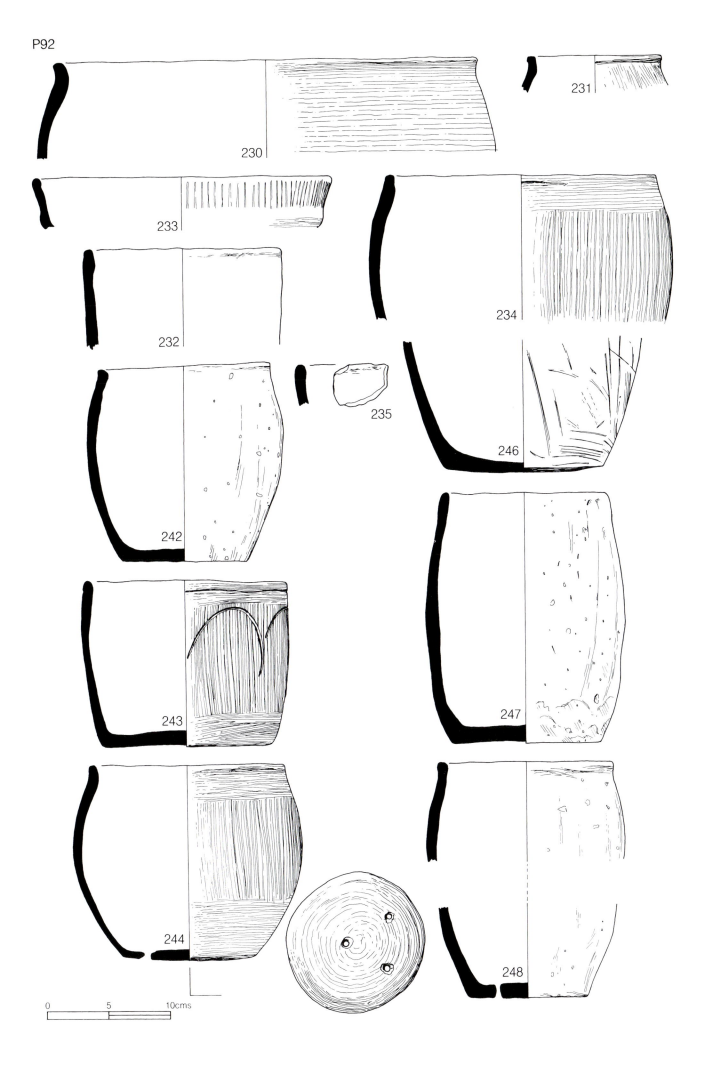

230

231

233

234

232

242

235

246

243

247

244

248

0   5   10cms

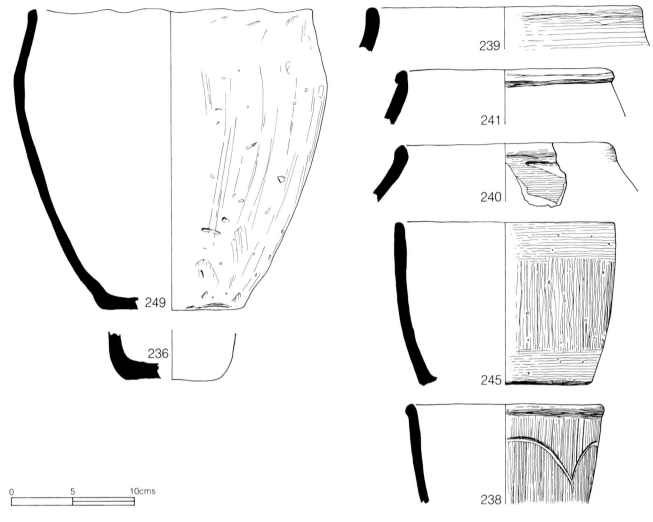

0   5   10cms

Fig. 3.50 Pottery

P120

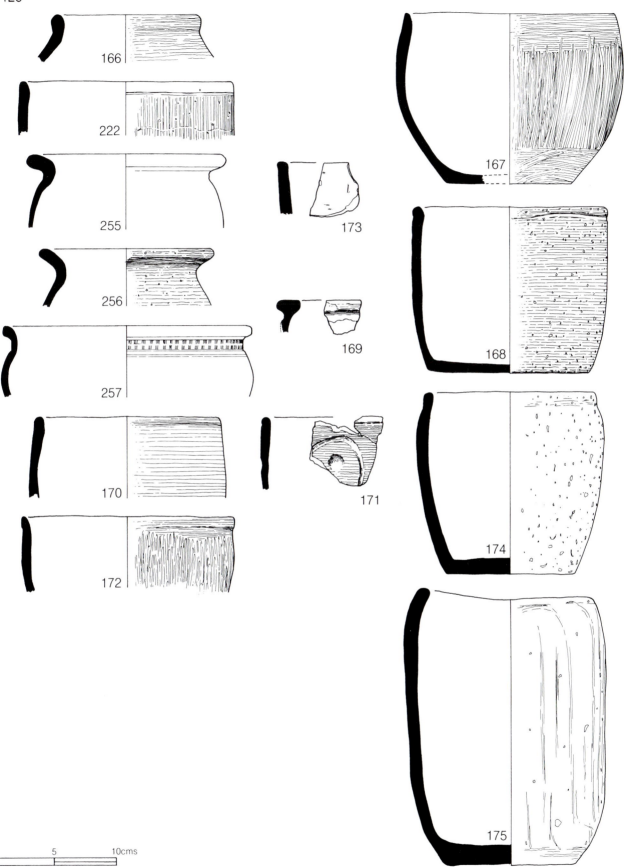

Fig. 3.51 Pottery

0   5   10cms

77

P104

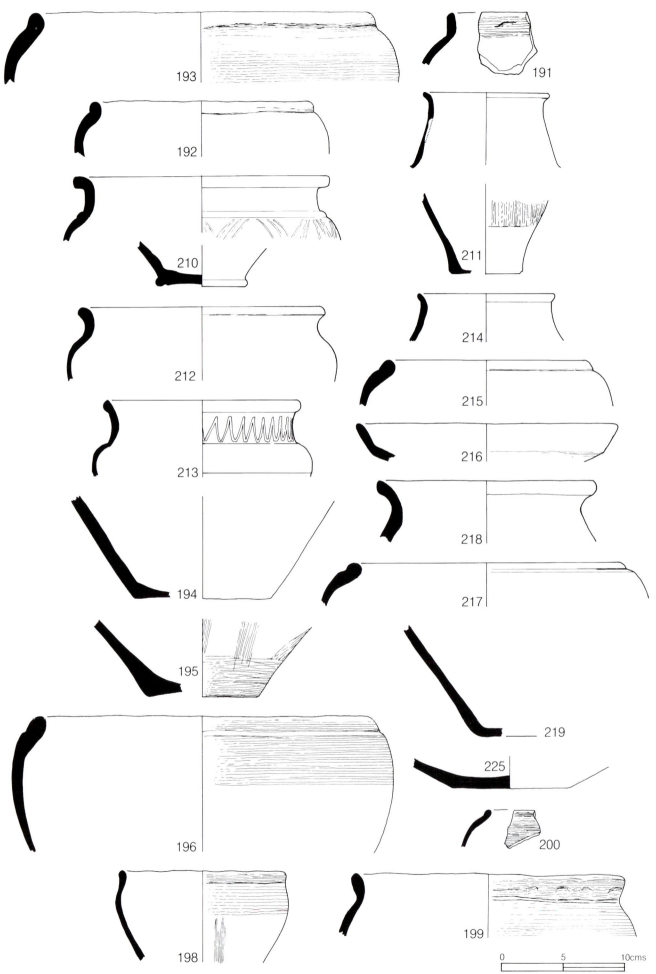

P104 (cont.)

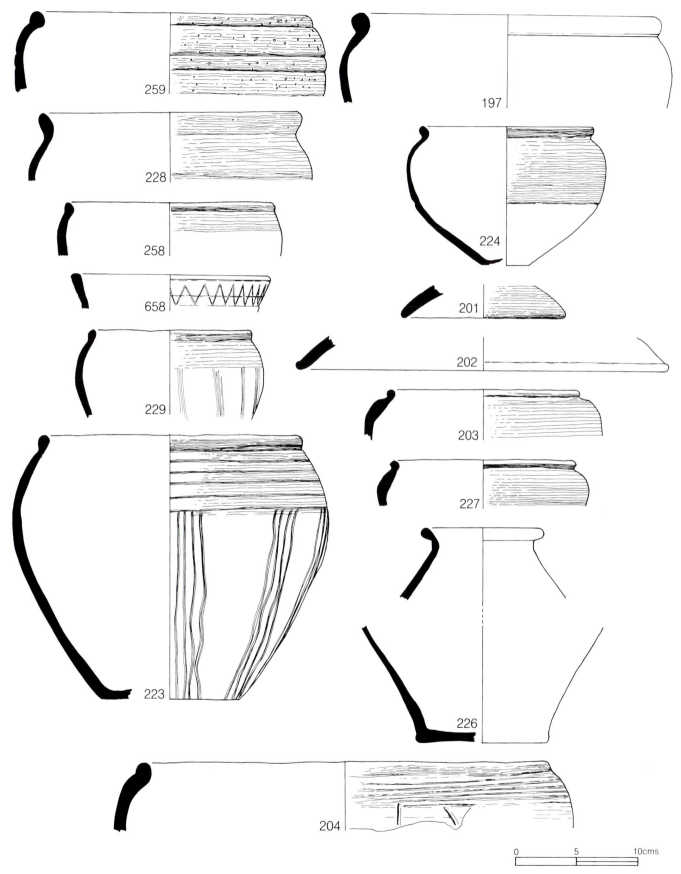

259

228

258

658

229

223

197

224

201

202

203

227

226

204

0   5   10cms

Fig. 3.53 Pottery

Fig. 3.52 (left) Pottery

79

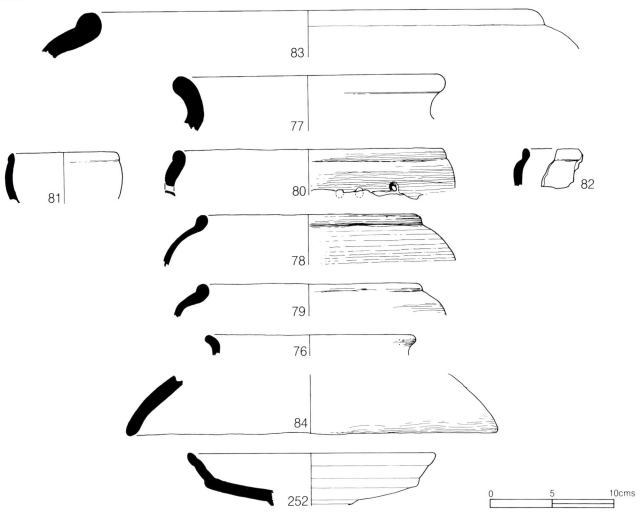

83

77

81

80

82

78

79

76

84

252

0   5   10cms

Fig. 3.54 Pottery

Fig. 3.55 (right) Pottery

P119

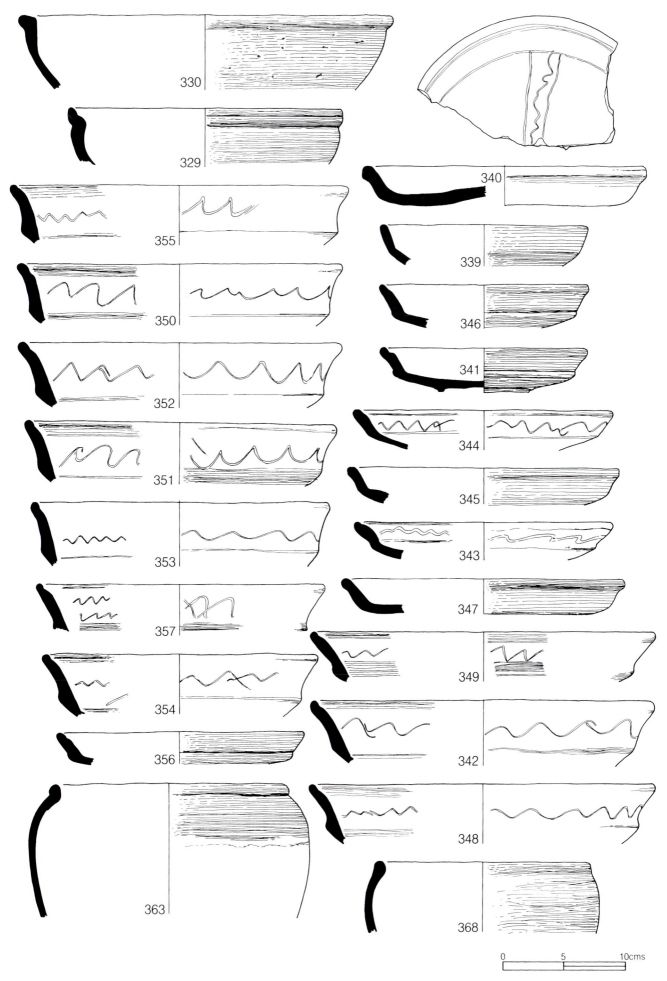

330

329

355

350

352

351

353

357

354

356

363

340

339

346

341

344

345

343

347

349

342

348

368

0   5   10cms

P119 (cont.)

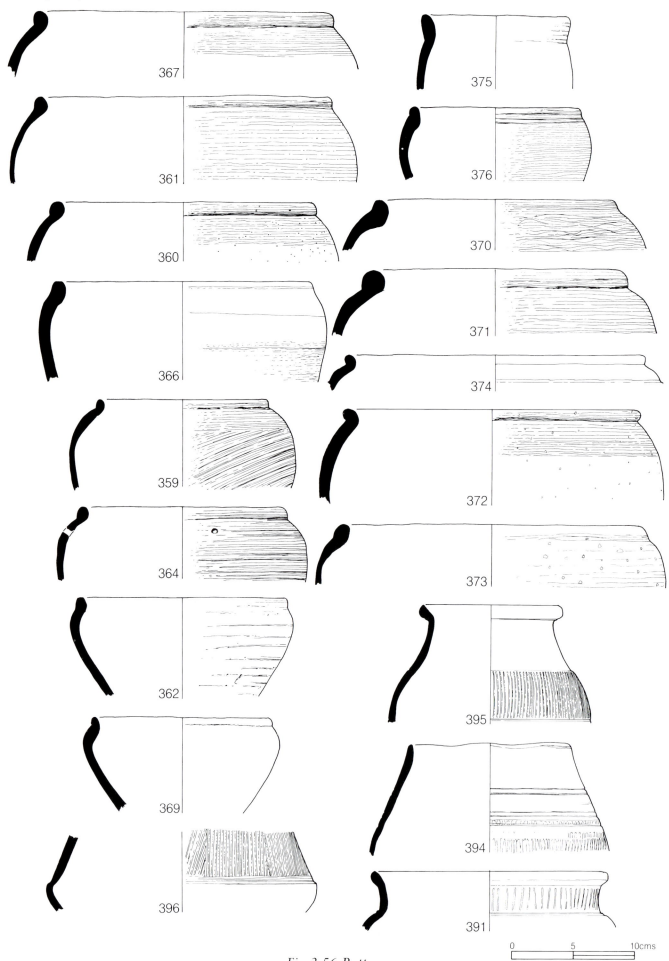

Fig. 3.56 Pottery

P119 (cont.)

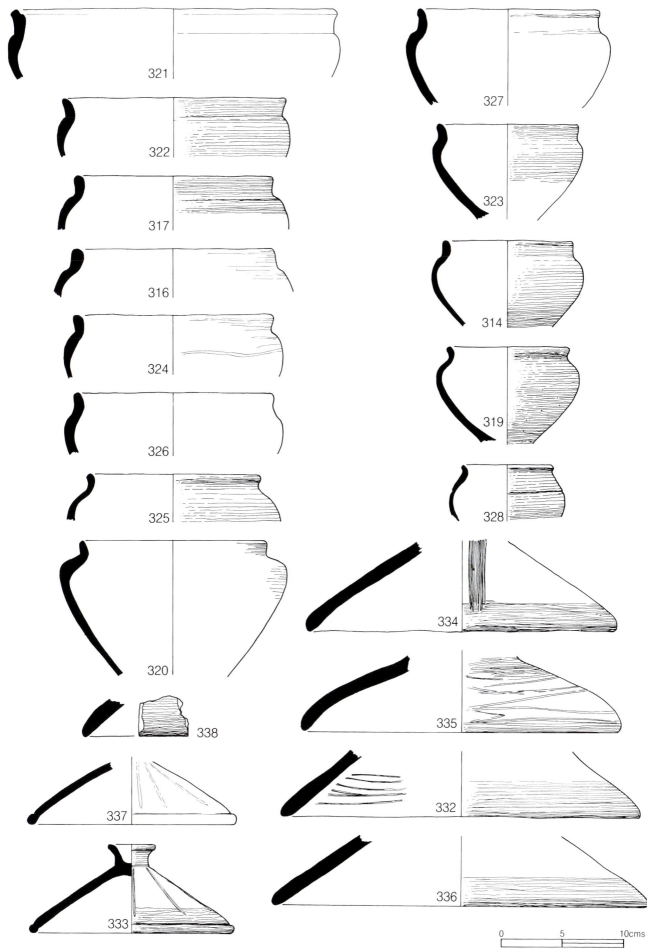

Fig. 3.57 Pottery

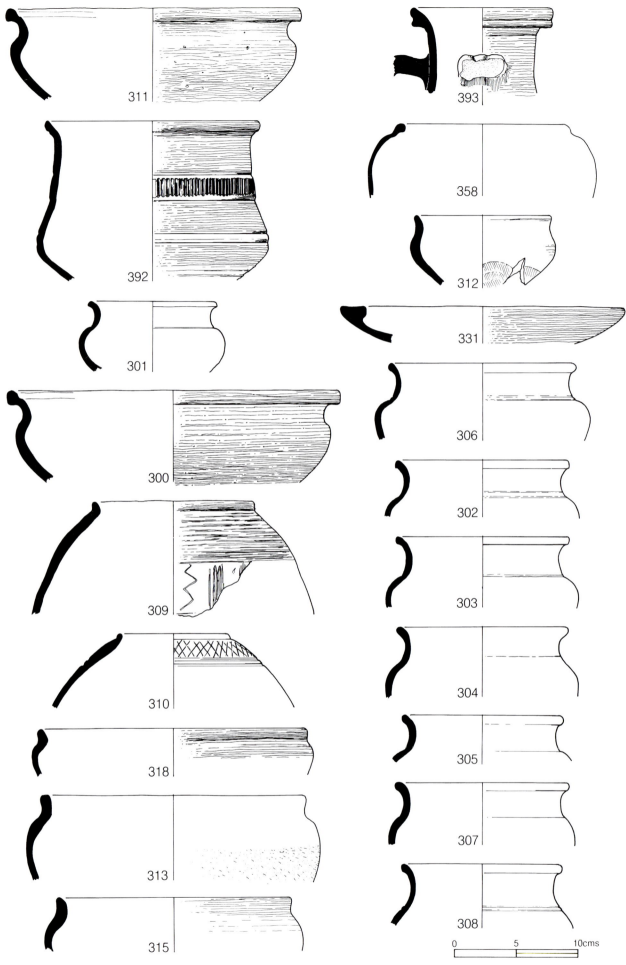

Fig. 3.58 Pottery

P119 (cont.)

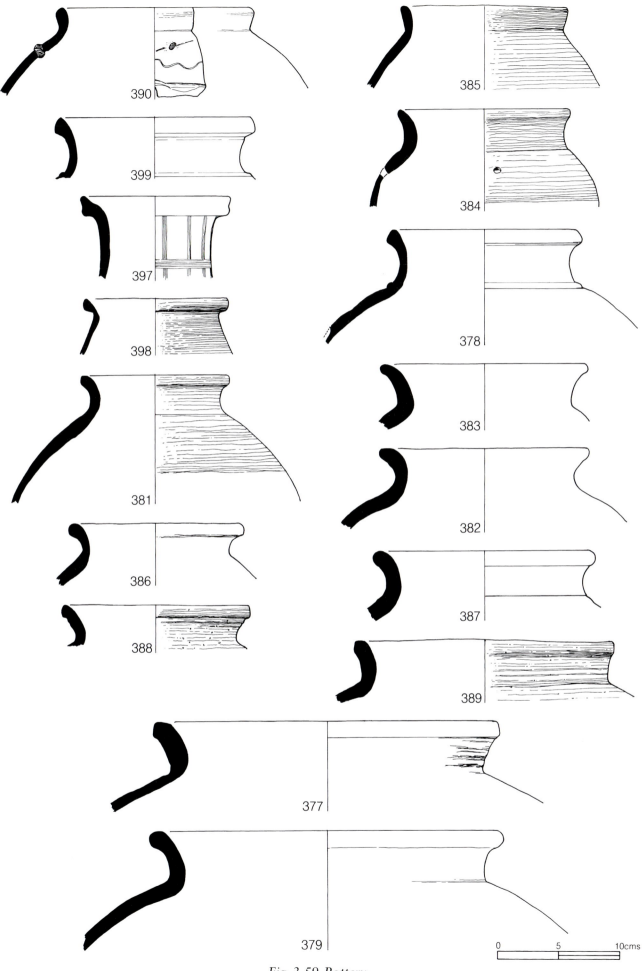

Fig. 3.59 Pottery

85

P125

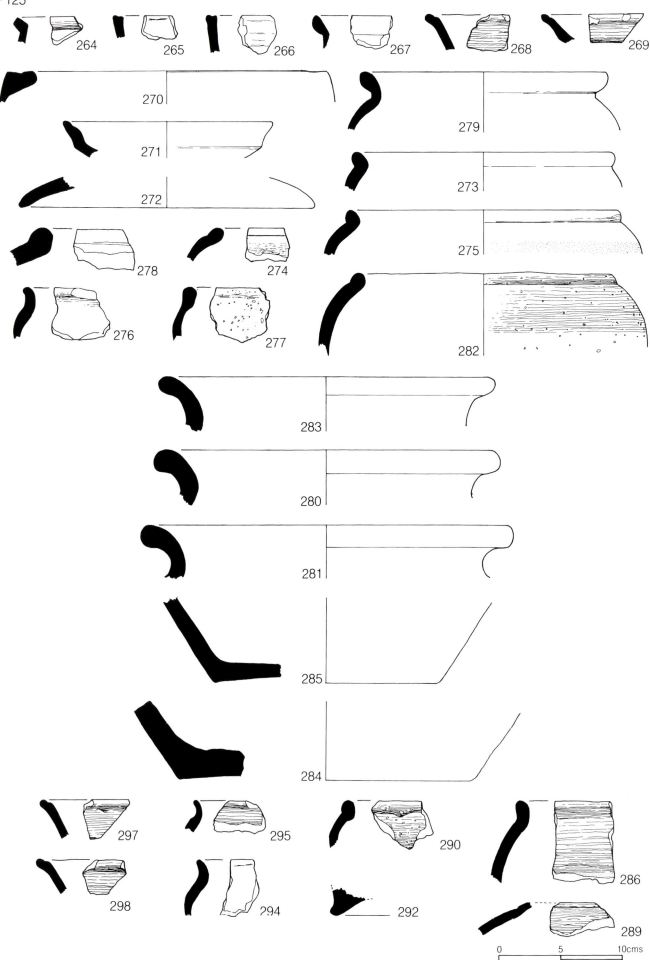

264
265
266
267
268
269
270
279
271
273
272
278
274
275
276
277
282
283
280
281
285
284
297
295
290
298
294
292
286
289

0   5   10cms

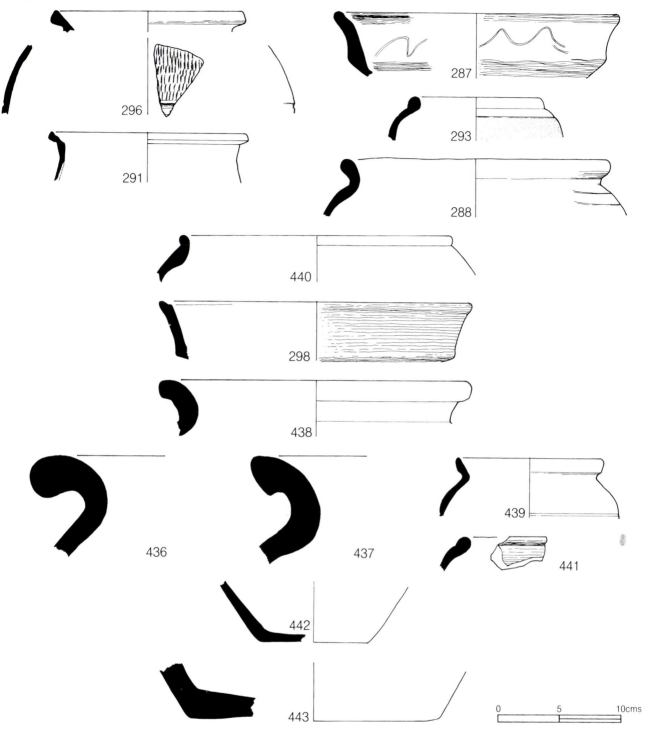

Fig. 3.61 Pottery

Fig. 3.60 (left) Pottery

F64

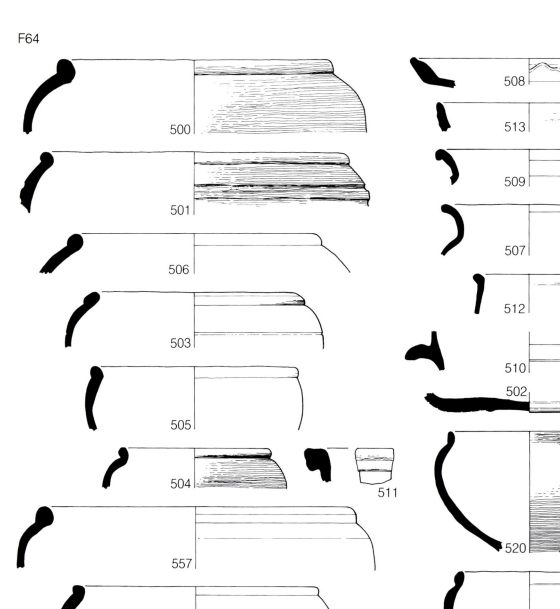

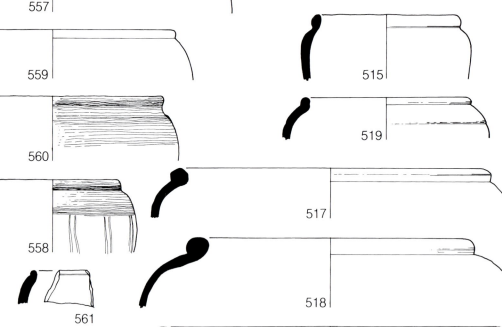

0   5   10cms

Fig. 3.62 (above) Pottery

Fig. 3.63 (right) Pottery

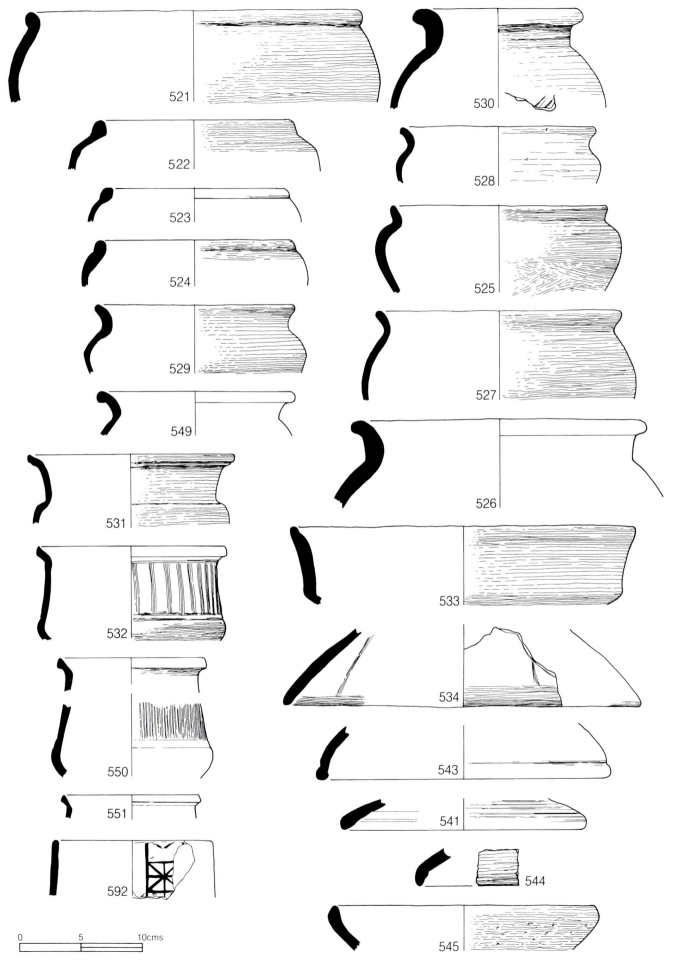

0   5   10cms

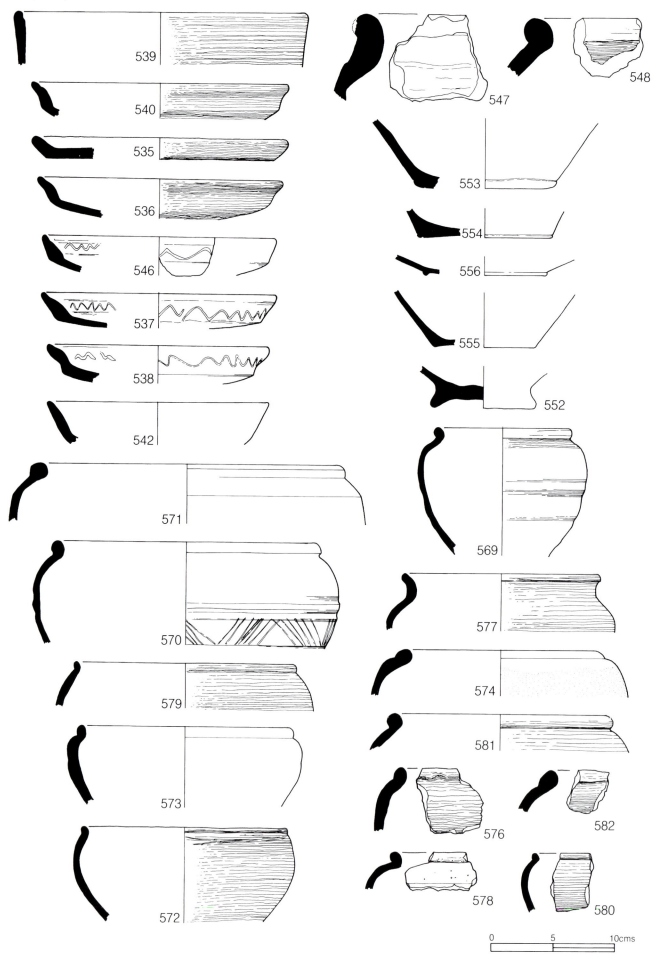

539

540

535

536

546

537

538

542

571

570

579

573

572

547

548

553

554

556

555

552

569

577

574

581

576

582

578

580

0 5 10cms

F64 (cont.)

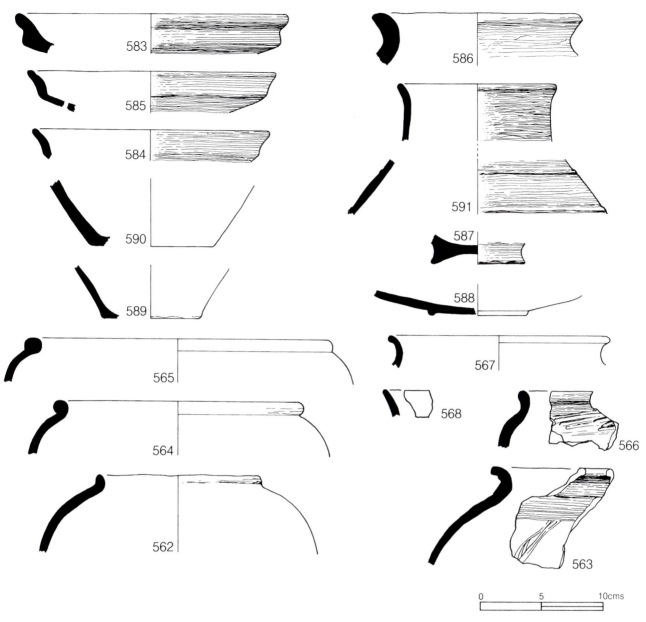

Fig. 3.65 Pottery

Fig. 3.64 (left) Pottery

F66

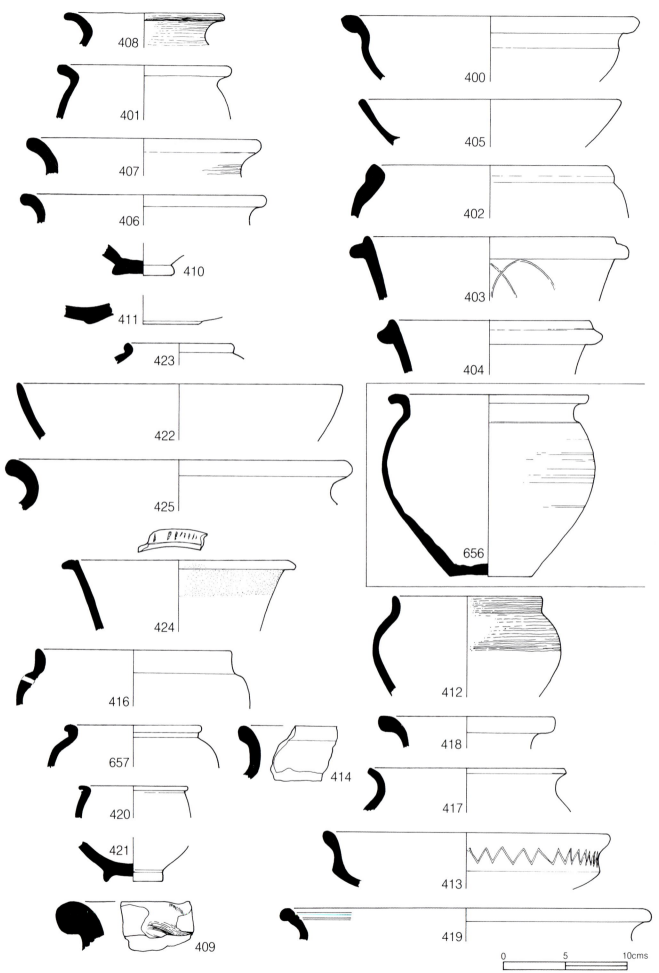

408

401

407

406

410

411

423

422

425

424

416

657

420

421

409

400

405

402

403

404

656

412

418

417

413

419

0   5   10cms

F66 (cont.)

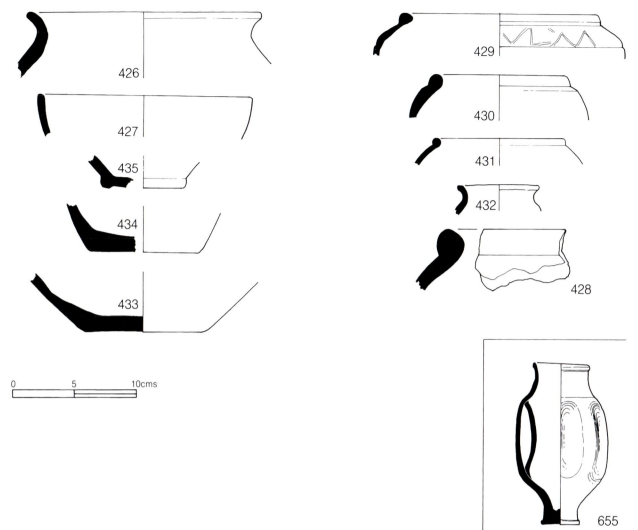

426

427

435

434

433

0   5   10cms

429

430

431

432

428

655

Fig. 3.67 Pottery

Fig. 3.66 (left) Pottery

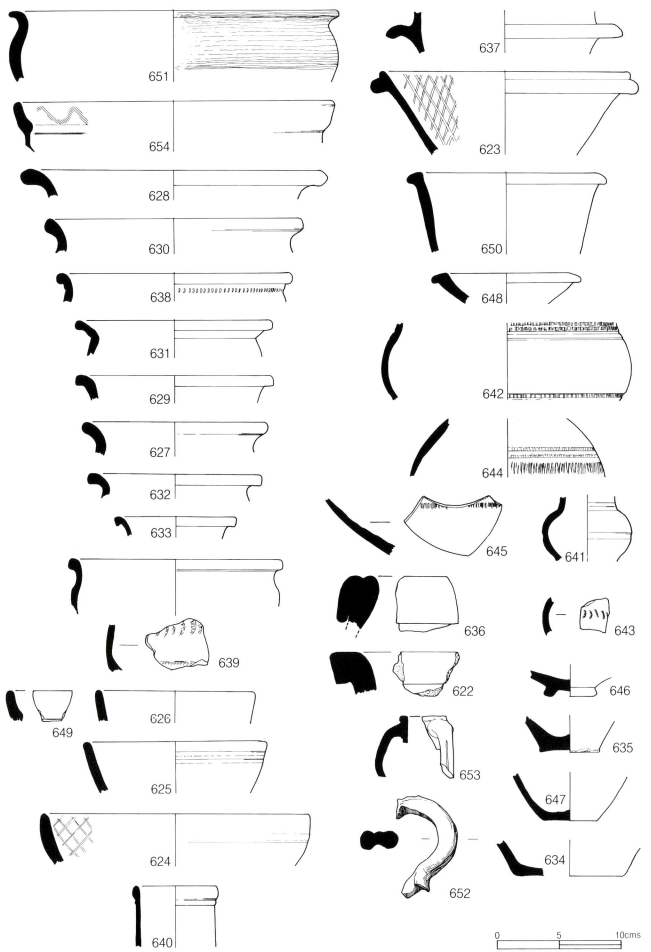

651
654
628
630
638
631
629
627
632
633
639
649
626
625
624
640
637
623
650
648
642
644
645
641
636
643
622
646
653
635
647
634
652

0   5   10cms

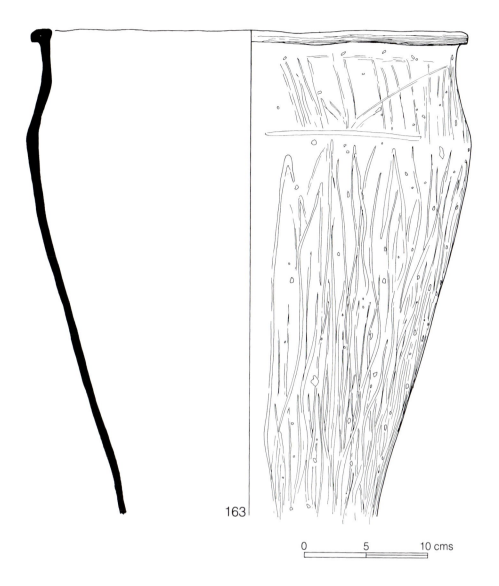

163

0   5   10 cms

Fig. 3.69 Pottery

Fig. 3.68 (left) Pottery

F400

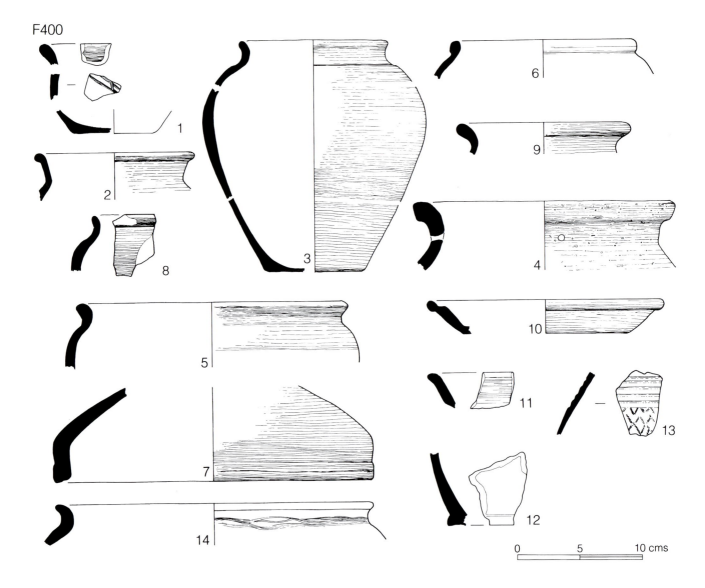

Fig. 3.70 Pottery

F409

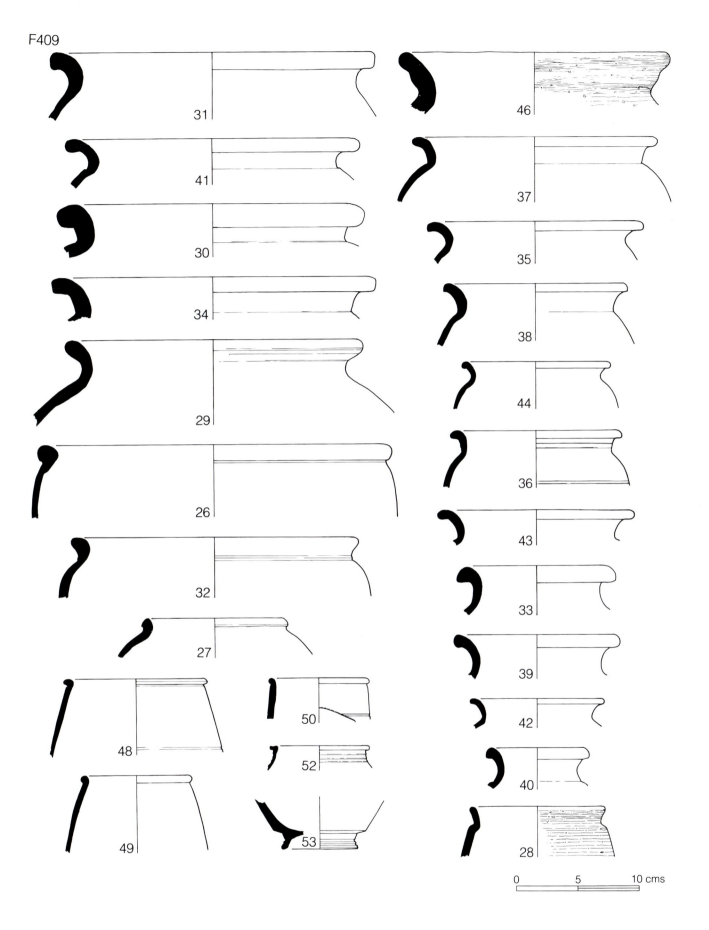

Fig. 3.71 Pottery

F409

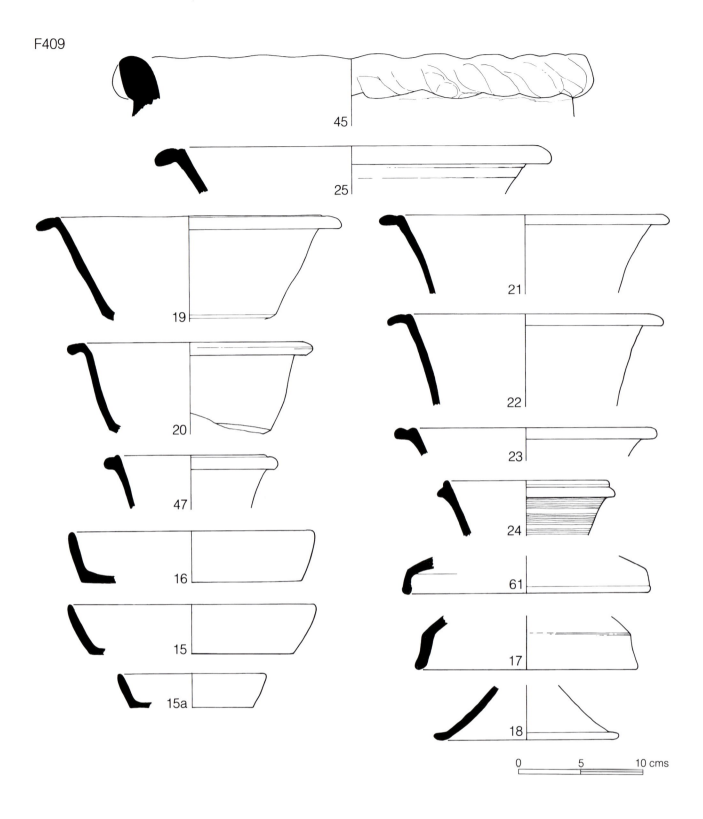

Fig. 3.72 Pottery

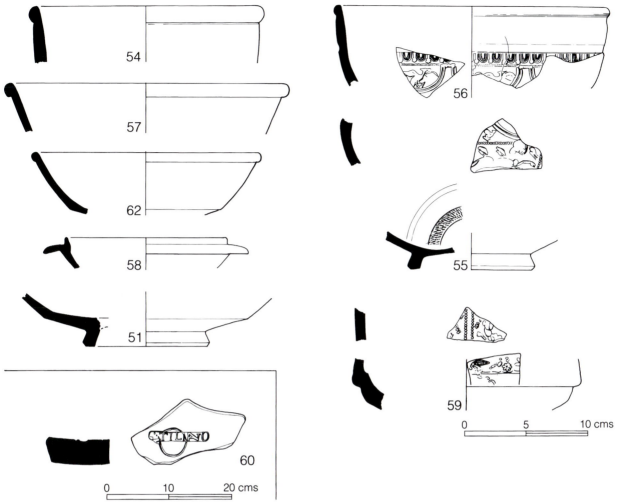

Fig. 3.73 Pottery

F421

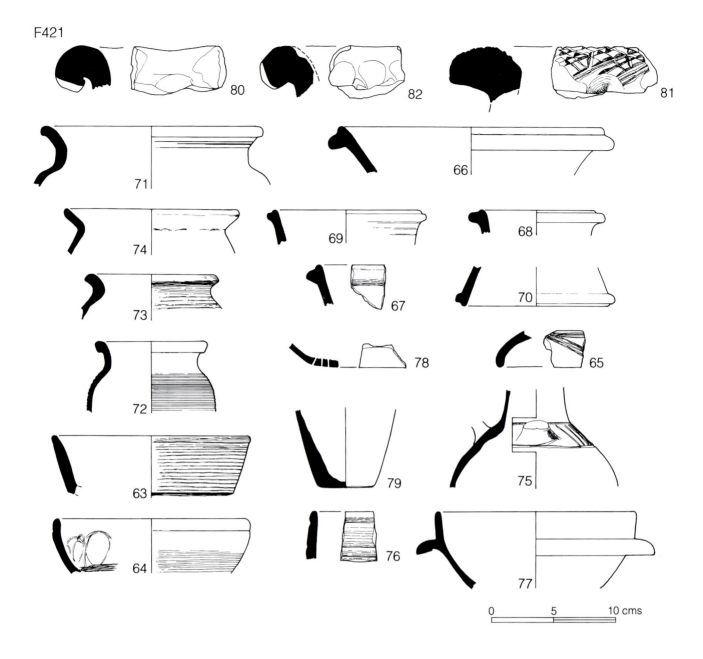

Fig. 3.74 Pottery

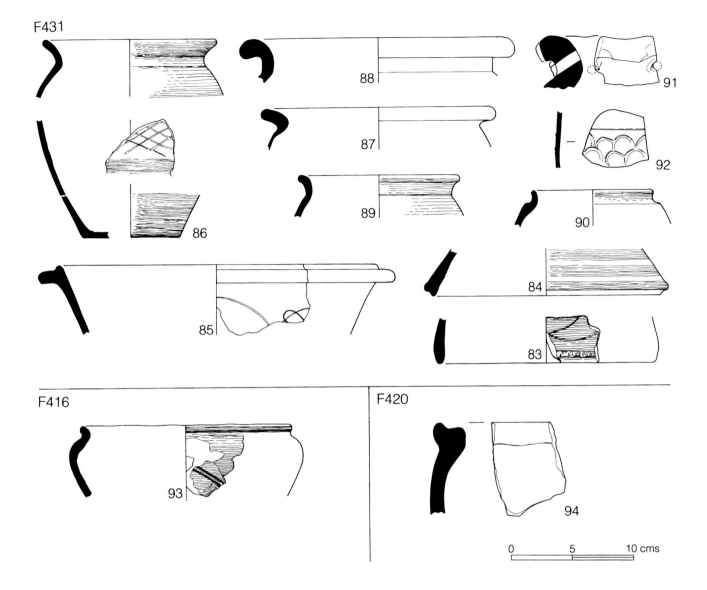

F431

88

87

89

86

91

92

90

84

83

85

F416

93

F420

94

0   5   10 cms

Fig. 3.75 Pottery

suggests that the latest recut of the feature may have been entirely filled between the mid first century BC and mid first century AD, whilst the sequence in the outer ditch (F66), although overlapping, continued into the third century AD.

The evidence for occupation within the enclosure is less clear. No structures survived the later ploughing, but a number of pits and a shallow hollow (F49) produced assemblages dating to the first century. Most of the pottery comprising the substantial first century component (72%, in fact) derived from two pits alone, with most of the remainder coming from the ditches. These pits, P119 and P125, like the ditches, were not strictly contemporary but overlapped in date, P119 corresponding to the inner ditch chronologically and P125 to the outer. The characteristic which they share, however, is that their fills contained a vast quantity of potsherds. Layer 3 of P119 was, in fact, composed almost entirely of sherds. The deposits of mostly fragmentary, non-joining sherds, appear to represent a 'shovelling out' from an unidentified deposit rather than a 'special deposit' of the more usual sort. The mere presence of such a large quantity of pottery fragments indicates intensive occupation of some sort in the immediate vicinity.

Continuity of occupation from the LIA through to the fourth century AD can be argued although the evidence for the second century is tenuous. The ceramic sequence from the outer ditch suggests a second century element, mostly in the form of flat-rimmed dishes with incipient flanges (Form BO1.9a) and several sherds of Savernake type and Alice Holt cable-rimmed jars with a proposed date of 180+ were recovered from pits and 'working hollows' along with a sherd of Trajanic samian ware. The large cable-rimmed pots with wall perforations (e.g. Fiche 5:D9, ph181, no. 447) figure prominently on the site, several examples having been recovered from the 1996 excavations, and their proposed function as beehives may help to define the nature of the settlement during this period.

A relatively large quantity of New Forest colour-coated wares were recovered from both the 1991 and 1996 excavations and reduced ware jars with cavetto rims (including BB1) point to fairly intensive occupation in the third and fourth centuries. That activity of this period extended beyond the area of the enclosure was demonstrated in the 1996 excavations. Several ovens and hollows produced pottery of this date and, although features of this description which were revealed in the area of the 1996 trench were not excavated, it is safe to guess that they may be roughly contemporary with those within the enclosure. Light rural industrial activity of some nature seems to have been a feature of this Roman settlement.

In summary, the ceramic evidence does not rule out continuity of occupation at Suddern Farm from the earliest Iron Age through to the late Roman period. For certain phases, however, particularly the Early Iron Age, the late Middle Iron Age and the second century AD, the evidence is slight or debatable.

Deposition

The large size of the ceramic assemblage allows for detailed consideration of the circumstances of deposition. Other material evidence, including articulated animal bone, deposits of skulls and numerous quern fragments indicates deliberate deposition in many of the pits. The ceramic evidence is equally convincing.

Deliberate deposits of large sherds or complete vessels did not occur frequently in the EIA at Suddern Farm. The earliest recognizable such deposit was recovered from P87 (cp 3/4) which produced a complete pot of form JB2.2 in 121 fragments within layers 3 and 4 (Fig. 3.69, no. 163). The remaining 35 sherds from the pit were essentially small abraded fragments with no indication of special deposition. P197 (cp 4/5) contained a large number of joining sherds representing up to 40 vessels. Most of the complete or near complete vessels were recovered as large fragments which were scattered throughout the pit, from the primary to the ultimate fill, indicating that the filling took place as a single operation and suggesting that the deposit was composed of curated rubbish. By cp 6–7 it appears to have become common practice to place whole pots or large fragments in a deliberate way within pits. The manner of deposition varied: complete or near complete pots placed upside down, sometimes over a lens of charcoal or ash, pot bases filled with burnt material, large sherds of a single pot stacked together before deposition, pots or large sherds placed in specific relation to other pots or objects such as animal skulls or legs, quern fragments, burnt flints, probably organic material (which is not preserved) or a combination of these objects.

P140 provided the best example of a special deposit. Three hundred and twenty-nine sherds representing 95 or so vessels were recovered. Within the basal fill (layer 3) ten complete or near complete pots were placed in association with horse mandibles, quern fragments and burnt flints. One complete, unusual, richly decorated pot, no. 33, appears to have been thrown onto the bare pit base where it shattered into dozens of fragments. The pottery, much of which was the Wiltshire-style decorated type, would suggest a date of cp 6 or 7 for the pit.

The anomalous nature of the deposit in P92 has been noted above. Although the date of the ceramics has been confused by the association of chronologically inconsistent types, the circumstances of deposition are clear. Once three layers of fill had accumulated, by whatever means, eight near complete vessels were placed on the top of the fill around the pit edge. P194 presented another interesting chronological question. Large sherds and near complete vessels of typologically early form (cp 3–5) directly overlay a complete vessel (no. 158) and a decorated sherd (no. 156) in fabric D15 (the Wiltshire glauconitic ware) which are decorated with the distinctive wave motif. The dating evidence for these wares, however contentious, would normally place them in about the third century BC (cp 6). The specific form of no. 158, however, corresponds to the pedestalled jar form, JD2, which is a rare, undecorated type at Danebury. This wave decorated, glauconitic ware globular jar may be an early example, or precursor, of the Wiltshire saucepan pot tradition more commonly encountered at sites in the region. This particular ceramic group was deposited with other materials including large quantities of oven daub and an animal burial, and several of the sherds lay on a bed of ash.

The evidence of this specific behaviour continuing into the first century BC–AD is not particularly convincing. P104 produced a large assemblage of cp 8/9 type sherds but, although there were some large joining fragments present in the central fill, the overall deposit more closely resembles those from P119 and P125 – a large number of small to medium sized fragments, most of which were non-joining, constituting, in some layers, a large component of the fill. These deposits appear to resemble those within the ditch fills, with which they are contemporary. Although the large late Roman assemblage from F47, a shallow hollow, was associated with four ox skulls, the sherds were fragmentary and abraded and appeared likely to be a rubbish accumulation, whilst the skulls may be products of butchering activities. There was no other evidence for the practice of special deposition in the Roman period.

Stratified assemblages

Introduction

The illustrated ceramic assemblages presented in the following pages demonstrate the chronological and typological range of material recovered from the site. As a result of agricultural activity from Roman times, stratified deposits, as such, did not survive except within features such as pits, hollows and ditches. The groups recovered from such features appear to provide a reasonable degree of chronological and typological integrity, although in the case of shallower features, allowance must be made for disturbance and intrusion of more recent material. The best assemblages have been presented in the main text and an additional group (P84, P113, P132, F47, F48, F49, F63, F79, Ph181) can be found in Fiche 5:C14–D9.

The assemblages are presented in chronological order. In those cases in which material from the top of the feature appears to be of significantly later date than that from the lower fills, this is indicated and dating adjusted as necessary. Groups normally contain at least 50 sherds but smaller assemblages, such as P91 and P212, have been included because no larger groups belonging to those phases were recovered. Details of fabric, form, surface treatment, decoration and context are provided in table form for each illustrated sherd and basic quantification summarized for each group.

P91 (Fig. 3.43)   cp 1/2

Sherd	Form	Fabric	SF/Dec.	Layer
205	JA	D0	B3	1
206	JA	A1	A3	1
207	BA	A1	D furrowed	1
208	BA	D8	– furrowed	1
209	BA	A1	D	1

24 sherds representing 23 vessels.

Fabric	No.	%
B3	1	4.2
E0	2	8.3
D0	104	1.7
D8	1	4.2
D17	2	8.3
D18	2	8.3
A1	5	20.8
G2	1	4.2

A small assemblage from a subrectangular pit producing few finds. Although very fragmentary, the furrowed and fingertipped sherds in coarse fabrics indicate a date in the earliest Iron Age, corresponding to cp 1–2 at Danebury.

P135 (Fig. 3.43)   cp 3/4

Sherd	Form	Fabric	SF/Dec.	Layer
16	JB2.3	C0:1	B	1
17	BS5.5	A1	A	1
18	JB2.0	D5	A	1
19	JB2.1	D5	A	1
20	DA1.1	D15	E	1
21	BS5.1	D5	A	6
22	BB1.1	E0	E4	8
23	JB2/3	D16	B	8
45	JB3.1	D0	B	+

107 sherds representing 101 vessels.

Fabric	No.	%
A1	10	9.3
C0:1	4	3.7
D0	6	5.6
D5	39	36.5
D15	7	6.5
D16	2	1.9
D18	37	34.6
E0	2	1.9

A substantial early assemblage composed largely of shouldered jars in coarse fabrics with a single fragment of a cordoned bowl. No. 20, from the top fill, is a MIA dish in Wilts. type glauconitic ware, probably not contemporary with the rest of the assemblage. Pottery present throughout the fill.

P212 (Fig. 3.43)   cp 3/4

Sherd	Form	Fabric	SF/Dec.	Layer
60	BS5.1	E0	D	2
61	BS5.2	A1	A	2
62	JB4.1	D18	B	2
63	JB1.2	D5	A3	2
64	JB2.0	A1	A	2
65	BA2.3	E0	B	2

38 sherds representing 15 vessels.

Fabric	No.	%
A1	25	65.8
D5	2	5.3
D18	8	21.0
E0	3	7.9

A small EIA assemblage, most sherds datable to cp 3 but no. 62 possibly a slightly later type. All but five sherds recovered from layer 2, the main fill of the pit.

103

P194 (Fig. 3.44)   cp 3–5/8?

Sherd	Form	Fabric	SF/Dec.	Layer
151	PB1.1	B1	E	+
152	DA1.1	D0	E5.1a	2
153	BS5.1	D5	E	4
154	JA2?	D0	D	4
155	JA2	A1	B	4/5
156	–	D17.3	E10.1a	6
157	PA1.1	D0	B	6
158	JD2.2?	D17.3	E10.1a	6
159	JD2.0	D0	D	5/7
185	JC2.0	D0	E	5
186	BS5.5	D0	A	5

219 sherds representing 81 vessels.

Fabric	No.	%
A1	10	4.5
B1	1	0.5
C0:1	1	0.5
C2	1	0.5
D0	135	61.6
D5	7	3.2
D8	1	0.5
D9	1	0.5
D17.2	2	0.9
D17.3	21	9.5
D18	35	15.9
E0	3	1.4
G2	1	0.5

This large assemblage derived mostly from the bottom half of the fill. The dating is problematical due to the mixed typology of the vessels. Large jars nos. 154 and 155 could be cp 3 types, nos. 157 and 159, recovered from layers underlying 154 and 155, are similar to cp 4–5 forms, and nos. 156 and 158 are decorated Poole Harbour wares which, at the earliest, would be MIA Durotrigian forms. No. 158, a near complete vessel, lay near the base of the pit in association with an animal burial. No. 155, also near complete, and an apparently much earlier vessel, had been deposited as a stack of large fragments in the layer above 158. The date range of vessel type no. 155 must be reconsidered if it is not to be regarded as an example of curated rubbish, which appears unlikely in view of its condition.

P197 (Fig. 3.45)   cp 4/5

Sherd	Form	Fabric	SF/Dec.	Layer
176	PA2.1	D9	E	2/3/4/6/8
177	JC2.1	D0	B	2/3/4/6
178	PA1.2	A1	B	2/3/6/8
179	JB2.3	D0	D	4/6
180	PA2.1	A1	B	7
181	PA1.1	A1	D	7/8
182	JB4.1	D0	E	7
183	BS5.5	D0	E	7
184	PA3.1	A1	A	8
260	PB1.1	D0	E	2
261	PA2.1	D1	5	B7
262	PA1.1	D1	8	A7

232 sherds representing 40 vessels.

Fabric	No.	%
A1	74	31.9 (7 vessels)
D0	138	59.5 (27 vessels)
D5	7	3.0 (1 vessel)
D9	11	4.7 (1 vessel)
D18	2	0.9

This pit produced a large number of sherds many of which were joining sherds of a far smaller number of vessels. The near complete vessels were recovered as large fragments dispersed throughout the fill (see nos. 176–179) rather than as complete vessels or large fragments *in situ*. This would suggest that the pit was filled in a single operation, perhaps with curated midden material.

P108 (Fig. 3.45)   cp 6

Sherd	Form	Fabric	SF/Dec.	Layer	
105	JC2.3	D18	E	1	
106	JC1.1	D9	E	2/4	
107	JC1.1	A1	B	2	
108	Misc.	A2	–	2	
109	PB1.1	D18	D	4	
110	PB1.1	C0:1	B	4	
111	BS5.1	D15	E	5	perforated
251	BA5	9.1		5	2 Roman colour-coat

76 sherds representing 30 vessels.

Fabric	No.	%
A1	3	3.9
A2	1	1.3
C0:1	40	52.7 (1 vessel)
D0	3	3.9
D9	12	15.8
D15	2	2.7
D18	14	18.4
9.1	1	1.3

A small early MIA assemblage including undecorated saucepan pots and bipartite jars. Flint-tempered wares are entirely absent. The large proportion of shell-tempered fabric (C0:1) is misleading in that the 40 sherds belong to a single vessel. No. 251, a New Forest colour-coated base, is from the top fill of the pit.

P140 (Figs. 3.46 and 3.47)   cp 6/7

Sherd	Form	Fabric	SF/Dec.	Layer
24	BS5.3	A1	A	3
25	BC2.1	D15	E	3
26	PB1.1	D15	E5.1f	3
27	BS5.1	D15	E	3
28	JC2.2	D15	E	3
30	JC2.2	A1	D	3
31	JC2.2	D15	E	3
32	JC2.3	D8	E	3
33	PB1.1	D15	E5.1f Misc.	3

329 sherds representing 95 vessels.

Fabric	No.		%	
A1	8		2.4	
B1	2		0.6	
D0	18		1.5	
D5	5		25.6	
D8	22		5.5	
D15	133	319	40.4	97%
D16	57		6.7	
D18	84		17.3	

A large assemblage of which ten complete and near complete vessels were deposited on the primary fill. No. 33 was recovered as shattered fragments scattered across the pit top, no. 25 was deposited as a near complete vessel. These vessels were associated with horse mandibles, quern fragments and burnt flints.

104

P78 (Fig. 3.48)   cp 7

Sherd	Form	Fabric	SF/Dec.	Layer
139	PA2.1	D0	B	1
140	PB1.1	B1	E	2
141	PB1.1	B1	E	2
142	PB1.1	D18	E	3
143	BS5.1	B1	E	3
144	PB1.1	B1	E	3
145	PB1.1	B1	E	3
146	PB1.1	D0	E	3
147	DA1.1	D15	E5.2a	3
148	BS5.1	B1	E	5
149	JD3.1	B1	E5.3b	5
150	JC2.3	D8	E	5
250	JC2.2/3	B1	B	1
453	JC2.0	D15	E	1
455	PB1.1	B1	E	1

230 sherds representing 105 vessels.

Fabric	No.		%	
A1	3		1.3	
B1	53		23.0	
C0:1	3		1.3	
D0	8		3.5	
D8	105		45.7	(4 vessels)
D9	2		0.8	
D15	26	169	11.3	73.5
D16	3		1.3	
D18	25		11.0	
E0	1		1.3	
H0	1		1.3	

A large assemblage predominated by sandy fabrics, although most identifiable vessels (PB1.1) are in flint-tempered ware (B1). This group, unusually for the site, resembles the late MIA pit groups from Danebury (see decorated jar no. 149).

P92 (Figs. 3.49 and 3.50)   cp 6–7

Sherd	Form	Fabric	SF/Dec.	Layer
230	JC1.1	D0	E	1
231	JB2/4	D18	B	1
232	PA2.1	D0	A	1
233	PL (Misc.)	D17.2	D	1 very coarse copy
234	JC2.1/2	D0	E	2/3
235	PA1.0	A1	A	3
236	BS5.5	D0	A	7
237	JC1.1	A1	B	7
238	PB1.1	D15	E5.1f	7
239	JC2.0	D0	E	6
240	JC2.0	D15	E	6
241	JC2.0	D0	B	6
242	JC2.3	D0	B	4
243	PB1.1	D15	E5.1f	4
244	JC2.3	D0	E	4
245	PB1.1	D0	E	6
246	BS5.1	D0	B	4/6
247	PA1.2	A1	B	4/6
248	JC2.2	A1	A	4/6
249	JB4.1	A1	A	4/6

387 sherds representing 196 vessels.

Fabric	No.	%	
A1	173	44.7	(112 vessels)
B1	2	0.5	
D0)	143	37.0	(32 vessels)
D5)	7	1.8	
D9)	1	0.2	
D15)	30	7.8	54.8%(11 vessels)
D16)	2	0.5	
D17)	2	0.5	
D18)	27	7.0	

This assemblage has been discussed in some detail in the text (pp. 102–3). It comprises a mixture of cp 4/5 type vessels and cp 6 or 7 decorated Wiltshire forms in direct association, deposited as complete or near complete vessels around the pit edge half way up the fill. No. 244 was complete and no. 242 had been placed within 243. The uppermost and the primary fills produced smaller non-joining fragments.

P120 (Fig. 3.51)   cp 6 or 7

Sherd	Form	Fabric	SF/Dec.	Layer
166	JD2.0	D18	E	1
167	JC2.3	D18	E	1/2/5
168	PB1.1	B1	E	2/3/5
169	JA2?	D18	D	3
170	PB1.1	D18	E	3
171	PB1.1	D15	E5.1hi	1
172	PB1.1	D18	E	1/2/5/6
173	PB1.1	D0	B	2
174	JB4.1	A1	A	5
175	PA1.2	D0	A	5/6
222	PB1.1	D0	E5.1h	1
255	JD4.11	D4	E(w)	1
256	JD4.11	G0	D	1
257	BO3.3	9.2	5/15	1 Oxon. colour-coat: Young C.75

210 sherds representing 98 vessels.

Fabric	No.		%	
A1	33		15.7	
B1	15	17	7.1	8.1
B2	2		1.0	
D0	76		36.1	
D5	1		0.5	
D9	2	155	1.0	73.7
D15	4		1.9	
D18	72		34.2	
E0	1		0.5	
G0	2		1.0	
1.1	1		0.5	
9.2	1		0.5	

29 abraded sherds of LIA and Roman date from top fill not recorded.

The date of this pit is not clear because both of the decorated sherds are from the upper fill. The primary fill, however, yielded a fragment of a burnished saucepan pot (no. 172) which would indicate a date of cp 6 at the earliest. Sherds belonging to the same vessels were scattered throughout the fill, suggesting that the filling was undertaken as a single operation.

P104 (Figs. 3.52 and 3.53)   cp 8/9

Sherd	Form	Fabric	SF/Dec.	Layer
191	JD4.41	D17.2	D	1
192	JC3.1	D17.2	D	1
193	JC3.1	D17.3	E	1
194	BS5.1	D17.3	D	4
195	BS5.1	D17.2	D10.32	4
196	JC3.1	D17.2	D	3/4
197	JC3.1	D17.3	E	4/5
198	BC3.3	D17.3	D10.32	4
199	JD4.42	D17.2	E	4
200	BC3.3	D17.3	E	4
201	Lid	D17.2	E	4
202	Lid	D17.2	D	4
203	BC3.51	D17.2	E	8
204	JC3.1	D17.2	D10.4b	10
210	JE4.1	D4	D4,10.4a	1
211	BkB	D4	E8	1
212	JD4.42	D4	D(w)	1
213	BD2.11	D17.2	D10.4a	1
214	BkB	D4	E	1
215	JC3.1	D4	D(w)	1
216	PL1	D17.2	E	1
217	JC3.1	D4	D	1

218	JD4.11	D17.1	D	1
219	BS5.1	D4	B	1
223	JC3.1	G1	D6	4/5
224	BC3.3	D17.3	D4	4/5
225	BS5.1	G0	E(w)	4
226	BkB?	D17.2	E	10
227	BC3.3	D17.2	D	9
228	JD4.11	D17.2	E	4
229	BC3.3	D17.3	D10.32	4
258	BC3.2	D17.2	D	4
259	BD5.1	G2	E4	4
658	JE4.2	D17.3	D10.4a	4

288 sherds representing 235 vessels.

Fabric	No.		%	
B1	4		1.4	
B3	1		0.3	
D4	33		11.5	
D17.1	14		4.8	
D17.2	180	227	62.5	78.8
D17.3	33		11.5	
D18	2		0.7	
G0	2		0.7	
G1	16		5.6 (3 vessels)	
G2	3		1.0	

A deep cylindrical pit which produced a large assemblage, composed mostly of small, non-joining sherds. Poole Harbour wares (D17) represent a large proportion (nearly 79%) of the total, and these are present in the lowest fills indicating a date of first century +. The pottery does not appear to represent a special deposit.

P128 (Fig. 3.54)   First century BC

Sherd	Form	Fabric	SF/Dec.	Layer
76	JE4.0	D17.2	D	1
77	JE4.2	D17.1	D	1
78	BC3.3	D17.2	E	1
79	BC3.3	D17.2	E	1
80	BC3.3	D17.2	D	1 perforated wall
81	BC3.3	D17.2	E	1
82	BC3.3	D17.3	E	1
83	JC3.1	D17.3	E	1
84	Lid	D17.2	D	1
252	PL2	D20	E	1

174 sherds representing 151 vessels.

Fabric	No.		%	
D4	26		14.9	
D5	1		0.6	
D13	1		0.6	
D17.1	26		14.9	
D17.2	55	102	31.6	58.6
D17.3	21		12.1	
D20	1		0.6	
G0	19		10.9	
G3	24		13.8	

A large group of small, non-joining sherds. Poole Harbour wares predominate by a small margin. Sherds could be pre-conquest.

P119 (Figs. 3.55–3.59)   First century BC/AD

Sherd	Form	Fabric	SF/Dec.	Layer
300	BD4.1	G1	E	3
301	BD4.2	D4	E	1/3
302	BD2.1	D4	E4	3
303	BD2.1	D4	E4	3
304	BD4.2	D4	E	3
305	BD4.2	D4	E	3
306	BD2.1	D17.3	E4	3
307	BD4.2	D4	E	3
308	BD2.1	D4	E4	3
309	JC3.1	D17.2	D10.32/34	3
310	JC3.3	D4	E4,6.1h	3

311	BD4.1	G1	E	1/3
312	BC3.51	D17.2	D	1/3
313	BD4.2	D17.3	D	3
314	BC3.51	D17.3	E	3
315	BD4.2	D17.2	E	3
316	BD4.2	D17.3	D	3
317	BD4.2	D4	D	3
318	BC3.51	D4	D	3
319	BC3.51	D17.2	E	3
320	JC3.2	D17.2	D	3
321	BD4.1	D17.2	–	3
322	BD4.1	D20	E	3
323	BC3.51	D17.2	D	3
324	BD4.2	D4	D	3
325	BD4.2	D17.2	E	3
326	BD4.2	D17.2	E	3
327	BD4.2	D17.2	D	3
328	BD5.1	D17.3	E4	3
329	Lid(?)	D17.2	E	3
330	DA1.2	D8	E	3
331	Misc.			
	(Lid?)	D20	E6.1h	1/3
332	Lid	D17.2	D	3
333	Lid	D20	D6	3
334	Lid	D20	D6	3
335	Lid	D17.2	D10.7a	3
336	Lid	D17.2	D	3
337	Lid	D17.3	D	3
338	Lid	D17.1	E	3
339	PL1	D17.2	E	3
340	PL3	D20	E6.1a,h	3
341	PL2	D20	E	3
342	PL2	D20	E6.1h	3
343	PL2	D20	D6.1h	3
344	PL2	D20	D6.1h	3
345	PL3	D20	E	3
346	PL2	D20	E	3
347	PL3	D17.2	E	3
348	PL2	D20	D6.1h	3
349	PL2	D17.2	D10.4a	3
350	PL2	D20	D6.1h	3
351	PL2	D17.3	D10.1a	3
352	PL2	D20	D6.1h	3
353	PL2	D17.2	D10.1a	3
354	PL2	D20	D6.1h	3
355	PL2	D17.2	D10.4a	3
356	PL3	D20	E	3
357	PL2	D20	D6.1h	3
358	JC3.1	D4	D	1/3
359	BC3.3	D17.2	D	3
360	JC3.1	G1	E	3
361	JC3.1	D17.2	E	3
362	JC3.2	D17.2	B	3
363	JC3.1	D17.2	D	3
364	JC3.1	D17.2	D	3
365	PART OF 309			
366	JC3.2	D17.2	B	3
367	JC3.1	D17.2	D	3
368	BC3.3	D17.2	D	3
369	JC3.2	D17.2	E	3
370	JC3.1	D17.2	D	3
371	JC3.1	D17.2	E	3
372	JC3.1	G2	D	3
373	JC3.1	D8	D	3
374	JC3.1	D4	E4	3
375	JD4.11	G1	–	3
376	BC3.3	D17.3	D	3
377	JD5.1	G2	D	3
378	JE4.3	D20	E4	3 part of 399
379	JE4.2	D17.2	E	3
380	PART OF 379			
381	JE4.3	D17.2	D	3
382	JE4.2	D17.2	E	3
383	JE4.2	D17.2	D	3
384	JE4.2	D17.2	D	3
385	JD4.4	D20	E	3
386	JE4.3	D17.2	D	3
387	JE4.2	D17.2	E	3
388	JE4.2	G1	E	3
389	JD5.1	G2	D	3
390	JD4.42	D17.3	D	3
391	JE4.1	D17.2	E6.1j	3

392	C	D4	E4,5.1j	1/3
393	F	D4	E	1/3
394	BkA?	D4	E4,7	3 rim missing
395	BkA	D4?	E4,7	3
396	C	D4	E8	3
397	F	D4	D6	3
398	BkA	D20	E	3
399	JE4.3	–	–	3 part of 378

2581 sherds representing 2496 vessels.

This quantity represents 21.3% of site total by sherd count.

An additional 59 sherds, all abraded Roman, recovered from pit top.

Fabric	No.		%	
B1	1		0.04	
D0	4		0.15	
D4	834		32.31	
D8	8		0.31	
D15	3		0.12	
D17.1	24		0.93	
D17.2	1206	1303	46.73	50.5
D17.3	73		2.83	
D18	3		0.12	
D20	86		3.33	
E0	1		0.04	
G0	11		0.42	
G1	56	338	2.17	13.1
G2	211		8.18	
G3	60		2.32	

A fifth of the total site assemblage was recovered from this pit. Most sherds came from layer 3, in association with daub, quern fragments and non-articulated animal bone. Very few joining sherds and no complete vessels, indicating that ritual deposition was not intended. Durotrigian wares account for half of the total, fine sandy wares for much of the remainder. Copies of Gallo-Belgic forms – butt-beakers, girth beakers, and numerous platters – are present in association with a variety of jars, bead rim bowls and storage vessels.

P125 (Figs. 3.60 and 3.61)				First–second century
Sherd	Form	Fabric	SF/Dec.	Layer
264	BE4	5.2	1	1
265	BC3.51	D17.3	E	1
266	BC3.42	D17.3	D	1
267	BkA	D17.2	E	1
268	PL2	D20	E	1
269	PL2	D20	E	1
270	JC3 Misc.	D20	E(w)	1
271	PL2	D20	E	1
272	Lid	D17.2	D	1
273	JC3.1	D4	D	1
274	JC3.1	D20	D	1
275	JC3.1	D4	D	1
276	BD4.2	D17.2	B	1
277	BC3.3	G1	D	1
278	JC3.1	D17.2	D	1
279	JD4.41	D20	E	1
280	JR3.4	1.1	3	1
281	JR3.4	2.2	3	1
282	JC3.1	D8	E	1
283	JE4.2	D17.1	D	1
284	BA1	2.1	3	1
285	BS5.1	D17.1	D	1
286	JD4.41	2.1	E	2
287	PL2	D20	E6.1h	2
288	JD4.41	D20	E	2 part of 279?
289	JC3.1	D20	E	2
290	JC3.1	G2	D	2
291	BkA	D17.3	E	2

292	BS2.0	D17.2	E	2
293	BC3.3	D17.3	D	2
294	BC3.51	D17.1	B	2
295	BD4.2	D17.2	E	2
296	BkA	D4	E7	2
297	PL2	D17.2	E	2
298	PL2	D20	E	2
436	SJ3	2.4	3	3
437	SJ3	2.4	3	3 Savernake Type
438	JR3.3	2.2	2	3
439	BkA	D17.2	E	3
440	JC3.1	D17.2	D	3
441	JC3.1	D20	D	3 part of 274?
442	BS5.1	D20	D	3
443	BA1	2.1	2	3

929 sherds representing 906 vessels.

Fabric	No.		%	
A1	2		0.2	
D0	3		0.3	
D4	151		16.3	
D8	21		2.3	
D15	6		0.6	
D17.1	212	474	22.8	51
D17.2	262		28.2	
D17.3	15		1.6	
D18	1		0.1	
D20	32		3.5	
G0	25		2.7	
G1	155		16.7	
G2	32		3.5	
1.1	1		0.1	
2.1	2		0.2	
2.2	4		0.4	
2.4	2		0.2	
4.2	2		0.2	
5.2	1		0.1	

A substantial deposit of fragmentary sherds, many in abraded condition and mostly non-joining. Only the Savernake type storage jars (no. 437) from the primary fill would suggest a date of the late second century. The assemblage otherwise resembles P119, except that fine tableware forms are less common. Durotrigian wares represent just over half of the total.

F64 (Figs. 3.62–3.65)				First century (pre-Flavian)
Sherd	Form	Fabric	SF/Dec.	Layer
500	JC3.1	D17.2	E	1
501	BD5.1	D4	E4	1
502	BS3 Misc.	D4	E8	1/2
503	JC3.1	D17.3	E4	1
504	BC3.3	D17.2	D	1
505	BC3.3	D4	E	1
506	JC3.1	D17.3	E(w)	1
507	JE4.2	D4	E	1
508	PL2	D20	E6.1h	1
509	JE4.2	D4	E(w)	1
510	BO6	9.2	5	1
511	Misc.	4.2	1	1
512	BE2	9.1	5	1
513	DI1.9	1.3	1	1
515	JC3.1	D4	D	2
516	JC3.1	D17.1	E	2
517	JC3.1	D4	D	2
518	JC3.1	D17.3	D	2
519	BC3.3	D17.3	E(w)	2
520	BC3.3	D17.2	E	2
521	JC3.1	D17.2	E	2
522	JC3.2	D20	D	2
523	BC3.3	D17.3	E(w)	2
524	JC3.1	D20	D	2
525	JD4.4	D17.2	E	2
526	JE4.2	D17.2	E	2
527	JD4.4	D17.2	D	2
528	BD4.2	D4	E	2
529	JD4.4	D20	E	2

Sherd	Form	Fabric	SF/Dec.	Layer
530	JE4.3	G1	E	2
531	JE4.2	D17.3	E	2
532	C	D4 (oxidized)	D5.1j	2
533	PL2	D20	E	2
534	Lid	D17.2	D6	2
535	PL3	D17.2	E	2
536	PL2	D20	E	2
537	PL2	D20	D6.1h	2
538	PL2	D20	D6.1h	2
539	PL2?	D17.2	E	2
540	PL2	D20	E	2
541	Lid	D17.2	D	2
542	PL2	D20	E	2
543	Lid	1.2	1	2
544	Lid	G1	E	2
545	PL/Lid	D17.1	E	2
546	PL2	D20	D6.1h	2
547	JD5	D17.2	B	2
548	JC3.1	D17.1	D	2
549	JR3.5	1.5	1	2
550	BkA	D20	E8	2
551	BE4	4.2	1	2
552	BS1.2	D17.2	B	2
553	BS3.3	D17.3	E	2
554	BS3.3	D17.2	E(W)	2
555	BA1	1.5	1	2
556	BS3.3	D4	E	2
557	JC3.1	D4	D	3
558	BC3.3	D17.2	D10.32	3
559	BC3.3	G2	E	3
560	JD4.5	D17.2	D	3
561	BC3.3	G1	E	3
562	JC3.1	D17.1	D	4
563	JD4.4	D17.2	E10.32	4
564	JC3.1	D4	E	4
565	JC3.2	D4	D	4
566	JC3.1	B1	E	4
567	BD4.2	G1	E	4
568	BB1.1	E0	C	4
569	JC3.1	D17.3	D4	5
570	BD5.1	G1	D4,5.1b	5
571	JC3.2	D4	D	5
572	BC3.3	G1	E	5
573	JC3.2	D17.2	E	5
574	JC3.2	D20	D	5
576	JC3.2	D17.1	D	5
577	JD4.4	D20	E	5
578	BC3.3	G3	E	5
579	BC3.2	D18	E	5
580	BC3.3	G1	E	5
581	JC3.1	D4	E	5
582	JC3.1	D17.2	E	5
583	PL1	D17.2	E	5
584	PL2	D20	E	5
585	PL2	D20	E	5
586	JD4.11	D17.3	E	5
587	BS2.1	D17.2	E	5
588	BS3.2	D4	E	5
589	BS5.1	D4	E	5
590	BS5.1	D4	E(w)	5
591	BkB?	D20	E4	5
592	Misc.	4.2	2 (painted)	2 (SF 457)

970 sherds representing 966 vessels.

Fabric	No.	%
A0	1	0.1
A1	6	0.6
B1	20	2.1
B3	1	0.1
C3	1	0.1
D0	28	3.0
D3	1	0.1
D4	205	21.1
D5	1	0.1
D8	2	0.2
D9	3	0.3
D13	1	0.1
D15	28	3.0
D16	1	0.1
D17.1	16	1.7
D17.2	353	36.4
D17.3	23	2.4
D18	22	2.3
D20	25	2.6
E0	1	0.1
G0	19	2.0
G1	79	8.1
G2	1	0.1
G3	15	1.5
1.2	6	0.6
1.3	34	3.5
1.5	2	0.2
1.6	1	0.1
1.8	3	0.3
1.9	1	0.1
2.1	10	1.0
2.2	1	0.1
2.6	6	0.6
3.2	1	0.1
4.2	27	2.8
4.3	2	0.2
5.2	1	0.1
9.1	5	0.5
9.2	4	0.4
Amphora	1	0.1

A typical assemblage from a ditch fill, fragmentary sherds, many abraded. A wide variety of forms and fabrics. Only 19 sherds recovered from below layer 5. Most of these are Durotrigian wares and flint-tempered MIA sherds. Most sherds from layer 5 upwards could date to the first century BC/AD, a single residual EIA sherd (no. 568) in layer 4. Roman pottery present only in top layer.

F66 (Figs. 3.66 and 3.67)   Late first–early second century

Sherd	Form	Fabric	SF/Dec.	Layer
400	BO3.3	1.3	1	2
401	JR3.4	1.10	1	2
402	JR1.1	1.3	3	2
403	BO1.9a	1.1	2/8	2
404	BO1.9a	1.2	3	2
405	DI1.8	1.3	1	2
406	JR3.3	1.3	1	2
407	JD4.11	D4	E	2
408	JR3.4	1.1	3	2
409	SJ3	1.3?	4	2/3/6
410	BS4.1	E0	E(w)	2
411	BA3	5.2	–	2
412	BD4.2	D4	D	3/6
413	PL1	D4	D6.1d	3/6
414	JE4.2	D4	E	3/6
415	JR3.3	1.3	3	3/6
416	JD4.5	D4	E	3/6
417	JD4.11	D4	E	3/6
418	JR3.4	1.1	2	3/6
419	JE4.3	1.2	2	3/6
420	BE3	1.4	2	3/6
421	BA3	1.1	1	3/6
422	DI1.8	1.2	1	4
423	BE–	1.3	1	4
424	BO1.7	1.1	3 Misc.	5
425	JR3.4	1.3	1	5
426	JD4.11	D4	3	7
427	DI1.8	5.2	5	7
428	JC3.1	D17.2	D	8
429	Misc.	D17.3	D10.4a	8
430	JR1.1	1.3	3	8
431	BC3.3	D17.3	D	8
432	BE2	1.8	1	8
433	BS5.1	D4	E(w)	8
434	BS5.2	D0	D	8
435	BA3	3.1	1	8
655	BE1	9.1	5	9 Beaker accompanying inhumation burial
656	JR3.4	1.3	1	4 Cremation vessel
657	BE3	1.1?	1	3/6

446 sherds representing 442 vessels.

Fabric	No.	%
B3	1	0.2
D0	12	2.7
D4	17	3.8
D8	2	0.4
D15	6	1.4
D17.2	68	15.3
D17.3	11	2.5
D18	9	2.0
D20	6	1.4
E0	1	0.2
G0	2	0.4
G1	20	4.5
1.1	22	4.9
1.2	20	4.5
1.3	171	38.3
1.4	4	0.9
1.5	6	1.4
1.6	7	1.6
1.8	20	4.5
1.10	2	0.4
1.11	1	0.2
2.2	2	0.4
2.5	1	0.2
2.6	3	0.7
4.1	1	0.2
4.2	15	3.4
4.3	1	0.2
5.2	2	0.4
5.3	4	0.9
9.1	4	0.9
9.2	3	0.7

This assemblage resembles that from F64 in character – composed largely of small abraded non-joining sherds. Most of the pottery is of slightly later date, the majority of sherds apparently in Alice Holt reduced ware. No pottery present in lowest fills. Mid first century AD material present in layer 8. Second century type flanged bowls present in layer 2.

No. 655 is an indented beaker which accompanied the inhumation burial.

No. 656, a complete pot, contained cremated animal bones. The context is not clear. The vessel may have been placed in a feature cut into the ditch fill but no such feature was observed in excavation. Alternatively, the vessel may have been placed in the hollow of the partially filled ditch and subsequently covered.

F62 (Fig. 3.68)   Fourth century

Sherd	Form	Fabric	SF/Dec.	Layer
622	SJ3.13	2.4	3	1
623	BO1.9	1.8	2/5	1
624	DI1.8	1.3	1/5	1
625	DI1.8	1.3	1	1
626	DI1.8	1.3	2	1
627	JR3.4	1.1	1	1
628	JR3.4	1.8	1	1
629	JR3.3	1.3	1	1
630	JR3.4	1.3	2	1
631	JR3.5	4.2	1	1
632	JR3.4	4.2	1	1
633	JR3.12	4.2	1	1
634	BA1	1.8	2	1
635	BA1	4.2	1	1
636	Amphora	–	–	1
637	BO6.9	9.2	5	1
638	BO3.3	9.2	5	1
639	BO3.3	9.2	5/15,29	1
640	BE2	9.2	5	1
641	FL	9.1	5	1
642	BO3.3	9.2	5/15	1
643	–	9.2	5/29	1
644	–	9.2	5/15	1
645	–	9.2	5/15	1
646	BA3	9.1	5	1
647	BA1	9.1	5	1
648	BO2.9	3.2	–	1
649	BO2.14	3.2	–	1
650	BO1.6	5.2	3	2
651	JR3.4	1.1	6	2
652	HA4	1.3	1	2
653	FL1.1	9.1	5	1
654	BO1 Misc	3.3	38	1

329 sherds representing 312 vessels.

Fabric	No.	%
1.1	14	0.3
1.2	4	1.2
1.3	117	35.6
1.4	1	0.3
1.6	6	1.8
1.8	24	7.3
1.9	2	0.6
1.11	1	0.3
2.1	20	6.1
2.2	27	8.2
2.3	1	0.3
2.4	1	0.3
2.6	2	0.6
3.2	2	0.6
4.2	19	5.8
4.3	5	1.5
5.1	4	1.2
5.2	3	0.9
9.1	27	8.2
9.2	34	10.4
Misc.	1	0.3
B9	1	0.3
C0:1	1	0.3
D15	4	1.2
D17.2	7	2.1
D18	1	0.3

Non-joining, small, abraded sherds in a wide variety of forms and fabrics. Large proportion of New Forest and Oxfordshire colour-coated wares suggests a fourth century date. Most forms are coarse, utilitarian types. Small quantity of residual Iron Age material.

The 1996 assemblage

Introduction

The excavations produced a total of 2161 sherds weighing 31.88 kg. Of this number 1967 sherds (91%) are of Roman type, the remaining sherds dating to the Iron Age. An additional small quantity of pottery was recovered from the ploughsoil during machine stripping. These sherds were examined but not recorded.

Owing to the strategy of limited intervention on the site, excavation was minimal in relation to the size of the area surveyed and stripped. Only a few small features were completely excavated, and most of the pottery derives from segments of fill of major features such as ditches (F400) and shallow hollows (F409 and F421). The fill of F409, the hollow which formed over the infilled enclosure ditch, F400, produced over 70% of the total assemblage. Segments of the fill of F400, exposed in a number of small trenches along its width, produced 151 sherds (7%), and a deliberately created shallow hollow, F421, produced 127 sherds (6%). The corn drier, F431, produced 73 sherds (3%). The remainder of sherds occurred in small groups or individually within a number of other features. The cemetery exposed in trench 2 produced very little pottery, but the 30 sherds recovered from individual graves are almost all of EIA/MIA type. Most of the remainder of the pre-Roman assemblage is LIA material recovered from the fill of the enclosure ditch, F400.

Forms and fabrics (Table 3.9)

The pre-Roman assemblage is largely Late Iron Age and the bulk of this material derives from the top fills of the enclosure ditch, F400. Fabrics D17 and D20 occur in equal quantities and are essentially contemporary. Both types were common in the 1991 assemblage. Fabric D4, a comparatively ill-defined category, is also a LIA type, often represented by wheelmade necked jars and bowls. The grog-tempered wares (fabric G) are a first century BC introduction in the area, and the wares here defined as LIA examples overlap to some extent with the Roman types. Where vessel form is not classifiable, surface finish can sometimes be used as a chronological indicator, but specifically dating these wares is a notoriously difficult task, and it must be accepted that there is not always a clear distinction between Iron Age and Roman grog-tempered wares.

The fabric range indicates an Early to Middle Iron Age component, although few vessel forms of that date could be securely identified. Fabrics D15 and D18 continue in use in the LIA, but the flint-tempered wares (B), the two coarse mixed tempered sherds (A), and the fineware sherd (E) are clearly earlier. Most of the relevant sherds derived from burial fills or the quarry fill into which the graves were cut. Although no sherds were recovered which are diagnostic of form, the fabrics and the surface treatment of this small group of sherds are indistinguishable from EIA and MIA types at Danebury and other sites in the region.

A wide range of fabrics characterizes the Roman ceramic assemblage. The majority, just under 60%, are coarse reduced wares (fabric 1), most of which are likely to be products of the New Forest and Alice Holt potteries. Four per cent of sherds are Black Burnished Ware I, from the same Dorset source as Iron Age fabric D17. Orange and white firing wares (fabrics 3 and 4) represent 26% of the total Roman assemblage, and a small quantity of these may be products of the Oxfordshire kilns. Grog-tempered wares account for just under 8%. Finewares including New Forest and Oxfordshire colour-coated wares (fabrics 9.1 and 9.2 respectively) and terra sigillata form only 7% of the total. This paucity of finewares is paralleled in the Suddern Farm 1991 collection. The majority of terra sigillata sherds were recovered from the occupation-rich fill of F409 and most were severely burnt and abraded. This condition applied almost exclusively to the sigillata and suggests that those sherds originated from a specific location where a conflagration had occurred and were subsequently redeposited with other sherds in the area of F409.

Table 3.9.
Quantification of pottery from the 1996 excavation by fabric type

Prehistoric wares: 194 sherds

fabric	no. sherds	% total	vessel forms
A0	1	0.5	
A1	1	0.5	
B1	16	8	DA1/Lid
B3	2	1	
B4	1	0.5	
DO	8	4	
D4	18	9	BD4.4; JC3; JD3.11; JE
D5	4	2	BA2
D8	2	1	
D15	12	6	JD4.4
D17	46	24	JC3.1; JD; JE4.2
D18	26	14	JE4.0; PL/Lid
D20	46	24	BD4.2; JC3.1; JD4.4; JE4.0; JE4.2; PL1; PL2
E1	1	0.5	
GO	6	3	
G1	3	1.5	JE4.2
G2	1	0.5	

Roman wares: 1967 sherds

fabric	no. sherds	% total	vessel forms
1.1	84	4	BO1.9a; BO1.9b; JR1; JR3.3; JR3.4; DI1; Lid
1.2	336	17	BO1.6; BO1.7; BO1.9a; BO2.6; JR1; JR3.1; JR3.3; JR3.4; SJ; DI1
1.3	274	14	BO1.6; BO1.7; BO1.9a; JR3.11; JR3.3; JR3.4; SJ; HA4
1.4	8	0.5	BO1.2
1.5	14	0.5	BO1.9a; BO3
1.6	73	4	JR3.4; FL/BE; HA
1.7	2	0.3	JR3.4; Lid
1.8	85	4	BO1.6; BO1.9a; JR3.4; DI1; FL1
1.9	6	0.5	
1.10	223	11	BO1.7; BO1.9a; JR3.1; JR3.3; JR3.4; DI2; Lid
1.11	5	0.5	
1.12	7	0.5	JR3.4
1.13	39	2	BO1.9a; JR3.3; JR3.4; SJ3; HA4
2.1	30	1	SJ
2.2	22	1	JR1.2; JR3.4; SJ; DI1; DI2; Lid
2.3	1	0.1	SJ
2.4	1	0.1	
2.5	14	0.5	BO1.9a; JR1
2.6	94	5	JR3.2; SJ
3.1	2	0.3	JR3.3
3.2	15	0.5	BO2.9a; MO
4.1	3	0.2	
4.2	452	23	BO1.7; BO1.9a; JR1.4; JR3.3; JR3.4; SJ3.4; BE4; DI1
4.3	40	2	BI1.9b; JR3.4; DI1; BE
6	1	0.1	
9.1	54	2.5	BE; BE1; BE3; BO2.9b; FL2; DI2; Lid; HA
9.2	9	0.5	BO2.9b
samian	71	3.5	BO2; BA4; BA5
misc	2	0.3	cup?

The range of vessel forms is best appreciated by referring to the selected illustrated assemblages found elsewhere in this report. A form/fabric correlation is incorporated in the tables below. Few identifiable EIA or MIA vessel fragments were recovered. These include vessel BA2 in shell-tempered ware, D5, an example of an EIA coarseware shouldered bowl. Vessel DA1 in flint-tempered ware, B1, is a tentatively identified flat-rimmed bowl (although it could be a lid) of the type which occurs in the MIA (cp 5–7) at Danebury. Other Iron Age vessels are consistent with a date in the first century BC onwards. These are mostly necked jars and bowls, a small number of bead rim jars, and platters copying terra nigra forms.

The Roman assemblage is dominated by coarsewares. Necked jars with upright or slightly everted rims are more common by far than bead rim jars. Dishes (type DI) are relatively common in both BBI and a number of other coarse reduced fabrics. Straight-sided bowls with a variety of rim forms (flat, grooved, flanged) occur commonly in reduced fabrics, and the high, short, 'stumpy' flange on vessels of New Forest manufacture are particularly common. This profile is dated late in the BBI assemblage and should probably be regarded as correspondingly late (fourth century) amongst New Forest products (Malcolm Lyne, pers. comm.). Tablewares – flagons, beakers, platters, etc. – are uncommon even in local reduced wares. Sherds belonging to New Forest ware indented beakers were identified amongst the small quantity of imported colour-coated wares and F409 produced a small but significant group of samian ware, but pottery of this quality is rare. The site produced a number of sherds from large storage jars with cabled rims and pre-firing perforations in the neck and/or body. This type of vessel was produced at the Alice Holt and New Forest potteries but their precise function is uncertain since the perforations would preclude their use for many types of storage. It has been proposed that they may have functioned as beehives (Clark and Nichols 1960) and the concentration of a relatively large number of these vessels in a small area may suggest that bee-keeping was a significant activity at the site some time after the late second century.

Chronology

The ceramic evidence indicates occupation in some form from the EIA or MIA onwards. Linear ditches F402/F403 and the large quarry complex F410/F429 produced sufficient sherds of EIA to MIA date, and a corresponding paucity of Roman material in their lower fills to be as certain as is possible that they pre-date the enclosure ditch which, on the combined evidence of the 1991 and 1996 excavations, is dated fairly securely to the LIA. The quarry complex was clearly dug into in the Roman period as well as in the Early to Middle Iron Age, if only for the burial of a number of neonates, and a quantity of Roman pottery thereby ended up in the top of the quarry fills. Sufficient Iron Age sherds were recovered from the quarry fills and from the inhumation cuts to leave no doubt that the features are of Iron Age date. It was difficult to date many of the Roman features to precise phases within the Roman period because of the long lifespan of much of the coarseware assemblage, but the presence of a small but significant quantity of samian ware and New Forest colour-coated ware indicates a date span between the conquest and the late third/early fourth centuries at the very least. It is not possible to be certain on the basis of this assemblage whether there was a significant gap in occupation on the site at any time during the Iron Age or Roman periods.

Selected stratified assemblages

Little substantial excavation was undertaken with the result that few ceramic groups were available for detailed assessment. Four groups were selected for detailed presentation: F400 – the enclosure ditch, investigated in several small trenches, but nowhere excavated to its base; F409 – a shallow hollow overlying part of the enclosure ditch and containing occupation material; F421 – a shallow, roughly circular hollow containing occupation material; and F431 – a corn-drying oven.

F400 (Fig. 3.70) Pre-Flavian

Sherd	Form	Fabric	SF/Dec.	Layer
1	JE/BS5.1	D4	D10.4b	1
2	JE4.2	D17.2	D	1
3	JD4.4	D15	D	2
4	JE4.2	G1	D	2
5	JC3.1	D20	D	2
6	JC3.1	D20	E	2
7	LID?PL	D18	D	2
8	BD4.2	D20	E	2
9	JD	D20	E	2
10	PL2	D20	D	2
11	PL1	D20	D	2
12	BS2	D20	D	2
13	BE4	4.2	1/15	2
14	JD4.4	D20	D	3

Total sherds: 151

Fabrics: D4 – 2 (1.3%); D15 – 10 (6.6%); D17 – 19 (12.5%); D8 – 3 (1.9%); D20 – 34 (22.5%); GO – 6 (3.9%); G1 – 1 (0.6%); G2 – 1 (0.6%); 1.1 – 1 (0.6%); 1.2 – 3 (1.9%); 1.3 – 21 (13.9%); 1.5 – 2 (1.3%); 1.8 – 5 (3.3%); 1.9 – 2 (1.3%); 1.12 – 2 (1.3%); 2.1 – 3 (1.9%); 2.2 – 3 (1.9%); 2.5 – 4 (2.6%); 3.2 – 2 (1.3%); 4.1 – 1 (0.6%); 4.2 – 5 (3.3%); 4.3 – 3 (1.9%); 6 – 1 (0.6%); 9.1 – 14 (9.2%); 9.2 – 1 (0.6%).

Roman sherds account for approximately half of this assemblage, but this late material derives largely from the top fills of the ditch which, on the basis of the 1991 assemblage and of the relatively high proportion of LIA pottery, is likely to be an Iron Age feature. With no obvious exceptions, the Iron Age pottery can be accommodated within a date range of mid first century BC to mid first century AD, and this is consistent with the 1991 assemblage. The most common fabric in this group is D20, which was used in the manufacture of a distinctive range of platter copies (e.g. nos. 10 and 11) amongst other types. The Durotrigian ware component which is prominent in the 1991 outer ditch assemblage is smaller, but nonetheless apparent in this group. No.13 is a rare example of a beaker, but it is in a relatively coarse fabric and probably of near-local manufacture.

F409 (Figs. 3.71–3.73) Mid third century AD

Sherd	Form	Fabric	SF/Dec.	Layer
15	DI1	1.10	1	1
15A	DI1	1.8	3	1
16	DI1	4.2	1	1
17	LID	1.10	3	1
18	LID	1.10	1	1
19	BO1.9a	1.2	1	1
20	BO1.6	1.3	1/6	1
21	BO1.9a	1.5	1	1
22	BO1.9a	4.2	1	1
23	BO1.9a	1.3	1	1
24	BO1.9a	1.1	3	1

25	BO1.9a	1.2	3	1
26	JR3.1	1.10	1	1
27	JR3.1	1.2	7	1
28	JR1.2	2.2	2/3	1
29	JR3.4	4.2	1	1
30	JE4.2	D20	E(w)	1
31	JR3.3	1.3	1	1
32	JR3.1	1.10	2	1
33	JR3.3	1.2	1	1
34	JR3.3	4.2	1	1
35	JR3.4	1.10	1	1
36	JR3.3	1.10	1	1
37	JR3.3	1.3	1	1
38	JR3.3	1.10	1	1
39	JR1.4	4.2	1	1
40	JR1.4	4.2	1	1
41	JR3.4	4.2	1	1
42	JR3.3	1.2	1	1
43	JR3.4	1.3	1	1
44	JR3.4	4.3	1	1
45	SJ.17	1.2	1/4	1
46	SJ	2.2	3	1
47	BO1.9a	4.2	3	1
48	BE	9.2	5	1
49	BE3	9.2	5	1
50	BE	4.3	1	1
51	BA4	samian		1
52	BE	9.2	5	1
53	BA4	4.3	5?	1
54	BO2.1	samian		1
55	BA5	samian		1
56	BO2.1	samian		1
57	BO2.1	samian		1
58	BO2.9b	samian		1
59	dec. sherd	samian		1
60	stamp	samian		1
61	LID?	9.2	5	1
62	BO2.1	samian		1

Total sherds: 1539

Fabrics: D4 – 2 (0.1%); D20 – 6 (0.4%); E1 – 1 (0.1%); Misc. – 1 (0.1%); 1.1 – 48 (3.1%); 1.2 – 283 (18.3%); 1.3 – 203 (13.1%); 1.4 – 6 (0.3%); 1.5 – 1 (0.1%); 1.6 – 20 (1.2%); 1.8 – 60 (3.8%); 1.9 – 1 (0.1%); 1.10 – 202 (13.1%); 1.12 – 2 (0.1%); 1.13 – 12 (0.7%); 2.1 – 4 (0.2%); 2.2 – 7 (0.4%); 2.3 – 1 (0.1%); 2.4 – 1 (0.1%); 2.5 – 4 (0.2%); 2.6 – 82 (5.3%); 3.2 – 13 (0.8%); 4.1 – 1 (0.1%); 4.2 – 459 (29.8%); 4.3 – 29 (1.8%); 9.1 – 24 (1.5%); 9.2 – 2 (0.1%); samian – 64 (4.1%).

This group includes a wide range of fabrics, most of which are coarse reduced wares and a moderately coarse variety of an oxidized ware (4.2). Most of these types are typical of coarseware products of the New Forest and Alice Holt potteries and decoration of any sort is rare. The exceptions are a collection of samian wares and a small quantity of New Forest colour-coated wares. These include beaker sherds, including fragments from an indented beaker, which should date from the late third century onwards (Fulford 1975). A small colour-coated handle, probably from a flagon, was also recovered. Much of the collection could otherwise be consistent with a second century date, on the basis of the absence of cavetto rims and the paucity of wares treated with neutral slip, which seems to be a third century feature at both the New Forest and Alice Holt potteries (Lyne and Jefferies 1979, 35). Some of the coarseware bowls can be tentatively highlighted as late types, however, on the basis of their devolved short, stubby flanges. Conservatism of form, fabric and general treatment within the coarseware assemblage does, on the whole, render much of the group undatable. Even bearing in mind the relatively substantial collection of samian ware from this feature, it is probably best to view this assemblage as a mix of redeposited sherds from deposits of different dates, with an overall latest date of mid third century plus.

F421 (Fig. 3.74)   Fourth century AD

Sherd	Form	Fabric	SF/Dec.	Layer
63	DI1	1.1	3	1
64	DI1	?D20	4	1
65	LID	2.2	1/1	1
66	BO1.9a	1.1	3	1
67	BO1.9a	2.5	1/4	1
68	BO1.9a	1.3	1	1
69	BO/JR.7?	1.2	6	1
70	BO1.9a	1.1	3	1
71	JR3.3	1.10	1	1
72	JR3.3	3.1	1/43	1
73	JR3.4	2.2	2	1
74	JR3.2	2.6	4	1
75	F	9.1	6	1
76	Misc	1.5	5 or 6	1
77	BO2.9a	9.2		1
78	BA1	1.8	1	1
79	BA1	1.3	1	1
80	SJ 17	1.2	1/4	1
81	SJ 13	2.1	4	1
82	SJ 17	1.2	1/4	1

Total sherds: 127

Fabrics: D17 – 2 (1.5%); D18 – 2 (1.5%); D20 – 2 (1.5%); 1.1 – 10 (7.8%); 1.2 – 21 (16.5%); 1.3 – 13 (10.2%); 1.5 – 1 (0.7%); 1.6 – 6 (4.7%); 1.8 – 5 (3.9%); 1.9 – 3 (2.3%); 1.10 – 6 (4.7%); 2.1 – 9 (7.0%); 2.2 – 5 (3.9%); 2.5 – 2 (1.5%); 2.6 – 8 (6.2%); 3.1 – 2 (1.5%); 4.2 – 7 (5.5%); 4.3 – 2 (1.5%); 9.1 – 13 (10.2%); 9.2 – 4 (3.1%); samian – 4 (3.1%).

This assemblage broadly resembles that from F409 in character and range of fabrics, but proportions of fine colour-coated wares are higher, suggesting that the overall date of this deposit should be mid third century or later. The fineware sherds are fragmentary and abraded and, in most cases, vessel types were not distinguishable. Fragments of an indented beaker were identified, however, along with a rouletted sherd and a flanged bowl in Oxfordshire red colour-coated ware. No. 72, in a coarse, gritty buff ware resembles the rilled jars produced in the fourth century by the Alice Holt kilns (Lyne and Jefferies 1979, 45.) The range of forms within the coarseware assemblage, however, could be placed earlier in the Roman sequence. The possibility that the group represents a deposit of mixed date deriving from redeposited material must be allowed. On the other hand, many of the vessels types standard within the New Forest and Alice Holt coarseware repertoire had a long lifespan.

F431 (Fig. 3.75)   Late third or fourth century AD

Sherd	Form	Fabric	SF/Dec.	Layer
83	DI1	1.1	2/8	1
84	LID	1.8	2	1
85	BO1.9a	1.1	3/8	1
86	JR3.4	1.1	3/6	1
87	JR3.4	1.13	6	1
88	JR3.3	1.13	2	1
89	JR3.3	1.1	3	1
90	JC3.0	D4	D	1
91	SJ 17	1.3	1/4	1
92	BE	9.1	42	1

Total sherds: 73

Fabrics: B1 – 4 (5.4%); D4 – 1 (1.3%); D17 – 1 (1.3%); 1.1 – 8 (10.9%); 1.2 – 1 (1.3%); 1.3 – 5 (6.8%); 1.4 – 1 (1.3%); 1.6 – 25 (34.2%); 1.8 – 3 (4.1%); 1.10 – 7 (9.5%); 1.11 – 1 (1.3%); 1.13 – 7 (9.5%); 2.1 – 4 (5.4%); 4.2 – 2 (2.7%); 4.3 – 2 (2.7%); 9.1 – 1 (1.3%).

The coarsewares which dominate this small group are not closely datable, but include a few Late Iron Age types. The presence of a New Forest beaker with rusticated decoration (no. 92) within the fill must, however, point to a date in the late third to fourth centuries for the destruction phase of the corn drier. The Alice Holt type storage jar with cabled rim continued to be manufactured into the fourth century, and the less diagnostic jar types also have a wide date range.

Miscellaneous sherds (Fig. 3.75)

Sherd	Form	Fabric	SF/Dec.	Context
93	JC3.1	D17.1	D.7a	F416/1
94	JD3.11	D4	D	F420/1

Roman amphora sherds by David Williams

1. F64 layer 5
   Plain body sherd in a hard, rough sandy fabric containing visible inclusions of quartz, white felspar and some fragments of granite. Light red colour throughout (Munsell 10R 6/8). This sherd almost certainly has a Catalan origin and probably belongs to the amphora form Dressel 2/4, though it is possible that it may instead come from the earlier Dressel 1/Pascual 1 type which has a similar fabric (Peacock and Williams 1986, Classes 10 and 6). Both of these vessels would most likely have been used to export the local Catalan wine. A first century AD date either side of the Conquest period would seem appropriate.

2. P112 layer 1
   Small plain body sherd in a very hard, rough, somewhat sandy fabric. Light creamy-buff colour throughout (10YR 8/4). Difficult to be certain given the small size of the sherds, but probably from one of the southern Spanish amphora types which were used to carry various forms of fish produce (e.g., ibid., Classes 14 and 16/19). As a whole, this class of amphora appears to have been in common use from the second half of the first century BC until the second century AD.

Small finds

The small objects recovered have been listed and described in full in the fiche section (Fiche 5:D10–6:B14). Here a selection has been made for illustration and comment. Those that remain unillustrated are, for the most part, fragmentary or undiagnostic.

The flint assemblage by Ian Brooks

The collection from Areas 1 and 2 (1991)

A small assemblage of 196 flint artefacts was recovered from the excavation of Late Iron Age and Roman features from Suddern Farm. All of these artefacts are presumed to be residual from previous use of the site, although the presence of a Late Iron Age or Roman component within the assemblage cannot be ignored.

The source of the flint for the assemblage is assumed to be the immediate area, where both primary, chalk, and clay-with-flint resources are available.

The flakes have been divided into three broad categories for aid in description. These are primary flakes, with a totally corticated dorsal surface, secondary flakes with partially corticated dorsal surface and tertiary with no cortex present on the dorsal surface. The size and shape of these flakes demonstrate the mixed nature of the assemblage.

Because of the mixed nature of the assemblage it will be described as a whole and is summarized in Fiche 5:D10–12.

Flakes

Twelve primary, 81 secondary, 57 tertiary and 25 broken flakes were recovered. Of these four tertiary flakes and two secondary flakes could be considered blades, that is having a length/width ratio of greater than 5:2. The size of these blades would suggest an Early Neolithic component to the assemblage. A single flake with a partly polished dorsal surface was probably derived from a polished tool, such as an axe and would also suggest a Neolithic component.

Tools (Fig. 3.76)

Only three formal tools were found, two of these were scrapers and the third, a tertiary flake retouched to a considerable degree. A further 18 artefacts were modified to a minor degree of retouching. The three tools were:

1. A coarsely made end scraper on a tertiary flake. The tool was made in a mottled, semi-opaque grey/brown flint. From F66 layer 5.
2. An end/side scraper on a long tertiary flake of probable Neolithic date. The tool is highly patinated to a dense white colour. From F66 layer 3/6.
3. A tertiary flake, heavily retouched along both edges in the distal half of the tool. All of the retouch is unifacial in character with retouch from the dorsal surface. It is possible that this tool is the proximal end of an awl or point. From P215 layer 3.

Worked lumps and cores

Only two formal cores were recovered from the site; both of these were flake cores, one being a multiplatform core and the other a single platform core worked partly around the periphery. Both of these were found in the ditches which surround the site. Three core rejuvenation flakes were also found showing the limited level of knapping control on the site. Nine worked lumps were found also reflecting the *ad hoc* nature of the assemblage.

The collection from Area 3 (1996)

A small collection of 19 flint artefacts was recovered during the course of the excavation at Suddern Farm in 1996. All of the artefacts were found in the upper layers of the features or from unstratified contexts and are therefore not in primary contexts. They are, therefore, regarded as residual artefacts. The assemblage is summarized in Fiche 5:D10–12.

The flakes were separated into three main groupings: primary flakes with a completely corticated dorsal surface, secondary flakes with a partially corticated dorsal surface and tertiary flakes with an uncorticated dorsal surface. The description of the tools follows Inizan *et al.* (1992) and the flint colours are defined by the Geological Society of America's Rock-Color Chart (Goddard *et al.* 1948).

The majority of the artefacts were patinated to a sufficient degree to hide the colour and texture of the flint being used. However, the remaining eight artefacts varied between a dark grey (N3) flint with a moderate to poor translucency to a highly translucent dark yellowish-brown (10 YR 4/2).

Fourteen of the artefacts recovered were flakes of one form or another. Four primary, five secondary, three tertiary and two broken flakes were found. Of

these only one had been further modified by slight retouch and use damage. The majority of flakes were in the intermediate to long (l/w = 1.00 to 2.00) flake group, although two blades (l/w <2.5) were found.

No formal cores or core debris was recovered, although two crude worked lumps were found. One of these had a slightly battered appearance, suggesting it may have been reused as a hammerstone. The lack of formal knapping strategies displayed by the assemblage would suggest an *ad hoc* approach to the reduction process.

Three scrapers were found and are illustrated here (Fig. 3.76):

4. A scraper on a large pot-lid fracture with a cortical dorsal surface. This piece has a 80 mm long worked edge produced by a series of direct, semi-abrupt, scaled, short removals. The tool is slightly patinated to a pale grey colour and is on a semi-translucent, dark yellowish-brown flint. From F400 surface.
5. A convexed side scraper on a tertiary flake. The tool was produced by a series of direct, abrupt, sub-parallel, intermediate removals along the right hand edge. The bulb of percussion has been removed by a single flake removed from the ventral surface. The tool is patinated to a dense white colour. From F429 layer 1.
6. A convexed side scraper on a secondary flake. The tool was produced by a series of direct, semi-abrupt, scalar, short removals along the right hand edge. The tool is patinated to a pale grey and is heat damaged, presumably after use. From F429 layer 1.

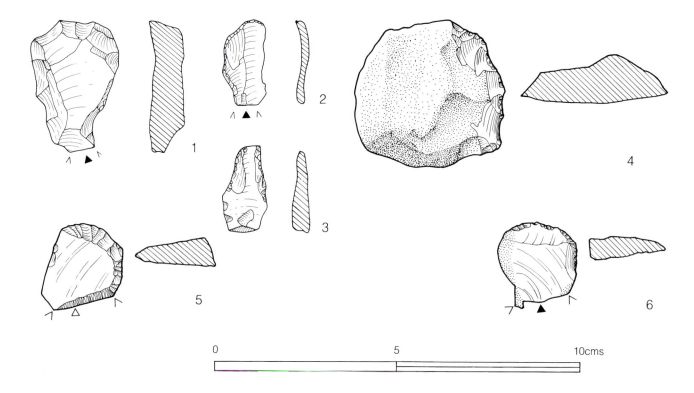

Fig. 3.76 Flints

Discussion

With a small assemblage such as that from Suddern Farm 1996 it is difficult to assign a date range with any certainty. However the form of the few tools and the relatively crude appearance of much of the flint-work would suggest a Late Neolithic to Bronze Age date for much of the assemblage. The 1996 assemblage can be compared to the assemblage from 1991, where 196 flint artefacts were recovered which, whilst it differs in detail is similar in character. Both assemblages have the appearance of *ad hoc* knapping strategy with no formal cores and a reliance on local derived flint sources. The assemblage from 1991 had only three tools (1.5%) from its assemblage, compared with three tools from 19 (15.8%) from 1996. These differences are probably related to differences in excavation and collection strategies between the two excavations.

The average size of artefacts from the 1996 excavation is relatively large (55.9 mm length). No sieving took place and much of the upper layers were excavated by machine, thereby biasing the assemblage towards the larger artefacts and the more obvious tools.

The coins by Cathy King

Coins from the excavations of 1991 and 1996

Three Roman coins were discovered in stratified positions during the excavation of 1991 and a further 22 were recovered from the topsoil, removed mechanically from the 1996 area, during routine screening with a metal detector. The details of the coins are given below. A list with small finds numbers will be found in Fiche 5:D13.

Of the 25 coins recovered from Suddern Farm, all but two (radiates of the period 260–86) belong in the fourth century between the years 330 and 402. The chronological distribution of the coins may be summarized as follows:

DATE	GEN.		IMIT.		TOTAL	
	No.	%	No.	%	No.	%
260–86	2	8.00			2	8.00
330–48	3	12.00	3	12.00	6	24.00
348–60	2	8.00	3	12.00	5	20.00
364–78	9	36.00			9	36.00
388–402	3	12.00			3	12.00
TOTAL	19	76.00	6	24.00	25	100.00

More than half (68%) of the coins fall in the years 348–402 which is a stronger representation than one might expect for this period. This emphasis on the later part of the century is made more pronounced by the scarcity of radiates of the years 260–86 which are normally found in large numbers on British sites and the relatively small numbers of coins minted between 330 and 348 which also tend to be abundant.

Roman coins from stratified contexts (1991)

1. AD 330–5   obv.: VRBS ROMA
rev.: wolf and twins
mint: Arles
From top of P164.

2. AD 348–60   obv.: illegible
rev.: [FEL TEMP REPARATIO]
falling horseman
mint: Trier
From top of P80.

3. AD 364–78   obv.: PN GRATIANVS AVGG
AVG.
rev.: GLORIA NOVI SAECVLI
mint: Arles T CON
From F66 layer 2.

Roman coins from unstratified topsoil (1996)

4. *c*.AD 270–2   obv.: DIVO CLAVDIO
rev.: CONSECRATIO, eagle
mint: Rome

5. *c*.AD 270–4   obv.: [   ] Tetricus II?
rev.: [   ] Illeg.
mint: Gaul

6. *c*.AD 330–48   obv.: VRBS ROMA
rev.: wolf and twins
mint: Trier; T R • P; ancient copy

7. *c*.AD 330–48   obv.: [CONSTANTINOPOLIS]
rev.: Victory on prow
mint: Illeg.

8. *c*.AD 330–48   obv.: [CONSTANT[INOPOLIS]
rev.: [Victory]
mint: Illeg; ancient copy

9. AD 335–41   obv.: IMP CONSTAN[   ]
rev.: GLOR[IA EXERCITVS]
1 standard
mint: Illeg.

10. AD 341–8   obv.: DN CONSTANS PF AVG
rev.: VICTOR[IAE DD
AVGG Q NN]
mint: Illeg.

11. AD 348–60   obv.: DN CONSTANS PF AVG
rev.: FEL TEMP REPARATIO
(phoenix, pyre)
mint: Trier, TR …; ancient copy

12. *c*.AD 348–60   obv.: CONS[   ]
rev.: [FEL TEMP REPARATIO]
falling horseman
mint: Illeg; ancient copy

13. c.AD 350–60　obv.: [　　　　] Mag. or Dec.
　　　　　　　　rev.: [FEL TEMP REPARATIO]
　　　　　　　　　　　emperor
　　　　　　　　mint: Illeg; ancient copy

14. c.AD 348–60　obv.: [　　　　]
　　　　　　　　rev.: [FEL TEMP REPARATIO]
　　　　　　　　　　　falling horseman
　　　　　　　　mint: Illeg; ancient copy

15. AD 367–75　obv.: DN GRATIANVS AVGG
　　　　　　　　　　　AVG
　　　　　　　　rev.: GLORIA NOVI SAECVLI
　　　　　　　　mint: Arles OF | ?
　　　　　　　　　　　　　　CON

16. AD 367–75　obv.: DN GRATIANVS AVGG
　　　　　　　　　　　AVG
　　　　　　　　rev.: GLORIA NOVI SAECVLI
　　　　　　　　mint: Arles T̄CON

17. AD 367–75　obv.: DN GRATIANVS PF AVG
　　　　　　　　rev.: GLORIA ROMANORVM
　　　　　　　　mint: Illeg. OFI|*
　　　　　　　　　　　　　?

18. AD 36　obv.: DN VALENS PF AVG
　　　　　　　　rev.: SECVRITAS REIPVBLICAE
　　　　　　　　mint: Arles OF | II
　　　　　　　　　　　　[ ] CON

19. AD 364–75　obv.: DN VALENTINIANVS PF
　　　　　　　　　　　AVG
　　　　　　　　rev.: SECVRITAS REIPVBLICAE
　　　　　　　　mint: Arles [ ] CON

20. AD 367–78　obv.: DN VALENS PF AVG
　　　　　　　　rev.: SECVRITAS REIPVBLICAE
　　　　　　　　mint: Illeg.

21. AD 364–78　obv.: [　　　　]
　　　　　　　　rev.: SECVRITAS REIPVBLICAE
　　　　　　　　mint: Illeg.

22. AD 364–78　obv.: [　　　　]
　　　　　　　　rev.: [SECVRITAS REIPVBLICAE]
　　　　　　　　mint: Illeg.

23. AD 388–402　obv.: [　　　　]
　　　　　　　　rev.: [　　　　] Victory l.
　　　　　　　　mint: Illeg.

24. AD 388–402　obv.: [　　　　]
　　　　　　　　rev.: [　　　　] Victory l.
　　　　　　　　　　　dragging captive
　　　　　　　　mint: Illeg.

25. AD 388–402　obv.: [　　　　]
　　　　　　　　rev.: [　　　　] Victory l.
　　　　　　　　　　　dragging captive
　　　　　　　　mint: Illeg.

Coins collected from the vicinity of Suddern Farm

A collection of coins recovered by a local metal detectorist was made available for study. They were from the 'general vicinity' of the Suddern Farm site and were picked up over a number of years. The assemblage comprises two Celtic coins (identified by P. de Jersey) and 30 Roman coins (identified by C.E. King).

The Celtic coins
1. Silver stater of the Durotriges.
　Van Arsdell 1235–1. Wt. 4.69 gm. Probably late first century BC.
2. Silver unit of Epaticcus, of the Atrebates.
　Van Arsdell 580–1. Wt. 1.28 gm. Probably c.AD 30–40.

The Roman coins

The 30 Roman coins in this group range in date from the second half of the first century to the last years of the fourth. Their metallic and chronological composition suggest that they do not represent a typical Romano-British site distribution; rather they look to be a selected group of above-average interest and condition. There are nine silver coins, seven denarii including a plated specimen of Trajan, and two clipped late fourth century siliquae of Arcadius and Honorius respectively.

If the coins are grouped into broad categories and tabulated, there are no peaks where one normally expects to find them, e.g. between 260 to 286, 330 to 348, and in some cases 364 to 378. Another unusual feature of so small a group of coins is the presence of two coins of Carausius, both in excellent condition.

DATE	GENUINE	IMITS	TOTAL
1st–2nd century	5	1	6
193–260	4	–	4
260–95	2	3	5
295–315	1	–	1
315–30	4	1	5
330–48	5	1	6
348–60	–	1	1
388–402	2	–	2
TOTAL	23	7	30

Objects of copper alloy (Fig. 3.77)

The descriptions of 1.1–1.3 were contributed by Dr. Martin Henig and of 1.10 by Dr. Helena Hamerow. Detailed descriptions of all items are given in Fiche 5:D14–E1.

1.1　Fibula of Nauheim derivative type with incipient wings, a six-coil spring and external chord secured by a hook. The bow is plain and the catch plate though broken appears to be solid. Claudio-Neronian.
　　From the uppermost fill of pit P119. First

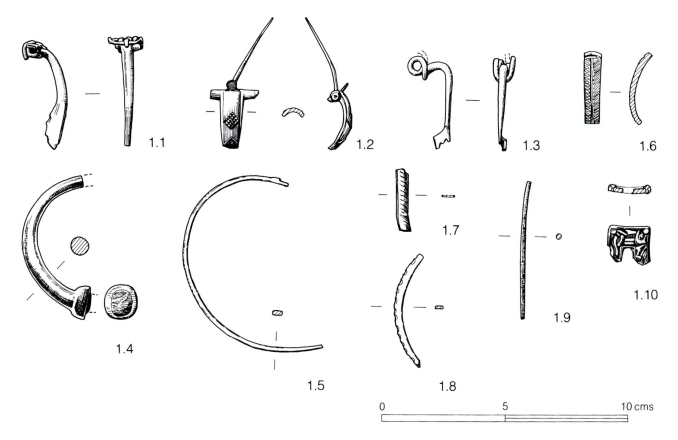

Fig. 3.77 Objects of copper alloy

century AD.

1.2 Fibula. Hinged T-shaped type with raised cross hatched lozenges on the wide flat bow. Foot plate missing. Mid second century.
From topsoil (1996).

1.3 Fibula of Nauheim derivative type. Simple rectangular-sectioned bow with four-coiled spring and plain foot plate. Claudio-Neronian.
From within the wall of oven F431 (1996).

1.4 Fragment of a terret ring of circular section with an undecorated stop.
From pit P104 cp 8–9.

1.5–1.8 Fragments of bracelets. All Roman from feature F47 except 1.6 which is unstratified. Late Roman.

1.9 Rod.
From pit P194 cp 3–5.

1.10 Fragment of a rectangular cast copper alloy buckle plate which would almost certainly have been gilded, with chip-carved Style I animal ornament. It is missing its central setting, which was almost certainly a piece of garnet or red glass. The design of two quadrupeds (the head of one and the tail of the other survive) is very closely matched by a buckle-plate from Apple Down Grave 63. Grave 63 was quite a rich burial (also containing a bucket, spear, seax, and purse), and the other parallels are also from fairly ostentatious burials at Alfriston, Mucking, Petersfinger and Pewsey. The date of manufacture is around the second quarter of the sixth century (Hawkes *et al.* 1974).

From topsoil (1996).
Not illustrated: three collections of fragments of sheet, all very corroded.

Objects of iron (Figs. 3.78 and 3.79)

Detailed descriptions of all items are given in Fiche 5:E2–7.

2.1 Key with looped end attached to a ring.
From the top of pit P204: Roman.

2.2–2.3 Tanged knives, one with a groove on one side. 2.2 is from pit P104 of cp 8–9; 2.3 is from ph 122 and may well be Roman.
Two other blade fragments, not illustrated, were also found, both from Roman contexts.

2.4 Socketed handle of a bladed implement of unknown form.
From feature F48: late Roman.

2.5 Horseshoe fragment.
From pit P191: Roman?

2.6 Spiral ring in two fragments: possibly an ox-goad.
From pit P117: cp 8–9.

2.7 Hook with looped end.
From F48: late Roman.

2.8 Harness ring of iron still retaining much of its copper alloy covering.
From feature F60: late Roman.

2.9 Ring.
From feature F79: late Roman.

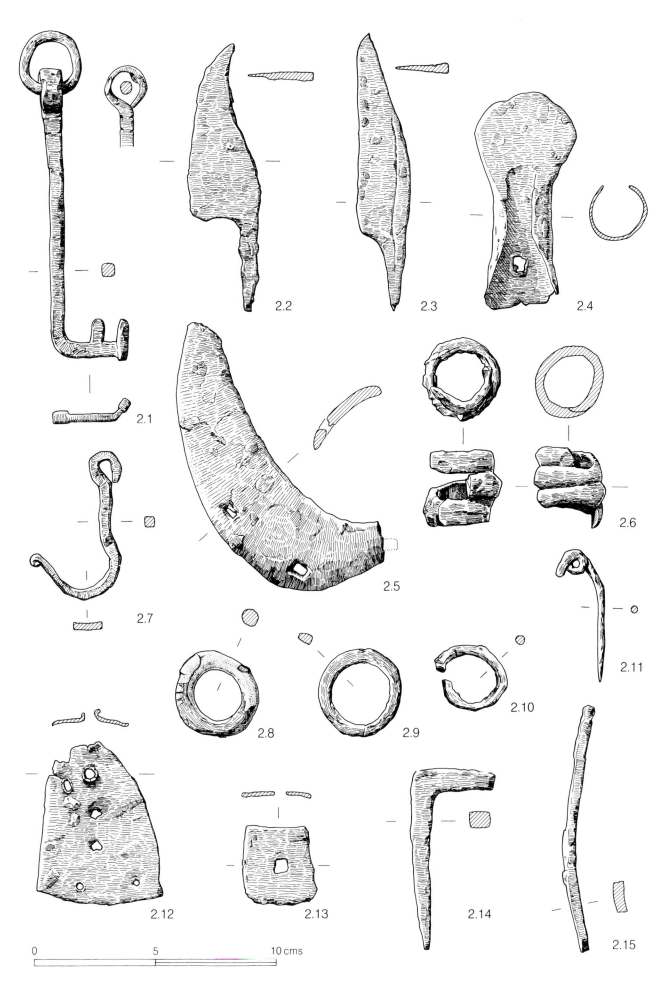

2.1

2.2

2.3

2.4

2.5

2.6

2.7

2.8

2.9

2.10

2.11

2.12

2.13

2.14

2.15

0   5   10 cms

Fig. 3.78 Objects of iron

Fig. 3.79 (right) Objects of iron

118

2.10 Ring.
  From feature F44: late Roman.
2.11 Pin and part of the spring of a fibula.
  From feature F64: first century, pre-Flavian.
2.12–2.13 Fragments of sheet with perforations. 2.12 came from the top of pit P125 (Roman), while 2.13 came from the top of pit P152 (undated).
2.14 Point with head bent at right angles.
  From feature F60: late Roman.
2.15 Strip.
  From the top of pit P107: cp 3–6.
2.16 Involuted fibula much corroded. Found with skeleton in grave F447. Corresponding to Stead's type D 'long involuted' (Stead 1991, 83). Of La Tène II type, i.e. late fourth to late second century.
2.17 Curved iron strip possibly fragments of a spiral coiled ring.

Found with skeleton in grave F441.
2.18–2.21 Cleats of varying sizes and forms. 2.18 from feature F66 (early Roman); 2.19 and 2.20 from feature F62 (late Roman); 2.21 from pit P119 (first century AD).
2.22–2.28 Selection of the 76 iron nails recovered, all from probable or certain Roman contexts. Twenty of them were from the Roman burial. Details including measurements are given on Fiche 5:E8–11.

Not illustrated: in addition to the identifiable nails and the two blade fragments mentioned above 24 other fragments of iron were found. These were mostly fragments of rods (possibly broken nails), sheets and strips. The majority came from certain or probable Roman contexts.

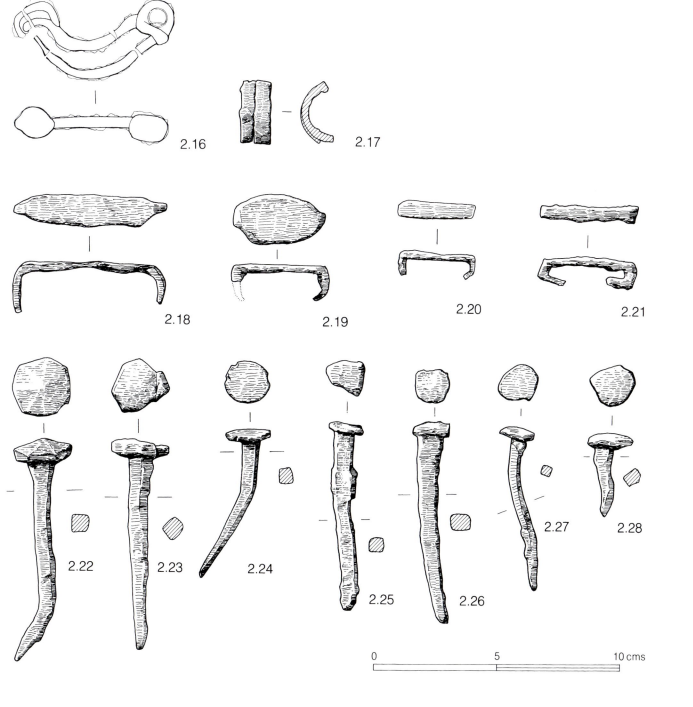

2.16 2.17
2.18 2.19 2.20 2.21
2.22 2.23 2.24 2.25 2.26 2.27 2.28

0   5   10 cms

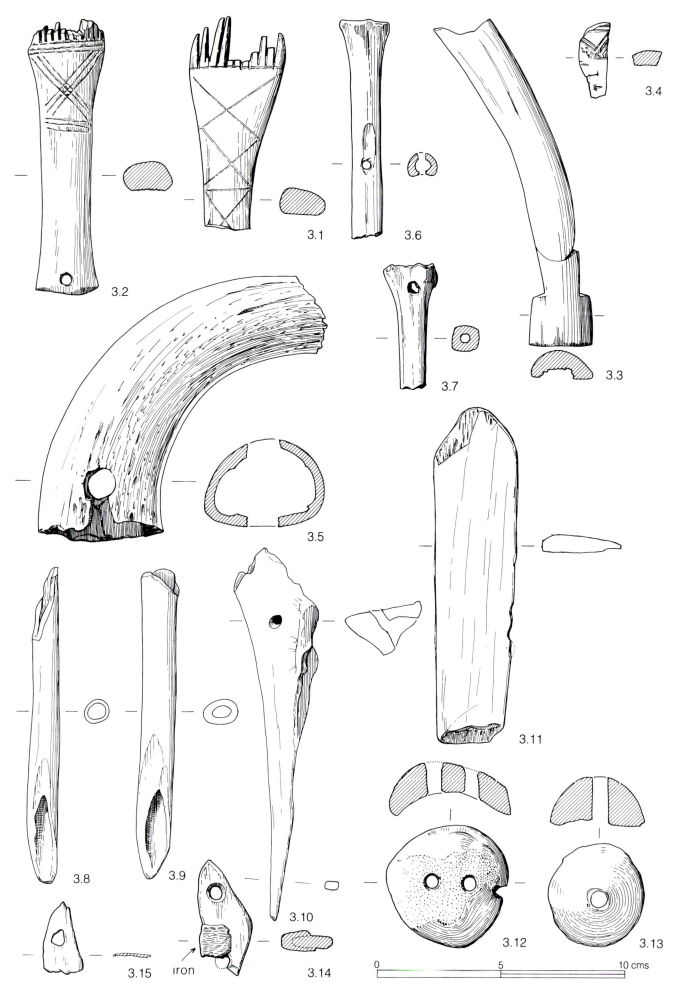

3.1

3.2

3.3

3.4

3.5

3.6

3.7

3.8

3.9

3.10

3.11

3.12

3.13

3.14

3.15

iron

0   5   10 cms

Fig. 3.80 Objects of bone and antler

Objects of bone and antler (Fig. 3.80)

Detailed descriptions of all items are given in Fiche 5:E12–14.

3.1 Comb with an unusually wide head. Decorated with simple crossing diagonal lines throughout the length.
From pit P101 layer 1: Roman.

3.2 Comb with simple head, perforated. A zone of inscribed decoration lies immediately behind the teeth.
From pit P101 layer 1: Roman.

3.3 Comb, considerably distorted, with square handle: undecorated.
From pit P140 layer 3: cp 6–7.

3.4 Fragment of decorated bone probably part of a comb.
From pit P119 layer 1: first century AD.
Not illustrated: comb tooth. Unstratified.

3.5 Perforated long bone.
From pit P92 layer 3: cp 6–7.

3.6 Tibia/metapodial of sheep with perforation through the centre of the shaft.
From pit P89 layer 4: cp 8–9.

3.7 Tibia of sheep with perforation through the shaft towards the epiphysis.
From pit P131 layer 1: cp 3.

3.8 Gouge made from sheep's tibia.
From pit P107 layer 2: cp 3–6.

3.9 Gouge made from sheep's tibia.
From pit P211 layer 2: cp 6/7.

3.10 Point made from cow's ulna.
From pit P83 layer 2: cp 7.

3.11 Rib knife.
From F64 layer 2: cp 9.

3.12 Roundel cut from pelvis(?) bone with two perforations.
From pit P78 layer 3: cp 7.

3.13 Roundel cut from the proximal articular end of a cow's femur with central perforation.
From pit P104 layer 9: cp 8–9.

3.14 Triangular plate of bone with perforation through two apexes. A fragment of iron is attached suggesting that the bone may have served as a handle for an iron tool.

From pit P82 layer 3: cp 4/5.

3.15 Pierced bone fragment.
From pit P194 layer 4: cp 3–5.

Not illustrated are seven fragments of worked antler from a variety of contexts and two utilized ribs.

Objects of shale (Fig. 3.81)

Detailed descriptions are given in Fiche 5:F1.

4.1 Fragments of shale bracelet, hand cut.
From pit P132 layer 1: cp 6.

4.2 Fragment of shale bracelet, hand cut.
From pit P139 layer 2: cp 3–4.

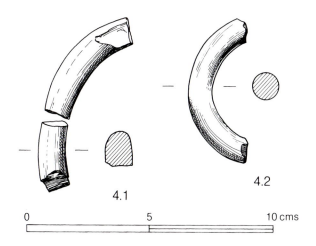

Fig. 3.81 Objects of shale

Objects of glass (Fig. 3.82)

Detailed descriptions are given in Fiche 5:F1.

6.1 Glass ring: yellow glass.
From pit P120 layer 1: Roman.

Not illustrated: four sherds of vessel glass from Roman contexts.

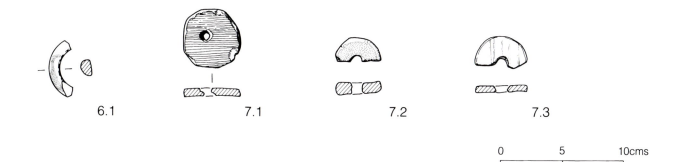

Fig. 3.82 Objects of glass and ceramics

121

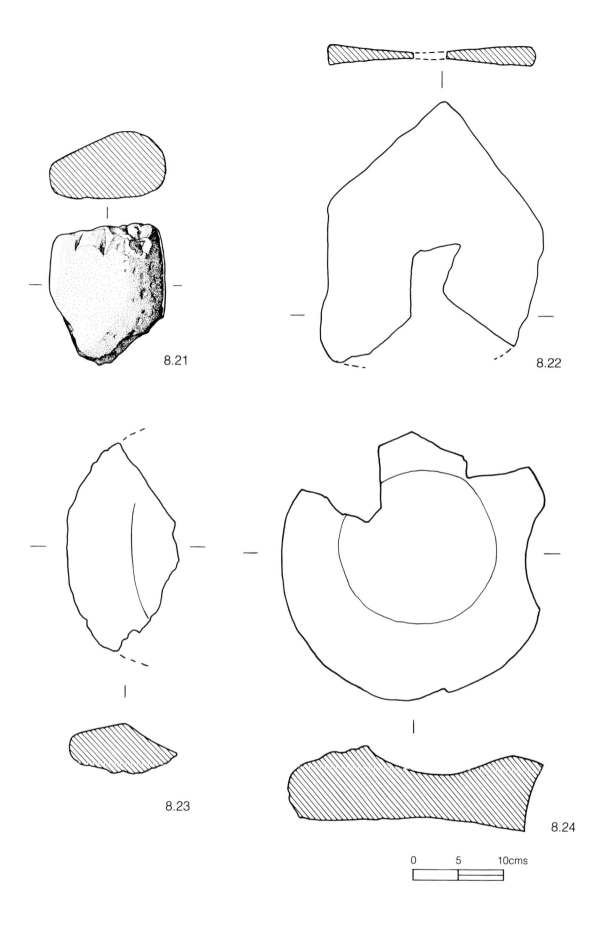

8.21

8.22

8.23

8.24

0   5   10cms

Fig. 3.86 Miscellaneous items of stone

Objects of baked clay (Fig. 3.82)

Detailed descriptions are given in Fiche 5:F2.

7.1 Perforated disc.
    From pit P104 layer 4: cp 8–9.
7.2 Perforated disc.
    From F448 layer 1: Roman.
7.3 Spindle whorl.
    From F401 layer 1: Roman.

Four other pottery discs were found. Of the total collection, three were of Roman date; the remaining four were from Late Iron Age contexts.

Objects of stone by Emma Durham

Whetstones (Fig. 3.83 nos. 8.1–8.10)

Eight whetstones were recovered of which the majority were elongated pebbles of subrectangular to circular cross section. Two were probably of Staddon Grit. Three were micaceous sandstone from the Coal Measures and two were probably of Kentish Rag. The other is of unidentified sandstone. One came from a cp 4/5 context, one from cp 6 while the rest were Roman. Eight are illustrated (nos. 8.1–8.8).

Several flat stones (e.g. no. 8.9) were also used for sharpening.

One hammerstone, of sarsen (no. 8.10), was recovered from an early Roman context.

Details are given in Fiche 5:F3–4.

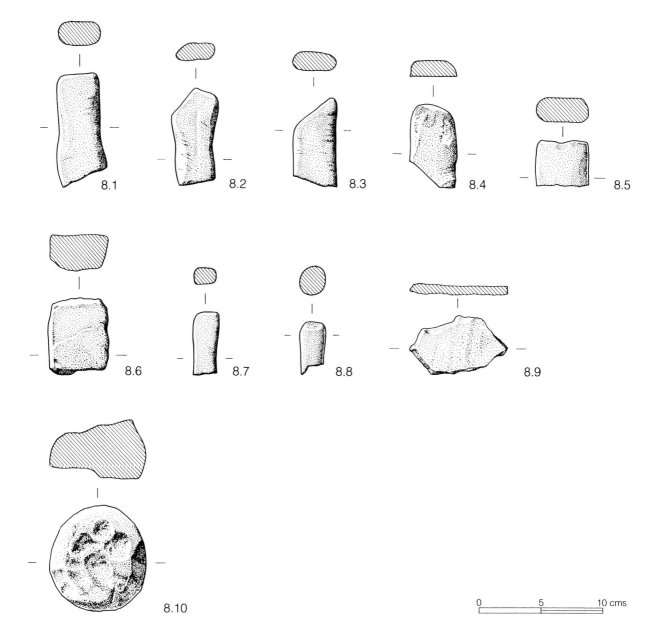

Fig. 3.83 Objects of stone

Querns (Figs. 8.84 and 8.85)

Quernstones of both rotary and saddle type are represented by 157 fragments of stone. Of these 42 saddle querns are represented by 47 fragments and 14 rubbers are represented by 19 fragments. The 66 rotary querns account for 92 fragments. In addition to this there are 92 fragments of stone of indeterminate shape which were probably quern fragments.

All of the rotary querns and many of the saddle querns were made of greensand of which several varieties have been identified. Lower Greensand is the predominant type much of it coming from the Lodsworth quarries near Midhurst (Peacock 1987).

Details of the querns are given on Fiche 5:F5–G6.

Rotary querns

Upper stones of rotary querns were divided into seven types: R1–R6 were identified at Danebury (Vol. 2, 412–18) but R7 is a new type defined here. A selection are illustrated in Fig. 3.84.

R1 Five examples: one Upper Greensand; four Lower Greensand. All cp 8–9 to Roman (Fig. 3.84 nos. 8.11 and 8.12). In the original definition the type was described as having a hopper but the definition should be modified to allow for those without hoppers as well.

R2 Two examples both Lower Greensand. Both first century AD (Fig. 3.84 no. 8.13).
    There are two examples of either R1 or R2.

R6 One example: Lower Greensand. First century AD.

R7 Six examples: all greensand and from late Roman contexts. These querns are flat (18–28 mm thick) and have a large central hole. In fragments they are difficult to distinguish from lower stones except that the lower stones tend to be thicker (35–47 mm). Many of the stones show evidence of tooling with radiating toolmarks on the grinding surface and/or peck marks (Fig. 3.84 nos. 8.14 and 8.15).
    Also tentatively assigned to this category is a fragment of top stone with a basin-shaped hopper. The upper surface has radial tooling (Fig. 3.84 no. 8.16).

Unclassified: Sixteen fragments all of greensand. The earliest comes from a cp 6 context.

Lower stones: In total 21 fragments of lower stones were found. Of these seven were of type R7, the rest were unclassified. All were of greensand. The earliest context was cp 8–9. All the R7 types came from late Roman contexts. Of the generalized type only two were large enough fragments to allow their diameters (330 mm and 340 mm) to be accurately measured. Thicknesses varied from 57–120 mm. They generally have a flat base and a convex grinding surface often with a raised rim around the central socket. There is little evidence of tooling and the bases were roughly finished. A selection are illustrated (Fig. 3.85 nos. 8.17–8.20).

Saddle querns and rubbing stones

Saddle querns and their associated rubbing stones account for about 40% of the querns from the site although the number is probably over-represented because of the highly fragmented nature of this type. Of the total 27 querns (69%) were of greensand and eight querns (20%) were of sarsen. Sandstone and gritstone each account for 5%.

Two types of saddle quern have been distinguished, as at Danebury: larger block-shaped querns and smaller querns rather more carefully finished. The grinding surfaces are usually flat, sloping or concave and sometimes the base and sides are worn from contact with the ground.

The majority of the saddle querns come from pits the earliest being of cp 3. A number were found, presumably as strays, in late Roman contexts.

Thirteen rubbing stones were found; 6 are of sandstone, 1 of gritstone, 3 of greensand and 3 of sarsen. Nine of these come from pits the earliest dating to cp 3. One has been selected for illustration (Fig. 3.86 no. 8.21).

Other objects of stone (Fig. 3.86)

Hexagonal roof slabs

In all 131 fragments of limestone roof slabs were found. Many of them showed traces of wear suggesting secondary use possibly as paving. The majority come from well-dated Roman features. One example (Fig. 3.86 no. 8.22) was heavily worn on the surface suggesting that it may have been used for sharpening or grinding.

Mortars

Two possible mortars were discovered both of Lower Greensand. Their upper surfaces were worn into a deep regular-shaped hollow by a circular grinding motion. One was early Roman, the other was unstratified (Fig. 3.86 nos. 8.23 and 8.24).

Chalk weights (Fig. 3.87 nos. 8.25–8.31)

Eight chalk objects were found, including three spindle whorls, one spindle whorl/disc and three discs. All the objects are similar to those found on other contemporary sites in the region.

The spindle whorls vary from 27–56 mm in diameter and have subrectangular or sub-square cross-sections. One (no. 8.27) is decorated on both sides with nine grooves radiating from the centre. Other spindle whorls with this type of decoration have been found at various sites such as Danebury and Maiden Castle.

The spindle whorl/disc and discs vary in diameter from 62–100 mm. The spindle whorl/disc has flat faces and a rectangular cross-section while the discs have slightly curved faces. Also recovered was one small piece of chalk which may be a disc fragment.

Further details are provided in Fiche 5:G7–8.

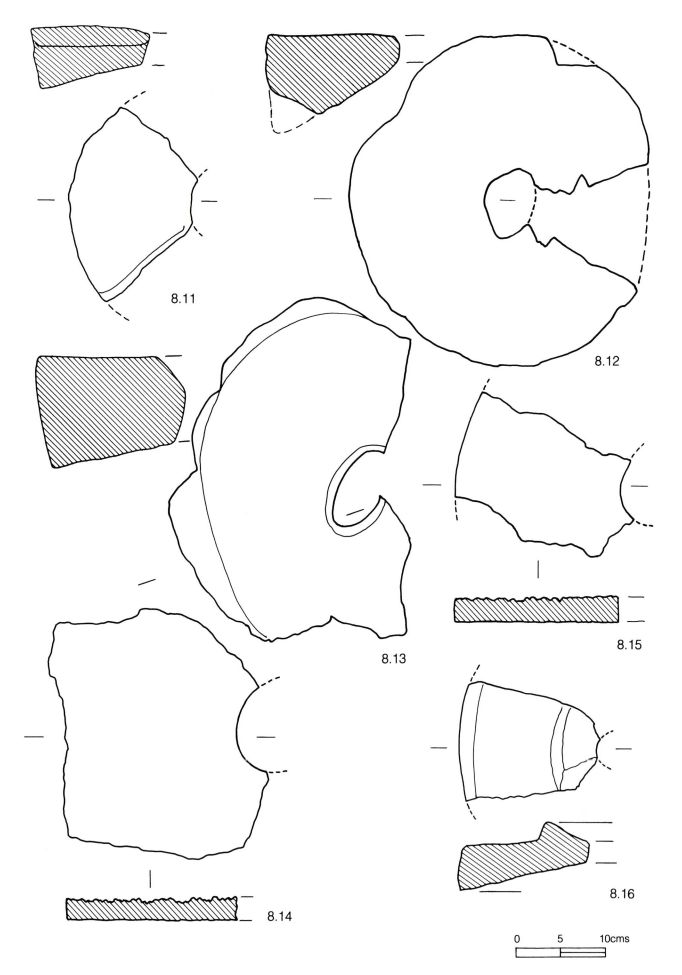

8.11

8.12

8.13

8.14

8.15

8.16

0 5 10cms

Fig. 3.84 Querns

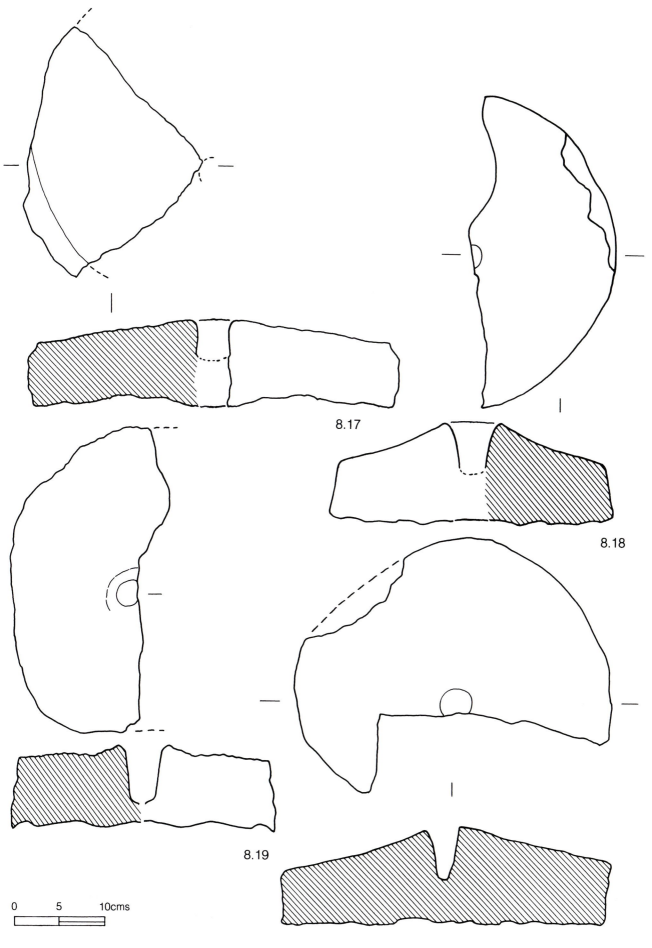

0   5   10cms

8.17

8.18

8.19

8.20

Fig. 3.85 Querns

125

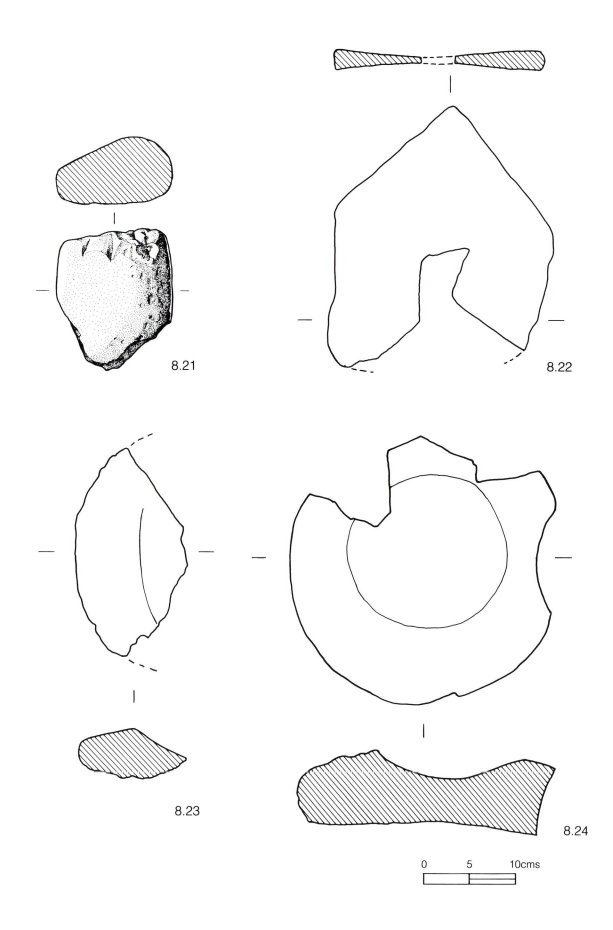

Fig. 3.86 Miscellaneous items of stone

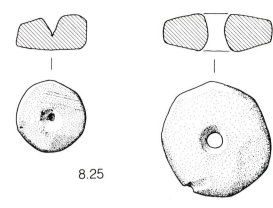

8.25

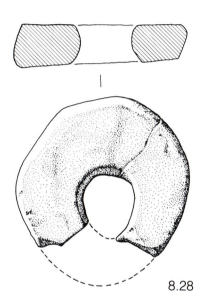

8.26

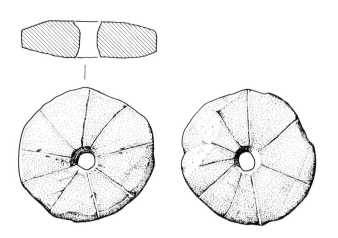

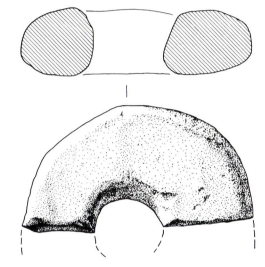

8.27

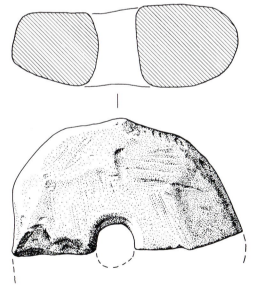

8.28

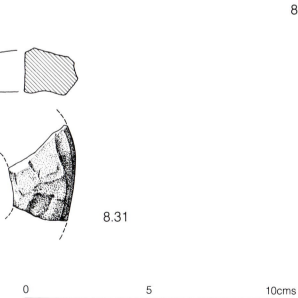

8.29

8.30

8.31

0   5   10cms

Fig. 3.87 Objects of chalk

127

Structural oven daub by Cynthia Poole

The 1991 excavations at Suddern Farm produced a total 532.25 kg of structural daub, by far the largest quantity of any of the Environs sites. It included three very large groups: 170 kg from P120, nearly 146 kg from P194 and 53 kg from P165, which accounted for three-quarters of all the daub, and a fourth rather smaller one of 16 kg from P119. Material collected from the *in situ* Roman ovens weighed between 1 and 11 kg per oven, but this represents a sample, not the total from each oven. These accounted for 5.5% of the daub. (All percentages quoted are based on weight rather than fragment count, though some of the tables have both.)

The daub occurred in 96 features representing 204 individual contexts. The majority (over 90%) of the daub was found in storage pits with only small quantities occurring in bowl pits, hollows, post-holes, quarry hollows, working hollows, slots and the ditches. The distribution is quantified in Fiche 6:A3. It can be seen that during the Iron Age pits accounted for 95–100% of the daub, whilst in the Roman period though pits remained important for recovery of daub in secondary situations, the ovens produced two-thirds to three-quarters of the total recovered.

Daub occurred in phases dating from cp 3 in the Iron Age through to the late Roman period. The greatest quantity occurred in the MIA, closely followed by LIA. However if one excludes the four largest groups from single pits the pattern which emerges is a gradual decrease in quantities from the EIA onwards and continues in the Roman period if material from the *in situ* ovens is excluded. The quantities of daub in relation to phase, together with feature type, form and fabric are summarized in Fiche 6:A3–6. More detailed information on form and fabric for each phase is provided in Fiche 6:A7–11.

There is a greater density of features containing daub in the western central section of the site, but the pits containing the very large groups lie more to the east. The pattern does not appear to have any particular significance except to reflect the preference for deposition in pits.

Table 3.10.
Size of daub samples with diagnostic types

Sample size	No. features with diagnostic daub	without diagnostic daub
<100 gm	6	30
100–499 gm	6	5
500–999 gm	8	2
1–5 kg	14	2
5–20 kg	7	0
>50 kg	4	0
Total	45	39

The size of the daub sample within a feature bears a direct relation to how likely it is to contain diagnostic material. Few samples under 100 gm were identifiable with regards to function and below 0.5 kg samples were unlikely to contain more than one diagnostic variety. Above this the variety of diagnostic material

appeared to bear no relationship to the quantity of daub overall.

The average fragment size in grams has been calculated for each sample and details appear in Fiche 6:A12–B14. The overall averages in relation to fabric and form are presented in Fiche 6:A4. This shows that all forms of structural oven daub, especially in fabrics A, C, D and E tend to survive as larger fragments (70–200 gm) by contrast to the unidentifiable fragments which are generally less than 30 gm. Fragment size probably depends on a number of factors: the strength or fragility of the fabric, whether it was fired, the size of the structure and events after its use. The upper wall daub tends to break up into smaller pieces (12–120 gm) than other structural areas (50–200 gm). Smaller individual objects or oven furniture are more likely to remain more complete, unless deliberately smashed, but will be relatively small to begin with. Certain fabrics tended to survive better than others: the clays and sandy clays (A, F, G, H, J, K, L) tended to be smaller than the coarse tempered daub fragments (C, D, E). Considering how fragile much of the daub is it is likely that most of the better preserved and more diagnostic samples were placed fairly directly in pits from their primary position, whilst the smaller amorphous fragments probably spent some time on floors, yards or in middens, but not excessively long as such material would quickly disintegrate if trampled.

The fabrics

The fabric categories used are those originated for Danebury and subsequently used for all Environs sites. A range of eleven fabrics were observed, but no new fabric types were identified at Suddern Farm. They can be broadly divided into three groups: fairly pure clays – J, K, L, N; fine tempered sandy clays – A, F, H; and coarse tempered daub – C, D, E. The quantification of the fabrics in relation to phasing and form can be found in Fiche 6:A4–5.

The most common of the clays was fabric K, red or slightly purplish red in colour with grey or creamy streaks or mottles and occasionally might contain a little quartz sand, flint grit or organic material. It was present in all phases, forming only a small proportion of the daub in the Iron Age, but a higher proportion in the Roman phases. This clay is thought to derive from the Reading Beds, the nearest sources lying about 10 km to the south.

Fabrics J and L were yellowish-brown clays, sometimes containing small flint grit. Though present from EIA to early Roman, they never formed more than a tiny proportion, less than 1%, of the daub. Fabric H, a green sandy clay, occurred as a single small fragment in the EIA. At other sites it has been identified as the raw form of fabric A and this also appears to be the case with the oven cover in fabric A in P194.

Fabric N is thought to derive from a local source of clay with flints, being a brown clay containing small subangular flint grit and gravel up to 25 mm size. Some of the samples showed evidence of being utilized possibly, but it was more often used probably as the basis for the coarse tempered daub fabrics. Samples only occurred in EIA and MIA when it formed less than 5% of the daub.

The sandy clay fabrics A and F occurred in all phases. Fabric A, a dark brown coarse sandy clay was sometimes tempered with coarse oyster shell or small flint. The majority of it was used to make oven covers, 86% of which was accounted for by the single sample from P194, but it had also been used for one triangular oven brick.

Fabric F, a fine sandy clay varying in colour through shades of red, reddish yellow and brown occurred in all phases, usually only accounting for about 1% of the daub in each phase, but rising to 6% in the LIA. It was used for all forms of structural daub, but most frequently for triangular oven bricks and to a lesser extent wall daub.

The coarse daub fabrics, C, D and E formed nearly 90% of all daub. Fabric G a very soft, pale pink/brown chalky daub was insignificant (less than 1%) occurring only in LIA and early Roman phases. Fabrics C and E, as suggested for other Environs sites, were probably variations of a single fabric. Fabric C was generally yellow or pale brown in colour and less baked or fired, whilst E was red, reddish yellow or dark brown and baked to highly fired. Both contained a high proportion (up to 40%) of coarse chalk and flint temper, together with small quantities of snail shell, burnt chalk and flint, marcasite, clay pellets and charcoal, which may indicate soil was added to the clay base to provide the temper. The difference in colour may be purely a feature of firing or it may relate to different clays used as the base (fabrics N, J, L perhaps forming fabric C, and fabric K or K and a mix of the others forming E).

Fabric D is very similar to C and E, but is differentiated by the addition of small burnt chalk grit, which appears to be a deliberate addition as usually it occurs in conjunction with unburnt fragments, suggesting it is not just a result of intense firing, though D is normally well fired.

Fabrics C and E were the most common varieties through all phases. Fabric C accounted for three-quarters of all EIA daub, but decreased to a fifth of the daub of the late Roman period. However in terms of actual quantities the largest amount was present in the MIA (over 100 kg) with somewhat lower, but roughly equal quantities (70–75 kg) in EIA and LIA, compared to a mere 22 kg (8% of fabric C) in the Roman period. Fabric E however formed 14% in the EIA, increasing to 45% in the LIA; the increase is reflected in actual quantities during the Iron Age, but thereafter the amount decreases. Fabric D remains small actually and proportionately (less than 1%) except in the MIA when it was boosted to 37% by the large sample in P120.

All the major fabrics that occur in any quantity appear to have remained in use throughout the occupation of the site, though there is a distinct decrease in the quantities recovered from the Roman period. This is most likely owing to the decrease in the number of pits, as well as perhaps a change in attitude to the placing of special deposits.

The forms

All the key elements of oven structure were present: namely lower walls/base, upper walls, oven plate and oven cover. Triangular oven bricks were the only oven furniture found and other associated material comprised a few small samples of furnace lining, straw impressed disc and possibly a fragment of funnel/bellows' guard. A full catalogue of all the daub arranged by phase and feature appears in Fiche 6:A7–11 together with a separate section of more detailed descriptions of diagnostic pieces (Fiche 6:A12–B4). The three large groups in P119, P120 and P194 are described in detail separately below.

All forms are quantified in relation to fabrics and phasing in Fiche 6:A4–6.

Oven base – lower walls

The *in situ* Roman oven bases are described elsewhere (pp. 39–46, Fiche 4:F5–14) and the material considered here was all found in secondary contexts. Oven base was the most prolific form accounting for nearly 300 kg of daub. It occurred in all Iron Age phases being proportionately greatest in the EIA (83%) decreasing to 38% in the LIA, though the greatest actual amount was nearly 100 kg in MIA contexts. The majority (82%) were constructed in fabric C followed by fabric E (15%) and minimal amounts in fabrics D, F, G and K. The best preserved examples with the greatest variety of characteristics occurred in P120 and P194 and these are the only samples to be described in detail. The other large group of oven base was found in P165 and though comprising nearly 53 kg of daub few diagnostic features beyond the minimum were present.

The general characteristics of oven base include remnants of at least one smooth surface, sometimes both inner and outer, evidence of the daub being above average thickness, i.e. over 50 mm and frequently in the region of 80–120 mm, impressions of (or more rarely actual) large flints embedded in the interior and a low density of isolated wattle impressions. More rarely a curving surface with semicircular profile may indicate the presence of a stokehole. P165 had some fragments with parts of circular perforations, but it was not clear whether these were holes in the oven wall (e.g. for a bellows) or derived from some other part of the oven such as a plate or cover.

The majority of fragments are assigned to this category because of thickness of the daub together with one surface often showing some indication of heating or burning. In the larger samples it is clear there can be considerable variation in the degree to which the daub has been heated ranging from a slight pink tinge on the surface to well fired to some depth, or sometimes only blackening or sooting of the surface. Firing is usually most intense around the stokehole arch. Wattle impressions were generally small falling in the size range of 7–12 mm diameter.

Upper walls

Material from the upper walls is described in detail for P119, P120 and P194; as these are very typical the fiche descriptions of the remaining samples record only wattle sizes.

Upper wall daub was only found in the MIA and LIA, utilized fabrics D, E, F and G and was up to about 50 mm thick. The daub is typified by impressions of interwoven wattles composed of horizontal rods, mostly 7–15 mm diameter and vertical sails 15–25 mm. In the five MIA samples there was a total of 54 rod and 5 sail impressions and in the three LIA samples 17 rod impressions.

On present available evidence it is not possible to detect whether the wattle work was prefabricated like an inverted basket or whether the sails were set in the lower walls and the basketry woven *in situ*. It could be argued that the wattle impressions found in the lower walls are compatible with the latter hypothesis, except that their sizes are smaller than the sails in the upper wall daub.

Generally only one surface, frequently well fired or burnt, survives and this is considered to be the interior surface of the oven. Occasionally where daub has squeezed between wattles there is evidence of it being smoothed off on the other side. It is likely that any outside surface remained under fired and as a result did not survive.

One sample (P104) had a white, possibly lime-based, coating forming a thin veneer over the surface. This also occurred on the oven plate from the same pit. This characteristic was also observed in upper wall material from P119, oven base from P92 and an unidentified form from F64.

Oven plate

This formed 5% (just over 27 kg) of all daub deposited and occurred in a total of nine pits ranging in date from EIA to early Roman, though represented by only single fragments in the earliest and latest phases. The largest amount, nearly 20 kg, was deposited in the MIA most of it in P120 and similarly most of the LIA material derived from P194. Oven plate was constructed in fabrics C, D, E and F.

The form is well exemplified by that from P120 and P194. It generally takes the form of a flat plate roughly 50 mm thick with a smooth upper surface pierced by vertical circular holes *c*.30 mm in diameter and with a rough underside frequently covered in impressions of straw and/or criss-crossed wattles and planks. The perforations and impressions are considered the key characteristics for identification, though some samples have been tentatively identified as oven plate purely on the general character of fabric, surface and burning.

Oven cover

A total of 19 samples were identified and formed about 8% of all daub. It was fairly evenly distributed from EIA to late Roman apart from the LIA, when a distinct rise occurred with the large sample in P194. This was the most complete sample and best preserved of any oven covers found at Danebury or the Environs sites, though it may be of atypical design. It is fully described on pp. 135–38.

Two designs of oven cover are apparent and both have been recognized at other sites. The simplest variety (designated type 1) confined at Suddern Farm to the Iron Age phases and made in fabric K (as appears to be the norm at other sites) took the form of a flat or convex plate about 30 mm thick pierced by a single circular hole or flue 110–20 mm in diameter. A variant of this appears to be just the circular flue moulded as an individual unit in the form of a circular collar with a thin flange or projecting edge on one side as though intended to fit over a damaged flue or to decrease the size of the opening.

The type 2 oven cover (originally designated type 2 oven plate at Danebury) took the form of a flat or convex plate about 25–30 mm with a large circular hole 120–80 mm diameter encircled by 6–12 small perforations about 25 mm in diameter. No outer edges of the cover survived in any samples from Suddern Farm, though the evidence from other sites indicates that they could be individual movable objects moulded with an outer edge or could be set into a more substantial oven wall.

The sample from P194 had this basic type of cover, which formed the top element of a more substantial structure possibly best regarded as a portable oven rather than an oven cover. It is fully described and discussed on pp. 135–38.

At other sites type 1 oven cover has had impressed circular or rectangular decoration, but no evidence of such occurred at Suddern Farm. However two fragments, which may be parts of oven covers, had evidence of impressed lines in a herringbone pattern (Fig. 3.88, Ov. 13 and Ov. 14). Both appeared to occur close to an edge.

Triangular oven bricks

Triangular oven bricks (traditionally called clay loomweights) accounted for 3% of the daub and occurred in all phases except the early Roman period, though the only sample from the late Roman phase is uncertain. They were made in a variety of fabrics most frequently F and C, followed by E, K, J, A and D.

Eleven samples of triangular oven bricks, representing at least 20 individual objects, included a large group of ten from P119 and two from P194. The remaining pieces were mostly small fragments generally corners with part of the perforation(s) surviving. Only one was more complete with three perforations surviving, one across each corner, but was very fragile and fragmented. All appeared to be of average size, 60–80 mm thick with perforations of 10–16 mm diameter. The more complete one weighed 1900 gm. Most fragments were fired or baked to some extent though a couple appeared to be unburnt or unbaked in any way.

The hypothesis that these objects were some form of oven furniture as opposed to loomweights has been discussed elsewhere (Danebury Vol. 6, 285–6) and the arguments will not be repeated here. The evidence from Suddern Farm does nothing to invalidate the hypothesis, though no new evidence has come to light to explain how they were used. Most were found in association with other forms of oven daub and most had been fired. One from P119 had a small groove at the edge of one perforation, but the extent of the groove is not compatible with suspension for any substantial period of time (Fig. 3.91, sf 1430).

Discussion

The daub from Suddern Farm is dominated by the four large groups, probably all special deposits placed in pits and without these the collection would be insignificant. The material from P194 covers the widest range of structural forms and may represent one complex structure or two separate structures, probably used in close association. This includes evidence of a new variety of structure not previously recognized, which may be interpreted as a variant of type 2 oven cover or a portable oven.

The Iron Age daub occurred almost exclusively in pits with no *in situ* oven bases apparent in contrast to the Roman ovens/furnace bases. The Roman ovens had none of the various structural forms associated suggesting a different function.

The Iron Age material suggests more complex structures, though probably domestic in function and it is likely that they included structures for baking and cooking in pots. The deliberate deposition of some virtually whole ovens may indicate use in some ritual activity, either prior to or during deposition in the pit. The association with a human cremation in P119 may possibly indicate the oven was used in activities relating to the funeral, such as ritual feasting.

Apart from oven cover the traditional Iron Age structural forms (upper wall, oven plate and triangular oven brick) do not appear to have continued significantly into the Roman period. This may represent a change in the type of structures used for baking, though the presence of oven covers may indicate that cooking in pots continued in the same manner: the oven cover could have been rested on some form of supports of another material over a simple hearth. Alternatively the lack of oven material in the Roman period may indicate the main centre of domestic and cooking activity had moved to another part of the settlement.

Analysis of large groups

P120 (cp 6–7) (Fig. 3.88)
This pit contained a very large quantity of oven daub, over 170 kg in total, and is the largest group from any individual feature from all the Environs sites – it is nearly twice the size of the largest deposit from Danebury. The daub was distributed throughout all six layers of the fill but with a greater amount in the lower half.

This collection of daub comprised all the most typical elements of an oven, with more than 98% of the daub being identifiable to form. Nearly half appeared to be from the lower oven walls including the stokehole, over 40% from the upper wattle supported walls and 10% from the oven plate. The only other material included some fragments of straw impressed discs and possibly some oven cover.

The lower/basal walls and stokehole

There was a total of 80,087 gm and over 210 fragments (the discarded fragments from layer 5 were not counted, it merely being noted that it amounted to 'hundreds', probably *c*.350 on the basis of average fragment size of 139 gm for the whole pit).

A high proportion of fragments were entirely featureless and others only retained a roughly finished or smoothed flat or convex surface. On some pieces there was evidence of burning with the surface of the daub reddened. On the broken surfaces there were sometimes impressions of large broken flint nodules, which were often laid within the lower oven walls of *in situ* structures at Danebury. Additionally in the interior of the daub were scattered impressions of wattles or split or squared poles: the roundwood wattles ranged from 6–21 mm in diameter. The daub was up to 150–60 mm thick.

Several pieces had a rounded semicircular profile forming both a straight and curved edge, suggesting these formed part of an arched opening in the wall of the oven, probably for a stokehole. On some fragments were interwoven wattles 17 and 18 mm in diameter and a split timber over 32 mm wide. These stokehole fragments were between 80 and 100 mm thick.

A few fragments from one sample had pieces of green fabric H and brown fabric N clay embedded in the daub. It was not clear whether this was merely a form of temper, a post-depositional effect with clay compressed onto the daub or remnants of an oven cover built into walls.

The daub fabric was the basic coarse chalk- and flint-tempered daub variously designated C, D and E, this basically reflecting the intensity to which the daub was heated. Unsurprisingly the pieces of stokehole arch (fabric D) were the most highly fired. The same basic daub fabric was used for the upper walls and also for oven plates.

The upper walls

There was a total of 723 fragments of wall daub, weighing 70,438 gm. This material is characterized by the impression of an interwoven wattle framework on one side of the daub fragments.

The outer moulded surface of the daub fragments (probably in fact representing the interior surface of the oven itself) was generally well smoothed, but varied from extremely smooth, sometimes with fine striations from wiping to rather more irregular, sometimes with shallow finger ridging, but large protrusions, depressions and irregularities were rare. The surface could be flat or curving, being both convex and more often concave. Occasional impressions of cereal grains or grass seeds and straw- or grass-stem impressions were observed. On one fragment a plank impression pierced the daub and was placed at right angles to the wattle rods. The plank may have formed support for an oven plate, possibly where it crossed the stokehole and had no supporting wall. The daub bulged around the plank and had four horizontal lines of fingernail impressions (Fig. 3.88, Ov. 1). Their purpose is unclear: they may represent decoration, doodling or may have provided information relating to manufacture.

A small number of fragments had both an inner and outer surface preserved with a total thickness of daub between 25 and 50 mm: the impression is that one surface was not as well fired or baked and in general character was more akin to the lower oven wall material, having a rougher more powdery surface. From this evidence it can be surmised that generally the outer coating forming the exterior of upper walls on the outside of the wattle frame was relatively thin, poorly fired or baked and rarely survived.

The daub ranged from 2–50 mm thick, though most commonly averaged 25–35 mm and very rarely reached as much as 65 mm.

The diagnostic features of upper wall daub are the impressions on the interior surface of closely inter-woven wattles (Fig. 3.88, Ov. 2). On the larger fragments the rods woven alternately under and over the sails are clear. The spacing of the sails varied with examples of 100 mm, 120 mm and c.190 mm. It is assumed that the wattles were woven into a hemispherical/dome shape to form a framework to support the daub. Alternative shapes might have been cylindrical/truncated cone or arched. Moreover one might question whether the wattle framework was really a support, as the daub was apparently placed on the interior of the framework. It was possibly done to make the upper structure lighter: in the process of initial firing of the oven the wattles may have been burnt out. This may have been a relevant factor if the upper part of some ovens were portable or designed to be dismantled.

The wattles comprised horizontal rods ranging in diameter from 4–30 mm, but with the main peak at 10–14 mm and vertical sails with diameters from 11–38 mm, the bulk fairly evenly spread between 12 and 21 mm. A small number of split timbers were noted amongst both rods and poles. Sixteen pairs of vertical poles were noted and many of these were of the same or similar diameter. Only one wattle had a leaf impression associated with it, suggesting that most were obtained when largely leafless or were deliberately defoliated.

Straw-impressed discs

This was the only example from the site of straw-impressed discs. They took the form of irregular lumps or a ball of sand-tempered clay covered in impressions of grass/straw stems as well as some being incorporated within the clay. Their formation or purpose is unclear.

The oven plate (Fig. 3.88, Ovs. 3–5)

There were 149 pieces of daub identified as oven plate, which weighed in all 17,765 gm. The oven plate took the form of a flat ?circular plate, possibly prefabricated, with a flat upper surface and irregular underside covered in impressions of the supporting framework and pierced by circular holes. The upper surface of the plate was generally smooth, flat and well finished, but curved up at the edge to join with the oven walls. There was little sign of burning on the surface, though the daub was well fired; the base of the perforations generally showed more signs of burning. In the central area the plate ranged from 20–65 mm thick, but increased at the edge up to 105 mm, where it joined in to the oven walls. It was at its narrowest over the wide plank impressions.

The perforations piercing the plate vertically appear to have been randomly spaced at distances of 30–5 mm up to 55 mm and were circular or oval with cylindrical, funnel-shaped or biconical profiles. A total of 47 perforations were observed, of which 40 could be measured having the following diameters:

cylindrical
25 mm – 1, 26 mm – 1, 27 mm – 1, 30 mm – 1, 31 mm – 1, 35 mm – 3, 36 mm – 1, 38 mm – 1, 40 mm – 11, 50 mm – 3, 60 mm – 6, 70 mm – 3

funnel shaped
36 mm > 28 mm, 50 mm > 32 mm, 50 mm > 35 mm, 52 mm > 23 mm, 40 mm > 27 mm, 35 mm > 27 mm, 60 x 50 mm > 36 x 26 mm

On the basis of number, size and spacing of the perforations the minimum size of the oven plate must have been 0.6 m wide, but the evidence was inadequate to assess whether it was circular or rectangular.

The underside of the oven plate was densely covered in thin fine straw or perhaps grass impressions, often in wads lying parallel to each other but beyond this randomly arranged (Fig. 3.88, Ovs. 4 and 5). This formed a thin layer between the daub and the major supporting timbers, which took the form of roundwood poles 11–25 mm diameter and wider planks with a curved, convex surface and straight cut edges. The planks appear to have been 40–55 mm wide and were placed at intervals of 50 mm. They lay at right angles to the wall daub wattles.

There were several large blocks of daub from the junction of the oven plate and wall daub (Fig. 3.88, Ovs. 3–5). From these it can be seen that the oven plate was prefabricated to some extent as the straw-impressed surface clearly overlapped the wall daub.

From one well preserved block (Fig. 3.88, Ov. 4) the sequence of construction may be suggested: (i) on the lower walls of the oven base the wide planks or split poles were laid horizontally and smaller wattles laid over this; (ii) then the wattle framework for the upper walls must have been constructed, or at least the lower part woven. Whether the wattles were tied or joined in some way to the planks is not preserved by the impressions; (iii) the lower level of the wall daub was spread over the wattles and moulded to shape; (iv) the oven plate, in a partially or wholly prefabricated state was placed in position on the planks – it must have been during the prefabrication stage that the grass/straw was compressed onto the underside, presumably the means used to prevent the large slab of clay becoming stuck to the surface on which it was moulded; (v) the plate was smoothed and finished off with the edge sloping up and moulded in to join with the upper walls and probably the perforations were made at this stage. Once the oven plate was in position the remainder of the upper walls could be completed.

The oven design

There is sufficient material found in P120, all of which appears to derive from a single structure, to make an attempt at reconstruction possible. On the basis of ovens observed *in situ* at other sites the base was probably cut down below ground level with the floor formed of puddled chalk or daub. The lower walls were thick reinforced with courses of flints and possibly with some wattles used in the construction mainly around the opening in the side. The edge of the oven walls had a rounded profile and probably curved at the top to form an arched opening: the opening may have been multi-purpose – used for stoking the fire, removing cinders or perhaps placing the food or items to be heated.

On this base was placed the oven plate and the upper walls constructed around a wattle framework, in the manner described in detail above. The stokehole or opening may have continued above the level of the plate, as one fragment of oven plate had the straw impressions continuing up the side to join with the surface, showing that part of the edge was not built into the upper walls.

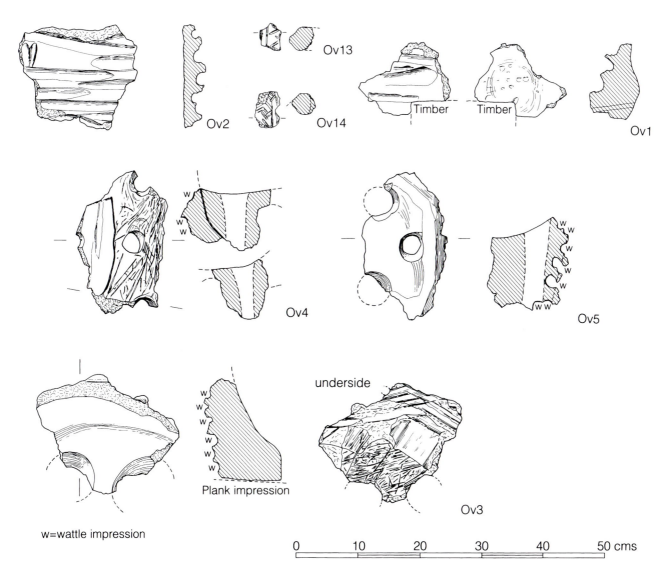

w=wattle impression

0 10 20 30 40 50 cms

Fig. 3.88 Structural daub

133

What form the top of the oven took is unclear. As none of the wall daub had a moulded edge of any form, a continuous domed top is perhaps most likely in the absence of other evidence.

Finally we must consider its size. It has already been suggested that the minimum size for the oven plate must have been at least 0.6 m and from the number of supporting timbers and their spacing a similar minimum size is indicated. The actual quantity in terms of weight might also be used to give some indication, but unfortunately there are no comparative data from Iron Age *in situ* ovens. An indication that the oven must have been considerably larger than this minimum is provided by comparing the weight to some small modern Spanish clay ovens: a portable oven of similar design to that suggested for P120 daub, measuring 0.23 m diameter and 0.26 m high weighed only 7 kg; a simple prefabricated domed bread oven 0.5 m diameter and 0.4 m high weighed 29 kg. Clearly there is some way to go to 170 kg, but it is perhaps not unreasonable to suggest that this oven was over 1 m in diameter and perhaps as much in height.

P194 (cp 8–9) (Figs. 3.89–3.90)
This pit produced 1210 fragments of daub, weighing 145,762 gm. The daub was clearly all derived from the same one or two oven structures and was distributed throughout the pit fill, but with the main concentration in layers 4 and 5.

All the major structural elements of an oven were present: the base/lower walls and upper walls occurred in roughly equal quantities, *c*.57 kg and 51 kg respectively, whilst oven plate was infrequent by comparison comprising just over 6 kg. There was additionally over 30 kg of oven cover/portable oven and two oven bricks.

The oven base/lower walls

This material comprised 460 fragments weighing 56,765 gm, but a large proportion (66%) of this had little in the way of diagnostic characteristics and was discarded. It was made of coarse chalk- and flint-tempered daub, fabric C/E, baked rather than fired in general.

Several of the fragments were very large (as much as 1–3 kg in a few cases) and exhibit a variety of features. One large block had two burnt surfaces, one flat, one concave diverging from 70 mm to 100 mm thickness. Other fragments had roughly flattened or curving surfaces, some burnt black or reddened, though much of the daub had been only lightly baked. On most pieces the thickness was incomplete but a few more complete fragments indicated a thickness in the region of 80–100 mm. There also appeared to be some thinner pieces 45–80 mm.

There were several fragments moulded to a rounded edge with a semicircular profile. These probably derived from the opening in the oven wall for a stokehole, probably in the form of a curving arch. The best preserved fragment (Fig. 3.90, Ov. 6)

probably represents the base of the arch: the underside on which it apparently stood was rough and irregular, as though bedded on soil. It was semicircular, measuring 140 mm diameter at the base narrowing to *c*.100 mm 50 mm above the base and decreasing to 90 mm at the top; it survived 185 mm in height. The curved surface had a series of horizontal ridges around it – probably the effect of the fingers moulding the curved edge. This daub was backed by the flat, smooth surface of a plank impression 70 mm wide and at least 150 mm long and it appeared the daub continued to either side to enclose the timber, though the surface of the plank impression had been burnt grey for most of its length. Across the broken top of this daub fragment was a small horizontal wattle impression 8 mm in diameter.

A low density of wattle impressions, 22 in all measuring between 4 and 25 mm, were observed but they do not form a coherent structure in comparison to the upper wall daub.

A few blocks of daub had an angled recess and in a few fragments there were remnants of type A daub embedded or smeared.

The upper wall

The majority of the wall daub was made in fabric E: 418 fragments weighing 50,615 gm. Only a small quantity, eight pieces weighing 590 gm, was designated fabric C and probably only represents a variation in the degree of baking or firing, deriving from the part of the oven that remained cooler.

Most fragments had a concave surface and less frequently flat or convex. They were generally smooth with only a few very slight irregularities and fine striations from smoothing. Finger ridging running parallel to the wattle impressions on the opposite side were present in a number of instances. The fragments ranged from 10–55 mm thick.

On the opposite side was the typical mass of interwoven wattle impressions. A total of 1369 horizontal rod impressions and 50 vertical sails were preserved. The rods ranged in size from 4 to 23 mm diameter with the main peak between 9 and 13 mm, whilst sails ranged from 12 to over 45 mm in diameter with an even spread of sizes. More than a quarter of the sails were split timbers and two pairs of sails were also observed. A small number of wattles had leaf impressions attached: though the veins of the leaves were visible the margins and stem were not, merely indicating a broad leafed species as opposed to a conifer. On the larger fragments, described below, the rods were very closely spaced and the sails are estimated to have been at distances of up to *c*.200 mm.

A number of particularly large pieces provide some details regarding the oven. One block had a distinctly concave surface, clearly indicative of it being the interior of the oven with a band of burning along one edge running parallel with the wattles: here the daub has been blackened on the surface from smoke, the clay itself turned grey and behind this redder; beyond this the daub was a more uniform light brown colour throughout. A distinct line of this sort would form along the lower part of the walls a short distance above the oven plate, essentially where the wall would have been in contact with the embers and implies there was some type of opening at the top as ovens with an entirely enclosed dome become entirely sooted and blackened.

Three other pieces, that may come from the base, all exhibited closely interwoven wattles and had all the characteristics typical of wall daub. Two were particularly thick – 100 mm, but were well fired to a yellowish-red colour. Another sizeable piece (Fig. 3.89, Ov. 7), 50 mm thick, had the usual interwoven wattles along the top half, but the lower half was irregular with chalk fragments embedded in the surface or pitted with voids where the chalk lumps had fallen out. At this point the daub is thinning with the pitted surface sloping in to a minimum thickness of 15 mm at the bottom. The general impression is that the base of the wall had been constructed on a surface of small subrounded chalk 10–30 mm that had perhaps been compacted in puddled chalk or just soil. The density and size of the chalk lumps are not consistent with that in the daub described above as lower walls and therefore the evidence suggests the wattle-framed walls represent a separate structure.

The oven plate

Oven plate formed a relatively small proportion of the group comprising 64 fragments weighing 6208 gm in fabric C and one fragment of 186 gm in fabric D. During the analysis of the oven plate the fragments were laid out closely spaced to obtain a rough idea of the area covered by the surviving plate. It was found to cover an area of about 2000 sq cm (an area of 0.45 x 0.45 m if square, or about 0.5 m in diameter if circular). These would be minimum measurements, as clearly the surviving fragments do not represent the whole plate: no evidence of the margins survived and many of the perforations were incomplete.

The upper surface was moderately smooth and flat or undulating, but with some more pronounced irregularities including rough finger ridging. It was pierced by a random spread of circular and oval perforations that were cylindrical or funnel-shaped in profile. There were 54 perforations observed, of which eight were too fragmentary to be measured; the remainder had the following diameters:

16 mm	2	30 mm	1	50 mm	1
>17 mm	1 (oval)	32 mm	1	>50 mm	2 (oval)
18 mm	2	33 mm	1	60 mm	1
19 mm	2	34 mm	2		
21 mm	2	35 mm	4	Funnel shaped	
22 mm	3	36 mm	1	24 > 15 mm	1
23 mm	2	37 mm	1	36 > 25 mm	1
25 mm	1	38 mm	2	38 > 33 mm	1
26 mm	1	40 mm	3	40 > 21 mm	1
27 mm	2	45 x 35 mm	1	50 > 40 mm	1 (oval)
28 mm	2	>45 mm	1		

The underside was very rough and irregular with no attempts made to smooth it off. It was covered by a pattern of criss-crossed (not interwoven) wattle impressions, mostly roundwood poles measuring between 6 mm and 22 mm in diameter with a slight peak at 16–17 mm. A total of 73 impressions were preserved. Scattered straw impressions were observed caught between the poles and the daub, but they did not occur in the profusion observed on the daub from P120. Straw was not used in the process of construction of the oven plate. The wattles rested on larger planks, which provided the main support for the oven plate. These planks could be either flat or slightly convex in profile with a straight or slightly rounded edge (probably the natural curvature of the outside of the timber). The width of the planks could rarely be measured in their entirety: the smallest complete one was 20 mm wide and the largest were in excess of 50 and 60 mm; they ranged between 8 and 60 mm thick. There were 25 plank impressions present.

With the oven plate were two fragments, which appeared to have formed part of a larger circular or oval opening or flue about 80–90 mm wide. They were not necessarily a part of the plate, though included in this sample in the general analysis of the daub. It is most likely that it would have been placed on the top of the oven walls as a type of support to hold a pot perhaps. One side (the top?) of the daub had a flat but irregular surface covered in finger ridging sweeping around the circular/oval rim, which curved under and back up, so that the area furthest from the flue rim formed a thin plate or collar to rest over a supporting edge. This has the appearance of being a portable item to fit on the top of an oven perhaps to create a different shaped opening or perhaps a means of repair for a damaged flue.

The oven cover/portable oven

This material could represent part of an oven, forming a single structure with the material described above or a completely separate oven. The question will be considered further in the section on design below. This part of the oven was constructed in the very distinctive dark brown sandy daub, fabric A, but yellow-green in its unfired state (fabric H). A total of 235 fragments weighing 29,838 gm were recovered from throughout the pit fill, but the majority (94%) were found in layer 5 and some joined with fragments from other layers indicating clearly that it all derived from the same structure.

The material was very fragile and crumbly in spite of conservation, particularly the daub away from the various openings and flues. Thickness varied from an average of 25–30 mm up to 45 mm maximum on the cover plate and 50 mm at the junction of the wall with the cover plate.

The overall form appears to have been roughly beehive-shaped with vertical walls sloping in to be truncated and covered with a flat top. The walls were gently convex, curving in slightly to the top at which point it was possible to estimate an external diameter of about 0.56–0.6 m (internal diameter c.0.5 m). The height must have been at least 0.42 m high. The top of the oven took the form of a type 2 oven cover possibly with a shallow ridge encircling it.

The interior of the oven walls was covered with long finger ridges frequently running in different directions and often ending in deeper fingertip depressions (Figs. 3.89–3.90, Ovs. 8, 9 and 10). The direction of smoothing can be identified on the larger blocks: the ridges run parallel to the vertical edge of the opening and then towards the top sweep off at a diagonal towards the joint with the oven cover plate. Along this joint where the daub is much thicker the ridges run horizontally along the joint and cutting across the top of the vertical and diagonal ridges (Fig. 3.89, Ov. 8b). On some other fragments from the top the diagonal ridges ran in different directions sometimes cutting through the horizontal ridges along the joint. The direction of movement of the finger ridges was from the base upwards, indicating that the oven was built up from the base. (This may seem an obvious statement, but if it had been made as a freestanding structure with an open base, as in the case of some Roman ovens, then it might have been easier to construct and fire it inverted.)

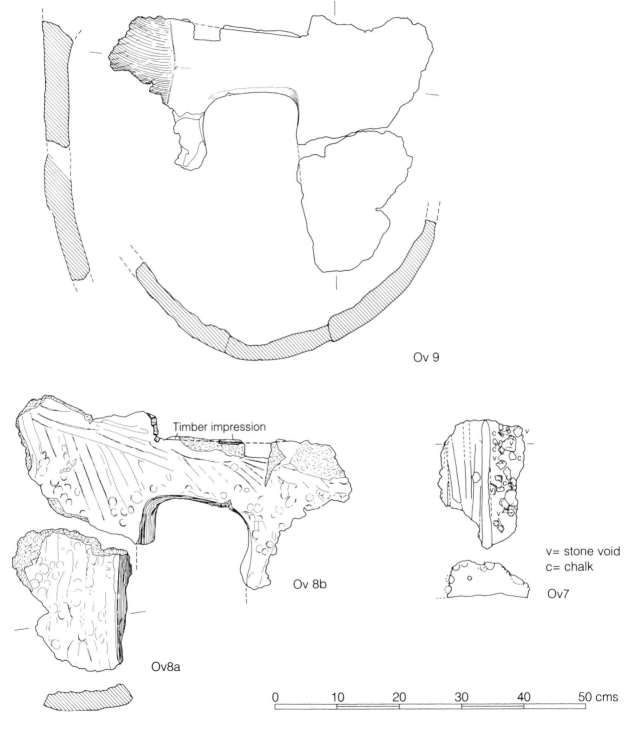

Fig. 3.89 Structural daub

The condition of the interior surface was very variable being most intensely fired with extensive burning and sooting around the opening, whilst fragments apparently some distance from this were virtually unfired with little or no blackening from smoke. Some pieces had been burnt and blackened to a depth of 5 mm then turning brown up to 20 mm from the inner surface with the remaining thickness apparently unaffected by heating maintaining the character of raw green clay. These fragments represent a relatively low proportion of the total, but indicate that in some areas the heat did not penetrate throughout the thickness of the wall, though there was intense blackening from the effects of smoke.

The pieces dominated by fingertip depressions (Fig. 3.89,Ov. 8a) rather than ridging appear to have come from the base of the wall suggesting a more static pressure was applied in this area. Many of the fragments covered exclusively in fingertip depressions were well fired and very blackened over the inner surface.

The exterior surface was smoother, gently undulating, with no finger ridging remaining (Fig. 3.89, Ov. 9): it was very fragile and a thin veneer had flaked off over much of the surface. Some fairly extensive areas of the exterior surface had been burnt or smoked black or grey. The most intense burning on the walls was around the opening in the side and the

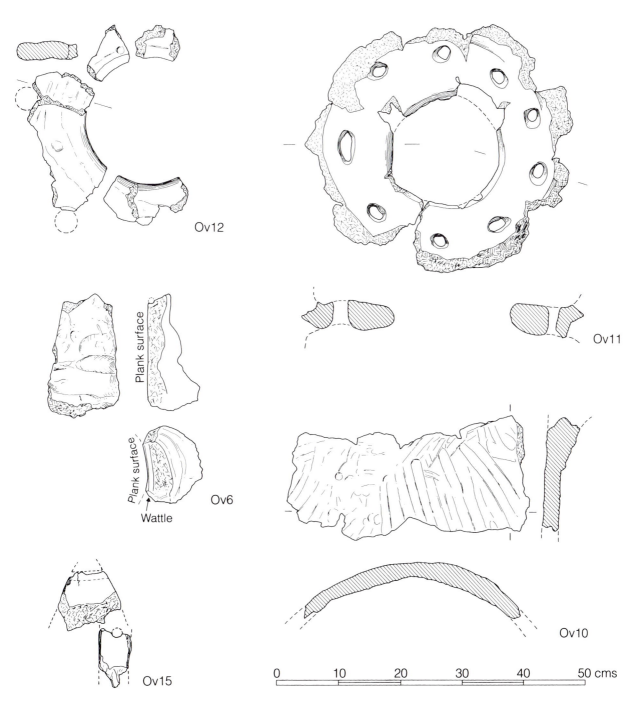

Fig. 3.90 Structural daub

137

burnt out timber. On one of the fragments with a burnt exterior there was a small area that appeared to have a textile impression on it.

In the side wall part of a large rectangular or trapezoidal opening survived (Fig. 3.89, Ovs. 8 and 9): it was about 150 mm wide at the top and at least 240 mm high, flaring out to the base, where it would have been at least 200 mm wide. It was straight sided with rounded corners and an undercutting flat edge. It was probably enclosed on all four sides as a single fragment with a rounded inturned lip is similar to the top edge (which survives complete) and probably is part of the opposite edge. About 100 mm above this opening was a horizontal void left by a burnt out timber/plank measuring at least 0.22 m long by 40 mm or more high. The purpose of this void is unclear, but may have related in some way to the control of the air flow.

The top of the walls thickened (Figs. 3.89–3.90, Ovs. 9 and 10) where they join with the type 2 oven cover or plate, which formed the top (Fig. 3.90, Ov. 11). This took the form of a typical type 2 cover having a large circular central hole 200–30 mm in diameter encircled by nine small perforations. These perforations were circular or oval in shape with cylindrical, funnel or biconical profiles and ranged in size from 20 x 25 mm up to 24 x 48 mm and 26 x 40 mm. The distance between perforations was 55–85 mm and the distance from the lip of the central flue was 44–65 mm.

Blackening on the cover plate is most accentuated around or behind the perforations. On the underside there was a ridge of clay encircling the perforations that had clearly formed from the clay that had been pushed through in the process of forming the perforations. Outside the ring of perforations the surface of the daub slopes up to a slight ridge. It is clear that both walls and plate thickened where they joined, though this joint was clearly a weak point as all fragments had broken away along this joint. It possibly implies the cover plate was prefabricated and set into the top of the walls. One of the plate fragments appeared to have a small flat surface from a plank impression, which was probably the top of the timber void observed in the wall fragments.

Two other fragments are best interpreted as being part of a shallow rim that enclosed the cover plate. These were very blackened on both sides with the intensity of the heat resulting in a crazed pattern of polygonal cracks. The original surface would have been well smoothed. The fragments were 20–5 mm thick with a flat rim at right angles or sloping in slightly angled. The more informative fragment indicates a slightly convex exterior surface, which is cut 62 mm from the rim by a probable plank impression. The interior surface is more overtly curved forming a concave surface diverging to the base to form a thicker wall of 35 mm. It would appear from this that the oven wall formed a continuous gently curving surface that stopped slightly above the cover plate, so that it was set down about 50 mm below the top of the wall.

Oven bricks

A partial triangular oven brick (Fig. 3.90, Ov. 15) was found in layer 4. The surviving fragment came from the central area of the body and weighed 390 gm. It measured over 90 mm in height with the sides estimated to have a minimum length of 150 mm and was 50 mm thick. One perforation, 10 mm in diameter, was present and it is possible there were no others originally, as one might have expected some evidence of them to survive. It was made in fabric A, though unlike the oven cover material it did not appear to contain any shell and so may have come from a different batch of clay. The brick had been partly baked and an area of surface blackened.

A second object that may have been some form of oven brick weighed 500 gm and was made in fabric J. It was a yellowish greeny brown colour and was unbaked. (This clay may have formed the basis for fabric A, as it bears some similarity to the unbaked areas of the oven cover.) It was probably roughly oval or circular: it measured 95 mm wide and 60 mm thick and something over 90 mm in length. One face was convex, the other slightly sunken in the centre and the sides rounded.

Both bricks were found amongst the oven daub, implying they had some function integral with the oven(s). Neither was intensely baked or fired implying they were not used close to the heat source.

The oven design

The various elements described above, when taken individually, are all very typical elements of structural oven daub, except for the oven 'cover', which though the top is typical the lower part has not been observed before in the Danebury area. It is the combination of the different elements, as well as the new characteristics observed that make this an unusual collection and not entirely easy to interpret. Two possibilities present themselves:
  – the material represents one 'normal' oven of the type described for P120 above and a second 'portable oven', or
  – the material represents a single structure.

The bulk of the daub – the lower wall/base, stokehole, upper walls and oven plate – clearly formed a structure in the same form as that already outlined for P120. The only difference, not observed in other daub collections, is the fragment of upper wall daub that appeared to be set into a chalk or chalky soil and so implying that particular fragment formed part of the lower walls. One explanation might be that the oven was terraced into a slope or bank, resulting in the upper wall being constructed directly on the contemporary ground surface at the back. An alternative explanation is that one oven was entirely wattle-framed with typical wall daub forming the entire structure, except that the daub was rather thicker than normal at the base. The fragments of flue collar may have belonged with such a structure indicating an opening in the top.

The oven cover could represent the upper part of an oven, possibly integral with one of the types described above or alternatively some form of portable oven. The basic design remains the same whether part of a structure or freestanding. It was a truncated inverted cone in form with a large trapezoidal opening in the side wall a short distance above which was a horizontal timber void. The top was enclosed by a type 2 oven cover in the form of a flat plate with a central hole encircled by small perforations and the whole enclosed by a shallow wall. The central hole probably held a cooking pot, on analogy with a contemporary small traditional portable oven from southern Spain and the encircling holes allowed smoke to escape. The opening in the wall was presumably a stokehole.

The base of the walls of this oven cover/portable oven do not survive, so one may speculate about possible alternatives. One option is that it was freestanding, the walls continuing slightly further but not preserved because of lack of firing. Another is that the cover was set on or into some thicker low walls made in the coarse chalk-tempered fabric C/E. There is some limited evidence to support this idea in that some of the wall base daub had small fragments of type A or H daub adhering or inset into it. The recessed ledge in some of this wall base also implies something was laid on it. Of course it is possible that the ledge was intended to hold the oven plate, rather than the oven cover or both. An alternative is that the oven cover could be placed on the oven plate within the upper walls if these were entirely open at the top, rather than resting on the top of the upper walls.

Whatever the exact arrangement of the various oven parts it is most likely that the actual fire was set on top of the oven plate which acted as a grate and the chamber below this would have allowed space for ash to accumulate during firing and to allow a good flow of air. The opening in the lower oven walls/base must have been for cleaning out rather than stoking. Stoking the fire would have been done either through the top of the oven if it was open or through a side vent.

The oven cover, whether a movable or permanent part of the oven, would have held a cooking pot in the top and the side opening probably allowed stoking of the fire to take place during use as well as items to be placed inside if the interior chamber was used for baking at the same time. The oven plate and upper walls were the part of the oven(s) that were most intensely fired, whilst firing of the oven cover was generally less so and variable, with shallow burning and blackening from smoke more common. Firing, smoking and burning were invariably greatest around flues, vents, stokeholes or perforations indicating that the air flow drew the heat out of all the openings. To prevent heat loss it was probably necessary to have a means of blocking these up and oven bricks may have sometimes been utilized for this.

P119 (cp 8–9) Fig. 3.91

This pit produced a total of 441 daub fragments weighing 16,322 gm. Three-quarters of this was in the form of oven bricks in a number of different fabrics and the remainder was wall and oven base. There were at least ten triangular oven bricks identified and fragments of several others and possibly a cylindrical oven brick. All came from layer 3 which filled the lowest two-thirds of the pit. All the pit fill and its artefacts may be associated with a cremation burial.

SF1428
Frags: 1 Wt: 890 gm Completeness: 50% or less
Fabric: F
Length: *c*.205 mm Height: 180 mm Width: >60 mm
Perforations: none surviving

The surviving fragment had been split down the centre, so only one triangular face was present; two corners had broken off. The surface was smooth and even with rounded corners and angles. There were some fine straw or chaff impressions on the surface. Heating of the brick had been variable with the clay ranging from raw green clay in the central body through baked reddish brown to fired black and light brown fabric at the surviving corner. It is likely much of the missing part was poorly fired. It is not clear whether originally there were any perforations or not: if they are postulated it would make the total width very thick at over 120 mm.

SF 1429
Frags: 23 Wt: 1720 gm Completeness: ? Fabric F
Length: >100 mm (estimated total 180–200 mm)
Width: 90–100 mm
Perforations: (i) 15 mm (ii) 14 mm–17 mm (at side) (iii) 20 mm at side (iv) 19 mm at side (v and vi) 7 and 9 mm (placed side by side)

Fifteen of the fragments probably came from the same object (or two very similar ones possibly). The remaining eight pieces were very small and do not certainly belong with this. None of the fragments actually join possibly indicating it was deliberately smashed or broken in antiquity. The surfaces are smooth, even, but with occasional hollows or rounded protrusions; edges and corners were rounded but fairly sharp.

Although five fragments exhibited remains of perforations, some of these could be parts of the same one. One fragment had two perforations side by side piercing the surface at the same angle, which indicates the two cut across the same corner. Alternatively some could belong to a second brick.

SF1433
Frags: 5 Wt: 1140 gm Completeness: 50–70% Fabric F
Length: >165 mm (estimated 170–180 mm) Width: >60 mm (est. 80–90 mm)
Perforations: (i) 17–18 mm (ii) 21 mm (iii) 19 mm (iv) 20 mm

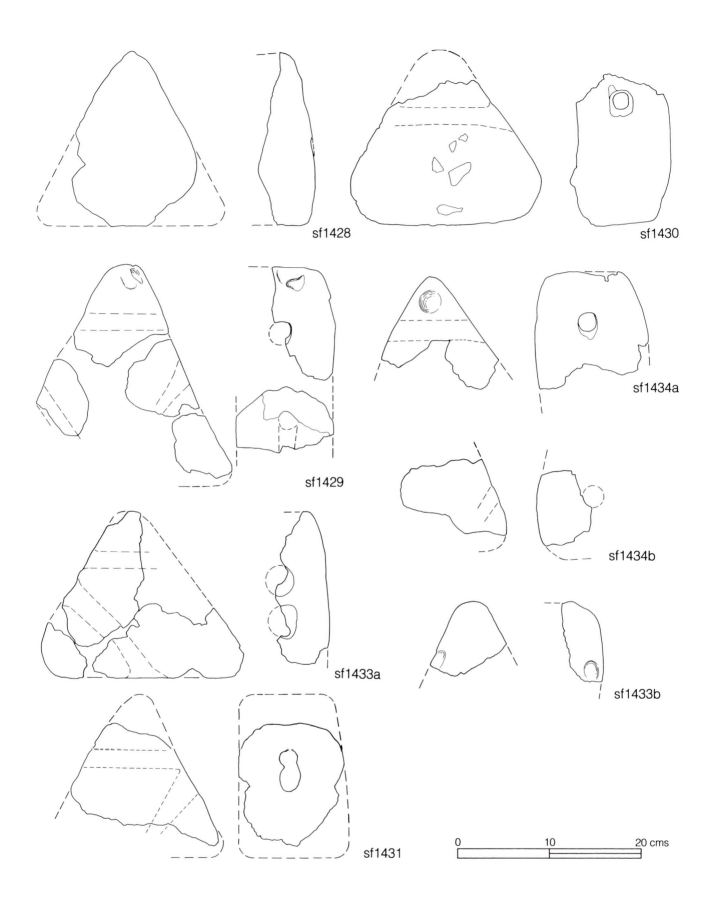

sf1428

sf1430

sf1429

sf1434a

sf1434b

sf1433a

sf1433b

sf1431

0   10   20 cms

Fig. 3.91 Triangular oven bricks

These five fragments do not join, but are all similar and likely to derive from the same object. The surfaces were smooth, even and generally flat with rounded but sharp corners and edges. Fine organic impressions of chaff or straw were sparsely scattered over the surface. Although it is possible to arrange the fragments to form one object it is perhaps more likely that they in fact represent two bricks. The total number of perforations is also uncertain as some might be opposite ends of the same one.

SF1434

Frags: 7x and 14 Wt: 1245 gm Completeness: 35–40% Fabric F
Length: >120 mm (estimated 200–220 mm) Width: 110 mm
Perforations: (i) 25 x 20 –17 mm (ii) c.13 mm

The joining fragments form one corner and another large fragment comes from the central body of the brick with a small part of a perforation. The surface was fairly smooth and even, but with some slight irregularities; the triangular face was convex and the corners and edges rounded but fairly sharp.

SF1437

Frags: 1 Wt: 390 gm Completeness: 10–15% Fabric F
Length: >90 mm Width: 100–110 mm Perforations: none surviving

This fragment is part of an angular and fairly sharp corner with well smoothed flat surfaces; the triangular face slopes out from the corner to give a distinct bowed effect.

S470

Frags: 40 Wt: 630 gm Fabric F
Perforations: (i) 11 mm (ii) 15 mm (iii) 8 mm (iv) 13 mm
The surfaces were smooth and even with slight undulations and irregularities.

These fragments probably derive from the TOBs described above made in the same fabric. The fragments were fired to a light brown at the surface becoming dark grey/brown in the interior.

SF1430

Frags: 1 Wt: 2500 gm Completeness: 70% Fabric C
Length: 210 mm Height: 185 mm Width: 60–100 mm
Perforations: (i) 18–20 mm

This was a large heavy object fired to a light/greyish brown. The surfaces were smooth and flat with occasional chaff impressions. The width narrows substantially to one side, making it rather unbalanced. There was only one perforation slightly closer to the apex than base. The top corner was missing with one end of the perforation damaged as a result. The other end of the perforation has a slight groove on the top left side, which may be the result of suspen-

sion at some stage. Owing to the asymmetric placing of the perforation this appears to be the natural position the thread would take as opposed to centrally above. The groove appears to have formed before the object was fired.

SF1431

Frags: 2x + 2 Wt: 1070 gm + 315 gm Completeness: 50% Fabric C
Length: c.190 mm Width: 80–120 mm
Perforations: (i) 23 x 25 > 20 < ? mm (ii) 20 x 18–20 x 25 mm

This was a large heavy object made in a very coarse daub fabric fired light–dark greyish brown and similar in character to SF1430. It had suffered a lot of damage and it is uncertain whether a third perforation existed. The surviving surfaces were smooth, rather undulating on the sides and convex on the triangular face. A shallow rounded ridge encircled one perforation, probably resulting from the clay pushed out in making the perforation being smoothed around it. One of the perforations was figure-of-eight shaped. One of the smaller fragments with a perforation of 19 mm diameter has been allocated to this object as it came from a brick at least 95 mm thick.

SF1432

Frags: 8 Wt: 845 gm Completeness: 30%+ Fabric C
Length: >100 mm Width: >70 mm (estimated 90–100 mm)
Perforations: (i) 15 mm (ii) 20 mm (iii) 20 mm

The main fragment is a corner with perforation, which had smooth, even surfaces and rounded angles. All the other pieces assessed with this need not necessarily be part of this as opposed to others made in fabric C (SF 1431 and 1438): it is impossible to assign the small fragments with any certainty.

SF1438

Frags: 21 Wt: 730 gm Fabric C
Width: 90–100 mm Perforation: 15 mm

The surfaces were moderately smooth and even with corners and angles well rounded; occasional organic impressions occurred on the surface. These fragments could all form an individual object, but it is more likely that some belong to other incomplete TOBs made in the same fabric (SF1430–1432). It is probable that a minimum of four different objects are represented, but it is impossible to allocate the smaller, less diagnostic, fragments with any certainty.

All four triangular oven bricks made in fabric C were clearly very similar made in the same coarse chalk- and flint-tempered fabric and of similar size. They probably all measured c.190 mm long, 90–120 mm wide and their total weight is estimated at about 3500 gm each. The fragmentary broken nature of these triangular oven bricks suggests they were broken in antiquity, possibly being deliberately smashed immediately before or during placing in the pit, rather than a result of accidental damage.

SF1439
Frags: 1 Wt: 82 gm Fabric K
Length: >63 mm Width: >50 mm Perforations: none surviving

This fragment had two flat surfaces at right angles joined by a sharp rounded edge. It had no diagnostic features, but the fabric and quality of finish suggest it may have been a fragment of oven brick.

S634
Frags: 2x Wt: 870 gm Fabric E
Length: >185 mm Breadth: >95 mm Width: >90 mm
No perforations

Roughly cylindrical-shaped object with well smoothed curving surface. It is incomplete and could be interpreted as oven brick or edge of stokehole.

Upper and lower wall daub

A small sample of wall daub of just over 1 kg was identified, made in fabric G, a soft powdery chalky clay material. In this sample a total of 32 wattle impressions, some clearly interwoven, were present with an even spread of measurements between 8 and 25 mm diameter. Two vertical sails of 26 and 30 mm were also identified.

A second sample of Fabric F was slightly larger (1306 gm). It retained impressions of 39 wattles ranging from 4 to 22 mm diameter and at right angles six poles 15–26 mm including split timbers and a larger plank over 40 mm wide. In this latter sample the wattles are not unequivocally interwoven, but appear rather to criss-cross. Such evidence together with the larger plank is more typical of oven plate. However no other diagnostic features typical of oven plate were observed. The surface was mostly very flat and smooth, though with some irregularities, and a large proportion of fragments had evidence of a white, ?lime based, coating over this surface. A few fragments with plank impressions also appear to have this white veneer over the surface.

A slightly larger sample of 1683 gm appeared to derive from the lower oven walls or base. It was made in coarse chalk- and flint-tempered fabric E fired to a reddish yellow-brown colour. Smooth flat surfaces were most usual and many retained evidence of a thin coating of the same white render. A total of 11 wattle impressions were observed measuring between 10 and 20 mm, together with two split timbers larger in size than this.

Discussion

The material from this pit clearly represents only a small proportion of an oven, though it apparently includes fragments from both upper and lower walls and possibly a fragment of oven plate. Together with

this rather token sample of oven daub was a large collection of at least ten triangular oven bricks made in three different fabrics – F, C and an uncertain one in fabric K. There appears to be two sets present of slightly differing sizes. Approximate sizes have been estimated where possible, though the very fragmented nature of the remaining daub made this difficult. Those in fabric C were perhaps slightly larger and heavier and a more standardized group than those in fabric F, which appear to have a wider range of side length and thickness and were probably somewhat lighter. The very broken nature of the objects suggests that they were deliberately smashed at the time they were placed in the pit or very shortly before. The associated material in this pit, as well as the way the oven bricks were treated, suggests some ritual activity was involved, possibly some form of funeral rites relating to the cremation placed in this pit.

The briquetage by Cynthia Poole

Four samples of briquetage were identified from three storage pits and a shallow hollow. They amounted to a total of eight sherds weighing 58 gm. Two of the samples occurred in MIA context, one in LIA and one in a late Roman context. Three of the samples were made in fabric X1 a fine chaff-tempered clay all with an oxidized yellowish-red surface and reduced black-grey interior and one in X3 a yellowish-red sandy clay oxidized throughout. The form could only be identified for one sample: this appeared to be a body sherd from a cylinder with a diameter of c.140 mm and walls 11 mm thick.

The presence of these few sherds of briquetage indicates that salt was being traded to the site from at least cp 6 possibly until the late Roman period. The very small quantity in contrast to Danebury suggests it was obtained for the use of the occupants rather than for redistribution.

		Table 3.11. Summary of briquetage samples				
Context	*Sherd no.*	*Weight*	*Fab.*	*Form*	*Wall size*	*Phase*
P92 (8)	1	16 gm	X1	S1	11 mm	cp 6–7
P101 (1)	5	24 gm	X1	–	5–10 mm	Mid C3–C4 AD
P132 (1)	1	6 gm	X1	–	9 mm	cp 6
P136(1)	1	12 gm	X3	–	14 mm	cp 8–9

Roman tile

A small sample of Roman tile was recovered from the excavations of 1991 and 1996 (Fiche 6:C1–2). Two complete flanged roof tiles were found in the filling of the end flue of the T-shaped oven excavated in 1996 and had evidently been used to control the draught. The rest of the tile was in small fragments and came from a variety of Roman features. *Tegulae*, *imbrices* and box tile were identified. It is probable that the tile was brought to the site for reuse from a masonry building in the vicinity.

4 Behaviour and Beliefs

The excavation at Suddern Farm produced an unusually rich array of evidence relevant to belief systems. Special deposits in pits and other features were prolific in the Early and Middle Iron Age and continued through the Late Iron Age into the Roman period suggesting that a certain conservatism may have prevailed. A wide range of deposits were encountered including the deliberate placing of whole and partial human bodies.

Outside the settlement the discovery of a cemetery of Early–Mid Iron Age date provides a rare example in central southern Britain of what might be regarded as a normal burial rite complementing deposition in pits.

Finally two inhumation graves and a cremation found close together in the vicinity of the outer ditch hint at the possible existence of an area set aside for burial in the Roman period.

The special burials will be considered first all together. Then follows a detailed consideration of the Iron Age and Roman cemeteries.

Special deposits by Cynthia Poole

A total of 182 special deposits were identified in 34 out of the 78 pits (44%). In addition 10 deposits were found in bowl pits, quarry hollows and working hollows. The distribution and type categories of special deposits according to fill cycle, phase and pit type are shown in Tables 3.16–3.18.

Table 3.12 provides a summary of numbers of special deposits in relation to pit numbers according to phase. Though there is a gradual decrease of pits containing special deposits from EIA to Roman, the peak in actual numbers of special deposits occurs in MIA, this being the period with the highest average number of special deposits per pit and also has the largest number of special deposits in a single pit. The average number of special deposits per pit is higher than the values for Danebury and Bury Hill, where the figure is about two, whilst compared to the non-hillfort sites it is similar to New Buildings (4.3) and Nettlebank Copse (4.6) whilst Houghton Down was distinctly higher at 9.

It is clear that the placing of special deposits was most intense in EIA and MIA, but remained significant into the LIA, though declining noticeably thereafter. However the fact that the custom continued into the early Roman phase, though not beyond the second century AD, is unusual and indicates the continuity of native customs and beliefs.

Table 3.12.
Quantification of special deposits in relation to pit numbers according to phase

Phase	EIA	MIA	LIA	FIRST CENT. BC/AD	Ro	Total
Pits with sp. dep.	12	8	8	4	2	34
No. of sp. dep.	60	70	39	11	2	182
Av. no. sp. dep. p. pit	5	9	5	3	1	5.4
Av. no. p. total pits	2.4	4.7	3	0.6	0.3	2.3
Pits with single sp. dep.	4	1	3	2	2	12
Pits with mult. sp. dep.	8	7	5	2	–	22
Quantity range of multiple deposits	2–20	2–24	2–8	3–4	–	–

The majority of deposits occurred in pits with fill cycle 2 (17 pits) or 2c (10 pits) with the remainder occurring in 1a and 1d (2 pits each) and 1b, 2a and 2b (one each). A small number of deposits occurred in other features dating from LIA to Roman and included a bowl pit, a quarry hollow and two working hollows.

A listing of all special deposits is given in Fiche 4:G5–5:C10.

Types of special deposits

The range of categories is limited in comparison to those present at Houghton Down and Danebury, the latter having the greatest variety of deposits of all the surrounding settlements. When compared to Suddern Farm, the other Environs sites tended to have a more limited range of deposits, where the main emphasis was on animal and pottery deposits, with considerably fewer in other categories.

Human

Only one human deposit in a pit was recognized on site, though other material has been recognized during analysis of the animal bone.

A full listing of all the human remains is provided below (p. 152).

In P78 a near complete human body occurred at a basal level in association with many animal deposits. In the bowl pit, F68, a human pelvis articulated with a few vertebrae had been placed. Both types of deposits were encountered at Danebury. Amongst the animal bone a deposit of human skull and another of isolated bone have also been identified and it is likely that more is present. An unusual deposit is a mass of burnt human bone in association with much burnt animal bone in P119, together with charcoal and metal fittings, much pottery, quern and oven daub. It is possible that this deposit represents a cremation burial rather than a special deposit.

In contrast to all the other Environs sites Suddern Farm is the only one to produce a significant amount of human bone in the context of special deposits in pits. As the cemetery for the Iron Age settlement was found in the 1996 excavations, one can be fairly certain that disposal in pits was not the normal rite.

However the quantity of human bone in pits is still low compared to Danebury.

Animal (Pls. 3.11–3.14)

The full range of animal deposits was present and accounted for 118 or 64% of all deposits. Animal skulls were the most common category, though all varieties of deposits were frequent. A sub-section of skull deposits has been added to the classification to accommodate horn cores, in particular of goat. Goats are otherwise particularly rare on all Environs sites. The category of significant single bones (R71), though mainly referring to long bones, includes pelvis and scapula as well and sometimes includes more than one bone.

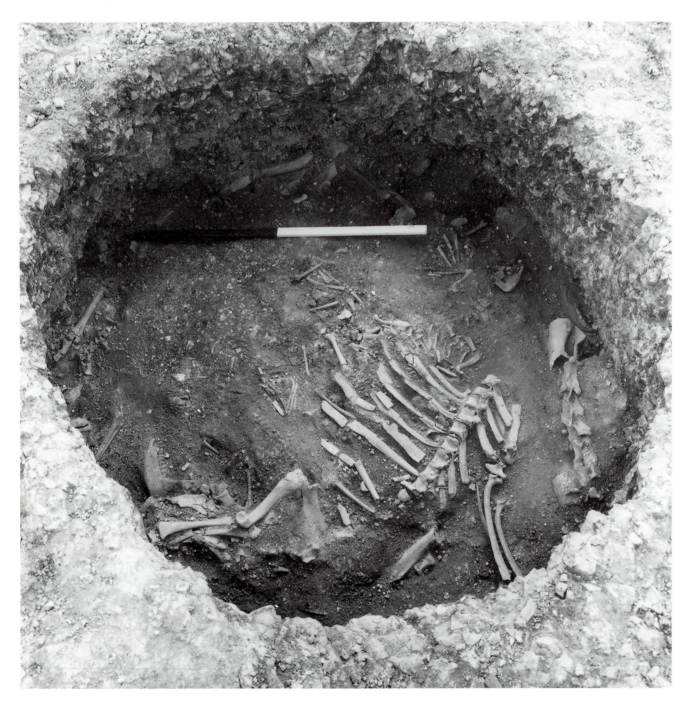

Pl. 3.11 Special burial in pit P159

For most of the animal deposits the highest number occurred in the basal position with a distinct decrease above this and none above secondary, apart from a single deposit of a mandible in the top level and an unarticulated bone dump in tertiary. The only exceptions were whole animals which were distributed equally in base, primary and secondary and animal legs, which showed a distinct decrease in primary with a slight increase in secondary.

All the usual species of domestic animals were present as special deposits together with a smaller number of less common or wild species, including hare and fox and possibly some bird. No rodent, small mammal or bird bone concentrations were observed on site, though the bone analysis has produced evidence of these animals, some perhaps being placed as special deposits.

Table 3.13.
Numbers of animal species used in different deposit types in pits. Large = cattle, horse; medium = sheep, pig, young of large, * = ?calf; small = dog, fox, lamb, piglet. A ? indicates uncertain on-site identification not yet cross referenced to bone analysis. F = foetal

	R35 Whole	R36 Limb	R37 Partial	R38 Skull	R39 Mandib.	R71 Single	Total
Sheep	1(F)	3+?1	–	4	?2	–	11
Cattle	2	4+?2	1	11+?1	1+?1	4	25
Horse	–	2+?6	–	8+?3	3+?2	2	26
Pig	1	–	1	–	–	–	2
Goat	–	–	–	a:3	–	–	3
Dog	4	1	3	3	–	–	11
Fox	1	–	?1	1	–	–	3
Hare	1	–	–	–	–	–	1
Bird	–	–	?2	–	–	–	2
Large	2	6	3	2	4	8	25
Medium	1*	–	2	–	4	–	7
Small	3	–	6	–	1	–	10

Pl. 3.12 Special burial in pit P135

145

A recurring theme in the deposits at this site is the association of skulls and limbs, either as complete articulated legs, partial legs, feet or single long bones. This has been noted with sheep, cattle and horse. It is the main form of deposition for the large animals with horse additionally represented by mandibles and cattle with a few examples of whole and partial animals as well as some mandibles and other single bones.

Complete or partial (usually torso plus some legs and/or skull) deposits tended to be small and medium sized animals with dog dominating both categories. Of the mandibles only cattle and horse were identified with any certainty, though it is likely on the grounds of size some other species are also represented in this category. Only cattle and horse are represented in the single bone category, possibly because the larger size makes them more apparent on site. However the curious deposit in P122 included a dog baculum together with skull and mandibles, suggesting that parts of the anatomy of smaller animals may have been selectively deposited together.

For most categories of deposit the highest number occurred in EIA contexts with a gradual decrease thereafter except for skulls which had their peak in the MIA and whole bodies, which were equally distributed through E–M–LIA. Only partial animal and skull deposits occurred as late as the first century BC/AD.

Most animal deposits occurred in beehive and barrel pits, with a small number of most categories in subrectangular pits and virtually none in cylindrical,

Pl. 3.13 Special burial in pit P197

though most of the unarticulated bone dumps occurred in cylindrical pits. Four or more cattle skulls together with other bones were found in F47 and two horn cores of cattle were observed in F48, both being late Roman working hollows. A cattle sacrum with lumbar vertebra was noted in a LIA quarry (P110).

Pottery

This was the second major category of deposit with 42 examples forming 23% of the total. Differentiating between complete unbroken and broken pots has not been easy, as none were found in one piece. It was therefore a matter of judgment how deposition occurred: where most of a pot appeared to be in a closely confined area it was assumed to have been placed complete, unless it was obvious that it had been first broken and then stacked as large sherds. It was clear in some deposits, where there were more discrete pot groups than vessels, that some of the pots must have been broken prior to deposition and placed in separate positions. The small number of groups of small non-joining or abraded sherds may be indicative of the deposition of midden material, rather than representing a pottery deposit *per se*.

The majority of deposits occurred in base and primary levels with the peak at primary followed by a considerable drop in numbers above this. Only a single deposit each occurred in tertiary and top of, respectively, a partial broken pot and small sherd dump.

Most of the pottery deposits occurred in E and MIA phases with a small number in LIA and only partial

Pl. 3.14 Special burial in pit P87

pots continuing into the first century AD and Roman phases. Dumps of small non-joining sherds occurred only in LIA.

The majority of the pottery deposits were placed in beehive and barrel pits with considerably fewer, all partial vessels, in cylindrical and subrectangular. The dumps of small sherds occurred in barrel and cylindrical pits only.

Other artefacts

Deposits of artefacts were limited to oven daub, triangular clay oven bricks, quernstone and possibly metal artefacts. In total fifteen deposits of artefacts were identified representing 8% of all deposits.

The single deposit of metal artefacts in P119 may have been associated with a lens of charcoal and may represent the fittings left from the wooden artefacts that were burnt. This particular group is associated with a possible cremation burial, so may not be a true special deposit in the sense in which we have defined it.

Oven daub occurred in all levels except the top, though clay oven bricks only occurred in the lower levels. Fragments of the same oven daub frequently occurred throughout the pit fill. Most deposits covered the whole area of the pit or a substantial central area and one group covered the northern half of the pit; but there was only one discrete deposit placed close to the pit edge. Special deposits occurred in all phases but that in the first century BC/AD was associated with the possible cremation in P119 and may not have been a true special deposit. The Roman example is unlike the earlier deposits being a small discrete deposit of oven cover debris; all the earlier deposits represent extensive dumps of all forms of oven daub. The oven daub and brick deposits occurred mainly in beehive pits with fewer in subrectangular pits.

The few quern deposits identified were also restricted to beehive and subrectangular pits with a deposit each in EIA, MIA and the first century BC/AD. They were confined to base and primary level in the pit fill cycle.

Organic

Evidence for organic deposits is fairly limited. Two deposits of carbonized grain occurred on the pit base of a LIA subrectangular pit and a MIA beehive pit; these could relate either to the primary use of the pit as a silo or be a deliberately placed deposit. There was only one other deposit of carbonized grain at secondary level in a LIA barrel pit, where it was mixed with charcoal and other occupation debris. Only two layers of charcoal occurred on pit bases, one associated with the cremation already mentioned and the other in a MIA beehive pit.

It is hard to gauge whether other layers of charcoal represent special deposits or not. Many clearly related to oven debris or, in association with burnt flints, were almost certainly debris raked out of ovens. Burnt layers deposited in pits may have related to ritual activity taking place outside the pit.

Occupation-rich layers could represent the deposition of curated midden material. These layers are usually soily layers characterized by a high proportion of burnt debris or artefacts or a combination of the two. Large dumps of small abraded potsherds or animal bone may be particularly indicative.

Activity

The only deposits in this category were groups/piles of stones all relating in some way to other special deposits. There were five examples. In two cases stones had been used to cover over other deposits: a horse skull was covered by a mound of large flint nodules and chalk and flint blocks covered another animal deposit. Flint nodules and burnt flints were associated with the multiple animal deposits in P78, though their precise arrangement was not recorded. A large flint nodule had also been carefully placed on its own as part of the same group of deposits. A bed of burnt flints had formed a platform for a horse skull. The deliberate placing of deposits on a bed of burnt flints was noted at Houghton Down and at Suddern Farm the placing of pottery deposits on small patches of ash or charcoal may represent a variant of the practice. A large number of flint nodules and quernstone fragments were associated with the cattle skulls in the later Roman working hollow F47.

The arrangement of special deposits

The deposits can be viewed at three levels: the disposition of the deposit in isolation, its position in the horizontal plane in relation to the pit plan and its position vertically in relation to the internal stratigraphy and fill cycle of the pit. In addition a broader spatial pattern of different deposit types in relation to the overall site plan may also produce a significant pattern.

Disposition and arrangement

The variety of positions and ways in which most deposits can be placed is limited: upright, inverted or on its side/edge. For animal/human whole or partial bodies the usual positions are lying on back, front or side (L/R). The direction in which a skull or head is facing may also be significant, since it is sometimes clear the head has been placed in a deliberate manner that is not the expected position from the overall arrangement of the body. The bodies range from tightly contracted to splayed; some of the smaller animals appeared to be curled up like a sleeping dog or cat. There are instances in the multiple animal deposits of one apparently enclosing another (P197), which may have a similar significance to the placing of one pot inside another (P140). Sometimes the outer pot may be inverted over the inner pot. Some pottery vessels had clearly been smashed by being thrown onto the pit floor (P140), but in other cases the pot had been broken up first and the sherds stacked on top of each other (P194, P151). There were no examples of potsherds or other artefacts being placed on edge as was observed at Houghton Down, apart from a pot base leaning up against the pit wall (P165).

The practice of arranging deposits in a ring (annular or penannular) was apparent in P78 and P197 in the placing of skulls and limb bones. It is also possible some of the pots in P140 were placed in this way.

Spatial arrangement within the pit
(Tables 3.14 and 3.15; Fig. 3.92)

The area within the pit has been notionally divided in two ways: as concentric rings separating the centre, off-centre, intermediate and peripheral areas and into wedges radiating from the centre to the pit wall in relation to the compass points (N, NE etc). This divides the pit into twenty-five separate areas.

There is a clear preference for the periphery with nearly half the deposits placed in this area, followed by nearly a third in an intermediate position and 16% in the centre. Only 6.5% of deposits covered the whole area, though multiple deposits in P78, P159, P197 and P140 recorded individually could be regarded as whole area deposits when grouped together.

A total of 165 deposits (88% of all deposits) could be allocated a position, which is quantified in Tables 3.14 and 3.15 and in diagrammatic form in Fig. 3.92. In these no attempt has been made to separate deposits according to phase or pit type, though if such factors are relevant the overall pattern will inevitably be dominated by that of beehive(/barrel) pits of E–MIA.

No striking pattern stands out: the initial impression is that most types of deposits occurred in most sectors. However if one takes overall quantities it is apparent that SE and SW sectors were most favoured, followed by N and centre. The SE/SW preferences may relate to the same factors affecting the position of house doors in the Iron Age (though no houses were actually exposed at Suddern Farm itself). Most of the other sectors had similar number of deposits except for the western sector in which only five deposits were observed.

Table 3.14.
Quantity and types of special deposits in relation to pit in plan.
See Table 3.16 for key to deposit codes. Figure in brackets is total for that cell

	Whole	Centre	Intermediate	Periphery	Total
North	R44/R52(2)	R37 (1)	R36 R38 R41x2 (4)	R36 R37x2 R39 R38x3 R38/71 R38/53 R40 R50 R51 (14)	21 13%
NE			R35 R36 R38 R41 (4)	R35 R37 R39 R38/71 Q71 Q53 R40 (8)	12 7%
East		R71 (1)	R36x3 R37 R38x2 R39 (7)	R35 R38x3 R71 R41 R50x2 R53 (9)	17 10%
SE		R36 (1)	R36x3 R37x2 R39 R54 R45 (8)	R35 R37x3 R36/38 R38x3 R39x2 R71 R40 R41 R50x3 R51x2 (19)	28 17%
South		R39, R37 (2)	R35x2 R39 R41 R50 (5)	R35 R36 R37 R38 R39x2 R40 R41 (8)	15 9%
SW		R38, R50 (2)	R32 R35x2 R36x3 R37 R38/71 R40 R41 R52 (12)	R36 R37 R38 R38/71 R39x2 R51x2 (9)	23 14%
West			R45 R38a (2)	R35 R36 R39 (3)	5 3%
NW			R38x2 R39 R71 (4)	R35 R37 R39 R38x2 R36x2 R50 R51 (9)	13 8%
	R54x2 R53 R41x2 R52x6 (11)	R35x2 R36x3 R37x3 R38x2 R71x2 R41x2 R39 R50 Q51 R60x3 (20)			31 19%
Total	13 8%	27 16%	46 28%	79 48%	165

149

In terms of particular types of deposits, no one variety appears to prefer any particular location: all sectors contain a variety of deposits with no particular type or material being dominant. Separating material from cylindrical and subrectangular pits does not materially alter the picture. It is possible that by grouping deposits from all phases variations through time might be masked though a quick appraisal did not suggest any obvious pattern. This implies either that the placing of deposits was entirely random, except perhaps in relation to centre v. periphery, or reasons for placing a deposit in a particular position were so subtle or personal that we cannot possibly hope to perceive a pattern.

However, looking at the distribution in relation to the fill cycle (Table 3.15) there is a hint, with some types of deposit, of a different emphasis on position according to the level in the fill cycle. For example whole bodies on the pit base appeared to prefer the western half of the pit, but above this, in primary and secondary, had a NE round to S focus. Partial animals on the base covered the whole area of the pit but in primary and secondary tended to focus on SE–SW. Whole unbroken pots had a northerly focus on the base, but a southern focus at primary level, neither of which was apparent with the broken whole pots. Partial pots preferred the SE and E sectors at basal level, at primary tended to move to S, SW and central areas, and at secondary–tertiary tended to have a northern emphasis. These changes in position with the level of the fill may reflect a lapse of time with other events in the calendar such as movements of sun or moon having an influence on position. Since this particular pattern has not yet been studied at the other sites it is unclear how widespread, if at all, the pattern was.

Table 3.15.
Positions of special deposits in relation to plan and fill cycle of pits

	Base	1°	2°	3°/Top	Total
North	R36 R37x2 R38x3 R38/53 R38/71 R40 R41x2 (13)	R38 (1)	R36 R37 R38 R50 R51 (5)		19 11.5%
NE	R36 R37 R38/71 Q71 Q53 R40 R41 (8)	R35 R38 (2)	R35 R39 (2)		12 8%
East	R36x2 R37 R38x4 R39 R71 R41 R50 R53 (12)	R71 (1)	R35 R36 R38 R50 (4)		17 10%
SE	R36x2 R37 R38 R36/38 R39 R71 R41 R50x2 R51x2 R45 (14)	R35 R36 R37x2 R38x2 R39x2 R40 R50 (10)	R36 R37x2 R54 (4)		28 16%
South	R35 R37x2 R38 R39x2 R41 (7)	R35 R36 R40 R50 R41 (5)	R35 R39x2 (3)		15 10%
SW	R32 R35x2 R36x2 R37 R38 R38/71 R38/71 R39 (12)	R38 R40 R41 R50 R51x2 (6)	R36x2 R37 R52 (1) R39 (4)		23 15%
West	R35 R39 (2)	R38a R45 (2)	R36 (1)		5 3%
NW	R35 R36 R37 R39 R38x3 (7)	R50 R71 (2)	R36 R38 (2)	R51 (2) Top: R39	13 8%
Centre/ Whole	R36x2 R37x3 R52 R41x4 (10)	R39 R71x2 R54 R50 Q51 R60 R44 R52x2 (10)	R35x2 R36 R52 R54 R53 R38x2 R60 R52x3 (3)	Top: R60 (10)	33 20%
Total	85 51.5%	39 23.5%	35 21%	6 4%	165

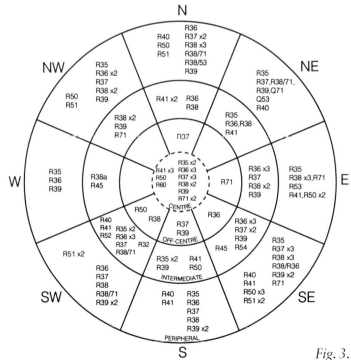

Fig. 3.92 Location of types of special burials in pits

Position in the fill cycle (Table 3.16)

A total of 185 deposits have been identified which can all be allocated to a position in the fill cycle (Table 3.16). Those identified solely from post-excavation analysis can sometimes only be allocated to a layer, which on occasions may be imprecise if a layer was particularly thick or in fact made up of several lenses that could be subdivided. On occasions one may suggest that the animal or object was placed at the interface of layers, where material had been allocated to contiguous layers.

Table 3.16.
Numbers of special deposit types through the pit fill cycle

Figures in italics refer to deposits in features other than pits

Deposit type	Base	1°	2°	3°	Top	Total	%
R31 Human skull	–	–	1	–	–	1	0.5%
R32 Human body	2	–	–	–	–	2	1%
R33 Human partial	–	–	–, *1*	–	–	–, *1*	–
R34 Unartic. hu. bone	–	1	–	–	1	2	1%
R35 Animal body	5	5	6	–	–	16	9%
R36 Animal limb	13	3	8	–	–	24	13%
R37 Partial animal	12	3, *1*	3	–	–	18, *1*	10%
R38 Animal skull	21	6, *4*	5	–	–	32, *4*	17%
R38a An. horn core	–	2, *2*	1	–	–	3, *2*	1.6%
R39 Animal jaw	6	2	2	–	1	11	6%
R71 Single bones	7	3	–	–	–	10	5.5%
R54 Unartic. bone	–	1	2	1	–	4	2%
R40 Whole pot	2	4	–	–	–	6	3%
R41 Broken pot	9	6	–	–	–	15	8%
R50 Partial pot	1	4	2	–	–	7	4%
R51 Part. broken pot	3	5	2	1	–	11	6%
R60 Potsherd dump	–	–	2	–	1	3	1.6%
R44 Daub oven brick	1	2	–	–	–	3	1.6%
R52 Oven daub	1	2	3	2	–	8	4.4%
R45 Quern	1	2, *1*	–	–	–	3, *1*	1.6%
R47 Metal objects	1	–	–	–	–	1	0.5%
R53 Stone piles	4	–, *1*	1	–	–	5, *1*	2%
Total no. in features	–	*9*	*1*	–	–	*10*	
Total no. in pits	89	51	38	4	3	185	
Percentage in pits	48%	28%	20%	2%	1.5%		

Patterns of deposition in relation to particular types of deposit have been noted to some extent above. Taking all deposits, the broad pattern is that nearly half were deposited on the base or in basal layers and just over a quarter in primary levels. A fifth occurred in secondary layers but only a handful, less than 5%, above this in tertiary and top layers. This is very similar to Houghton Down and New Buildings but contrasts with Danebury (taking the data on beehive pits with fill cycle 2 only) and Nettlebank Copse, where deposits in basal and primary were almost equal with a slight increase in primary, and with Bury Hill where most deposits were at tertiary level. The pattern seems to indicate a single major phase of deposition occurring in the lowest levels with considerably reduced deposition thereafter.

The majority of deposits followed this general pattern, but a few diverged. Whole animals were equally divided between base, primary and secondary, whilst animal limbs produced a bimodal pattern with a minor rise in secondary. Unarticulated bone and small potsherd dumps tended to concentrate in the upper half of the pit and oven daub and bricks had their main concentrations in primary and secondary.

Most of the pottery categories, except for whole broken pots, had their main peak at primary level.

A few pits appear to show a cycle of activity with a series of deposits at several levels often involving deposits of oven daub (P120, P194) and animal deposits (P122, P135, P155). A total of eight pits had deposits at three or four different levels and the same number at two different levels. Other pits had deposits at a single level only: six pits each at base and primary, two at secondary and one each only at tertiary and top.

Discussion (Tables 3.17 and 3.18)

The major characteristics of the special deposits at Suddern Farm are the large multiple groups of animal remains or pottery generally close to the base of the pit (P78, P87, P89, P92, P140, P159, P197) and the common practice of placing animal skulls and legs in close proximity. The pottery deposits were unusual in respect of some rare forms and the juxtaposition of early and late forms together (P194 cp 4–5 types with Durotrigian). It implies that objects were deliberately retained over long periods of time perhaps specifically for deposition.

Table 3.17.
Numbers of special deposit types by phase

* deposits may be part of cremation burial; figures in italics refer to deposits in features other than pits

Deposit type	EIA	MIA	LIA	FIRST CENT. BC/AD	Ro	Total
R31 Human skull	1	–	–	–	–	1
R32 Human body	–	1	–	1*	–	2
R33 Human partial	–	–	–, *1*	–	–	1, *1*
R34 Unartic. hu. bone	2	–	–	–	–	2
R35 Animal body	5	5	6	–	–	16
R36 Animal limb	15	7	2	–	–	24
R37 Partial animal	11	5	1, *1*	1	–	18, *1*
R38 Animal skull	10	13	8	1	–, *4*	32, *4*
R38a An. horn core	1	–	2	–	–, *2*	3, *2*
R39 Animal jaw	3	6	2	–	–	11
R71 Single bones	1	6	3	–	–	10
R54 Unartic. bone	3	–	1	–	–	4
R40 Whole pot	1	2	3	–	–	6
R41 Broken pot	1	14	–	–	–	15
R50 Partial pot	1	–	4	2	–	7
R51 Part. broken pot	2	4	2	2	1	11
R60 Potsherd dump	–	–	3	–	–	3
R44 Daub oven brick	2	–	–	1*	–	3
R52 Oven daub	1	3	2	1*	1	8
R45 Quern	1	1	–	1*	–, *1*	3, *1*
R47 Metal objects	–	–	–	1*	–	1
R53 Stone piles	1	4	–	–	–, *1*	5, *1*
Total no. in features	–	–	*2*	–	*8*	*10*
Total no. in pits	62	71	39	11	2	185
Percentage in pits	33%	38%	21%	6%	1%	

A similar attitude or wish to maintain traditional customs may be inferred from the continuation in the practice of placing special deposits in pits not only into the LIA but into the early Roman period and possibly as late as the fourth century AD, though at a much reduced level of activity.

The largest number of deposits (69%) occurred in beehive pits, but barrel pits had an unusually high proportion (15%) for the quantity of pits (6.5%). Most types of deposits occurred in beehive pits and the range in barrel pits covered most animal and pottery deposits. Cylindrical pits contained a very limited range comprising partial pots and sherd dumps and single or unarticulated animal bones. Subrectangular pits appeared to have a wider spectrum of deposits, but if the cremation and associated material is excluded then they were limited largely to skulls and articulated animal remains and partial pots.

The greatest variety of deposits were placed in the EIA with the range becoming increasingly limited by the Roman period, though each of the major groupings (human, animal, etc.) is represented. It is only from the LIA that a wider range of features received deposits and it could be argued that the animal deposits in the fourth century AD working hollows could be waste produce relating to activity undertaken rather than being special deposits.

Table 3.18.
Quantities and types of special deposits in different pit forms and features

deposits may be part of cremation burial

Deposit type	BH	BA	CYL	SR	HE	WH	QH
R31 Human skull	1	–	–	–	–	–	–
R32 Human body	1	–	–	1*	1	–	–
R34 Unartic. hu. bone	2	–	–	–	–	–	–
R35 Animal body	10	5	–	1	–	–	–
R36 Animal limb	19	4	–	1	–	–	–
R37 Partial animal	15	–	–	3	–	–	1
R38 Animal skull	24	6	–	2	–	4	–
R38a An. horn core	2	1	–	–	–	2	–
R39 Animal jaw	7	2	1	1	–	–	–
R71 Single bones	9	–	1	–	–	–	–
R54 Unartic. bone	–	–	3	1	–	–	–
R40 Whole pot	5	1	–	–	–	–	–
R41 Broken pot	9	6	–	–	–	–	–
R50 Partial pot	3	1	3	–	–	–	–
R51 Part. broken pot	6	–	2	3	–	–	–
R60 Potsherd dump	–	2	1	–	–	–	–
R44 Daub oven brick	1	–	–	2*	–	–	–
R52 Oven daub	7	–	–	1*	–	–	–
R45 Quern	2	–	–	1*	–	1	–
R47 Metal objects	–	–	–	1*	–	–	–
R53 Stone piles	5	–	–	–	–	1	–
Total no.	128	28	11	18	1	8	1
Percentage	69%	15%	6%	10%	0.5%	4%	0.5%

The high density of deposits, especially the large multiple deposits together with the presence of human remains placed in the pits may be interpreted as implying a relatively wealthy community based on agricultural activity, but without the easy access to imported luxury/specialist items that were apparent at Danebury. Though the deposits can be regarded as typical, the emphasis on certain groupings or arrangements suggests a community could select or adapt from an acceptable range of deposits as appropriate to their needs or resources.

The use of, and traditions associated with, pits were long lived at Suddern Farm remaining fairly strong through the LIA, but diminishing as Roman influence made its mark on the settlement. It is possible to interpret the evidence as an important local community upholding their traditions in the face of a new system, but gradually becoming something of a backwater stubbornly clinging to old fashioned methods, values and beliefs. Alternatively one may prefer to see it in a more heroic light as evidence that the native beliefs and lifestyle could not be entirely overwhelmed by the imposition of Roman bureaucracy and culture.

Human remains from Iron Age contexts within the enclosure

Human remains were not particularly prolific in Iron Age pits within the enclosure but the two significant deposits both from Late Iron Age contexts may be briefly listed:

P78 (cp 8). A partial skeleton of an adult male aged 17–25 was found on the pit bottom. The arms and lower legs were missing and there is some evidence to suggest that the skeleton may have been partially defleshed before deposition. The individual had been killed by sword thrusts to the lower abdomen.

P119 (first century AD). A partial skeleton of an adult female(?), aged 25–35 lacking the lower limbs, incompletely cremated. Associated with quantities of burnt animal bone and much domestic debris.

In addition, isolated human bones were found in P113, P150, P200 and F60 all belonging to cp 3–4. The bone of a neonatal infant was found in P190 dating to cp 6.

Details of the skeletal remains are given in Fiche 6:C3–7.

The Early–Middle Iron Age cemetery

(Figs. 3.93–3.96 and Pls. 3.15–3.23)

Introduction

A large, and somewhat amorphous, quarry (F429) developed outside the ditched enclosure in the Early to Mid Iron Age. It appears to have respected the linear boundary ditch F402/F403/F413 but it cut through, and removed a considerable length of, the earlier linear boundary ditch F411. The quarry probably developed over a period of time as the small-scale winning of chalk gradually expanding outwards from the initial pit. This process created a large irregular hole with a very uneven bottom where individual delves had dug deeper. During the process of quarrying unwanted spoil was thrown back from the working face into abandoned parts of the old workings. In this way the lower parts of the quarry became filled with chalk-rubble and silt, from processes of natural erosion, will have added to it. It

Suddern Farm 1996, Trench 5, Cutting 2
Inhumations

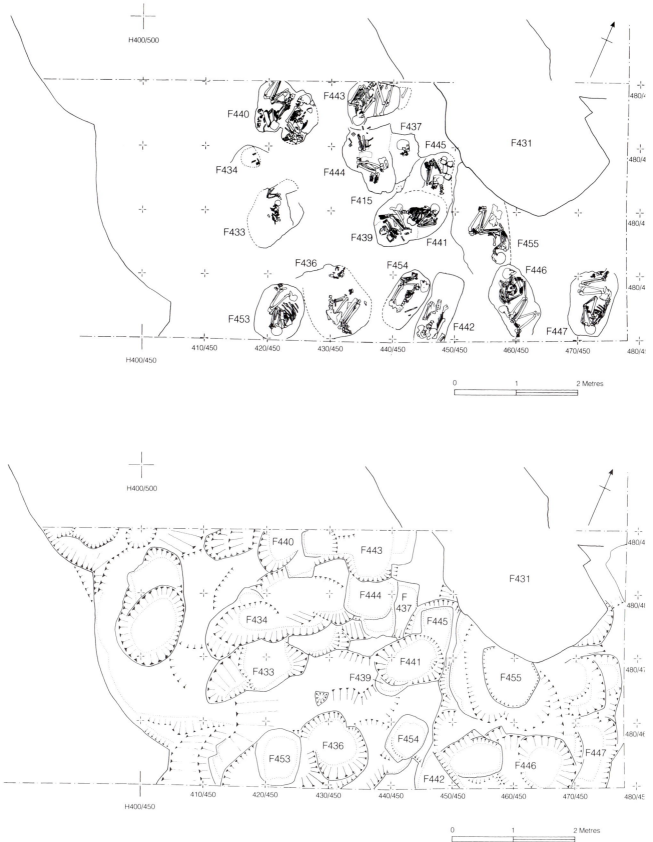

Fig. 3.93 Plan of Iron Age cemetery. The lower plan shows the quarry hollow after complete excavation

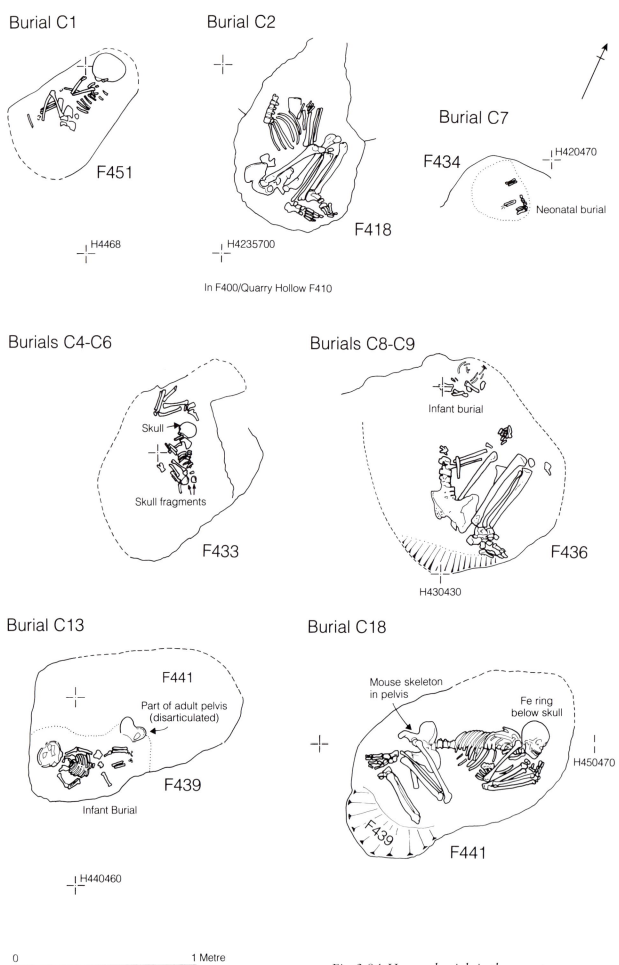

Burial C1

F451

H4468

Burial C2

F418

H4235700

In F400/Quarry Hollow F410

Burial C7

F434

H420470

Neonatal burial

Burials C4-C6

Skull

Skull fragments

F433

Burials C8-C9

Infant burial

F436

H430430

Burial C13

F441

Part of adult pelvis
(disarticulated)

F439

Infant Burial

H440460

Burial C18

Mouse skeleton
in pelvis

Fe ring
below skull

H450470

F439

F441

0   1 Metre

Fig. 3.94 Human burials in the cemetery

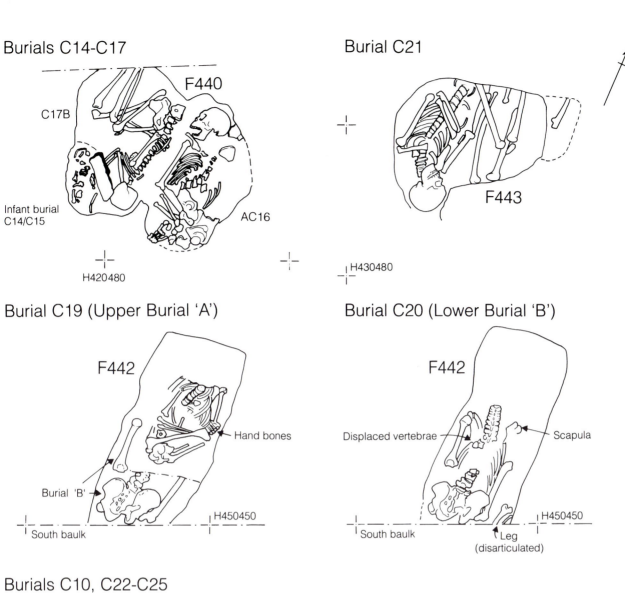

Burials C14-C17

F440

C17B

Infant burial
C14/C15

AC16

H420480

Burial C21

F443

H430480

Burial C19 (Upper Burial 'A')

F442

Hand bones

Burial 'B'

South baulk

H450450

Burial C20 (Lower Burial 'B')

F442

Displaced vertebrae

Scapula

South baulk

Leg
(disarticulated)

H450450

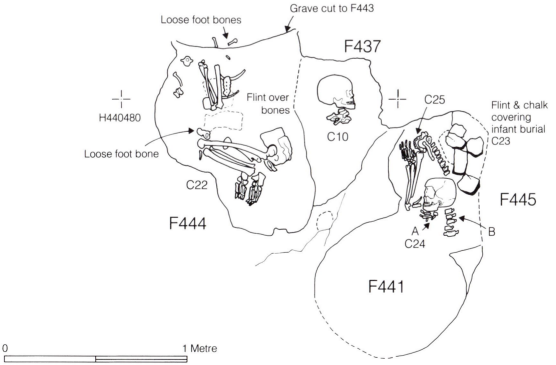

Burials C10, C22-C25

Loose foot bones

Grave cut to F443

F437

Flint over
bones

H440480

Loose foot bone

C10

C25

Flint & chalk
covering
infant burial
C23

C22

F445

F444

A
C24

B

F441

0   1 Metre

Fig. 3.95 Human burials in the cemetery

155

Burial C26

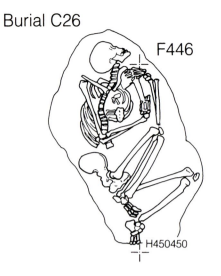

F446

H450450

Burial C27

Fe fibula

F447

H470450

Burial C28

H420460

F453

South baulk

Burial C30 (Upper Burial 'A')

H440460

F454

Burial C32 (Upper Burial 'A')

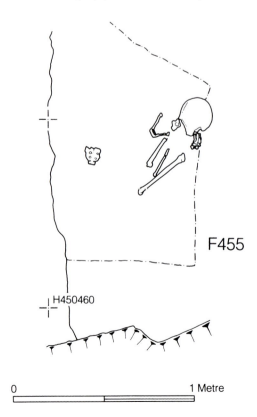

F455

H450460

0   1 Metre

Burial C33 (Lower Burial 'B')

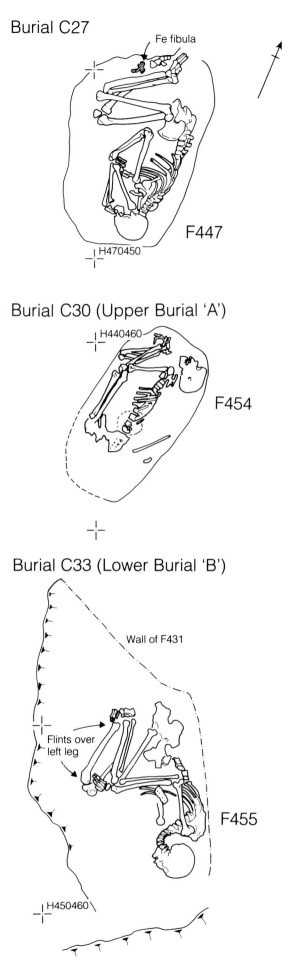

Wall of F431

Flints over
left leg

F455

H450460

Fig. 3.96 Human burials in the cemetery

156

Pl. 3.15 The Iron Age cemetery: burials C13 and C18

Pl. 3.16 The Iron Age cemetery: burials C10 and C24/C25

Pl. 3.17 The Iron Age cemetery: burial C21

Pl. 3.18 The Iron Age cemetery: burials C26 and C27

Pl. 3.19 The Iron Age cemetery: burial C27

Pl. 3.20 The Iron Age cemetery: burial C26

Pl. 3.21 The Iron Age cemetery: burial C28

Pl. 3.22 The Iron Age cemetery: burials C19 and C30

Pl. 3.23 The Iron Age cemetery: burials C19 and C20

was into this abandoned and partially silted quarry that a number of small pits were dug over a period of time for the disposal of human bodies. In some cases the grave pits were sufficiently deep to penetrate the natural chalk of the quarry floor but the majority of the burials were retained within the quarry fill.

In the Late Iron Age the quarry was dug through by the outer enclosure ditch (F400). In the Roman period a large corn-drying oven (F431) was cut into it together with several shallower disturbances.

The quarry was encountered in four trial trenches (trenches 1, 2, 9 and 11) (Fig. 3.31). Human remains were found in trenches 1, 2 and 9 which were sufficiently widely spaced to suggest that much, if not all, of the quarry had served as a burial ground. Trenches 1 and 9 were dug to examine other features with the result that they removed little of the quarry filling. In trench 1 two adult burials were found (C2 and C3) both partially cut away by the later ditch. In trench 9 a single burial of a young child (C1) was encountered in a shallow pit cut into the fill of the linear ditch F411. Trench 2 produced the largest number of burials (C4–C34). Initially the excavation across the quarry was planned as a 2–m wide cutting along the south edge of the area excavation with the explicit purpose of seeing whether any trace of the linear ditch F411 survived in the base of the quarry. Work began using a JCB to remove the upper deposits of the quarry. As soon as human bones were seen machine work stopped but not before some superficial burials were disturbed. After a brief period of hand digging it became clear that the area was densely packed with burials and to obtain a large sample the cutting was widened to four metres. In all some 31 complete or near complete burials were recovered of which 12 were neonates. In a number of cases burials were disturbed by later burial and large quantities of disarticulated bone from completely disturbed burials indicate that the cemetery was in use over a considerable period of time.

The hand excavation had, of necessity, to be rapid because in previous years, at New Buildings and Houghton Down, partially excavated skeletons had been stolen at night by an unidentified clandestine local collector. Even so each of the major deposits was carefully excavated and drawn and photographed before lifting. Neonatal burials once isolated were removed without drawing or photography. In this way, and working late in the evenings, the entire sample within the limits of trench 2 was excavated without interference.

Inventory of burials

During the excavation the burials were recorded in relation to the individual grave pits in which they were found, multiple burials being distinguished by letters. To simplify discussion we have assigned unique numbers to each individual body prefixed by 'C' to denote cemetery and thus to distinguish them from other burials found elsewhere on the site. The inventory is based on feature numbers, which are integral to the site recording system. Within each feature the burials are separately described and the presence of disarticulated bones from disturbed burials is briefly noted. Full anatomical descriptions of the skeletal remains are given in Fiche 6:C8–E6 together with a complete listing of disarticulated material.

All the burials in the following inventory come from the area of quarrying. C1 was found in trench 9, C2 and C3 were found in trench 1 while the remainder, C4–C34, were found in trench 2. Taking into account the disarticulated bones Bari Hooper estimates that at least 31 adults, 9 children and 20 infants are represented in the sample.

F415 (Tr. 9) Shallow grave pit cutting into the fill of ditch F411.

    C1 Child about 4 years. Complete.

        Lying on R side face downwards with back aligned along SE side of grave. L arm tightly flexed against chest, hand under chin. R arm extended and bent slightly at elbow below L arm. Legs contracted at right angles to spine, R foot under ankle of L leg. A large chalk block had been placed over the head and there were a few flints and larger chalk blocks around the skull.

F418 (Tr. 1) Base of irregular quarry cut by ditch F400.

    C2 Adult. Partial: head, part of vertebral column and hands missing; probably removed by ditch.

        Oriented N–S with head at N. Flexed with knees up to elbows. Lying on L side.

    C3 Adult, probably female, 18–20 years. Partial, including vertebrae, L arm and L leg. Rest removed by ditch.

F433 (Tr. 2) Pit cuts into natural chalk in quarry base.

    C4 Infant, c.18 months. Largely complete but disturbed.

        Slightly flexed lying on L side.

    C5 Neonate, 0–6 months. Largely complete, articulated but disturbed.

    C6 Neonate, 0–6 months. Isolated bones: L and R femur and R ulna. Different from C4 and C5.

F434 (Tr. 2) Small pit cut into quarry fill.

    C7 Neonate, 0–6 months. Complete.

        Slightly flexed, lying on L side.

F436 (Tr. 2) Pit cuts into natural chalk in quarry base.

C8 Adult male, 25–30 years. Largely complete but missing skull and part of torso and upper arms. Disturbed by mechanical excavator.

Flexed lying on L side with heels to pelvis. L arm bent with hand to chest. R arm extended with hand at knee.

C9 Neonate, 0–6 months. Once complete but disturbed.

F437 (Tr. 2) Pit cut into natural chalk, partially cut away by F444.

C10 Adult, probably male. Only skull, neck, left clavicle and a rib remain of what was probably a complete burial.

Head to N. Lying on L side and facing E.

F438 (Tr. 2) Shallow pit.

C11 Neonate, 0–6 months. Complete.

Aligned SE–NW with head to E.

F439 (Tr. 2) Pit cutting into top of fill of F441.

C12 Foetus. Partial because of disturbance.

C13 (Pl. 3.15) Neonate, 0–6 months. Partial because of disturbance.

Extended on back. Head to W. Arms slightly flexed, hands to pelvic area.

– The fill of the grave pit contained many isolated bones from a young person and adult presumably disturbed from earlier graves.

F440 (Tr. 2) Irregular pit. The adult burials are probably of different dates. The neonates are certainly later than the adult. There is a large upright flint in the pit containing the neonates.

C14 Neonate, 0–6 months.

C15 Neonate, 0–6 months.

C16 Adult, probably male. 30–35 years. Complete.

Flexed lying on back with head to N facing W. Knees so tightly drawn up that they must have been bound. R arm extended to elbow then flexed with hand to front of pelvis.

C17 Adult male. About 25 years. Complete.

Loosely flexed lying on L side, head to S.

F441 (Tr. 2) Grave pit cutting F445 and cut by F439.

C18 (Pl. 3.15) Adult female, 25–30 years. Complete but disturbance to L leg.

Body aligned E–W on L side. Flexed with heels to pelvis, hands to lower jaw.

Iron ring (Fig. 3.79, no. 2.17) near head.

(Mouse skeleton in pelvis area. Rodent teeth marks evident on some bones.)

F442 (Tr. 2) Rectangular grave pit with one body upon another but not necessarily a contemporary deposit.

C19 (Pls. 3.22 and 3.23) Young female(?), about 16 years. Partial, lacking skull, and R leg below knee probably due to later disturbance.

Lying on back, tightly flexed. Head to N.

C20 (Pl. 3.23) Adult male, 30+ years. Almost complete but lacking skull and leg disarticulated.

Lying face down with arms tightly flexed beneath chest. Legs also flexed.

– Collection of loose bones from fill includes adult skull fragment, temporal of child, mandible and neonatal bones (full listing is given in the fiche).

F443 (Tr. 2) Grave pit, partially excavated. Cuts F444.

C21 (Pl. 3.17) Adult male, about 25 years. Complete.

Body aligned NE–SW with head to S. Lying on back with legs flexed to right, knees bent. L arm bent across chest. R arm straight with hand to pelvis.

– Large collection of loose bones from grave fill representing a number of disturbed burials listed in the fiche.

F444 (Tr. 2) Irregular pit cuts F437 and cut by F443.

C22 Adult, possibly male, 20+ years. Articulated but partial because of disturbance by F443, lacking head.

Aligned N–S with feet to S. Lying on R side flexed with heels to pelvis.

– Other bones loose in grave fill included skull fragments and mandible and bones of hands and feet representing at least three individuals (listed in fiche).

F445 (Tr. 2) Small grave pit cut by F441. Neonate in small pit cut into fill and covered with flint and chalk blocks.

C23 Neonate 0–6 months. Complete.

C24 (Pl. 3.16) Adult, possibly male, 18–20 years. Skull and three cervical vertebrae only. Rest probably removed by F441.

C25 (Pl. 3.16) Adult, probably male, 35+. Partial, including mandible, spine, arms and some leg bones. Probably complete body disturbed and partially dispersed when C24 was buried.

F446 (Tr. 2) Isolated grave pit.

C26 (Pls. 3.18 and 3.20) Adult, male, 20–25. Complete.

Aligned NW–SE with head to N. Lying on L side, flexed. R knee to elbows, L knee less flexed. Hands to throat. Head bent back.

– Other bones loose in grave fill include some foetal bones and bones of youth. Fully listed in fiche.

F447 (Tr. 2) Grave pit cut partly into natural chalk of quarry bottom.

C27 (Pls. 3.18 and 3.19) Adult, female, 40+ years. Complete.
Aligned SW–NE, head to S. Lying on L side, flexed with R hand to mouth, L hand to R elbow, elbow to thigh. An iron fibula (Fig. 3.79, no. 2.16) found in the grave fill near the feet.

F453 (Tr. 2) Oval grave pit cut into chalk in quarry base.

C28 (Pl. 3.21) Adult, probably female, 25–30 years.
Aligned SW–NE with head to S. Lying on L side tightly flexed with hands to face.

F454 (Tr. 2) Elongated oval grave pit cut into chalk in quarry base. The three burials were successive with the neonate the most recent.

C29 Neonate, 0–6 months. Disturbed.
C30 (Pl. 3.22) Adult male, 35+. Once complete but disturbed by later burial.
Aligned NE–SW with head to NE. Lying on R side, head back. Legs tightly flexed with knees to chest. Elbows to knees with hands in front of the face.
C31 Child, 10–12. Partial. Much disturbed by cutting for C30. Parts of arms only.

F455 (Tr. 2) Irregular pit cut into quarry base. Cut by Roman oven F431. Two successive burials in fill.

C32 Adult, probably male, 30+ years. Partial due to later disturbance.
Aligned NE–SW, head to N. Arms flexed, hands to mouth.
C33 Adult male, 40+ years. Complete.
Aligned N–S with head to S. Lying on L side. Legs tightly flexed. R arm along chest and flexed with hand on knee. Head sharply bent back.

F456 (Tr. 2) Shallow pit cut into quarry floor.

– Collection of loose disarticulated bones, listed in fiche.

F457 (Tr. 2) Small pit.
C34 Neonate 0–6 months.

The nature of the cemetery

The above descriptions provide ample evidence of the nature of the burial tradition practised by the community in the Middle Iron Age. The rite involved the inhumation of bodies in individual grave pits. The pits were not dug to any preconceived norm but were simply holes, just large enough to contain the flexed body, dug with little or no regard of earlier grave pits. The legs were always flexed sometimes so tightly as to suggest that they had been bound. Arms were often flexed with hands close to the face. Orientation was generally N–S but there seems to have been no particular preference for which end the head lay nor for the side upon which the body was placed. Only two items, which may possibly have been grave goods were found, an iron ring below the skull of C18 and an iron fibula close to the feet of C27. It may be significant that both were adult females.

One point of considerable interest that does emerge is that all the neonatal burials were in the uppermost levels and where they could be related to other burials they were always the latest. While it could, of course, be argued that any earlier neonatal burials would have stood little chance of surviving, given the number of larger grave pits that were being dug, the evidence does show that in its latest stage this part of the burial ground had been used solely for the disposal of the new born. Too much significance should not, however, be placed on the fact. It could simply mean that this part of the cemetery was considered to be too full for further adult burials only much shallower, neonatal, graves being allowed. Contemporary adult burial may have taken place elsewhere.

It is impossible to estimate the size of the cemetery from such a small sample but *if* the entire quarry hollow was as densely packed with burials as the excavated sample then it could have held in the order of 300 adults, 80 children and 180 infants.

There is little direct evidence for the date of the cemetery except to say that, in terms of the sequences exposed in the 1996 excavation, it belongs to the Early to Middle Iron Age say within the bracket 500–250 BC. The few sherds of pottery recovered from the quarry and grave fills are consistent with this as is the date of the fibula found in grave C27. The evidence for recutting and disturbance suggests that the part of the cemetery examined in the excavation was in use over a significant period of time.

The cemetery population by Bari Hooper

Fifteen more or less complete skeletons were excavated at the site, but the odd skulls, bones and fragments of bones, which were also found in the grave pits, indicate that many more people were represented at the site. It is impossible to arrive at a precise figure for the number of people buried here, but a tentative figure of at least 31 adults (17 years +),

9 children (2–16 years) and 20 infants (0–2 years, inclusive of 6 which were probably still at the foetal age at time of death) is probably a fair estimate.

The sex of some of the skeletons was difficult to assess due either to ambiguity in their sexual dimorphism or to incompleteness of the remains. Of the complete or nearly complete skeletons, six are clearly male, five probably male, one female and four probably female. The sex of some of the odd bones has been suggested in the inventories (Fiche 6:C8–E6), but most remain unsexed.

Estimates of the age at which each individual died were determined by the degree of epiphyseal union and development of the teeth in the sub-adults and by the appearance of the symphyseal face of the pubis, dental attrition and chronological changes of a degenerative nature in the adults. Twenty adult skeletons provided sufficient evidence for age estimations to be made. Eight males and three probable males range from 17 to 40+ years of age, with the average age at death being 29 years. The range for the five females (inclusive of the four probable females) is from c.16 to 40+ years, with an average at death of 28.6 years. The age at death of four unsexed skeletons ranges from 25 years to c.40 years, an average of 30 years.

Estimates of stature were made using the standard regression equation formula (Trotter and Gleser 1952, 1958). The long-bones of 14 individuals: 6 males, 2 probable males, 1 female and 3 probable females, and 2 unsexed remains yielded the following information. The height of the eight males (inclusive of the two probable males) ranges from 152.7 cm to 175.9 cm, the average for the group being 165.7 cm; the range for the four females (inclusive of the three probable females) is from 150.9 cm to 160.7 cm, the average for the group being 156.8 cm.

The fragmentary condition of most of the skulls allowed only a very small number of basic cranial measurements to be taken, with only five skulls being of sufficient wholeness to enable the cephalic index to be calculated. Three of these skulls were found to be dolichocephalic, having indices of 68.3, 72.9 and 73.1; the remaining two are mesocephalic, having indices of 75.5 and 77.4.

Minor morphological variations are commonly noted in skeletons, but it is those that occur in the skull which usually receive the most attention, and a large amount of statistical material for the comparative study of the incidence of cranial differences among different populations is available. Although some cranial variants may be of pathological origin or a consequence of extrinsic influences, most are thought to be inherited, and as such they are termed epigenetic variants. Since the frequency of any particular variant appears to be constant in a given race, their occurrence is of value in comparing peoples within a major racial grouping. The frequency of these variants in each of the skeletons is appended to each individual description in the fiche.

The shape of the proximal shaft of the femur is expressed as an index calculated from the antero-posterior and transverse diameters. This index, known as the meric index, is a measure of the antero-flattening of the bone below the subtrochanteric portion of the shaft. An index of above 85.0 indicates eumeria; from 75.0–84.9 indicates platymeria, a flattening frequently noted in earlier populations, and an index of below 74.9 is indicative of hyperplatymeria a more extreme antero-posterior flattening. With the tibia, the transverse flattening of the bone at the level of the nutrient foramen is indicated by the cnemic index calculated from the projective transverse and maximum antero-posterior diameters. An index of above 70.0 indicates eurycnemia; from 63.0–69.9 indicates mesocnemia; from 55.0–62.9 indicates platycnemia, a condition also found frequently in earlier populations, sometimes in association with platymeria; and an index of below 54.9 is indicative of hyperplatycnemia.

Platymeria has been ascribed to a number of different causes, including excess mechanical stresses upon the bone during childhood and adolescence and as a physiological response to calcium or vitamin deficiencies in the diet. Various explanations have also been advanced for platycnemia, including as a response to habitual squatting. None of these hypotheses is wholly satisfactory, and to date there is no broad consensus of opinion as to the causes of these conditions. At Suddern Farm, of 27 measurable femora, 25 (92.5%) are hyper-platymeric, the remaining two being platymeric. And of 24 measurable tibiae, ten (41.6%) are mesocnemic; nine (37.5%) are eurycnemic; and five (20.8%) are platycnemic.

Cervical ribs were inferred in burial C10, and in burial C26 an actual cervical rib was found to be present. A fibrous or bony cervical rib formed unilaterally or bilaterally by the over-development of the costal process of a cervical vertebra may vary in size, shape and mobility from a small protrusion to a fully developed supernumerary rib. Cervical ribs are the most important of the small number of variations among the ribs, and when they occur they are usually sited at the level of the 7th cervical vertebra. In life they may be symptomless, but clinically they are important, for they can give rise in early adulthood to neurological and/or vascular problems. Parts of the subclavian artery and brachial plexus which cross over the rib may become compressed in so doing, causing neurological manifestations in the forearm. In modern clinical practice mild cases of cervical rib symptoms may be treated by physiotherapy. In severe cases the offending rib or ribs are now surgically removed.

Lumbarisation of the 1st sacral vertebra, as noted in burials C18 and C26, is one of several congenital sacral variations mentioned in standard textbooks of anatomy. The process being genetically influenced, it is of value here insomuch as it suggests a close blood relationship between these two individuals.

Eleven adult skeletons (6 male and 2 probable male; 1 female and 2 probable female) have osteoarthrotic lesions, principally focused in the lumbar vertebrae. The disease is manifested either at the intervertebral articulations or at the articulations between the vertebral bodies, these last lesions being termed osteophytosis. Of the 37 affected vertebrae, eight cervicals (29.6% of total affected vertebrae) and three thoracics (8.1%) have osteoarthrosis at their intervertebral articulations; and 24 lumbars (64.6% of total affected vertebrae) have osteophytosis. Most of the lesions are slight to medium, although in two instances of cervical and two instances of non-vertebral osteoarthrosis there is some eburnation of the articular surfaces. Non-vertebral osteoarthrosis was noted in the right shoulder and elbow joints of burial C33, in the left elbow of burial C20, in the 1st toe of burial C8, and in an odd right clavicle designated C21.

Schmorl's nodes, cavities in the vertebral body surfaces resulting from pressure following rupture of the intervertebral discs, were found in six spines (3 male, 1 probable male, and 2 probable female). Of 23 affected vertebrae, six (26.0%) are located in the lower thoracic region and 17 (73.9%) in the lumbar region. The degeneration of the discs usually occurs in adolescence perhaps through excessive strain being exerted upon them during the course of hard labour before they have had time to solidify.

Osteochondritis dissecans was noted in burials C8, C22 and in an odd left foot in the grave fill of F418 and in an odd scapula in the grave fill of F429. This lesion of uncertain aetiology is probably a consequence of an impairment of blood supply to the affected area of the articular cartilage and underlying bone. The affected portion of the articular surface separates from the bone to form a loose body in the joint (popularly known as a 'joint-mouse'), which in extreme cases, especially after exercise, can cause pain and recurrent locking of the joint. The cavity from which the loose body came may in time become filled with osseous tissue which may rise above the joint surface, predisposing the joint to the later onset of osteoarthrosis. Osteochondritis dissecans is common in modern orthopaedic practice, particularly amongst adolescents and young adults, commonly affecting the medial femoral condyle, the capitulum of the humerus, and less commonly the head of the femur and the talus. In earlier populations it affected a wide variety of joints.

Eight adult skulls exhibit slight manifestations of the strainer-like perforations in the roof of the orbit known as cribra orbitalia. This lesion, which has been frequently noted in early populations, has long prompted discussion, and a number of conflicting theories have been advanced as to its aetiology and importance. A consensus of current literature on the subject suggests that it is a consequence of iron-deficiency anaemia. At Suddern Farm the cribrous lesions are found either in both or in only one orbit, but in all cases the perforations are only at an early stage of development, suggesting that if iron-deficiency anaemia is the principal cause of the condition, it was not particularly severe among these people.

Periostitis, a surface inflammation of the bone, affecting the left tibia and fibula, and to a lesser extent the right tibia, was noted in burial C22. Periostitis, as a disease in its own right, is uncommon. It is usually part of, or a reaction to, a specific disease syndrome (the symptoms of which may be unrecognizable in dry bones) or it may even be a consequence of trauma. In modern clinical practice it is not often seen, except perhaps in syphilis, but its occurrence has been frequently noted in the archaeological record, especially focused in the tibia and fibula. Why this should be is not clear, but it is perhaps significant that periosteal reaction in syphilis, for instance, is usually found on the tibia and the skull, bones that lie close to the skin and are cooler than more heavily enclosed bones. Much of the tibia is particularly close to the surface, and people engaged in non-mechanized agriculture, both in the past and at the present, were and are susceptible to recurrent minor trauma to its sharp anterior crest. Such lesions can easily provide an entry for pathogenic bacteria, but in the present instance the fact that the periosteal reactions are bilateral may rule out trauma as the origin of the condition.

A few healed traumatic lesions were noted among the material. Burial C25 suffered a depressed fracture of the skull, most probably as a consequence of being either struck by a stone or a blunt instrument. This same individual also sustained a broken right tibia, which healed without any serious misalignment. The only broken long-bone noted is a Colle's fracture at the distal end of an isolated radius designated C2, an injury most likely to have been caused by a fall upon the outstretched hand. A single broken rib was also noted amongst the same material with this last designation. Two broken fingers of the left hand sustained by burial C30 healed without complication. An unhealed fractured rib designated C18 could have been sustained either at the time of death or at any time after. A partial lower spine found with burial C21 has a compression fracture of the 1st lumbar vertebra.

The few complete dentitions were found to occlude in either an edge-to-edge bite or less commonly in a slight overbite. Tooth-wear was severe in some of the older persons, with in some instances teeth being reduced to their roots. In 442 identifiable tooth positions only 333 (75.3%) teeth are present, 53 (15.9%) having been lost ante-mortem as a consequence of dental disease, and 54 (16.2%) lost post-mortem. Caries cavities were found in 26 (7.8%) of the teeth and 9 (2.7%) periodontal abscesses were noted.

Roman burials

In all five Roman burials were found:

- Burial 1: adult inhumation in coffin (P207): late third–fourth century AD
- Burial 2: cremation in small jar: second century AD
- Burial 3: neonate in small pit (ph 244): undated
- Burial 4: neonate in top of small pit (P169): first century AD
- Burial 5: neonate in top of small pit (P170): second–third century AD.

The inhumation, cremation and neonate (burial 3) were found close together in the immediate vicinity of the filled in outer ditch (F66) suggesting that the area may have been set aside for burial purposes. Details of the skeletal remains are given below (p. 174).

Burial 1. Adult inhumation (P207)
(Fig. 3.97 and Pl. 3.24)

Male aged 25–35 (for details see Fiche 6:E7–9).

The inhumation had been placed in a grave dug wholly within the filling of the outer ditch (F66) at the top but cutting into the solid chalk of the ditch side at the bottom. The grave was rectangular in plan and was cut to the depth of 1.8 m below the surface of layer 4. Towards the bottom a step had been formed along the two long sides leaving a central slot 0.25 mm deep for the body so that it would lie wholly below the level of the top of the step.

The body, of an adult male, lay extended, face downwards with left arm extended down his side and right arm folded beneath. He had been buried in hobnailed footwear and with a New Forest folded beaker placed on the back of his neck. The burial was aligned WNW–ESE with the head to the WNW.

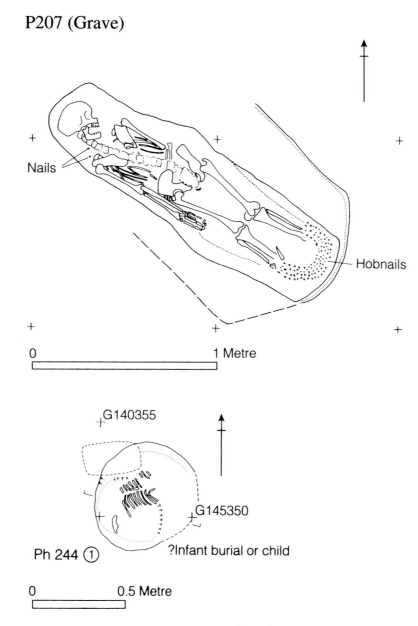

P207 (Grave)

Nails

Hobnails

0   1 Metre

G140355

G145350

Ph 244 ①

?Infant burial or child

0   0.5 Metre

Fig. 3.97 Roman burials

A number of nails found in the filling above and around the body suggest that it was covered with a wooden nailed structure presumably laid horizontally and resting on the ledges clear of the body. The grave was filled with redeposited chalk and silt and was sealed by the accumulation of layer 2. (For further details of fill see Fiche 4:G2).

The pottery vessel (Fig. 3.67 no. 655)

New Forest folded beaker of late third or fourth century date.

The nails of the plank grave-cover (Fig. 3.98)

Twenty-two nails were recovered from the lower part of the grave. These are described in detail in the fiche section (Fiche 5:E11) and a selection are illustrated here.

Fourteen of the nails were found above the body at the level of the ledge mostly towards the feet end (ESE) of the grave. They were largely of Manning's type 1 and were clinched at depths varying from 10 to 40 mm the majority suggesting planks 27–40 mm thick. Many showed traces of wood grain preserved in the corrosion products: in all cases the grain was horizontal. Eight nails were found below the level of the ledges, mostly at the head (WNW) end where they had presumably fallen as the body and the planking rotted. They showed similar grain patterns to the higher group.

Pl. 3.24 Roman burial P207 cut into the fill and side of the outer enclosure ditch

NAILS FROM GRAVE (P207)

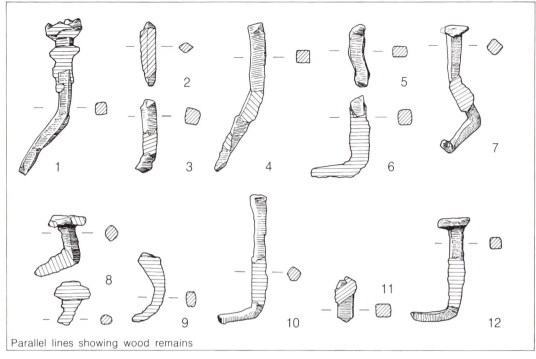

Parallel lines showing wood remains

HOBNAILS FROM BURIAL (P207)

Left foot

Right foot

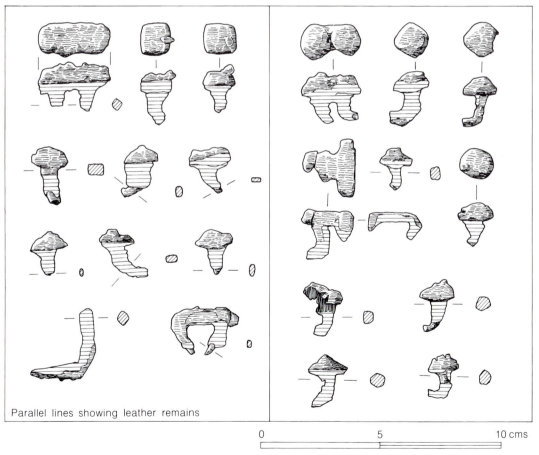

Parallel lines showing leather remains

0   5   10 cms

Fig. 3.98 Iron work from Roman burial in P207

The hobnailed footwear (Fig. 3.98)

A large number of hobnails were found around and above the feet of the skeleton. Examination during conservation in the Laboratory of the Institute of Archaeology, Oxford revealed the presence of collagen, presumably from the leather of the footwear. Boot plates found with the hobnails also bore traces of collagen, together with traces of organic matter, possibly leaves or twigs, on the underside and resin on the prongs. The resin may have been used to glue sheets of leather together while the vegetable traces suggest that the footwear may have been dirty when the body was interred.

In all there were 187 hobnails, 30 fragments and three fittings all of iron from the vicinity of the feet. A selection are illustrated in Fig. 3.98 and may be summarized as follows:

	left foot	right foot	total
complete hobnails	93	94	187
fragments	10	20	30
fittings	1	2	3
mean length of hobnail	16.2 mm	15.6 mm	
median length of hobnail	16 mm	17 mm	
mode length of hobnail	15, 19 mm	20 mm	
range of sizes	9–23 mm	8–23 mm	

Detailed listings are given in Fiche 5:E11.

The evidence is insufficiently distinct to allow the type of footwear, whether *calceus* (studded shoe), *solea* (sandle) or *caliga* (military boot) to be distinguished.

Hobnail footwear is comparatively common in late Roman contexts. At Lankhills, Winchester, hobnails were found in 144 out of the 375 intact graves (Clarke 1979, 178–80). Locally burials have been recorded at Conderton (*JRS* 54 (1964), 166), and Middle Wallop (Piggott 1949, 60–3).

Burial 2. Cremation

The cremation had been placed in a small jar of late first or early second century type (Fig. 3.66, no. 656) which had presumably been set in a shallow pit dug into the filling of the outer ditch. The pit was not identified during excavation but it must have been sealed by layer 2 in the filling of F66 and was probably dug from the surface of layer 5.

The cremation was contained in vessel 656 (Fig. 3.66).

Burial 3. Infant inhumation (ph 244) (Fig. 3.97)

A shallow hollow 0.36 m in diameter and 0.14 m deep had been dug into the natural chalk and quarry fill. The filling was of a grey brown soil containing small fragments of chalk.

The inhumation lay on the bottom of the hollow.

Burial 4. Infant inhumation (P169 layer 1)

Neonate aged 0–6 months.

Burial 5. Infant inhumation (P170 layer 1)

Neonate aged 0–6 months.

5 The Environment and the Agrarian Economy

The local environment

Suddern Farm occupies a gently sloping spur above the valley of the Wallop Brook which lies just one kilometre to the east. To the west the land rises steeply to Suddern Hill with the higher ridge of downland, reaching 170 m OD, just beyond. The flank of the Wallop Brook is a prime location. The land is among the best arable in the region while at the same time it has easy access to two other valuable resource potentials – the well-watered pastures of the valley, suitable for cattle rearing, and the open high down where sheep could be run.

The linear earthworks are best interpreted as land boundaries, possibly associated with animal husbandry, bounding and dividing the lower undulating land of the valley flank. No direct evidence of field systems has been recognized in the vicinity of the site but this may well be the result of obliteration by medieval agricultural regimes.

The animal bones by Julie Hamilton

Introduction

This report deals with the larger mammal and bird bone from the settlement at Suddern Farm. Remains of small mammals and amphibians were counted, but not further analysed, except that the jaws and teeth of small mammals were identified to species where possible. Bird bone was identified by Dr Colin Harrison. No fish bones were found.

The settlement at Suddern Farm seems to have been more or less continuously occupied through the Early, Middle and Late Iron Age (E, M, LIA) and first century BC/AD into the Roman period. The material was divided into these five periods for analysis, and any differences found are discussed as they appear, but there is no obvious point at which a clear division can be made.

The great majority of EIA and MIA material came from pits, but in the later periods around a third came from occupation deposits in the inner ditch, and in the Roman period most came from a variety of features (e.g. scoops, work hollows). Material from postholes, gullies and other small or poorly dated features was not examined.

Over 26,000 fragments were recovered by hand excavation, of which over 12,000 (47%) were identified to species (Table 3.19). Most of these were of the principal domestic animals, and it is on these that the report concentrates, with an emphasis on 'population' age and sex structures and comparisons between periods and types of deposits. In order to maintain comparability with Danebury, methods compatible with those of Grant (1984a, 1991) were used.

Central to any economic interpretation of the age-at-death/sex structures of the animal 'populations' is the question of whether the deposits examined can be taken as representative of the 'death population', or whether they are, rather, a subset of this which was selected for deposition in pits and/or ditches. This has been further discussed in Volume 1. Here, the assumption is made that over time the deposits are broadly representative, with the usual caveats about differential preservation which may lead to underestimation of juvenile animals. This approach may lead to anomalous results, e.g. on this basis the EIA sheep population structure was not sustainable, which suggests that there was some effect of selective deposition. Similarly, the sheep age data show some evidence of seasonality, but whether this reflects seasonal mortality or seasonal use of pits is not certain.

Distribution of the bone

The numbers of fragments recovered from different phases and feature types of the site are shown in Table 3.19.

Of the 14,245 fragments from the EIA (3044) and MIA (10,321) (plus 880 from E/MIA contexts), 10,322 (72%) were identified (to species) or classified (to size-class). Only 2% of fragments were from features other than pits (quarries). In the LIA, 2749 (71%) of 3858 fragments were identified or classified; 67% of fragments were from pits, 32% from the enclosure ditch, and <1% from scoops and quarries. For first century features, 2601 (67%) of 3880 fragments were identified or classified; 65% of fragments were from pits, 29% from the enclosure ditch, and 6% from other contexts, mainly scoops and work hollows. In the Roman period 2624 (65%) of 4053 fragments were identified or classified; only

Table 3.19.
Numbers of fragments in different phases and context types

PHASE	EIA				E/MIA		MIA			
CONTEXT TYPE	PIT		QUARRY		PIT		PIT		QUARRY	
Species	NIF	%	NIF	%	NIF	%	NIF	%	NIF	%
Cattle	350	14.3	5	15.2	166	29.9	1081	15.1	20	16.4
Sheep	393	16.1	8	24.2	92	16.5	2836	39.6	33	27.0
Pig	498	20.4		0.0	6	1.1	132	1.8	10	8.2
Horse	131	5.4	1	3.0	59	10.6	312	4.4	9	7.4
Dog	248	10.2		0.0	33	5.9	80	1.1	2	1.6
Goat	2	0.1		0.0		0.0		0.0		0.0
Deer	1	0.0		0.0		0.0		0.0	4	3.3
Fox	5	0.2		0.0		0.0	2	0.0		0.0
Weasel		0.0		0.0		0.0	2	0.0		0.0
TOTAL IDENTIFIED	1628	66.7	14	42.4	356	64.0	4445	62.0	78	63.9
Human	5	0.2		0.0		0.0	3	0.0		0.0
Small mammal	15	0.6		0.0	24	4.3	25	0.3		0.0
Bird	53	2.2		0.0	6	1.1	2	0.0		0.0
Amphibian	18	0.7		0.0	2	0.4	3	0.0		0.0
TOTAL	91	3.7	0	0.0	32	5.8	33	0.5	0	0.0
Large	276	11.3	5	15.2	28	5.0	733	10.2	14	11.5
Medium//Small	447	18.3	14	42.4	140	25.2	1958	27.3	30	24.6
TOTAL CLASSIFIED	814	33.3	19	57.6	200	36.0	2724	38.0	44	36.1
TOTAL I+C	2442	100.0	33	100.0	556	100.0	7169	100.0	122	100.0
UNIDENTIFIED	525	17.7	44	57.1	324	36.8	2945	29.1	85	41.1
TOTAL FRAGMENTS	2967		77		880		10,114		207	

PHASE	LIA						IA (unspecified)		IA Total	
CONTEXT TYPE	PIT		SCOOP/QUARRY		DITCH		PIT		ALL	
Species	NIF	%	NIF	%	NIF	%	NIF	%	NIF	%
Cattle	418	23.2	1	14.3	271	28.7	12	21.8	2324	17.7
Sheep	443	24.6	2	28.6	266	28.2	20	36.4	4093	31.2
Pig	48	2.7		0.0	45	4.8		0.0	739	5.6
Horse	55	3.1		0.0	42	4.4	3	5.5	612	4.7
Dog	304	16.9		0.0	16	1.7	7	12.7	690	5.3
Goat	1	0.1		0.0		0.0		0.0	3	0.0
Deer	2	0.1		0.0	8	0.8		0.0	15	0.1
Fox	89	4.9		0.0		0.0		0.0	96	0.7
Weasel		0.0		0.0		0.0		0.0	2	0.0
Hare	25	1.4		0.0	1	0.1		0.0	26	0.2
TOTAL IDENTIFIED	1385	77.0	3	42.9	649	68.8	42	76.4	8600	65.5
Human		0.0		0.0		0.0		0.0	8	0.1
Small mammal	3	0.2		0.0		0.0		0.0	67	0.5
Bird	23	1.3		0.0	29	3.1		0.0	113	0.9
Amphibian	4	0.2		0.0		0.0	3	5.5	30	0.2
TOTAL	30	1.7	0	0.0	29	3.1	3	5.5	218	1.7
Large	113	6.3		0.0	146	15.5	1	1.8	1316	10.0
Medium//Small	270	15.0	4	57.1	120	12.7	9	16.4	2992	22.8
TOTAL CLASSIFIED	413	23.0	4	57.1	295	31.3	13	23.6	4526	34.5
TOTAL I+C	1798	100.0	7	100.0	944	100.0	55	100.0	13,126	100.0
UNIDENTIFIED	803	30.9	4	57.1	302	24.2	30	35.3	5062	27.8
TOTAL FRAGMENTS	2601		11		1246		85		18,188	

PHASE	First century								Total first century	
CONTEXT TYPE	PIT		DITCH		WORK HOLLOW		OTHER		ALL	
Species	NIF	%	NIF	%	NIF	%	NIF	%	NIF	%
Cattle	119	7.4	169	19.8	11	18.0	13	17.1	312	12.0
Sheep	860	53.3	381	44.7	26	42.6	22	28.9	1289	49.6
Pig	23	1.4	32	3.8	3	4.9		0.0	58	2.2
Horse	33	2.0	19	2.2	1	1.6		0.0	53	2.0
Dog	100	6.2	5	0.6		0.0	2	2.6	107	4.1
Goat(?)	2	0.1		0.0		0.0		0.0	2	0.1
Deer	1	0.1	2	0.2		0.0		0.0	3	0.1
Hare		0.0	1	0.1		0.0		0.0	1	0.0
TOTAL IDENTIFIED	1138	70.6	609	71.5	41	67.2	37	48.7	1825	70.2
Human	65	4.0		0.0		0.0		0.0	65	2.5
Small mammal		0.0		0.0	1	1.6		0.0	1	0.0
Bird	2	0.1	2	0.2		0.0		0.0	4	0.2
TOTAL	67	4.2	2	0.2	1	1.6	0	0.0	70	2.7
Large	94	5.8	85	10.0	6	9.8	28	36.8	213	8.2
Medium//Small	313	19.4	156	18.3	13	21.3	11	14.5	493	19.0
TOTAL CLASSIFIED	474	29.4	243	28.5	20	32.8	39	51.3	776	29.8
TOTAL I+C	1612	100.0	852	100.0	61	100.0	76	100.0	2601	100.0
UNIDENTIFIED	913	36.2	278	24.6	45	42.5	43	36.1	1279	33.0
TOTAL FRAGMENTS	2525		1130		106		119		3880	

PHASE	Roman								Total Roman	
CONTEXT TYPE	PIT		WORK HOLLOW		DITCH		OTHER		ALL	
Species	NIF	%	NIF	%	NIF	%	NIF	%	NIF	%
Cattle	46	10.1	437	54.6	228	21.9	109	33.3	820	31.3
Sheep	142	31.1	110	13.7	393	37.8	76	23.2	721	27.5
Pig	17	3.7	7	0.9	16	1.5	17	5.2	57	2.2
Horse	11	2.4	47	5.9	30	2.9	4	1.2	92	3.5
Dog	77	16.9	4	0.5	22	2.1	3	0.9	106	4.0
Deer		0.0	1	0.1	1	0.1		0.0	2	0.1
TOTAL IDENTIFIED	293	64.3	606	75.7	690	66.3	209	63.9	1796	68.5
Human	13	2.9		0.0		0.0		0.0	13	0.5
Small mammal	4	0.9	1	0.1		0.0		0.0	5	0.2
Bird	2	0.4		0.0	7	0.7		0.0	9	0.3
TOTAL	19	4.2	1	0.1	7	0.7	0	0.0	27	1.0
Large	44	9.6	129	16.1	158	15.2	21	6.4	352	13.4
Medium//Small	100	21.9	65	8.1	185	17.8	97	29.7	447	17.0
TOTAL CLASSIFIED	163	35.7	195	24.3	350	33.7	118	36.1	826	31.5
TOTAL I+C	456	100.0	801	100.0	1040	100.0	327	100.0	2624	100.0
UNIDENTIFIED	238	34.3	512	39.0	409	28.2	270	45.2	1429	35.3
TOTAL FRAGMENTS	694		1313		1449		597		4053	

PHASE	Unspecified		Grand Total	
CONTEXT TYPE	ALL		ALL	
Species	NIF	%	NIF	%
Cattle	21	21.8	3477	18.8
Sheep	63	33.7	6166	33.3
Pig	2	1.1	856	4.6
Horse	1	0.5	758	4.1
Dog	1	0.5	904	4.9
Goat		0.0	5	0.0
Deer		0.0	20	0.1
Fox	11	5.9	107	0.6
Hare		0.0	26	0.0
Weasel		0.0	2	0.2
TOTAL IDENTIFIED	99	52.9	12,322	66.5
Human		0.0	86	0.5
Small mammal	1	0.5	74	0.4
Bird		0.0	126	0.7
Amphibian		0.0	30	0.2
TOTAL	1	0.5	316	1.7
Large	10	5.3	1891	10.2
Medium//Small	77	41.2	4009	21.6
TOTAL CLASSIFIED	88	47.1	6216	33.5
TOTAL I+C	187	100.0	18,538	100.0
UNIDENTIFIED	93	33.2	7863	29.8
TOTAL FRAGMENTS	280		26,401	

Notes: NIF: number of individual fragments
Percentages are %TOTAL I+C (identified+classified) except for UNIDENTIFIED, where %TOTAL FRAGMENTS is given
Large:Cattle/Horse-size rib, vertebra and longbone fragments
Medium//Small:Sheep/Pig//Dog-size rib, vertebra and longbone fragments

17% were from pits, 36% were from enclosure ditches and 47% from various other contexts, mainly scoops and work hollows. For comparisons between phases, total numbers for all features are used unless otherwise indicated. For comparisons between feature types, the categories used were pits, ditches, and others (mainly quarries, scoops and work hollows).

Site factors

Types of deposit

The types of deposit ranged from apparently unstructured butchery or domestic waste, with unconnected broken, butchered and/or burnt bone, to deposits of skulls or limbs or of complete skeletons, or even large groups of skeletons. In many cases the positioning of skulls, limbs, or skeletons in pits seemed deliberate, justifying their classification as special deposits, but this is not necessarily always so. Some apparently structured deposits might represent opportunistic disposal – the foetal pigs and dogs spring to mind – or large-scale disposal of e.g. butchery waste; and what appears to be a standard 'rubbish' layer might itself be a special deposit.

A high proportion of the material, particularly in the MIA, is derived from large groups of material which may well be special deposits. This introduces problems for analysis in several ways. For the smaller animals, especially sheep, a high proportion of complete skeletons may be included, which may therefore count disproportionately in the overall statistics. For the larger animals, particular parts of the skeleton may have been selected. On the other hand, there is no consistent way to distinguish special deposits.

There has therefore been no attempt to separate them in the analysis, although the effect of inclusion or exclusion of whole skeletons, or foetal material, has been considered where relevant. Some obvious adjustments have been made: for large groups of material (e.g. the sheep from P159/2) measurements and other data from the right side only were used, and the effect of excluding or including whole skeletons on overall species numbers and proportions is shown in Table 3.20. All the individuals that had apparently been deposited complete were from pits, rather than ditches or other features.

Table 3.20.
Major species quantified in terms of numbers of individual fragments (NIF), epiphyses-only (EPIF) and minimum numbers of individuals (MNI)

Phase: EIA

	All except 'whole' skeletons						All 'Whole' skeletons						All Inclusive					
Species	NIF	%	EPIF	%	MNI	%	NIF	%	EPIF	%	MNI	%	NIF	%	EPIF	%	MNI	%
Cattle	322	34.5	102	43.2	7	22.6	33	4.7		0.0	1	11.1	355	21.7	102	26.6	8	20.0
Sheep	294	31.5	69	29.2	13	41.9	107	15.3	21	14.2	1	11.1	401	24.5	90	23.4	14	35.0
Pig	108	11.6	9	3.8	3	9.7	390	55.7	67	45.3	3	33.3	498	30.5	76	19.8	6	15.0
Horse	132	14.1	14	5.9	2	6.5		0.0		0.0		0.0	132	8.1	14	3.6	2	5.0
Dog	78	8.4	42	17.8	6	19.4	170	24.3	60	40.5	4	44.4	248	15.2	102	26.6	10	25.0
Total	934	100	236	100	31	100	700	100	148	100	9	100	1634	100	384	100	40	100

Phase: MIA

	All except 'whole' skeletons						All 'Whole' skeletons						All Inclusive					
Species	NIF	%	EPIF	%	MNI	%	NIF	%	EPIF	%	MNI	%	NIF	%	EPIF	%	MNI	%
Cattle	1036	50.3	208	50.9	18	30.0	65	2.6	15	2.3	1	3.2	1101	24.4	223	20.8	19	20.9
Sheep	579	28.1	108	26.4	25	41.7	2290	93.2	620	93.5	28	90.3	2869	63.5	728	67.9	53	58.2
Pig	98	4.8	21	5.1	5	8.3	44	1.8	18	2.7	1	3.2	142	3.1	39	3.6	6	6.6
Horse	321	15.6	61	14.9	9	15.0		0.0		0.0		0.0	321	7.1	61	5.7	9	9.9
Dog	25	1.2	11	2.7	3	5.0	57	2.3	10	1.5	1	3.2	82	1.8	21	2.0	4	4.4
Total	2059	100	409	100	60	100	2456	100	663	100	30	100	4490	100	1072	100	91	100

Phase: LIA

	All except 'whole' skeletons						All 'Whole' skeletons						All Inclusive					
Species	NIF	%	EPIF	%	MNI	%	NIF	%	EPIF	%	MNI	%	NIF	%	EPIF	%	MNI	%
Cattle	690	40.6	125	39.8	17	25.0		0.0		0.0		0.0	690	36.1	125	36.5	17	23.9
Sheep	691	40.7	145	46.2	40	58.8	20	9.4	18	64.3	1	33.3	711	37.2	163	47.7	41	57.7
Pig	93	5.5	14	4.5	5	7.4		0.0		0.0		0.0	93	4.9	14	4.1	5	7.0
Horse	97	5.7	30	9.6	4	5.9		0.0		0.0		0.0	97	5.1	30	8.8	4	5.6
Dog	128	7.5		0.0	2	2.9	192	90.6	10	35.7	2	66.7	320	16.7	10	2.9	4	5.6
Total	1699	100	314	100	68	100	212	100	28	100	3	100	1911	100	342	100	71	100

+25 NIF from 1 hare

Phase: First century

	All except 'whole' skeletons						All 'Whole' skeletons						All Inclusive					
Species	NIF	%	EPIF	%	MNI	%	NIF	%	EPIF	%	MNI	%	NIF	%	EPIF	%	MNI	%
Cattle	312	26.6	65	21.5	12	21.8		0.0		0.0		0.0	312	17.2	65	17.0	12	19.4
Sheep	732	62.5	195	64.4	36	65.5	557	86.1	59	73.8	5	71.4	1289	70.9	254	66.3	41	66.1
Pig	58	4.9	7	2.3	3	5.5		0.0		0.0		0.0	58	3.2	7	1.8	3	4.8
Horse	53	4.5	19	6.3	3	5.5		0.0		0.0		0.0	53	2.9	19	5.0	3	4.8
Dog	17	1.5	17	5.6	1	1.8	90	13.9	21	26.3	2	28.6	107	5.9	38	9.9	3	4.8
Total	1172	100	303	100	55	100	647	100	80	100	7	100	1819	100	383	100	62	100

Phase: Roman

	All except 'whole' skeletons						All 'Whole' skeletons						All Inclusive					
Species	NIF	%	EPIF	%	MNI	%	NIF	%	EPIF	%	MNI	%	NIF	%	EPIF	%	MNI	%
Cattle	820	47.7	109	54.2	12	20.3		0.0		0.0		0.0	820	45.7	109	46.4	12	19.0
Sheep	721	41.9	66	32.8	36	61.0		0.0		0.0		0.0	721	40.1	66	28.1	36	57.1
Pig	57	3.3	7	3.5	2	3.4		0.0		0.0		0.0	57	3.2	7	3.0	2	3.2
Horse	92	5.4	15	7.5	3	5.1		0.0		0.0		0.0	92	5.1	15	6.4	3	4.8
Dog	29	1.7	4	2.0	6	10.2	77	100.0	34	100.0	4	100.0	106	5.9	38	16.2	10	15.9
Total	1719	100	201	100	59	100	77	100	34	100	4	100	1796	100	235	100	63	100

Features of dubious/mixed date omitted

Condition of the bone material

Bone was recovered by hand excavation. Skeletal representation data for whole skeletons suggest that there was some loss of small bones, such as those from limb extremities of sheep and dogs. Nevertheless some small and fragile bones such as those of foetal individuals, small mammals and birds were recovered, though undoubtedly there was bias against these smaller elements.

The bone was generally in good condition, though there was enough post-depositional surface alteration by 'rootlet' marks and other unspecified factors (recorded as 'erosion') to reduce the identifiability of fragments and obscure other surface alteration due to e.g. butchery or gnawing. Rootlet erosion (>10% of surface) was recorded on 29% of fragments overall. Its incidence varied markedly with depth, from 75% of fragments in the topmost layer of pits, to 15–25% in the next four layers, to <5% in deeper layers. Similarly, in the enclosure ditches 54% of fragments in the top layer showed rootlet erosion, 37% in the next layer, and <5% in deeper layers. In the generally shallower scoops, quarries and work hollows rootlet erosion was seen on around 80% of fragments throughout. Up to half of fragments overall came from features/layers with enough rootlet erosion to potentially affect recording of other surface alteration.

Other indices of preservation also vary with depth. The percentage of unidentified fragments was highest (around 40%) in the topmost layer of pits and ditches, and throughout other features. In lower layers of pits and ditches it was 20–30%, except for the lowest layer where it rose again to 35–45%. Perhaps this was due to an accumulation of small unidentified fragments by trickle-down, or crushing by higher layers. The percentage of loose teeth was generally higher in ditches and other features (9–10% overall) than in pits (6%), but here the numbers are too low to interpret variation by layer.

Overall, differences in preservation between features should not greatly affect comparisons. Preservation does vary with depth in pits and ditches, but apparently in a similar way, and is noticeably lower in the shallower quarries, scoops and work hollows which are here taken together as 'other features'. These only contribute a significant amount of bone in the Roman period, where, indeed, overall preservation is somewhat worse.

Butchery, burning, gnawing and fragmentation

Butchery marks were found on bones of sheep, cattle, pig, horse, dog, fox, hare and deer, on large- and medium-sized ribs, vertebrae and longbone fragments, and on unidentified fragments. Detailed patterns of butchery for each species are described in the individual species sections below. Overall butchery marks were recorded on 2.4% of all fragments, 3.3% of identified+classified fragments and <1% of unidentified fragments. They were commoner on bones of large species (excluding ribs, vertebrae and teeth: cattle 12%, horse 11%) than small species (sheep 3%, pig 2%, dog 1%). The same pattern was seen for size-classified elements (ribs, vertebrae, longbone fragments: large 3%, medium 0.5%). Most likely it reflects the greater degree of processing required for larger carcases.

Cut marks were much commoner than chop marks on Iron Age and first century fragments (c.90% cut marks), but not on Roman period fragments (c.45%), reflecting changes in butchery techniques (see sections on cattle and sheep). Saw marks were very rare and were probably related to the use of bone/antler/horn as raw material.

The percentage of fragments with butchery marks varied from layer to layer in pits (2–9%). Possibly the lower percentages in the upper two layers are related to the high proportion of fragments with rootlet erosion, which could obscure butchery marks. Apart from this there was no clear patterning, perhaps reflecting the episodic nature of deposition in the pits. In ditches overall percentages were lower, again with lower percentages in the top two layers (c.2%) and variation with no clear pattern (<1–4%) below that, and in other features percentages were always low at around 1%.

Overall about 7% of fragments showed traces of burning. Percentages were generally greater in pits (8%) than in ditches (2%) or other features (4%), and this was consistent for the later periods where direct comparisons could be made (LIA: 6% in pits, 3% in ditches; first century: 16% in pits, 5% in ditches; Roman: 24% in pits, <1% in ditches, 3% in other features). It is not easy to see any pattern in layer-by-layer distribution of burnt fragments: in all contexts, they are commoner in the surface layer than the next, and then vary widely. This latter is probably due to episodes of deposition of material including burnt bone, which does not occur in all deposits, while at least some of the burnt fragments in the top layer may result from events after the main fill has accumulated, for instance use for fires/kilns. In one case (P119) the burnt fill with human and animal bone may come from a cremation. Apparently pits were more likely than ditches to acquire burnt material, as the pattern of preservation in the two feature types is quite similar, and should not affect the comparison.

Traces of gnawing, probably by dogs, were seen on 4% of fragments overall. A few bones, mainly from sheep extremities (tarsals, phalanges, and also radius and humerus fragments) had a semidigested appearance and may well have survived passage through a dog digestive tract; an unknown number of other fragments must have disappeared or been rendered unrecognizable by the same means. In pits (and also 'other' features), percentages of gnawed bone vary from 0 to 5%, with little discernible pattern, except that <1% of fragments from the deepest layers show any gnawing. In the ditches percentage gnawing is variable, but consistently higher than in pits (7–22%). This could reflect greater accessibility of discarded bone in ditches than pits, but if this were the only factor one would expect similar percentages of gnawing in the top layers, which is not the case. 'Other' features should also have higher percentages of gnawing, which they do not, though this might be due to rootlet erosion obscuring traces of gnawing. It may be that bone deposited in the ditches had previously been more exposed to gnawing by dogs than that deposited in pits.

The overall state of fragmentation of skeletons and bones depends on a complicated interaction of the inherent physical properties of bones, the treatment and disposal of animal remains and preservational factors such as those just discussed. A fragmentation index (FI=NIF/MNI) allows comparison between species. When whole skeletons are removed from the analysis, FI seems generally to be higher for larger species, reflecting better recovery of identifiable elements: cattle 48, horse 33, sheep 20, dog 19, pig 14. The figure for horse may be lower than that for cattle because only part of the horse skeleton was usually deposited, whereas most of the cattle skeleton eventually reached the deposits: this would point to a difference in treatment between the two species. The low FI for pig may be because of generally worse preservation of this species, partly reflecting the high proportion of juvenile bone. Including the whole skeletons, not surprisingly, raises the FIs for sheep, pig and dog (to 33, 39, and 28 respectively).

Fragmentation for individual elements was generally higher for cattle and sheep (FI averaging around 3) than pig and horse (FI averaging around 2) or dog (averaging around 1). This could reflect more intensive use of cattle and sheep carcases. The FI for pig may be lower because fewer (recognizable) pieces per element survive, i.e. poorer preservation. If this is so, then there is a contrast between the major food species and horse and dog, even though butchery marks are found on all of them.

While FIs for individual elements varied widely (from <1 to 7 over all species, phases and elements), they were clearly higher in the Roman period for the species that were common enough to analyse, cattle and sheep. This could reflect the generally worse preservation in this period, and/or more intensive processing of carcases.

Distribution of bone within the pits

The bone contents of pits vary greatly, from pit to pit and layer to layer within pits. There are layers rich in bone and layers with little or no bone, suggesting that deposition was episodic. This is also suggested by the distribution of small mammal and amphibian remains, which probably accumulated while pits were open, acting as pitfall traps. They rarely occur in the top layers, perhaps because these were not too deep to escape from, but occur almost as often in middle layers as in the deepest layers of the pits, suggesting that the pits may sometimes have remained only partially filled.

Some layers with animal bone contained mainly fragmentary bone, sometimes with traces of butchery and/or burning, and these might represent domestic or butchery waste. Some other patterns of deposition were also noticeable: in some cases it was clear from the site record that elements had been deliberately placed, in others they were noted during post-excavation analysis and could not always be related to on-site observations. Undoubtedly some 'special deposits' of individual elements were missed, because there was nothing to distinguish them from 'background' deposits, and others may seem special (e.g. skulls) but in fact be simply waste. The patterns noted here, then, are somewhat arbitrary. For the larger animals, horse and cattle, deposits of whole skeletons were exceptional, and occurred only in pits with masses of other bone deposits. However, skulls, mandibles, and partial limbs or feet of both these animals, and horse innominates, sometimes with (partial) hind limbs or spines, were regularly found. Another pattern involved groups of longbones which were not in fact articulated or from the same animal, although at first sight they appeared to be so. These could, however, be the remains of some processing activity. For the smaller animals, sheep and pigs, there were deposits of whole and partial (or partially recovered) skeletons, as well as skulls and/or mandibles; it should be borne in mind, though, that articulated limbs or feet of these species might be less likely to be preserved in a recognizable state. Both dog and fox occurred mainly as whole or partial skeletons, with an additional pattern involving skull and mandibles only. For dog, two instances were noted of skull+mandibles+first two cervical vertebrae+ baculum (P122/1, P155/6). There was also a hare skeleton, and much of the bird bone, particularly crow/rook and raven, consisted of whole or partial skeletons. There were also groups of foetal/neonatal bone, generally of several dogs or pigs or one lamb, which could simply be the result of perinatal mortality, though this does not necessarily preclude their being special deposits. Some unusual isolated finds of goat horncores – there was no other definite goat material, and one had saw marks – and large ram horns, also with saw marks, may have been special deposits, or the waste from horn working. The same could apply to deer antler fragments; deer bone was uncommon, and mostly occurred as isolated longbones.

Finally, there were some pits which were unusually rich in bone, and these invariably included some deposits of the patterns just described. These generally date to the Iron Age (P113, P122, P135, EIA; P78, P89, LIA; lower layers of P155) or first century (P119), and the two most notable examples, P159 and P197, with over 4000 and over 1000 fragments, respectively, are MIA. P159 contained the skeletons of at least 23 sheep and lambs, four cattle skulls and at least partial skeletons, plus 'extra' cattle limb bone, a horse mandible, forelimb and femur, a few foetal/neonatal dog bones, a partial pig skull, and a ram horncore. P197 contained probably a whole juvenile cattle skeleton, and post-cranial material from at least two adult cattle; three skulls of old horses, the spine, innominates and hind limbs from at least one adult and one juvenile horse, an articulated forelimb from one adult horse, but no horse phalanges; the paired mandibles and probably skull and skeleton of a sheep about 2 years old, plus skulls, mandibles (all with periodontal disease), post-cranial material, probably whole skeletons of two older ewes, one mandible with periodontal disease from a much older sheep, and bones of at least three foetal/neonatal lambs. There was a juvenile pig skeleton on the bottom of the pit. These two pits are remarkable not only for the quantity of bone, but also for its composition. The sheep from P159 could be a single deposit of neonatal, 1-year-old, 2-year-old and older sheep that all died within a short space of time in spring (judging by the presence of newborns), while the concentration of old horses and broken-mouthed sheep in P197 is also peculiar.

Animal bone special deposits are only one aspect of a phenomenon that includes human bone, pottery, stone, weapons, tools, ornaments and no doubt other more perishable materials. Here, the focus is on economic interpretations, taking the view that the animal remains are broadly representative of the economy of the settlement, while acknowledging that there may be considerable selectivity in individual deposits.

Results: the animals

Species present

The domestic species present were cattle, sheep, goat, pig, horse and dog. Goat was represented by three horncores, and no other definite goat bones, so 'sheep/goat' will be referred to throughout as sheep. There was no evidence for wild boar, so all pig bone is counted as domestic pig. Some small canid bones could have come from either dog or fox; these are included in 'Medium/Small' in Table 3.19.

Wild mammals found were red deer (*Cervus elaphus*), fox (*Vulpes vulpes*), weasel (*Mustela nivalis*), and hare (*Lepus* sp.). The field vole (*Microtus agrestis*), water vole (*Arvicola terrestris)* and wood/yellownecked mouse (*Apodemus* sp.) were identified among the small mammal remains. There was no evidence of house mouse or rat.

Bird species present were domestic fowl (*Gallus gallus*), mallard (*Anas platyrhynchos*), pintail (*A. acuta*), wigeon (*A. penelope*), carrion crow (*Corvus corone*), raven (*C. corax*), common buzzard (*Buteo buteo*), and greenfinch (*Carduelis chloris*) (probably recent) (Fiche 6:G14). There were also a number of bones that could have been either crow or rook (*Corvus frugilegus*), which are difficult to separate on post-cranial characters.

Species proportions

Species proportions are rather inconsistent, varying with method of quantification and inclusion/exclusion of whole skeletons or large groups (Table 3.20). In all phases sheep and cattle dominate (70–80%), followed by pig, horse and dog in varying proportions; wild animals and birds make up only a very small proportion, however quantified.

Domestic mammals

Sheep

Size/type

The sheep were small and slender, similar to those from other Danebury Environs sites. Withers heights (calculated from lengths of complete limb bones) ranged from 0.50 to 0.62 m, averaging around 0.55 m. Measurements are given in Fiche 6:E10–G14. There were generally not enough measurable bones from later phases to test for size changes over time, though the few Roman period bones were near or beyond the upper end of the range for earlier periods. Where there were significant differences, EIA and MIA measurements were generally smaller than those of LIA or first century material; however, the pattern is not absolutely consistent, and many of these measurements came from the large special deposits within which there was considerable potential for distortion (due e.g. to non-independence or selection of individuals for deposition).

Both sexes were horned, and two hornless skulls were found (one EIA, one MIA); this anomaly occurs at low frequency in, for instance, Soay sheep (Clutton-Brock *et al.* 1990). It is difficult to quantify the proportion of hornless skulls at Suddern Farm because it is difficult to count skulls, but it is no more than 2%. There were also two strikingly large sheep horncores, both with saw marks (MIA), which could have come from old rams, or possibly from another, larger-horned type of sheep. There was also a partial skull (LIA) with the bases of a pair of similar large horns.

Age

The two mandible ageing methods (Grant 1982; Payne 1973) and epiphysial fusion (Fiche 6:E13–F2) give consistent age-at-death profiles indicating that sheep were killed relatively young. The general picture is similar across periods, except that in the EIA sheep were younger at death and in the Roman period older. A high proportion of MIA material came from one deposit (P159/2), but the age profile within this pit was very similar to that for all other MIA features taken together, so it was not separated in the analysis.

The mandible data (Payne's method) show that mortality at the earliest stage, within a few weeks of birth, was up to 5% (0 in the Roman period, up to 10% in the EIA). It is difficult to follow the pattern of mortality over the first year closely, because the two different methods give confusing results, but 30–40%

181

(EIA $c.60\%$, Roman period $c.5\%$) were dead by the end of the first year. A further 20% (10–15% in the Roman period) were dead by the end of the second year. Only 10–20% (EIA 0, Roman period 30–40%) were over 3 years old at death, and very few individuals were over 6 years old at death. The 'young' profile in the EIA is not due to exceptionally high perinatal mortality, but reflects high mortality over the next few months, and the absence of animals over 3 years old. It is based on far fewer mandibles (16–18, compared with around 50 for all other periods). The 'old' Roman period profile reflects generally lower mortality over the first 2 years.

The epiphysial fusion data are in general agreement with the mandible data, though it is always difficult to correlate these two sources of information exactly. Mortality before the end of the first year was 20–40% (0 in the Roman period), and by the end of the second year 50% ($c.80\%$ in the EIA, 40% in the Roman period); 20–30% of sheep were over 3–3.5 years old at death (EIA 6%, Roman period 50–60%). The same pattern of considerably higher mortality at a younger age in the EIA and considerably lower early mortality in the Roman period can be seen, though there are some inconsistencies of detail.

It is possible that the lack of younger animals in the Roman period is due to differential preservation; preservation overall was lower in this period, and the more fragile juvenile mandibles and unfused long-bones would be more likely to be lost. It is true that fewer than expected of the mandibles (X^2, $P<0.01$) come from 'other' features (not pits and ditches), where preservation is worse, but there is no discernible difference in the age profiles. For fused/unfused epiphyses (not including the foetal dog from P183/1) any effect is in the opposite direction, with relatively more unfused epiphyses from the 'other' features (X^2, $P<0.05$). It therefore seems unlikely that this effect could explain the different age profile for sheep in the Roman period.

About half (MNI) of the sheep from MIA contexts were from the pit P159 (layer 2). The age profile is quite compatible with all of these having been deposited together over a short period. There was one neonatal animal – which would suggest the deposit took place in spring – a group of juveniles with M2 erupting, $c.1$ year old, a group with M3 and P4 erupting, $c.2$ years old, and a group 3 years old and older. This pattern with distinct peaks is, in fact, found over the MIA as a whole, even if the material from P159 is excluded. It is most simply explained as seasonal mortality taking place in spring. This season might have been important both for lambing and for wool-gathering (e.g. Grant 1984a, 507). Some of the mortality of adult sheep could be associated with lambing, and it is also possible that sick animals and males were culled, taking advantage of the gathering of the flock for lambing. There is very little evidence for an autumn cull as suggested by e.g. Ewbank et al. (1964). Of course, if the pits were only open or used seasonally, only part of the sheep mortality might be represented.

How general is this pattern? To deduce anything about seasonal mortality, MWSs of 28 and over (Grant 1982) when all teeth are in wear are probably too long-lasting to be of use. The appearance of peaks in the age profile may to some extent be illusory if the stages in between are fleeting. They seem very clear in the MIA sheep age profile, at around 10 for 1-year-olds and 22–25 for 2-year-olds, but less so in the other phases. The sparse EIA data show higher mortality of young lambs and a peak around 1 year; these are also visible in the LIA, but there is no clear later peak, and there is an additional peak at MWS 5, perhaps lambs slaughtered in late summer/autumn. In the first century data, and still more so in the Roman period data, mortality below stage 10 is very low, though possibly there is a peak around 2 years which could represent deaths in late winter/spring. The sheep age profile at Danebury shows similar peaks, and while these may to some extent be an artefact of the method, Grant (1984a, 508) suggests that while annualized mortality rates may seem fairly steady, this is not incompatible with peaks at particular times of year.

Sex

Measurements of horncores and metapodials failed to give any clear evidence of morphometric variation attributable to sex. Perhaps this was because a high proportion of the material was from younger animals in which development was not complete. Observations of innominates suggested that females predominated among the older animals (e.g. acetabulum rim depth: of 16 sexable innominates, 1 was male, 12 female, and 3 uncertain; overall, by all available criteria, for 82 sexable fragments there were 6 male, 38 female, and 38 uncertain). This was consistent for all phases. For the large group from P159/2 there were 3 male, 10 female and 8 uncertain.

Pathology

Much the commonest pathology was periodontal disease, and related irregular tooth wear. Periodontal disease was observed in 26/309 mandibles with teeth, 8% overall. The incidence of periodontal disease was highly skewed towards older mandibles: 60% of cases were in mandibles over Grant mandible wear stage (MWS) 35, though these constituted only 11% of staged mandibles. There was some variation between phases (Fiche 6:F3–4): generally the incidence of periodontal disease was higher in the EIA (12%; in spite of the low proportion of old mandibles) and MIA (14%) than the LIA (2%) and Roman periods (5%; in spite of the high proportion of old mandibles), but in the first century it was 10%, so the trend is not consistent.

About half of all the MIA mandibles come from the large deposits in pits P159/2 and P197/7, and if sheep with periodontal disease were preferentially included, this would affect the incidence for the whole period. The incidence in P197/7 is certainly high (5/7 NIF, 3/4

MNI), but that in P159/2 (4/43 NIF, 3/23 MNI) is not significantly different from that for all other MIA features combined (not including P197; 3/42 NIF, 3/26 MNI). If P197/7 is omitted the overall incidence in the MIA is 9%, still fairly high. So, with the exception of the special deposit in P197, the distribution of mandibles with periodontal disease follows that of mandibles overall.

A mandible (MIA, P159/2) had a fractured tooth, with the fractured piece retained between the fourth premolar and first molar (cf. Baker and Brothwell 1980, 199, fig. 5e).

Apart from dental pathology, traces of disease or abnormality were infrequent (0.1–0.2% of NIF), suggesting that the sheep were generally in good condition, or that animals in poor condition were not kept long enough for traces to develop in the skeleton.

Early Iron Age. A humerus had a distal lateral exostosis (cf. 'pen elbow', Baker and Brothwell 1980, 127). A radius seemed to have the proximal epiphysis fusing prematurely, i.e. at too small a size. Another immature radius which may have been its pair lacked the epiphysis, but showed signs that it was starting to fuse. Other immature bones which may have come from the same animal showed no abnormality.

Middle Iron Age. A cranial fragment had a hole in it similar to those described by Brothwell *et al.* (1996) in cattle. A pair of forelimbs from a whole individual both showed bony projections and remodelling around the elbow joint (cf. 'pen elbow'). A tibia had a healed fracture in the distal part of the shaft. A metatarsal showed expansion and remodelling in the region of the distal epiphysial fusion line, possibly due to infection or stress, and a first phalanx showed expansion and remodelling at the proximal end, with a sinus anteriorly which could indicate endosteal infection.

First century. A metacarpal had an area of slight exostosis on the posterior shaft. An innominate showed an area of exostosis on the wing of the ilium, on the surface opposite the sacro-iliac joint. These could be due to ossification of muscle/tendon insertions, perhaps a result of stress.

No skeletal pathology (except in mandibles) was observed in LIA and Roman phases. The total numbers involved are so small that it is not possible to say whether the variation in incidence between phases is more than a chance effect: it is noticeable that, expressed on an MNI basis, the pattern is similar to that seen for periodontal disease alone (1/14, 5/53, 0/41, 2/41, 0/34 for EIA–Roman, respectively). All the MIA examples of skeletal pathology come from the large special deposits in P159/2 and P197/7, and one could argue that this reflects selection of clearly diseased animals for inclusion. On the other hand, these deposits contain the majority of the bone (80% NIF, 53% MNI) and so might be expected to include most of the pathological bone.

Congenital and other variation
There were two definitely hornless skulls (see Size and type) (Fiche 6:F4).

A pair of mandibles (first century, P155/7) both showed crowding and irregularity in the premolar region, so symmetrical that a congenital or developmental origin is likely. A first phalanx (Roman, F66/4) had a depression in the medial surface, with no sign of bone formation, remodelling or necrosis, of uncertain origin.

Butchery, fragmentation and skeletal representation
Butchery marks were seen on 2% of sheep fragments overall. Butchery appears to have proceeded mainly by dismemberment and meat stripping: the great majority of butchery marks were cuts, often around the joints, and joints were not generally chopped through. For the Iron Age phases taken together there was only one example of a limb bone (distal humerus) with chop marks (out of >100 butchery marks), while chop marks were commoner on skull (4/4), mandible (1/5), vertebrae (3/21) and innominate (1/6). Those on the skull may have been related to removal of horncores, and the others mainly to primary division of the carcase.

In the sheep from the MIA pit P159/2 there was a strong concentration of cut marks in the tarsal region (seen on 29/30 astragali, 1/32 calcanea, and 4/39 distal tibiae). These could have been due to skinning; the feet were not removed with the skin, however, as they remain in the deposit. The only other butchery marks here were on 1 distal humerus, 4 first cervical vertebrae (ventral) and 1 innominate (out of *c*.23 individuals), so there is little evidence for conventional butchery of these carcases.

Only ten butchery marks were seen on Roman period bones, but among these chop marks were relatively much commoner (4/10), especially on limb bones (2/5). This probably represents a real change in the handling of the carcase, but the evidence is too scanty to discern any detail. The pattern of butchery on the first century material seems similar to that in the Iron Age, with chop marks less common (7/35) and confined to skull and vertebrae.

Fragmentation seems generally to follow the pattern expected from the robustness of the various elements, while the proportion of a particular element with butchery marks is not correlated with the fragmentation index (NIF/MNI) – quite the contrary, in fact, particularly for tarsals, with high proportions butchered and low fragmentation. Phalanges, also, tend to be complete, not surprisingly for such small elements. The rather high fragmentation indices for radius, metapodials and tibia may partly reflect the recognizability of small fragments of these elements.

Fragmentation seems particularly low in the MIA, and this is largely due to the high proportion of material from special deposits in pits, especially P159/2 and P197/7. Conversely, it is noticeably higher in the Roman period, which may reflect the low proportion of material from deep pits or ditches, or, possibly, greater fragmentation of the carcase before disposal. The greater fragmentation of small elements such as phalanges, which are not usually broken during butchery, suggests that the effect is due to preservation rather than more extensive carcase division.

Skeletal representation (Fiche 6:F2) is affected both by the composition of the material originally discarded and by preservation. All parts of the skeleton are represented. The commonest element (on which MNI is therefore based) is usually the mandible, followed generallly by robust limb bone parts such as distal humerus, distal tibia, or proximal radius. It is clear that limb and skull fragments are much less common relative to mandibles where preservation is worse (high percentages of loose teeth; e.g. Roman period). If the MIA material is separated into that from the pits P159 and P197, where several whole skeletons were deposited, and that from other MIA features (also mainly pits), the former has far higher rates of skeletal representation in relation to mandibles for all elements, with only the most fragile (skull facial) and smallest elements (second and third phalanges) falling below 50%. It is likely, then, that for sheep differences in skeletal representation across features or periods are due to preservation rather than selective deposition.

Interpretation

The major potential products of sheep were wool and milk in life, and meat, skins or fleeces, and other carcase products in death; their function in manuring would also be important. The generally early age at death suggests that the production of meat was important. Only animals 2 years old or older would have provided more than one fleece, or, in the case of females, have produced lambs (and milk, if there was any surplus). The higher proportion of older animals in the Roman period could be explained as due to the greater importance of wool (and possibly milk); it might be worth keeping sheep for longer than the economic age for meat production if wool had a higher value. It is likely that most of the older animals were female, which would be necessary for flock replacement. Combining the age and sex profiles, there seem to be just enough older ewes to replenish the flock from the MIA onwards, but not enough in the EIA (because of the lack of older animals). Perhaps this is due to selective deposition; however, this explanation clearly undermines the whole basis of the argument. Taking the data at face value, the EIA flock does not seem capable of self-replacement.

There is some evidence of a seasonal peak in sheep mortality in spring, particularly in the MIA. It should be borne in mind, however, that this could be due to seasonality in activities at the settlement, so that only part of the 'true' mortality profile is represented. Late winter/spring would be a time of nutritional stress for sheep, as well as the lambing season, so a peak in mortality at this time is not unexpected, even if no deliberate culling took place. It might also be a

reasonable time to slaughter the yearling rams for meat, so that the available forage could go to the breeding ewes and lambs, and possibly also to slaughter the older animals in poor condition – this could explain the high incidence of periodontal disease in the older age-groups, if broken-mouthed animals were culled.

Goat

There is clear evidence for the presence of goat in the form of three horncores, two from EIA pits (P87/3, large horncore with saw marks at base; P122/2, small horncore, chopped or sawn through at base and partially burnt) and one from a LIA pit (P89/4, large horncore). No other skull or limb bones were definitely identified as goat, though a scapula in P89/4 could have been.

It seems unlikely that goat was present in large numbers at the site, and there is a 'token' quality to the deposits (cf. deer antler, large ram horncores, also often with saw marks), particularly the two from EIA pits. At Danebury, also, goat was found in all phases but at very low frequency.

Cattle

Size/type

The cattle were short-horned (Armitage and Clutton-Brock 1976). There was one skull with an unusually high frontal arch (EIA, P215/3; cf. Portchester, Nettlebank Copse), which was also hornless. A skull with very short, knobbly horncore stumps (MIA, P159/2), possibly polled, and another fragment of a hornless skull were also found (MIA, P210/6).

The cattle were small and slender, with measurements within the range for Danebury and similar to those from other local Iron Age sites (Fiche 6:F5–6). Estimated withers heights (von den Driesch and Boessneck 1974) ranged from 0.93 to 1.23 m with a mean of 1.07 m (n=74). There were no clear differences in measurements between periods, and certainly no indication that Roman period cattle were larger.

Age

The mandible data (Fiche 6:F7) indicate that around 20% of the cattle were under 1 year old (about half of these under 2–3 months) and 60% over 3 years old at death, with most mortality occurring in MWS 35–45, probably 4 years and older. Numbers of mandibles were too low for comparisons between phases except for MIA (n=26) and LIA (n=20), which differ mainly in the greater proportion of mandibles from very young (MWS 1–5) calves in the LIA (c.20%). The only phase in which no very young mandibles were found was the Roman period (n=9). After this early (perinatal?) mortality peak, rates were low until around MWS 30 or later.

Overall, the epiphysial fusion data (Fiche 6:F8–9) give similar results, with c.90% of cattle over 1 year old at death and 55% over 3.5–4 years – given the uncertainties and biases inherent in both methods, this is close agreement. There are differences in detail between the phases. In the EIA there were no unfused epiphyses from cattle under 1 year old, and over 90% were over 3.5–4 years old at death. In the MIA and LIA there was higher than average mortality in the 3rd–4th year, leaving only c.40% over 3.5–4 years old at death. This latter is perhaps paralleled in the MWS results, though these are the only two phases where there are enough data for comparison, and for mortality under 1 year the two methods do not correspond. This could reflect a greater importance for meat in the later Iron Age, with more cattle slaughtered at a younger age.

Of the 18 aged horncores (excluding 1 of each pair), there were 1 infant (<1 year), 2 juvenile (1–2 years), 4 sub-adult (2–3 years), 9 young adult (3–7 years), and 2 adult (7–10 years) (Armitage 1982), which again corresponds reasonably well, particularly for older age classes.

To summarize, the pattern of mortality seems to show peaks in the infant and young adult stages, with fewer sub-adults and old adults.

Sex

Measurements of metapodials failed to show any patterning clearly due to sexual differences. A few horncores could clearly be identified as male or female, but again the majority could not be clearly sexed. Males predominated among the older animals (acetabulum rim depth: of 16 sexable innominates, 7 were male, 2 female, and 7 uncertain; overall, by all available criteria, for 53 sexable fragments there were 23 male, 9 female, and 21 uncertain). This was apparently consistent over different phases, though there was only really enough material from the MIA.

Pathology

There is no clear pattern of variation between phases or types of deposit (Fiche 6:F10–12).

Mandible pathology was not as common in cattle as in sheep. Periodontal disease was seen in only 4/84 staged mandibles, including one pair, giving a maximum overall incidence of <5%. In one of the two from the Roman period there was an abscess probably derived from the original periodontal infection. There were also two examples of mandibular teeth with uneven wear, three more of maxillae or maxillary teeth, and one maxilla which had lost a tooth and healed over, though these were not necessarily due to periodontal disease. One maxilla (Roman period) possibly had stage 1 periodontal disease (pitting of alveolar margin but no recession). Three lower third molars with uneven wear appeared to lack the third cusp (see next section).

Skeletal pathology other than periodontal disease, however, was much commoner (1.5–2% of NIF) than in sheep, reflecting the longer lifespan of cattle and perhaps also greater stress due to their use as draught animals.

Deep grooving was noted on one pair and two other horncores (first century and Roman); a similar phenomenon in sheep may be due to nutritional stress (Albarella 1995). The skull with the pair of horncores also had an area of exostosis near the base of the right horncore, possibly due to trauma e.g. from tethering.

Six skulls with posterior perforations, like those described by Dobney et al. (1996) at Lincoln and Brothwell et al. (1996), were found (2 MIA, 3 LIA, 1 first century).

Two mandibles had deposits of platy bone on the ramus, possibly a reaction to oral infections, and two others had arthropathies at the articulatory condyle.

Arthropathies, including osteoarthritis and remodelling of bone around joints as a result of stress, were concentrated around the hip joint, and otherwise at limb extremities (ankle joint, metapodials), where there is also a concentration of traces of trauma/infection. Fractures seem commoner in the axial skeleton (vertebrae and ribs) and there is also a pattern of reaction to trauma/stress on the scapula.

It is plausible to interpret the high proportion of skeletal pathology (compared with other domestic species, including horse) as related to the use of cattle as draught animals, with trauma and repeated stresses on particular parts of the skeleton leading to many of the observed pathologies. Damage to the spine may be caused by yoking or loading, and Brothwell et al. (1996) suggest that yoking may be a factor in the development of parietal/occipital perforations. Tethering might also account for some damage to horns and lower limbs, and heavy-handed treatment for fractured ribs.

Congenital and other variation

Two skulls (EIA) were hornless ('polled'), and one of these had an unusually high frontal arch (see Size and type) (Fiche 6:F10–12).

Three lower third molars (1 EIA, 2 MIA) had the third cusp definitely absent, and four more (2 MIA, 2 Roman) apparently had reduced third cusps which had led to irregular wear on the posterior part of the tooth – though it is possible that this irregular wear had removed an otherwise normal third cusp. The overall incidence was therefore somewhere between 4 and 10% (3–7/68). With such small numbers no variation between phases is detectable. One mandible (MIA; MWS 45–46) with irregular wear of M3 also lacked the second premolar, but in such an old animal this is not necessarily a congenital feature.

One pair of maxillae (EIA) had a number of holes in the enamel and dentine of the occlusal surface of the teeth, so symmetrical that a developmental defect seems likely; they also showed abnormal wear on M3 that might indicate absence of the opposing cusp (lower M3 third cusp).

One mandible (EIA) had a double anterior foramen, and another (LIA) had the facet of the articular condyle split into two, slightly misaligned, facets; there was no appearance of bone remodelling or other disturbance, and this was probably a developmental variation (cf. Baker and Brothwell 1980, 113–14).

A lumbar vertebra (MIA) had the left-hand ventral foramen much larger than the right, probably a developmental asymmetry.

Butchery, fragmentation and skeletal representation
Overall butchery marks were seen on 9% of cattle fragments. As for sheep, there was a clear difference between the Iron Age and the Roman period in the proportion of chop marks, and the pattern in the first century was so similar to that in the Iron Age that they have been analysed together. In the earlier phases, joints were not chopped through, and butchery appears to have proceeded via dismemberment and flesh stripping. Chop marks were relatively commoner on the head and spine (12% of marks), particularly on the mandible, both on the horizontal and vertical rami. On the rest of the body (7% of marks) they were concentrated on the innominate and scapula (especially the neck), and also the proximal radius, distal humerus, distal tibia, proximal metatarsal, and first phalanx. These could represent early stages in the division of the carcase. Cut marks were seen at horncore bases, perhaps resulting from horn removal, and groups of cut marks were particularly common on the frontal bone, as though it had been skinned. They were also very common on the mandible, both anteriorly and around the jaw articulation, from removal of the cheek muscle and perhaps the tongue. On the rest of the skeleton they were concentrated around joints, e.g. distal scapula, distal humerus/proximal radius, acetabulum/proximal femur, distal tibia/calcaneum/astragalus/tarsal. They were also common on the blade of the scapula, from flesh-trimming, and on the first phalanx, perhaps from skinning or separation of feet from the leg.

The distribution of butchery marks over the skeleton was similar in the Roman period, perhaps with a higher proportion on the lower hind limb and fewer on the skull, but a much higher proportion were chop marks (40% on head and spine, 63% on rest of skeleton). Nevertheless, joints were not often chopped through and vertebrae were not halved. Though the technology and technique of butchery may have altered, the basic procedure was probably similar.

Overall, fragmentation varied with part of the skeleton: smaller elements, such as tarsals and phalanges, were much less fragmented. Fragmentation was not, however, strongly related to the concentration of butchery marks, reinforcing the impression that these were mainly related to disjointing and meat stripping rather than breaking up bones. There was no consistent pattern in fragmentation of particular longbones. There was some variation with period, with fragmentation particularly high in the Roman period. This could be because of poorer preservation in features that were shallower and therefore more exposed to later disturbance. The percentage of complete longbones was particularly high in the EIA and MIA, in which the great majority of bone was from pits; this could reflect better conditions of preservation, but perhaps also the nature of the original deposits. These were the phases in which deposits of whole/partial individuals in pits were particularly common.

All parts of the skeleton were present, though representation of skeletal elements, expressed as percentage of the commonest element (usually the mandible), was affected by both preservation and recovery (Fiche 6:F9). For instance, the more robust and earlier-fusing distal humerus, proximal radius and distal tibia were consistently commoner than the other ends of these bones, while smaller elements such as phalanges were consistently under-represented. Skull parts were generally well represented, in part reflecting the deposition of whole skulls. There were some differences between periods and feature types. To some extent these reflect preservation: those elements that are always relatively uncommon are even more so as preservation (measured as % loose teeth) worsens. In first century pits (but not ditches) and Roman period ditches (but not pits, scoops and hollows, taken together), skull parts, and even mandibles, are less common relative to limb bones, indeed the commonest elements are proximal radius and distal humerus, respectively. This could reflect a difference in the original composition of deposits, with skulls perhaps deposited elsewhere. Representation of limb elements generally seems particularly high in the EIA, perhaps reflecting good preservation, and similar in pattern, though overall lower, in MIA and LIA pits. LIA ditches perhaps have lower representation of skull parts than LIA pits, but there is no strong contrast in the pattern.

Interpretation
Cattle could provide milk and traction in life, and meat, hides, horn and other carcase products after death, and the manure they produced would also be important. Cattle were breeding at the site, as evidenced by the remains of very young calves, and a high proportion of cattle were fully mature at death. The mortality pattern does not suggest a concentration on meat production. The proportion of young calves killed (around 20% of total) seems higher than at other Danebury Environs sites, though not higher than at Danebury, and, taking the age data at face value, this could imply higher production of milk for human consumption. The rather limited evidence for sex ratios suggests that, in contrast to the sheep, the majority of older animals were male (possibly including castrates, for which there was no positive evidence). Presumably these animals were mainly used for traction, enough cows being kept to maintain the herd and possibly to supply milk. The high incidence of skeletal pathology reflects the use of cattle for heavy work.

Pig

Size/type

As is often the case, there were very few measurable mature pig bones. As far as the evidence goes, it suggests that the pigs were small, slender and long-limbed, conforming to the usual Iron Age type (e.g. Danebury), and there was no evidence for the presence of larger individuals that could have been wild boar.

Age

The mandible wear stage data, though scanty, show no pigs over 2 years old at death, with the majority dying early in the second year of life (Fiche 6:F13). There were only two jaws from the first century (<6 months, 1–2 years) and two more from the Roman period (both 1–2 years).

The epiphysial fusion data (Fiche 6:F14–15) include somewhat more evidence of pigs over 2 years old at death (below 10% of the 'population' where there are enough to judge), with the occasional fully fused humerus or radius (1 MIA, 1 LIA, 1 Roman).

The EIA material included three juvenile individuals (1 <2 months, 1 <6 months and 1 around 15 months), and the MIA material one juvenile individual (<6 months), but this does not greatly affect the overall picture. Consistently, for all periods, there was some mortality of pigs in the first year, most died (early) in the second year, and a few survived to maturity.

Sex

Of 12 loose canine teeth sexed, 3 were female, 9 male: however, the male canine is much bigger and more conspicuous, and may even have been collected or saved for ornament, so probably this is not a good guide to population sex ratio. Of 9 canines attached to jaws (7 maxillae, 2 mandibles) 6 were female, 3 male, suggesting that females may have been commoner in the adult population.

Pathology

A mandible (EIA) showed possible periodontal disease with associated abnormal wear and crowding, and another (LIA) evidence of infection within the ramus, possibly an abscess; both of these were from immature animals in which the lower third molar was not in wear. A tibia of the juvenile individual in P197/8 showed evidence of endosteal myelitis, though no other bones of the skeleton showed any trace of infection (Fiche 6:G1).

Congenital variation

A lunar (carpal) (EIA) had a depression in the articular surface (Baker and Brothwell 1980, 110) (Fiche 6:G1).

Butchery, fragmentation and skeletal representation

The overall proportion of fragments with butchery marks is similar to that for sheep (c.2%), but because pig bones are much less frequent this is based on only 16 fragments with marks: there is therefore no scope for analysis by phase or context type. The marks are mainly cuts, and occur mainly on the scapula (4), humerus (5) and innominate (3), with single examples on ulna, astragalus and first phalanx. As for cattle and sheep, they indicate butchery by separating limbs from trunk followed by jointing and meat stripping.

The fragmentation indices for pig are generally low, particularly for the EIA (and to a lesser extent the MIA) which had a high proportion of material from individual skeletons, and a correspondingly high percentage of 'whole' bones (both ends present). Apart from these, there were almost no complete bones, and the low fragmentation index is probably due to low preservation/recognition of fragments. Since most pigs were skeletally immature when killed, and the more robust elements tend to have higher fragmentation indices, probably low preservation is the explanation.

In the EIA all parts of the skeleton are represented and skeletal representation is high, because of the high proportion of bone from complete skeletons (Fiche 6:G2). However, in the other periods, skeletal representation (as a proportion of the commonest element: mandible, or maxilla in first century and Roman period) is much lower, and often only the most robust limb elements (distal humerus, radius, distal tibia) have survived. This is consistent with the generally poor preservation of pig bones.

Interpretation

The age-at-death profile is consistent with pigs being used mainly for meat (and other carcase products such as hides). A few adult pigs would have been kept for breeding, and the great majority reared to an economic size and then killed. If pig births were seasonal – perhaps more likely under Iron Age conditions – the peak in mortality early in the second year would represent an autumn/winter slaughter. Meat could be preserved by smoking or salting, though no specific signs of this were seen. Pigs can use different resources from sheep and cattle, such as domestic/farmyard refuse, or wild resources such as acorns, and so help to increase the efficiency of resource use and widen the resource base.

Horse

Size/type

The horses were small and slender (Fiche 6:G3–4): estimated withers heights (von den Driesch and Boessneck 1974) ranged from 1.14 to 1.36 m with a mean of 1.24 m (11-1 to 13-2 hands, mean 12-2 hands, $n=30$).

There were not enough of any one element to test for size differences between periods. If all the estimated withers heights were used, it seemed that MIA and LIA horses were smaller on average by 5–10 cm ($P<0.05$), but the observations may not be independent (there could be more than one element from the same animal), and there could be systematic biases in withers height estimation from different elements, so no conclusion can be drawn.

187

Age

The great majority of longbone epiphyses were fused, so horses were usually skeletally mature at death (Fiche 6:G5–6). Only in the MIA were there any unfused epiphyses: 1 of 8 (MNI 5) fusing at 20–24 months, and 5 (MNI 2) of 33 (MNI 5) fusing at 3–3.5 years, suggesting the presence of a few younger horses, but there was no evidence for horses dying under 20 months old. Tooth height measurements (Levine 1982) gave a similar picture: less than 5% were under 3 years old at death, a further 10% were dead by 5 years old and under, a further 20% were 5–7 years old, and 60% of teeth/mandibles/maxillae for which age could be estimated were from animals 8–11 years old. Interestingly, the three horse skulls from the MIA pit P197 were from particularly old horses (≥14 years), while there were only two approaching this age from all the rest of the site (of 16 ageable skulls altogether).

Sex

Of 12 skulls with premaxillae, 6 were definitely male (judging by the canines), but since this is a rather variable feature it was not possible to say whether the others were male or female.

Pathology

Traces of skeletal pathology were uncommon (*c*.1.5% of NIF) and too few to check for variation over periods, though four of eight instances were from the LIA, which seems more than would be expected (Fiche 6:G6).

There was almost no dental pathology – one maxillary tooth with abnormal wear was found. Pathological changes were observed mainly around joints, and seemed likely to be due to stress (perhaps repetitive) rather than obvious infection or injury. Such changes were seen on a skull near the occipital condyle/paroccipital process on one side, on an ulna around the proximal articulation, and on two sets of tarsals. Two lumbar vertebrae were ankylosed. A distal humerus and a first phalanx showed exostoses which may have been ossified tendon insertions, again possibly caused by stress.

The incidence of pathology was much lower than in cattle, though the pattern is not dissimilar, which suggests that horses were not used for heavy work in the same way.

Congenital variation

None was observed.

Butchery, fragmentation and skeletal representation

Overall, butchery marks were seen on 6% of fragments (n=758) (7% excluding Roman period). These were mainly cut marks (90%), and the proportions of chop marks on head and limbs were similar. There were no butchered fragments from the Roman period, significantly fewer than expected by chance (X^2, P<0.02). A skull (EIA, P113/4) had cut and chop marks on the exoccipital and basioccipital probably caused by separation of the head from the neck. In the post-cranial skeleton, as for other animals, cut marks tended to occur around joints, and were seen on scapula, humerus, radius, innominate, femur, calcaneum, astragalus, metatarsals, and phalanges. It is not surprising to find evidence of disjointing, since many deposits of horse bone involved articulated segments of limb, sometimes including scapula or innominate. Long longitudinal cuts on the medioproximal area of one femur seemed to be due to flesh stripping. A skull (EIA, P87/3) had numerous small cuts over the facial region, and other skull fragments (EIA P122/2, MIA P108/5) had similar marks, which might be due to skinning. Other such marks were seen on metatarsals and phalanges, and one metatarsal (MIA, P140/2) had been sawn through and probably represented boneworking waste.

The fragmentation indices of horse bones were generally lower than for cattle, reflecting the robustness of horse bones, the low proportion of immature animals, and probably also the occurrence of special deposits of articulated limb parts. Similarly, the proportion of complete bones tended to be high, though numbers are too low for formal comparisons.

Overall, all parts of the skeleton were represented (Fiche 6:G7). Detailed interpretation of variation with phase is not appropriate, because numbers of fragments are low, but some features are clear. The commonest element was not at all consistent – maxilla and mandible in the EIA, pelvis in MIA and LIA pits, metatarsal in LIA ditches, calcaneum/phalanges in Roman ditches (other phases/feature types had too few). Skull parts were absent from first century and Roman ditches (though there were a few loose teeth). It seems likely that skeletal representation is affected as much by the original pattern of deposition as by preservation – the high representation of innominate is particularly striking.

Interpretation

The small horses found at Suddern Farm are typical of the local Iron Age horses, as seen at Danebury and the other Danebury Environs sites. There is little evidence that horses bred at the site, and the great majority were dentally and skeletally mature at death: tooth height evidence shows that most were over 8 years old at death, and some, with very worn teeth, probably over 12 years old. It is clear that the primary use of horses was not for meat, though the butchery evidence does suggest that their meat was eaten in the Iron Age, though possibly not in the Roman period. They could have been used for riding, for draught, or for pack-carrying; the lower incidence of skeletal pathology compared to cattle, though they lived as long or longer, suggests that they were not used for the heaviest work, thus suffering less from stress and strain on the skeletomuscular system. The common occurrence of horse skulls, mandibles, innominates, and limbs or parts of limbs as special deposits suggests a place in ritual practice.

Dog

Size/type

The dogs were typical Iron Age dogs (Harcourt 1974), judging by skull shape and general conformation (Fiche 6:G8–9). Estimated shoulder heights ranged from 0.45 to 0.59 m, with a mean of 0.53 cm, falling into the middle to upper range of Iron Age dog measurements in Harcourt (1974). A few smaller bones could not definitely be identified as dog or fox – one example, from F64/2, was about 10% larger than any definite fox bones (or comparative material), but considerably smaller than any definite dog bones, so there may have been a smaller variety of dog at the site.

Age

If the age data (Fiche 6:G10–11) are taken as a profile, it is distinctly U-shaped – that is, there is a group of foetal/neonatal deaths, very few juvenile animals (up to 1.5 years old), and the remainder are adults. It is not possible to subdivide this category further, though individual dentitions ranged from little or moderate to heavy wear, suggesting that it includes dogs of a range of ages. The great majority of foetal/neonatal bone comes from individuals, singly or in groups, in pits, and the juvenile individual was also in a pit. Adults were also in pits, sometimes as complete skeletons (at least three) and sometimes as skulls (±mandibles, cervical vertebrae, baculum), and these were also found in ditches in later phases. Other finds of dog were from adults, as far as it was possible to tell. However, it seems likely that this pattern is a result of deliberate selection by people of dog bone to deposit (not necessarily for ritual reasons), and so may not represent the age-at-death profile of the dog population.

Sex

Of the three individual adult skeletons from pits, two had bacula and so were definitely male. Altogether six bacula were found (for an MNI of 16 adult individuals), two with individual skeletons, two with skulls+mandibles+cervical vertebrae, and two not associated with other dog bones. This gives a minimum figure for the proportion of males; however, it is not possible to know how many bacula have been lost.

Pathology and congenital variation

The commonest form of pathology observed (Fiche 6:G12) was the development of periosteal exostoses, perhaps an inflammatory response to infection or trauma. These were seen on all three skeletons of adults: in that from P89/3 (MIA) only on the cuboid (tarsal), in that from P84/4 (first century) on a sternebra and calcaneum, while in that from P113/3 and 4 (EIA) porous, platy deposits of bone were widespread, and there may also have been osteomyelitis in the right tibia. This dog evidently survived the infection long enough for the bone to form, but must have been in poor condition for some time before it died. Small exostoses were also seen on a mandible, two ulnas, a radius, a fibula, and a second cervical vertebra, derived from a minimum of three other individuals. On an MNI basis, this pathology was thus seen in about a third of the adults. Two LIA skulls had damaged teeth. One (from F64/2), with heavy wear on all teeth, had lost three incisors and the first premolars, and one carnassial was broken through, with evidence of infection around the roots. The other (P104/5) had broken canines, with very little wear on the exposed dentine. A dog/fox mandible from F64/5 had lost the first premolar and the second premolar was broken, and there was evidence of alveolar infection as well as healing.

There were two examples of probably congenital tooth row disorders: an upper second incisor was absent or possibly displaced medially, since the alveolus of the adjacent first incisor was large and slightly irregular in shape, and a mandible had an alveolus for a supernumerary tooth behind the third molar, and showed crowding. The skull with the broken carnassial also had a small intercalary bone between the left nasal and premaxilla.

Considering the relative rarity of dogs at the site, particularly if the foetal material is ignored as being unlikely to show pathology in any case, the incidence of skeletal pathology is high. It may not be representative of the incidence in the live population, however, if sick (or just old) individuals were particularly likely to be deposited as a result of selection by people.

Butchery, fragmentation and skeletal representation

Butchery marks were seen on eight dog bones from MIA, LIA and first century phases. A humerus had a series of cut marks down the shaft mediodistally, a radius (also with pathology) had a cut near the distal end, and an innominate had chop marks on the ilium: these were all from the same context (P165/2) and could have come from the same individual. The marks on the innominate clearly indicate dismemberment and could not be due to skinning. Small cuts which could be due to skinning were seen on a LIA calcaneum and a first century distal ulna. A mandible (F64/4) had small cuts around the articulatory condyle, and an ulna from the same context had cuts near the proximal articulation, again indicative of dismemberment. A dog rib had cut marks at the proximal end. A dog/fox mandible (F64/5) had small cuts on the horizontal ramus near the symphysis. While it is not certain that dog flesh was eaten, it is a possibility, since not all the butchery marks can be explained by skinning.

Unsurprisingly, in view of the amount of material from individual skeletons, fragmentation of dog bones was low and the percentage of whole bones was high.

Patterns of skeletal representation (Fiche 6:G13) also reflect the effect of special deposits, with in some phases (notably LIA pits) even very small elements such as phalanges well represented, though usually carpals, tarsals and phalanges, and to a lesser extent metapodials, were under-represented. Skull parts were also well represented in MIA, LIA and first century contexts. Apart from this the pattern seems more or less what would be expected from the size and robustness of the various elements.

Interpretation

The occurrence of foetal/neonatal bone provides good evidence that dogs were breeding at the site. Apart from these, nearly all the ageable material came from adults, probably of both sexes, and some probably of considerable age. While the incidence of pathology (mainly periosteal exostoses) among the adults was high, they may not be representative of the general population. Butchery marks, not all due to skinning, were found, so the carcases may have provided both meat and hides, though this is unlikely to be a primary use. Such uses could include guarding of places, people or flocks and herds, and/or herding. The dogs were large relative to the domestic ungulates: their shoulder heights overlapped with those of the sheep, and were about half those of the cattle and horses. They could also have been used for hunting. The effect of dogs on the deposits is clear, with definite marks of gnawing on up to 13% of bone fragments in some contexts, and some semi-digested material from their faeces. This suggests that dogs were at least to some extent free-ranging about the settlement.

Wild mammals

Deer

Pieces of red deer (*Cervus elaphus*) antler were found in a MIA quarry pit (P103/1), two LIA pits (P89/4, P111/1), a first century pit (P119/3), a Roman period work hollow (F62/1) and ditch (F66/4), and in the LIA/first century ditch (F64/2) along with other elements: five metatarsal fragments from at least three bones (F64/4), a radius and femur (F64/6) and an ulna (F64/7; from the same limb as the radius). A third phalanx from an EIA pit (P87/2) may also be red deer. Two of the antler fragments had been sawn; one (F64/2) was a small fragment of a tine, and the other (P89/4) was a more substantial piece of shaft, sawn at both ends and with chop and 'peck' marks too, probably a waste piece from working. One piece (F66/4) included the pedicel and thus must have come from a dead animal rather than being a piece of shed antler. There were butchery marks on the radius (cuts near the proximal end) and femur (cuts near the proximal and distal ends). The impression is that pieces of antler, quite possibly waste from working, and parts of limbs/single bones were deposited. It is possible that some fragmentary red deer bones were not recognized, or were confused with cattle (Bourdillon and Coy 1980).

The overall frequency of red deer fragments is so small that little more can be said. It probably was present in the vicinity of the site throughout its occupation, as not all the finds are of shed antler, and may well have been hunted and eaten, if only occasionally, as well as supplying antler for working.

Fox

Only finds definitely identified as fox (*Vulpes vulpes*) are included here.

There was a complete fox post-cranial skeleton in a LIA pit (P78/4) and a set of skull and mandibles (P78/2) which probably belonged with it. The skull and mandibles had tooth damage and loss. On the left side, the maxillary second premolar had lost the anterior cusp, and the alveolus was healing, while in the mandible the canine was heavily worn, and the third incisor and third and fourth premolars were broken (with the exposed alveolus healing). On the right, the upper tooth row was normal, but in the mandible the canine was broken, and the first premolar was lost and the alveolus healing. The skeleton also had signs of pathology: both femora showed periosteal bone proliferation, particularly the left where there was exuberant proliferation near the distal epiphysis, as did the tibiae where exostoses were noted near the proximal fusion line, and both fibulae were fused distally to the tibiae. A second phalanx also showed bone proliferation at the distal articulation. Five ribs showed swelling, distortion, and new bone formation, perhaps healed trauma; in one rib which was broken post-mortem there was evidence of osteomyelitis, suggesting that infection was also involved; perhaps this had spread to the other sites via the bloodstream. In short, this was not a healthy animal, having suffered trauma(s) some time previously and probably subsequent infection: perhaps its poor condition had contributed to its capture and/or death.

A fox skull and mandible were found in an EIA pit (P131/1 and 2), with a calcaneum and two metatarsals, perhaps what was left of a foot; there was no trace of a third molar in the mandible. A mandible and skull fragment were found in a MIA pit (P92/8). Some skull fragments, a series of cervical vertebrae and a tibia were found in an undated quarry pit (P209/2).

Fox measurements are given in Fiche 6:G14.

The pattern of deposition, with a whole skeleton or skull/mandibles as the most common form, is reminiscent of that of dog. Foxes would have been a normal component of the wild fauna in the area, and would have been of use to people for their fur: the parallel of the style of deposition with that of dog suggests that their zoological kinship was in some way recognized.

Weasel

A pair of weasel (*Mustela nivalis*) mandibles were found in a MIA pit (P108/5). This small predator would also have been a normal component of the wild fauna in the area, and it is possible that, like other small mammals, it was accidentally trapped in the pit rather than deliberately placed there (though there were no other small mammals or amphibia found in that context).

190

Hare

The skull and larger post-cranial bones of a hare (*Lepus* sp.) – probably originally a complete skeleton – were found in a LIA pit (P104/9). There were butchery marks (cuts) on the innominate, on the ischium near the acetabulum, perhaps made by separation of the limb from the pelvis. A humerus and a mandible were found in the LIA/first century settlement ditch (P64/2, 5). Hare also is likely to have been a normal component of the wild fauna in the area, and may well have been used for meat and skins.

Small mammals

The field vole (*Microtus agrestis*) was the commonest species identified (by tooth characters), and water vole (*Arvicola terrestris)* and wood/yellownecked mouse (*Apodemus* sp.) were also found. There was no evidence of house mouse or rat. Small mammal remains probably accumulate in pits because the pits act as pitfall traps. Again these are normal components of the local wild fauna. The species present suggest the presence of some long grass and shrub cover in the vicinity of the settlement, or possibly hedgebanks or other ungrazed habitat.

Interpretation

The wild species found could all have occurred locally. Deer and hare could have been hunted or trapped for meat and skins, and deer antler was an important material for artefacts (e.g. combs). Fur could have been obtained from fox and perhaps weasel. Fox, deer and hare all appeared in contexts suggestive of special deposits, and may thus have had some symbolic importance to people. What is perhaps most notable, however, is the extremely small amount of material from wild animals, less than 1% of fragments. This could indicate that wild animals were of little importance to the economy, or perhaps that they were mainly consumed in other contexts/areas, or not disposed of in the same way as domestic animals.

Birds

A total of 126 bird bones were found (Fiche 6:G14). The species present were domestic fowl (*Gallus gallus*), mallard (*Anas platyrhynchos*), pintail (*A. acuta*), wigeon (*A. penelope*), carrion crow (*Corvus corone*), raven (*C. corax*), common buzzard (*Buteo buteo*), and greenfinch (*Carduelis chloris*). There were also a number of bones that could have been either crow or rook (*Corvus frugilegus*), which are difficult to separate on post-cranial characters. The greenfinch bones appeared to be of recent origin. Some fragments and incompletely ossified bones could not be identified and were recorded as indeterminate.

Fowl

A total of eight fowl bones came from LIA, first century and Roman period contexts. Although fowl bones have been found locally in earlier contexts (notably the complete skeletons from Houghton Down, EIA), they are generally only widespread on sites of LIA and later in this area (West and Zhou 1988), and rarely occur in large quantities. The fowl were small, comparable in size to modern bantams.

Waterfowl

Five duck bones were found, three mallard (2 MIA, 1 LIA), one wigeon (LIA) and one pintail (first century). These could all have occurred wild in the area, and all are known to use shallow water and/or terrestrial resources for at least part of the year. It is possible that the 'mallard' material was from domesticated ducks, but there is no positive evidence for this.

Corvids

Over half of all the bird bones (71) were identified as raven. There was a skeleton of one individual in P87/3 (EIA), and two partial skeletons were recovered from the LIA pit P78/5 and ditch F64/4, 5, 6. There were also a single ulna in P123/4 (E/MIA), and six incompletely ossified bones in the Roman period ditch F66/2 that may have been raven.

Twelve crow/rook bones (two definitely crow) were found in three pits (3 in P123/3, 4, E/MIA; 8, from at least 2 individuals, in P78/3, LIA; 1 in P119/3, first century).

The larger corvids would all be likely to occur locally. They have varied diets, including crops and scavenged material, and might be important to people as crop pests and scavengers of waste material, or even predators of young lambs. As scavengers, they might also be important in the context of disposal of bodies, especially if these were exposed.

Birds of prey

A partial skeleton of a buzzard was found in the LIA ditch F64/4, 5, 6. This was also likely to occur locally, and is both a predator (especially on voles) and a scavenger like the raven.

Interpretation

The low overall occurrence of birds, including domestic fowl, suggests that they were not of great importance in the economy of the site. All the wild species could have occurred locally, and the ducks and perhaps the corvids could have been eaten, though no butchery marks or signs of cooking were found. The presence of partial skeletons of the larger scavengers, buzzard and raven, and the high proportion of raven, may however point to some symbolic importance, perhaps connected with disposal of human remains. This pattern was also noted at Danebury (Coy 1984; Serjeantson 1991b).

Discussion

The economy of the settlement

The economy of the settlement was based on mixed farming, with cattle, sheep and pig as the major domestic animals; horses and dogs were also kept. Goat and domestic fowl occurred, but at very low frequency. The remains of wild animals form a very small proportion of the bone remains. The animals were of the Iron Age types familiar from other sites in the region. The age and sex structures of the flocks and herds suggest that maintenance was a priority, with most sheep killed relatively young for meat rather than kept to greater ages for wool, and that cattle were kept to greater ages because they were important for traction. Horses may not have been bred at the settlement, judging by the paucity of juvenile remains.

It is more than usually difficult to look at the proportions of different species because the figures vary quite widely by phase depending on method of quantification and inclusion of whole skeletons. Using the overall figures, sheep and cattle together make up 70–80% of the total, sheep generally outnumber cattle by 2 or 3 to 1, and pig numbers are no more than 10% of the total, except in the EIA where they are more frequent (but not if special deposits are excluded). Percentages of horse and dog also fluctuate, but not with any clear pattern. Using various combinations of species proportions, estimated meat weights, and age profiles as described above to allow for turnover, it is possible to estimate the meat weight contributions of the three major species. Because of their greater carcase weight, cattle contribute around two-thirds of the meat weight (±10%, depending on the assumptions), sheep contribute 15–30%, and pigs 5–15%.

The importance of animals does not depend on their meat alone. Carcases would have been fully utilized, providing hides, fleeces, fat, glue, and raw materials such as bone, horn and antler. These have been ignored in the calculations because they are more or less by-products from animals that would die anyway, but this does not mean they were not important. Equally, a scarce resource might assume a particular importance at particular times. For instance, a very small amount of fat may be of critical importance in the diet at a time of nutritional stress (Speth 1983), and pigs, for instance, might be valuable because they could provide this. Storage, and thus preservation, of products would be an important aspect of this, spreading the availability of, say, protein or fat outside the major season of production.

Animals also have their uses during their lifetimes. Sheep can provide wool, and sheep, cattle and horses could all potentially be milked. Cattle were also vital for traction and transport, and horses for transport – the pathology evidence suggests that they were not used for such heavy work as cattle. Pigs and dogs can also function as scavengers. Dogs could be valuable for guarding, herding and hunting. All the herbivores were also crucial to maintaining soil fertility: they would act as collectors of nutrients from areas that were only grazed, not cultivated. By collecting their dung and/or folding them on cultivated ground, people could apply these nutrients to growing crops. Without animals to renew fertility, the soil in this type of environment would soon be exhausted, and long-term settlement and exploitation of the area would be much less intensive.

Keeping several species of animal which use different resources both allows exploitation of different habitats – downs by sheep, wetter grasslands by cattle, woods (and waste) by pigs – and spreads the risk of depending on any one type of resource or animal.

Changes over time

There are changes in proportions of species between phases, but it is difficult to judge their significance because of the possibly distorting effect of large deposits and inconsistency between different methods of quantification. The NIF and epiphyses only methods show lower numbers of sheep relative to cattle+pig in the EIA, similar proportions in the MIA (if P159 is omitted; but much higher numbers if it is included), and numbers rising in the LIA, peaking in the first century, and lower in the Roman period. Relative to cattle only, sheep numbers rise to the first century and fall in the Roman period. The MNI method suggests a fairly steady rise in the proportion of sheep to cattle, or cattle+pig, across phases. The relative numbers of pig are higher by all methods in the EIA, but this effect disappears if special deposits (whole skeletons) are removed from the analysis. There is, therefore, uncertainty about differences between Iron Age periods, and a serious discrepancy between the methods for the Roman period, where the MNI method shows relatively fewer cattle than the other methods.

At Danebury there was a slight rise in the proportion of sheep over the Iron Age (Grant 1984a, 1991), but no great change in population structure: that is probably paralleled here (given the uncertainties of quantification). While it is not possible to be certain of the proportion of sheep relative to cattle in the Roman period at Suddern Farm, the sheep age structure did seem to be different, with more older animals, which could indicate a greater importance for wool in this period. While the Iron Age sheep husbandry would seem to be geared to the settlement's nutritional needs, in the Roman period wool, potentially an export product, assumed greater importance.

The cattle age structures suggested the possibility that meat production from cattle became more important in the later Iron Age, with more cattle slaughtered before 2–3 years old (which could also represent an increase in milk production). The data for the Roman period (though rather few) also suggest a peak in mortality before 4 years, which could represent slaughter for meat. If this was in fact coupled with a greater proportion of cattle being kept, the proportion of meat supplied by cattle would rise to *c*.80%, which would represent a considerable change in the economy in terms of both inputs and outputs.

Another difference between the Iron Age and Roman periods was the butchery technique. In the Iron Age (including the first century AD) butchery mainly proceeded by dismemberment and flesh stripping, and most of the butchery marks produced were cut marks, while in the Roman period chopping was much commoner. The bone was also noticeably more fragmentary in this period, possibly indicating more intensive use of carcases.

Finally, special deposits were not seen in the Roman period to the same extent as the Iron Age, if at all. Whether this is because of a change in the nature of the deposits excavated (because of e.g. a shift in activity areas) or a real change in behaviour is uncertain.

The charred plant remains
by Gill Campbell

Sixty-two samples were available for study. Of these 59 came from 20 pits ranging in date from the Early Iron Age to the third or fourth century AD. Another two samples were taken from a Roman oven and one from a scoop or hollow dated to cp 8/9. Eleven samples were selected for analysis following the usual procedure (see Volume 1). The results of the analysis are given in Table 3.21.

Results

Samples from Early Iron Age pits (cp 3–6)

Five of the sampled pits were dated to this period and samples from three of these pits were analysed. Pits phased up to cp 6, e.g. cp 3–6, are included in this section as they seem to form a coherent group.

The group is characterized by the presence of grass and cereal straw and tubers in addition to the more usual remains. Weed seeds tended to form the largest component in the assemblages with seeds of *Fallopia convolvulus* particularly frequent. One of the samples from layer 5 in pit P194 produced a single frond fragment of bracken. Several low-growing weeds were also present such as *Aphanes arvensis* (parsley piert) and *Anagallis arvensis* (scarlet pimpernel).

Samples from middle to late Middle Iron Age pits (cp 6, cp 6–7)

Four pits were sampled dating to this period, one dating to cp 6 (pit P132) and three to cp 6–7 (pits P92, P120, P140). Samples from pit P132 produced very little charred material. The sample from pit P92 did not contain any remains that could be identified. However it did produce a possible burnt concretion.

This may represent the contents of one of the pots found in this pit.

The samples from pit P140 produced very little material but those from pit P120 were more promising and the sample from layer 4 of this pit was analysed. It was very rich in weeds. Most of these weed seeds are typical arable weeds but some such as *Urtica dioica* (stinging nettle), *Hyoscyamus niger* (henbane), *Prunella vulgaris* (self-heal), *Gleochoma hederacea* (ground ivy), and *Onopordum acanthium* (Scotch thistle) associated with ruderal habitats such as hedgebanks and areas of rough ground. *Sambucus nigra* (elder), represented by three seeds in this sample, could have been growing in similar habitats.

Samples from Latest Iron Age pits (cp 8–9)

Five features dated to this period were sampled. The samples from pit P104 produced very well preserved charred remains in high concentration and two samples from this pit, sample 344 from layer 4 and sample 346 from layer 6 were analysed. The samples from the other four features also produced well preserved remains but in much lower concentrations. A single sample was analysed from each of these features.

In sample 335 from layer 3 in pit P89 weed seeds formed the largest component in the assemblage, some 60 per cent, while chaff fragments accounted for some 26 per cent and grain 14 per cent. Small grasses made up the majority of the weeds but members of the Polygonaceae were common including single seeds of *Rumex acetosa* (common sorrel) and *Rumex acetosella* (sheep's sorrel).

The sample from layer 1 in pit P128 was very different. There were very few weeds or chaff fragments. Barley grains were numerous in the sample, with hulled wheat grain also present, about half of which had germinated. In addition some fifty large legumes were recovered. Most could not be identified to species as they had lost both testa and hilum. However a few were sufficiently well preserved to be identified as pea. Some of these specimens were examined by Dr. Anne Butler (University College, London) who was able to confirm this identification and suggested that the seeds belonged to *Pisum sativum* ssp *sativum* or field pea. Also of interest was the single seed of *Anthemis cotula* (stinking mayweed).

The assemblage from layer 4 of pit P104 consisted mainly of spelt wheat with some hulled six-row barley and very few weeds. Some short spelt grains were recorded as well as a few possible emmer type grains. Emmer wheat chaff was absent.

Sample 346 from layer 6 of the same pit formed a complete contrast. Chaff accounted for some 80 per cent of the assemblage. Weeds were numerous and there was relatively little grain (3%). Most of the grain consisted of hulled barley but the odd naked grain was recorded. Barley chaff was also plentiful with some two-row barley rachis present as well as the more usual six-row. This once again probably represents variation within the six-row hulled barley population rather than presence of naked or two-row barley. Some 200 oat grains were also recovered and since some cultivated oat florets were also found it would seem likely that at least some if not all of this grain is from cultivated oat. Most of the wheat chaff would appear to be from spelt but some emmer chaff was also present with emmer type grain more numerous than spelt grain.

The weed assemblage was varied and included many poppies, at least three species, fumitory, and small legumes. A few species such as *Linum catharticum* (fairy flax) and *Ononis* cf. *repens* (common restharrow) are more typical of chalk grassland than arable fields. Also of interest were the few seeds of *Agrostemma githago* (corn cockle).

The sample from scoop F68 produced large numbers of charcoal fragments with very few other remains.

Samples from pits dated to cp 9

Two pits dated to this period were sampled. A single sample from layer 5 of pit P84 was analysed. Weeds made up 62 per cent of the assemblage, grain 27 per cent and chaff 12 per cent. The sample was similar to those from the Early Iron Age pits in that it contained culm nodes and bases etc., and tubers. Also in common with these pits a large component of the weed assemblage was made up of grasses with seeds of *Bromus* sp. (brome) particularly common.

Samples from Roman features

Six pits and one oven of Roman date were sampled. The samples from the oven produced numerous fragments of charcoal and some buds but no other remains. The samples from pits produced very little. One sample from a pit dated to the middle second century was analysed.

The sample contained spelt wheat chaff and hulled wheat grain as well as a little barley grain and a single barley rachis. Some oat grain, which could be from wild or cultivated oat was also recovered along with a small number of weed seeds.

Discussion

Spelt wheat and hulled six-row barley were the main crops throughout the history of the site. Short grain spelt wheat grains were recovered from both the early pits and the Latest Iron Age pits indicating that the spelt population was genetically diverse. Similar variation was exhibited by the barley recovered from the Latest Iron Age pits.

Traces of emmer wheat were found throughout the features. It is probably present as a contaminant. During the Latest Iron Age field pea and oat were also grown. In addition two weeds once regarded as

Roman introduction appear: *Agrostemma githago* and *Anthemis cotula* (Godwin 1975).

The presence of cereal and grass straw along with tubers in the samples from the early pits dated to cp 3–6 and in the cp 9 pit would suggest that crops were harvested along with their weeds by uprooting. The absence of this material in the samples dated from the Middle Iron Age and very late Iron Age may indicate a change in harvesting techniques. However the presence of low-growing weeds throughout the samples would argue against this case. There are two other possibilities either the material was not being brought to the site during these phases of occupation or it was not being burnt and therefore did not enter the archaeobotanical record.

There is some evidence from layer 6 of pit P104 that the by-products of threshing were present on the site in the Latest Iron Age. Over two thousand fragments of barley rachis were recovered from this sample. Since barley is a free-threshing cereal in terms of its processing, most of these are usually removed at threshing (Hillman 1984). However some would also be present in the chaff and cleaning store, i.e the by-products of winnowing and cleaning, and this may be the source of these fragments. As such it is possible that threshing took place off site while winnowing and cleaning took place at the settlement. Alternatively the by-products of winnowing, etc. could have been brought to the site from elsewhere for use as fuel, etc. Overall this assemblage might be interpreted as the remains of a crop of mixed barley and oats which was being dried prior to grinding with chaff and weeds from the cleanings or chaff store (Hillman 1984) being used as fuel.

The other assemblage from this pit, sample 344 from layer 4 would appear to represent a different stage of crop processing. The assemblage would appear to represent charred spelt still in its spikelet with barley present as a contaminant. It may have been charred whilst being parched prior to the removal of the grain from its spikelets.

Many of the samples from this site produced large weed assemblages. Sample 356 from layer 4 of pit P104 contained over a thousand making up 90% of the assemblage. Some of the weeds were more typical of ruderal habitats than of arable land. The close association of this sample with fragments of oven daub may help to provide an explanation. The material may be all that remains of plant material used as fuel or tinder in the oven. This may have included plant material cut or gathered from rough ground as well as chaff and weeds from crop processing, the relatively small assemblage of grain from the sample representing in turn some of the material that was dried or cooked in the oven.

Some of the other samples analysed also produced weed seeds more characteristic of other habitats than arable land. Sample 346 contained some species typical of chalk grassland, *Linum catharticum* (purging flax) and *Ononis* cf. *repens* (common restharrow).

Rumex acetosella (sheep's sorrel) (Sample 335) is confined to acid to circum-neutral soils and probably grew on the soils developed on gravels close to the river or on clay with flints (Jones 1984, 489). Its presence would suggest that these soils were exploited but given the preponderance of grasses in this sample it could indicate the use of this land for hay production or pasture rather than arable. The bracken from sample 382 may have been gathered from such areas.

Table 3.21.
Charred plant remains

TAXA			CP3	CP3–5	CP3–6	CP6–7	CP8–9	CP8–9	CP8–9	CP8–9	CP8–9	CP9	Roman mid 2nd C.
	Common name	sample context	358 P122/3*	382 P194/5*	362 P123/4*	356 P120/4*	335 P89/3*	363 P128/1	344 P104/4*	346 P104/6*	386 P68/1	332 P84/5*	340 F99/2
		context type	pit	pit	pit	pit	pit	pit	pit	pit	scoop	pit	pit
		fill cycle	2	2c	2c	2c	2c	2c	2c	2c	2a	2	2c
		% of sample sorted	100%	100%	100%	100%	100%	100%	3%	100%[1]	25%	100%	100%
Pteridium aquilinum (L.) Kuhn (frond)	bracken		–	1	–	–	–	–	–	–	–	–	–
Ranunculus acris/ repens/bulbosus	buttercup		6	1	–	7	–	–	–	–	1	–	–
Ranunculus Section *Ranunculus*	buttercup		–	–	–	1	1	–	–	–	–	–	–
Papaver argemone L.	long prickly-headed poppy		–	–	–	9	–	–	–	66	–	–	–
P. somniferum L.	opium poppy		–	–	–	1	5	–	–	91	–	1	–
P. cf. *somniferum* L.	opium poppy		–	1	–	–	–	–	–	–	–	–	–
P. rhoeas/dubium/ hybridium/lecoquii	poppy		–	–	1	9	–	–	–	135	–	–	–
Papaver sp.	poppy		–	–	1	4	–	–	–	21	–	–	–
Papaver sp. (capsule top)	poppy		–	–	1	–	–	–	–	1	–	–	–
cf. *Papaver* sp.	poppy		–	–	1	–	–	–	–	–	–	–	–
Fumaria sp.	fumitory		18	4	3	2	–	–	–	101	1	5	–
Brassica cf. *rapa* ssp. *sylvestris* (L.) Janchen	navew		–	–	–	–	–	–	–	–	–	1	–
B. cf. *nigra* (L.) Koch	black mustard		–	–	–	2	–	–	–	–	–	1	2
cf. *Brassica* sp.	mustard, cabbage, navew, etc.		–	–	–	1	–	–	–	–	–	1	–
Brassica/Sinapis sp.	mustard, cabbage, navew, charlock, etc.		–	2	–	–	–	–	–	–	–	–	3
Cruciferae (large) indet.			1	–	–	–	–	–	–	–	–	–	–
Viola cf. *arvensis* Murray	field pansy		–	–	1	–	–	–	–	–	–	–	–
Silene cf. *latifolia* ssp. *alba* (Miller) Greuter & Burdet	white campion		–	–	–	–	–	–	–	–	–	1	–
Silene sp.	campion		–	–	–	1	–	–	–	2	–	1	–
Agrostemma githago L.	corn cockle		–	–	–	–	–	–	–	5	–	–	–
Cerastium sp.	mouse-ear chickweed		–	–	–	3	–	–	–	–	–	–	–
Stellaria media gp.	chickweed		1	4	3	42	2	–	1	–	–	8	–
Caryophyllaceae (large) indet. (capsule frag.)			–	–	–	–	–	–	–	2	–	–	–
Caryophyllaceae indet.			–	–	1	7	1	–	–	1	–	–	1
cf. Caryophyllaceae indet.			–	1	–	–	–	–	–	2	–	–	–
Chenopodium cf. *album* L.	fat hen		–	–	–	4	–	1	–	–	–	4	–
Atriplex sp.	orache		14	12	3	57	3	1	1	26	–	4	–
Chenopodiaceae indet.			–	–	2	35	–	–	–	11	–	–	–
Linum catharticum L.	fairy flax		–	–	–	1	–	–	–	1	–	–	–
Medicago lupulina L.	black medick		–	3	–	24	–	–	–	13	–	–	–
Medicago type	medick, clover, etc.		3	3	2	19	–	–	2	76	–	2	1
cf. *Trifolium* sp.	clover, etc.		–	4	–	1	–	–	–	1	–	–	–
Pisum sativum L.	pea		–	–	–	–	–	5	–	–	–	–	–
Vicia/Lathyrus sp.	vetch or tare		–	2	1	1	6	2	1	–	–	–	11
cf. *Vicia/Lathyrus* sp.	vetch or tare		–	–	1	–	–	–	–	–	–	–	–
Vicia/Lathyrus/Pisum sp.	large legume		–	–	–	–	–	41	–	–	–	–	–
Ononis cf. *repens* L.	common restharrow		–	–	–	–	–	–	–	1	–	–	–
Leguminosae (large) indet.	large legume		–	–	–	2	–	–	–	–	–	–	–
Leguminosae (small) indet.	small legume		6	33	9	88	6	–	–	94	–	10	3
cf. Leguminosae (small) indet.	small legume		–	–	–	10	–	–	–	–	–	–	–
Potentilla/Fragaria sp.			–	–	–	–	–	–	–	–	–	1	–
Aphanes arvensis L.	parsley-piert		1	7	14	22	–	–	–	8	–	3	–
Sanguisorba minor ssp. *minor* Scop.	salad burnet		1	–	–	–	–	–	–	–	–	–	–
cf. *S. minor* ssp. *minor* Scop.	salad burnet		–	–	–	–	–	–	–	–	–	1	–

TAXA		CP3	CP3–5	CP3–6	CP6–7	CP8–9	CP8–9	CP8–9	CP8–9	CP8–9	CP9	Roman mid 2nd C.
Common name	*sample context*	358 P122/3*	382 P194/5*	362 P123/4*	356 P120/4*	335 P89/3*	363 P128/1	344 P104/4*	346 P104/6*	386 P68/1	332 P84/5*	340 F99/2
	context type fill cycle	pit 2	pit 2c	pit 2c	pit 2c	pit 2c	pit 2c	pit 2c	pit 2c	scoop 2a	pit 2	pit 2c
	% of sample sorted	100%	100%	100%	100%	100%	100%	3%	100%[1]	25%	100%	100%
cf. *Prunus/Crataegus* type (thorn)	sloe/damson/plum/ bullace/ hawthorn, etc.	–	–	–	–	1	–	–	–	–	–	–
Torilis nodosa (L.) Gaertner	knotted hedge-parsley	–	3	–	6	–	–	–	–	–	–	–
T. japonica (Houtt.) DC	upright hedge-parsley	–	–	–	4	–	–	–	–	–	–	–
Torilis sp.	hedge-parsley	–	–	–	–	–	–	–	18	–	–	–
Anthriscus/Torilis sp.	bur-chervil/hedge-parsley	–	–	–	2	–	–	–	–	–	–	–
Umbelliferae indet.		–	1	15	37	–	–	–	31	–	1	2
Euphorbia exigua L.	dwarf spurge	–	–	–	1	–	–	–	–	–	–	–
Polygonum aviculare agg.	knotgrass	2	–	–	3	–	1	1	–	–	1	–
cf. *P. aviculare* agg.	knotgrass	–	–	1	1	–	–	–	–	–	–	–
Polygonum sp.	bistort/knotgrass	1	–	1	–	–	–	–	–	–	–	–
Fallopia convolvulus (L.) A Löve	black bindweed	5	9	62	1	1	–	–	1	–	–	–
cf. *F. convolvulus* (L.) A Löve	black bindweed	–	–	–	2	–	–	–	–	–	–	–
Rumex acetosella agg.	sheep's sorrel	–	–	–	–	1	–	–	–	–	–	–
R. cf. *acetosa* L.	common sorrel	–	–	–	–	1	–	–	–	–	–	–
Rumex spp.	dock	10	6	8	32	7	1	–	9	1	4	1
Polygonaceae indet.		1	–	20	–	3	–	–	–	–	–	–
cf. Polygonaceae indet.		–	–	–	–	–	–	–	5	–	1	–
Urtica dioica L.	stinging nettle	–	–	–	64	–	–	–	–	–	–	–
Anagallis arvensis L.	scarlet pimpernel	3	–	–	–	–	–	–	–	–	–	–
Primulaceae indet.		–	–	–	–	–	–	–	1	–	–	–
Lithospermum arvense L.	corn gromwell	–	5	2	37	5	–	3	4	–	1	–
Hyoscyamus niger L.	henbane	–	–	–	8	–	–	–	–	–	–	–
Veronica cf. *arvensis* L.	wall speedwell	–	–	–	1	–	–	–	–	–	–	–
V. hederifolia L.	ivy-leaved speedwell	–	–	–	3	–	–	–	1	–	–	–
Euphrasia/Odontites sp.	eyebright/red bartsia	2	9	17	–	–	–	2	43	–	13	–
Prunella vulgaris L.	self-heal	–	–	–	1	–	–	–	–	–	1	–
cf. *Gleochoma hederacea* L.	ground-ivy	–	–	–	2	–	–	–	–	–	–	–
Labiatae (large) indet.		–	–	–	4	–	–	–	–	–	–	–
Plantago media/lanceolata	plantain	–	1	–	2	1	–	–	–	–	–	–
Sherardia arvensis L.	field madder	3	2	6	11	–	–	–	6	–	4	–
cf. *S. arvensis* L.	field madder	–	2	1	–	–	–	–	–	–	–	–
Galium cf. *aparine* L.	cleavers	6	2	26	22	3	2	–	19	2	5	2
Galium sp.	goosefoot, etc.	–	6	12	8	–	1	–	3	–	4	–
cf. *Galium* sp.	goosefoot, etc.	–	–	–	–	–	–	–	–	–	–	1
Sambucus nigra L.	elder	–	–	–	3	–	–	–	–	–	–	–
Valerianella rimosa Bast.	broad-fruited cornsalad	–	–	–	3	–	–	–	–	–	–	–
V. dentata (L.) Pollich	narrow-fruited cornsalad	–	2	1	22	1	–	1	11	–	9	–
Valerianella sp.	cornsalad	–	–	–	1	–	–	–	–	–	–	–
Anthemis arvensis L.	corn chamomile	–	–	1	254	–	–	–	21	–	1	–
A. cotula L.	stinking mayweed	–	–	–	–	–	1	–	–	–	–	–
Tripleurospermum sp.	mayweed	37	4	75	37	1	1	–	19	–	9	1
Carduus/Cirsium sp.	thistle	1	–	–	–	–	–	–	–	–	–	–
Onopordum acanthium L.	scotch thistle	–	–	–	1	–	–	–	–	–	–	–
Centaurea sp.	knapweed/cornflower	–	1	–	–	–	–	–	–	–	–	–
Compositae (large) indet.		–	–	–	2	–	–	–	–	–	–	–
Compositae (small) indet.		–	–	14	7	–	–	–	–	–	–	–
Eleocharis palustris type	spike-rush	1	–	–	–	–	–	–	–	–	–	–
Carex spp.	sedges	–	1	–	15	–	–	–	3	–	–	2
cf. *Carex* sp.	sedge	–	–	–	2	–	–	–	–	–	–	–
Cyperaceae indet.		–	–	1	1	–	–	–	–	–	–	–
Lolium sp.		–	–	–	1	–	–	–	62	–	–	–
Lolium/Festuca sp.		–	–	–	–	–	–	–	–	–	39	–
Poa annua type	annual poa	2	1	3	1	1	–	–	3	–	2	1
cf. *Poa annua* type	annual poa	–	–	–	3	–	–	–	–	–	–	–
Bromus sterilis type	brome	–	–	–	2	–	–	–	–	–	–	–
B. hordeaceus type	brome	39	–	–	1	–	3	12	4	–	16	–
Bromus not *sterilis*	brome	19	43	26	14	4	1	–	9	1	40	–
cf. *Bromus* sp.	brome	–	17	13	–	–	–	–	–	–	19	–
Avena fatua/sativa (floret base)	oat	3	–	–	–	–	–	–	–	–	–	–
A. sativa/strigosa (floret)	cultivated oat	–	–	–	–	–	–	1	4	–	–	–
Avena sp.	oat	–	–	–	–	1	–	2	204	–	2	–

TAXA	Common name	CP3 358 P122/3* pit 2 100%	CP3–5 382 P194/5* pit 2c 100%	CP3–6 362 P123/4* pit 2c 100%	CP6–7 356 P120/4* pit 2c 100%	CP8–9 335 P89/3* pit 2c 100%	CP8–9 363 P128/1 pit 2c 100%	CP8–9 344 P104/4* pit 2c 3%	CP8–9 346 P104/6* pit 2c 100%[1]	CP8–9 386 P68/1 scoop 2a 25%	CP9 332 P84/5* pit 2 100%	Roman mid 2nd C. 340 F99/2 pit 2c 100%
Avena sp. (twisted awn)	oat	–	–	–	–	–	–	–	3319	–	–	14
Avena sp. (floret base)	oat	–	–	–	–	–	–	–	10	–	1	–
cf. *Avena* sp.	oat	–	–	–	–	–	–	–	10	–	1	–
Arrhenatherum elatius spp. *bulbosum* (Wild.) Schubler & Marten (tuber)	onion-couch	5	–	–	–	–	–	–	–	–	2	–
Gramineae (large) indet.	grass	15	44	14	17	4	1	1	65	–	25	8
Gramineae (small) indet.	grass	30	3	25	251	113	–	6	421	19	39	12
cf. Gramineae (small) indet.	grass	1	–	1	–	–	–	–	–	–	–	–
Triticum dicoccum (Schrank) Schubl. (grain)	emmer wheat	–	–	–	–	–	–	–	12	–	–	–
T. dicoccum (Schrank) Schubl. (glume base)	emmer wheat	1	2	1	1	–	–	–	12	–	–	–
T. cf. *dicoccum* (Schrank) Schubl. (grain)	emmer wheat	–	–	–	–	–	–	7	8	–	–	–
T. cf. *dicoccum* (Schrank) Schubl. (glume base)	emmer wheat	2	1	1	–	1	–	–	–	–	1	–
T. cf. *dicoccum* (Schrank) Schubl. (spikelet fork)	emmer wheat	–	1	–	–	–	–	–	–	–	–	–
T. spelta L. (grain)	spelt wheat	–	2	–	4	–	5	235	1	–	–	–
T. spelta L. (short grain)	spelt wheat	–	–	–	–	–	–	35	2	–	–	–
T. spelta L. (glume base)	spelt wheat	12	35	4	37	15	1	134+9[2]	808	–	12	3
T. spelta L. (spikelet fork)	spelt wheat	–	2	1	1	–	–	34+6[2]	40	–	1	–
T. spelta L. (rachis internode)	spelt wheat	3	–	–	1	3	–	–	440	–	–	–
T. cf. *spelta* L. (grain)	spelt wheat	–	1	–	–	–	–	14	–	–	–	–
T. cf. *spelta* L. (short grain)	spelt wheat	–	2	–	–	–	–	3	–	–	–	–
T. cf. *spelta* L. (glume base)	spelt wheat	4	7	–	2	–	–	10	116	–	2	1
T. cf. *spelta* L. (terminal spikelet fork)	spelt fork	–	–	–	–	–	–	1	–	–	–	–
T. cf. *spelta* L. (rachis internode)	spelt wheat	–	1	–	–	–	–	–	–	–	–	–
T. dicoccum/spelta (grain)	emmer or spelt wheat	–	14	6	7	2	8	317	8	–	–	4
T. dicoccum/spelta (grain – germinated)	emmer or spelt wheat	–	–	–	–	–	8	–	–	–	–	–
T. dicoccum/spelta (glume base)	emmer or spelt wheat	140	67	55	63	15	1	75	3343	2	23	32
T. dicoccum/spelta (terminal glume base)	emmer or spelt wheat	–	–	–	–	–	–	2[2]	–	–	–	–
T. dicoccum/spelta (spikelet fork)	emmer or spelt wheat	25	19	6	–	–	–	6+4[2]	117	–	5	7
T. cf. *dicoccum/spelta* (grain)	emmer or spelt	–	–	–	–	–	–	–	–	–	6	–
T. cf. *dicoccum/spelta* (glume base)	emmer or spelt	–	–	–	–	14	–	–	–	–	–	–
Triticum, hexaploid sp. (rachis internode)	wheat	–	–	–	–	–	–	–	44	–	–	–
Triticum, hexaploid sp. (terminal rachis node)	wheat	–	–	–	–	–	–	–	2	–	–	–
Triticum, hexaploid sp. (basal rachis node)	wheat	–	–	–	–	–	–	–	8	–	–	–
Triticum sp. (grain)	wheat	22	45	12	8	1	31	161	2	2	36	13
Triticum sp. (glume base)	wheat	11	11	3	–	6	–	3	565	1	4	45
Triticum sp. (spikelet fork)	wheat	3	–	–	–	–	–	7	44	–	–	6
Triticum sp. (rachis node)	wheat	2	–	–	–	–	–	–	–	–	–	–
Triticum sp. (rachis internode)	wheat	4	–	–	–	–	–	–	159	–	–	–
Triticum sp. (basal rachis frag.)	wheat	–	–	–	–	–	–	1	–	–	–	–
cf. *Triticum* sp. (grain)	wheat	–	–	–	–	–	–	–	2	–	3	2
cf. *Triticum* sp. (awn – near base)	wheat	–	–	–	–	–	–	–	320	–	–	–
cf. *Triticum* sp. (rachis internode)	wheat	–	–	–	–	–	–	–	1	–	–	–
Triticum/Secale sp. (awn frag.)	wheat/rye	–	–	–	–	–	–	82	1	–	–	–

TAXA	Common name	sample context	CP3	CP3–5	CP3–6	CP6–7	CP8–9	CP8–9	CP8–9	CP8–9	CP8–9	CP9	Roman mid 2nd C.
		sample	358	382	362	356	335	363	344	346	386	332	340
		context	P122/3*	P194/5*	P123/4*	P120/4*	P89/3*	P128/1	P104/4*	P104/6*	P68/1	P84/5*	F99/2
		context type	pit	pit	pit	pit	pit	pit	pit	pit	scoop	pit	pit
		fill cycle	2	2c	2c	2c	2c	2c	2c	2c	2a	2	2c
		% of sample sorted	100%	100%	100%	100%	100%	100%	3%	100%[1]	25%	100%	100%
Hordeum vulgare ssp. *vulgare* L. (rachis)	six-row barley		6	4	–	–	1	–	3	782	1	–	–
H. vulgare ssp. *distichum* L. (rachis)	two-row barley		–	–	–	–	–	–	–	16	–	–	–
Hordeum sp. (hulled straight grain)	hulled barley		–	1	1	–	1	15	27	48	–	1	–
Hordeum sp. (hulled twisted grain)	hulled barley		–	2	–	1	–	34	44	75	–	1	–
Hordeum sp. (hulled grain)	hulled barley		1	3	6	1	2	84	92	54	–	5	–
Hordeum sp. (cf. hulled straight grain)	hulled barley		–	–	–	–	–	2	–	–	–	–	–
Hordeum sp. (straight naked grain)	naked barley		–	–	–	–	–	–	1	–	–	–	–
Hordeum sp. (cf. naked straight grain)	barley		–	–	–	–	–	1	–	–	–	–	–
Hordeum sp. (grain)	barley		6	5	–	2	–	–	26	23	2	2	4
Hordeum sp. (grain – germinated)	barley		–	–	–	–	–	–	–	–	–	–	1
Hordeum sp. (awn)	barley		–	–	–	–	–	–	–	17	8	–	–
Hordeum sp. (rachis)	barley		2	10	–	1	2	–	4	806	–	–	1
cf. *Hordeum* sp. (grain)	barley		2	38	–	–	–	–	–	–	–	3	–
cf. *Hordeum* sp. (rachis)	barley		3	–	–	1	1	–	–	16	–	–	–
cf. *Hordeum* sp. (basal rachis node)	barley		–	–	–	–	–	–	–	4	–	–	–
Secale/Hordeum sp. (rachis)	barley		5	5	4	–	7	–	3	679	–	1	–
Cereales indet. (grain)			49	136	122	14	32	110	79	3	54	74	20
Cereales indet. (grain – germinated)			–	–	–	–	1	–	–	–	–	–	–
Cereales indet. (glume base/rachis)			42	4	–	1	10	–	–	271	–	1	50
Cereal size (embryo – unsprouted)			–	–	4	–	–	–	17	5	–	–	–
Cereal size (culm node)			16	39	6	–	–	–	–	1	–	15	–
Cereal size (culm base)			6	16	–	–	–	–	–	–	–	3	–
Cereal size (rhizome)			14	27	–	–	4	–	–	–	–	22	–
Cereal size (culm base/rhizome)			–	–	11	–	–	–	–	–	–	–	–
Gramineae size (culm node)			39	36	5	–	–	–	–	–	–	–	–
Gramineae size (culm base)			1	–	–	–	–	–	–	–	–	9	–
Gramineae size (rhizome)			129	172	14	–	–	–	–	–	–	63	2
tuber type 1			2	2	–	–	–	–	–	–	–	2	–
tuber indet.			–	2	4	–	–	–	–	–	–	9	–
bud			1	1	–	2	–	–	–	6	–	–	–
abscisson pads			–	–	–	–	–	–	–	4	–	–	–
catkin			1	–	–	–	–	–	–	–	–	–	–
herbage			–	++	++	–	–	–	–	++++	–	–	+
IGNOTA			3	11	25	74	4	–	3	21	2	21	6
mineralized IGNOTA			–	1	–	–	–	–	–	–	–	–	+
Total number of items identified			794	965	682	1467	288	362	1497	13841	88	610	262
Items per litre			31.76	38.6	27.28	58.68	11.52	14.48	1999	553.64	14.08	24.4	10.48

1. Only 12.5 % of the 1–0.5 mm fraction of this sample was sorted. The number of specimens identified from this fraction was multiplied up accordingly.
2. Fragments with part of the rachis still attached.

6 *Overview*

The settlement at Suddern Farm has provided evidence of occupation spanning the period from the eighth or seventh century BC to the fourth century AD. For part of that time the nucleus of the settlement was enclosed by one or more ditches.

The structural sequence

Before attempting to outline the chronological development of the site it is necessary briefly to consider the problem of dating. It is self-evident, but worth restating, that the material from the filling of a ditch reflects the date after which the ditch ceased to be a fully maintained boundary feature. Thus the initial digging of a ditch may date to any period before the earliest date when silting began to be allowed to accumulate. The three ditches which surrounded the nucleus of the settlement exemplify the problem. The Middle Ditch is probably the earliest. Its profile, which opens into a splayed V-shape towards the top, suggests that a period of time had elapsed, during which the ditch had been kept clear of silt, before the final silting was allowed to accumulate. The only dating evidence comprises a few sherds of undiagnostic Early Iron Age pottery in the top of the silt before the hollow of the ditch was levelled with fresh chalk rubble. On this evidence the ditch is likely to belong to the Early Iron Age but it could have been dug at any time within cp 1–5.

The Inner and Outer Ditches are far more massive. The Inner Ditch shows some signs of having been recut and its splayed profile would suggest that a long period of erosion and clearance had preceded the final phase of silting which began, according to the pottery assemblage, in the mid first century BC and was completed with tips of rubbish in the mid first century AD. Thus the ditch would have been in use in the early first century BC and could have been dug even earlier.

The Outer Ditch is more problematical. In the 1991 section it proved to be flat bottomed with comparatively steep sides suggesting that it had not experienced a long period of erosion and clearance. This point is confirmed by the thick fresh chalk shatter which makes up its basal filling. Thus, as it stands, the evidence could be interpreted as a single phase of ditch cutting followed immediately by the erosion of the sides and the uninterrupted silting of the ditch. The layer immediately above the primary silting produced pottery of the middle of the first century AD.

On this evidence it might be argued that the Outer Ditch was dug after the Inner Ditch had been abandoned. The reality, however, may have been far more complex if it is allowed that the final profile of the Outer Ditch was a late recut of a slightly smaller earlier ditch. Some hint that this may have been the case is given by the magnetometer survey (Fig. 3.4 simplified in Fig. 3.5). This shows that the Outer Ditch, at the NE corner of the enclosure, closely followed the line of the earlier Middle Ditch. At the NW corner, where a principal entrance was sited, there is a clear indication of the recutting of the Outer Ditch to the west of the entrance, suggesting that in the latest phase the ditch was realigned 10 m or so to the SE of the earlier line.

Taken together the evidence from the magnetometer survey and the 1991 ditch excavation would indicate the following *possible* sequence (Fig. 3.99):

1   Middle Ditch and early version of Outer Ditch.

These are not necessarily contemporary. It could be that the Middle Ditch was dug first and the early version of the Outer Ditch succeeded it the chalk from its digging being used to complete the filling of the Middle Ditch. In this scenario period 1 would be subdivided into:
1a   Middle Ditch dug
1b   Early Outer Ditch dug and Middle Ditch filled.

2   Inner Ditch dug and maintained.

The Inner Ditch lies within the earliest circuit but does not follow its line too closely.

3   Outer Ditch redug.

The new ditch followed the line of the early Outer Ditch except at the NW entrance where divergence occurred. This would imply that the early Outer Ditch was still visible either as a partially silted hollow or a hedge line, or both.

In the sequence as outlined there may well have been a long period of time between phase 1b and phase 2.

Turning now to the question of the triple linear ditch examined in 1996, it is evident that the centre ditch and the eastern ditch are early in the sequence and may, most appropriately, be placed within period 1 of the enclosure sequence. It is tempting to suggest that the two linears may be correlated with the two phases of period 1. However, if it is accepted that the Outer Ditch of the enclosure was preceded by an earlier version (called period 1b above) then both the central and eastern linear ditches must pre-date it and therefore must be assigned to period 1a. The simplest explanation would be to see the central linear ditch as being continuous with the Middle Ditch of the west side of the enclosure. This would allow the end of the eastern linear to align roughly with the end of the Middle Ditch on the south side of the enclosure. The suggested arrangement (Fig. 3.99) has close similarities to the earliest phase of Danebury (Cunliffe 1995, fig. 3).

How long this arrangement lasted is unclear but the fact that the central linear was recut, possibly on several occasions, suggests that some elements of the system retained their significance and were maintained. That the quarry hollow, and its cemetery, destroyed the eastern linear but appears to have respected the central linear is a further indication of the longevity of the system.

The relationship of the hypothetical early version of the Outer Ditch of the enclosure to the linears is unclear. There are two plausible possibilities: either the enclosure ditch cut through the linears and the quarry, or it was interrupted at this point respecting the linears. On balance this latter explanation would seem to be the more reasonable but there is no way in which the matter can be further tested.

The western linear ditch would appear to be considerably later. It shows little sign of recutting and contained pottery of the first century AD. On these grounds it is likely to belong to the same general phase as the latest cutting of the Outer Ditch of the enclosure, a suggestion supported by the fact that it terminates just before the outer lip of the ditch.

Finally the possibility that a south gate was provided in phase 2 and phase 3 is worth considering. The magnetometer survey suggests the possibility of a road through the enclosure and the, admittedly obscure, air photographic evidence would allow there to have been a gate.

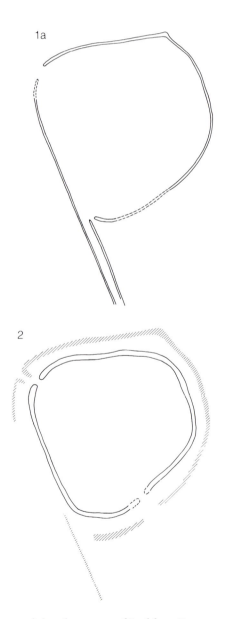
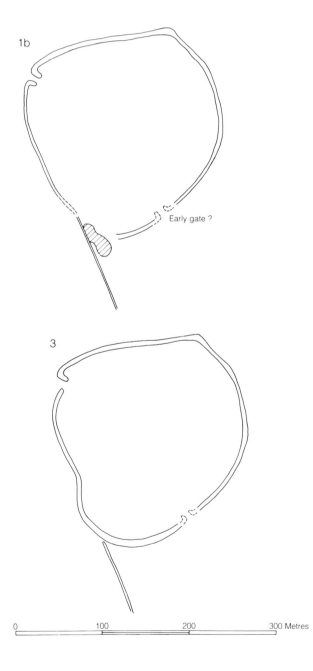

Fig. 3.99 Suggested development of Suddern Farm

Having presented a structural sequence based on the enclosure ditches and the linear ditches we may now consider the development of the settlement in broad chronological terms.

The Earliest Iron Age to the early Middle Iron Age (cp 1–cp 6)

The earliest occupation is represented by a limited assemblage of cp 1–2 pottery much of which was found in the rectangular pit P91. Thereafter the number of pits of cp 3–6 increases considerably (Fig. 3.29). They conform to the normal range of types and fills recorded elsewhere in the region. It is probably simplest to regard the sequence of occupation as continuous throughout this period (c.750–300 BC) with activity intensifying through time (assuming that the excavated sample is a fair reflection of the total occupation).

This early phase of occupation may reasonably be correlated with periods 1a and 1b of the enclosure ditch sequence.

The animal bones reflect an economy based on mixed farming with cattle, sheep and pig as the major animals. In broad terms cattle and sheep together amounted to 70–80% of the total with sheep two or three times more numerous than cattle. The sheep seem to have been reared primarily for meat with wool as a secondary product. The charred plant remains show that the agrarian economy was dominated by the production of spelt wheat and hulled six-row barley. There are indications that the crop was harvested by uprooting in the early phases but that cutting may have become more common in the early Middle Iron Age.

A matter of considerable interest is the treatment of the dead during this period. Two aspects of disposal are reflected in the archaeological record. Within the enclosure only a few isolated human bones were found in pits (four instances in cp 3–4 and one in cp 6). This contrasts dramatically with the 'cemetery' found in the quarry hollow just outside the enclosure where 15 more or less complete skeletons were found buried in individually cut graves together with a quantity of other human bones representing earlier disturbed burials. In all it is estimated that the cemetery could have held 300 adults, 80 children and 180 neonatal or very young infants.

The evidence from Suddern Farm is of considerable importance for understanding attitudes to death in the Iron Age of the region. It shows for the first time that regular burial grounds were in use and underlines the fact that bodies and body parts found in pits within the settlement reflect only one aspect of the complex rituals associated with the *rites de passage* of death.

The Middle Iron Age hiatus

The ceramic assemblage indicates that there was a cessation of occupation in cp 7 (c.270–50 BC). The suggestion rests upon the virtual absence of decorated saucepan pots and associated wares made in flint-tempered fabrics – an assemblage so prolific at nearby Danebury. In this Suddern Farm is similar to Nettlebank Copse and Houghton Down. The question of whether the absence of the typical cp 7 assemblage implies a chronological gap, or can be explained in other ways has been fully considered elsewhere (pp. 66–7). Suffice it to say that, on balance, abandonment is thought to be the more likely explanation.

The implication for Suddern Farm is that the early version of the Outer Ditch of the enclosure remained evident in some way throughout the period of abandonment as a partially silted hollow with a bank on the inside perhaps supporting a hedge. In all probability the line of the central linear was also marked by a hedge. If so it probably grew along its western side, the other side being occupied with the quarry and its cemetery.

The Late Iron Age to early Roman period (cp 8–first century AD)

Occupation recommenced some time towards the middle of the first century BC. In the area excavation this is represented by a number of pits and other small hollows (Fig. 3.30) producing typical Late Iron Age pottery assemblages of cp 8–9. It was probably at the beginning of the reoccupation that the Inner Ditch of the enclosure was dug inside the line of the earlier long-abandoned earthworks. Its profile and silting suggest that it was maintained for some time but began to silt up in the late first century BC. In the early decades of the first century AD tips of rubbish were being thrown into the top of the partially silted ditch. The deposit included sherds of amphorae and copies of Gallo-Belgic beakers indicating that a range of non-local goods were available to the occupants. One point of particular note is that more than 25% of the pottery comes from the Poole Harbour region. This implies that long-distance trade was now well established.

The economy of the settlement, as reflected in the animal bones, is much the same as in the earlier period but with an increase in the number of sheep relative to cattle. Cattle age structure suggests that meat production became more important in this period.

The charred plant remains indicate that spelt wheat and hulled six-row barley continued to be the main crops. The sample from P104 showed that the products of threshing were present on the site though this does not necessarily mean that threshing took place here since the waste could have been brought in for fuel or animal feed.

It is possible that the decision to throw rubbish into the Inner Ditch followed the recutting of the old Outer Ditch on a more massive scale some time in the early first century AD. Whether the redefence of the settlement was occasioned by the threat of the Roman invasion or was unrelated, pre-dating it by a decade or two, it is difficult to say but in any event the ditch does not seem to have been maintained and was left to silt up naturally. Internally the occupation of the Late Iron Age continued without a break into the second half of the first century AD.

Behaviour patterns involving the placing of propitiatory offerings in pits continued throughout the Late Iron Age and the use of human remains seems to have increased at this time. Two partial bodies were found in pits: one (P78) lacked arms and lower legs and had been killed by a sword thrust through the lower abdomen, the second (P119) lacking the lower limbs was partially cremated and buried along with large quantities of animal bone and pottery. Together these burials indicate something of the complexity of the belief patterns underlying ritual behaviour.

Early Roman occupation

It is to some extent arbitrary to separate the early Roman occupation from the preceding period, not least because occupation appears to have been continuous, but certain changes which took place in the late first century mark a break with the past. The most evident change was that the enclosure ditch no longer served as a significant boundary to the settlement and in the 1996 excavation there is evidence that its hollow was deliberately filled and levelled with chalk rubble. In the 1991 section a cremation burial in a pot of second century type was dug into the ditch fill. Another feature of change is that the classic storage pits were no longer in use though smaller and shallower pits were still being dug.

One of the new features introduced in the Roman period were the fenced enclosures found in the 1991 excavation (Fig. 3.30). Dating to the early Roman period is uncertain since, while none of the post-holes of the fence lines produced late Roman pottery, the possibility of a late Roman date must be allowed. Some, at least, of the ovens found within the fenced enclosures were of early Roman date.

In the 1996 area it was possible to distinguish several early Roman features including a narrow fence slot and a rectangular timber building. A group of pits, mostly unexcavated, may also have been of this date.

The nature of the early Roman occupation is difficult to characterize given that such a comparatively small sample of it was excavated and its boundaries have not been defined.

Late Roman occupation

Features of late Roman date were found in the excavations of 1991 and 1996. The 1991 area excavation produced several groups of small bread ovens together with a series of large subrectangular hollows cut (or worn) into the surface of the chalk. Since there is no structural evidence associated with these hollows they are best interpreted as open 'working floors' though there is nothing to suggest what activities were practised. Three similar features were found in the 1996 area where there was also evidence of a nearby trackway, worn into a hollow and subsequently metalled with flints. The only other features of note were the inhumation burial dug into the filling of the Outer Ditch and the corn-drying oven.

The late Roman occupation reflects a range of domestic activities appropriate to a rural settlement. There is little to indicate a status above a peasant level but it remains a possibility that the excavation chanced upon a zone of peripheral activities associated with a villa. Some slight support for this view is given by the discovery of hexagonal stone roofing slabs found reused in some of the ovens and various types of tiles scattered about the site.

The animal bones suggest that cattle had become important in the Roman period with the slaughter pattern geared to meat production. Taken overall cattle now provided some 80% of the total meat yield. Butchery techniques had changed when compared with the Iron Age with the greater use of the chopper for cutting joints. Greater fragmentation also implies that the carcase was more intensively used.

The date of the late Roman settlement may be indicated by the 25 coins recovered. Of these more than half fall in the period 348–402. The relative scarcity of coins belonging to the period 260–86 (normally prolific on British sites) and of coins minted between 330–48 suggest that the main phase of occupation lay in the second half of the fourth century. The possibility, therefore, is that there may have been a gap in occupation between the mid third and mid fourth centuries but again it is worth remembering that only a small area of the settlement has been sampled and it may not be typical of the occupation as a whole.

Finally the discovery of a small fragment of a decorated buckle plate of the early–mid sixth century is an intriguing hint of Saxon activity in the immediate vicinity.

The site at Suddern Farm reflects human settlement and endeavour over a period of 1000–1300 years though there may have been brief periods of abandonment during this time. Throughout the first part of this period from the seventh century BC to the mid first century AD the settlement was enclosed. Thereafter the ditched boundaries were abandoned and the area of occupation spread. From the small sample excavated it is difficult to chart the changing status of the settlement and the fortunes of its inhabitants but the consistency of its pattern of enclosures in the Iron Age and the maintenance of the linear boundaries associated with it suggest that it was a significant feature of the landscape and the massiveness of the enclosure ditches in the Late Iron Age may be indicative of its enhanced social status at this time. That the site was maintained throughout the Roman period may suggest some element of continuity in land holding.

7 Appendix

Commentary on the geophysical survey
(Fig. 3.4) by Andy Payne

The plough-levelled settlement site at Suddern Farm lies on a low spur of chalk at NGR SU 280377, 4 km to the west of Danebury. The site was first recorded by aerial photography in 1976 (Palmer 1984, 112) and consists of a roughly circular multiple-ditched enclosure (about 4 hectares in area including the ditches) constructed at a focal point on an extensive system of linear ditches. The site was selected for excavation in order to attempt to determine its status, function and evolution in relation to the larger hillforts and smaller enclosed settlements in the region. Detail of the internal utilization of the enclosure was generally lacking on the aerial photographic evidence, and it was hoped that magnetometer survey would be able to provide an enhanced level of information on the layout and nature of occupation of the site in advance of excavation. A sufficient area was surveyed in 1991 to investigate the form of the ditches defining the enclosure circuit and to assess the character of the internal area.

Enclosure ditches

In the magnetometer survey, the enclosure is defined by three concentric linear anomalies along most of its circuit. Two are evidently substantial ditches around 5 m wide at the top and roughly 10 m apart. Between them a narrower linear feature is present. These anomalies are interrupted at the north-western corner of the enclosure, marking the position of an entrance. Here the arrangement of the anomalies shows something of the complexity of the development of the enclosure features, suggesting several phases of ditch construction and recutting or modification (several different lines of ditches are recognizable that cannot all belong to the same period).

Excavation demonstrated that the inner and outer features were both massive ditches (F64 and F66), while the middle feature (F65) proved to be a smaller ditch earlier than the others (not a palisade trench as originally suspected). Where it was sectioned, the middle ditch varied in profile from 2.5 m wide at the top and 1.4 m deep to 3.4 m wide and 1.7 m deep (hinting that the ditch may have been recut during its life). In its final form it was allowed to silt naturally,

but at a later date was filled to the top with freshly cut chalk rubble (probably when the bigger internal and external flanking ditches were dug). The presence of the chalk rubble in the uppermost fill of the ditch would account for the relatively weak magnetic signal from this feature, which is only just above the threshold of detection in places.

Although different in profile, both the inner and outer ditches were of similar massive proportions (around 6 m wide at the top and 3 m deep). Where they were sectioned, the upper fills both included dumps of occupation rubbish containing organic material, ash, charcoal, burnt clay and broken pottery. The presence of this material explains the clarity of the magnetic response to these features, and areas where the magnetic anomaly from the ditch is locally more intense may indicate particular concentrations of magnetically enhanced material derived from occupation in the buried ditch fills (for example along the west and north-east sections of the inner ditch).

Excavation has demonstrated that the ditch features were not all in use at the same time, and the narrower middle ditch is probably the earlier of the three (perhaps contemporary with earliest occupation of the site belonging to the seventh century BC). The enclosure appears to have been redefined by one or both of the massive ditches in the Middle Iron Age (probably during the third or second century BC) following a period of abandonment. The site continued in use until the early first century AD when occupation was clearly of a high status and the rubbish accumulation in the inner ditch was taking place. The site appears to have been reoccupied again in the second half of the Roman period by a simple farming community which used the outer ditch for rubbish disposal. The cumulative effect of all this activity over many centuries is clearly reflected by the high density of occupation features mapped by magnetometry within the enclosure.

Internal occupation

The survey covered the northern three-quarters of the interior of the enclosure and revealed a multitude of positive anomalies representing pits and other occupation features packed together sufficiently densely to suggest intercutting and therefore sustained activity. A wide roadway is also evident crossing the interior of the site from the south-east to the entrance in the north-west corner of the enclosure. As at Bury Hill, the roadway is partially defined by an absence of other anomalies, but it has also produced a weak positive anomaly along part of its course. This indicates that the track survives as a silted-up feature heavily worn into the surface of the underlying natural chalk bedrock by passing traffic over a long period (similar to the southern linear at New Buildings (see below)). Because the road corridor has been avoided by occupation features, and the enclosure seems to have been designed with respect to it, the road may well have functioned throughout the lifetime of the settlement and perhaps after.

The 20 x 60 m area of excavation placed in the interior of the enclosure recovered evidence of a wide variety of occupation features cut into the natural chalk. These included (in order of the ability of the magnetometer to detect them): pits, quarry complexes, shallow scoops, small ovens, gullies, post-holes and stake-holes spanning four phases from the Early Iron Age to the Roman period with intervening phases of abandonment. The sheer variety and density of the occupation features represented in the excavated area provide a rare opportunity to compare geophysical instrument response with a wide range of different anomaly sources in the ground.

The majority of the features detected by the magnetometer were Iron Age pits (some 50–60 in the excavated area alone) of circular and rectangular plan dug 1–2 m into the chalk bedrock. A number of them retained their characteristic bell-shaped profile. Most had been filled with a combination of natural silting and erosion and the deliberate deposition of rubbish. They generally produced positive anomalies in the range of 4–6 nT. Good examples are P155 (Early Iron Age: 5 nT) and P92 (Late Iron Age: 5.5 nT). In addition to pits, several quarry complexes and some shallow hollows belonging to the Iron Age phases were also detected, but as weaker anomalies of around +2 nT.

Shallow Roman pits such as P66 and P125, present in small numbers in the excavated area, produced anomalies in the range of 7–8 nT, stronger and sharper in profile than their Iron Age predecessors. The main features characteristic of the Roman phase of occupation were 4–5 m wide shallow subrectangular hollows of unknown purpose (cut 20–30 cm into the chalk and filled with grey soil) and small ovens of hourglass plan. Both appear to be less susceptible to magnetic detection than the other types of feature found on the site. In spite of their shallow depth, the hollows were registered as slight positive anomalies while the survey apparently failed to detect the presence of the ovens. The lack of magnetic response over the ovens is surprising, but their small size must be a limiting factor. Similar ovens of Roman date also failed to register appreciable anomalies in the magnetometer survey at Houghton Down (see below). Analysis of the excavation results showed that the detection of the Roman period post-holes had been very selective and influenced by whether or not they lay directly beneath the line of an instrument traverse. Two post-holes less than 50 cm in diameter (situated 3 m north of pit P204 in the eastern part of the excavation) were resolved as very localized increases of about 1 nT in the magnetic field (just above the threshold of instrument noise). The reason these were detected is probably because they lay directly beneath the path of a magnetometer traverse across the site.

Further comparison of the plan of excavated features and the magnetometer data shows that anomalies from closely grouped individual pits and intercutting pits tend to coalesce into single composite anomalies. The results from Suddern Farm emphasize that compared to excavation, geophysical survey can only provide a relatively coarse picture representing a palimpsest of the main features resulting from the cumulative effect of activity on a site. The sheer density of activity revealed by the survey suggests prolonged occupation, but there are few clues to the actual phases of development involved. With the exception of the Roman pits it is impossible to differentiate groups of features belonging to any one phase of activity, although there seems to be some bias towards the detection of the widespread Early Iron Age pits (the excavated Middle and Late Iron Age pits generally show up less clearly in the data, possibly due to differences in size or composition). Only 35% of the features within the trench produced well defined anomalies and a further 27% only faint anomalies. Therefore 38% of features were not resolved, probably because they were too shallow and ephemeral (about 40% of the features were less than 30 cm in cross-section).

1996 survey

A second more limited excavation was carried out at Suddern Farm in 1996 to explore the junction of the enclosure with the group of triple linear ditches that approach the monument from the south. Magnetometer survey of a 60 m square area, south of the modern hedge-line crossing the site, successfully located the parallel ditches at the point where they articulated with the boundary ditches of the enclosure. This information enabled the excavation trench to be placed precisely over the main features of interest with minimal disturbance to the site. The magnetometer survey also enabled the archaeological complexity of the buried deposits in Area 3 to be correctly anticipated, helping to ensure that sufficient time and resources were allocated to the task of exploring as fully as possible the relationships between the numerous features present.

Although the survey suggested that the archaeology in Area 3 was far from simple, it failed to reveal the full range of archaeological features present due to the complex superimposition of deposits (the result of the cumulative effect of over a 1000 years of activity lasting from the Early Iron Age to the late Roman period). The eastern of the three linear features was not clearly defined in the survey as it had been obliterated by later quarrying (the extent of which can be traced from the magnetometer survey). The surprise discovery of an Early to Middle Iron Age inhumation cemetery in the fill of this quarry feature could not be predicted from the survey. The western and central linear ditches, which both produced weak linear positive anomalies approximately 3 nT in magnitude, were largely undisturbed by later activity and had fills which were mainly a product of natural silting.

In addition to containing the ditches and quarry located by the geophysics, Area 3 was also notable for the discovery of a series of Roman structures including a corn-drying oven (constructed mainly of flint set in a daub/cob matrix), and the worn floor of a rectangular timber building (F431 and F409). None of these features could be recognized in the magnetometer data either before or – with the benefit of hindsight – after excavation. Although the corn-drying oven was a substantial structure (c.1 m deep, with a 1.35 m square stoking chamber) and part of the flue showed evidence of having been heavily fired, it was filled with collapsed flint superstructure and chalky soil and rubble material. The overall magnetization of the feature might therefore not be particu-larly high. This combined with the deep burial of the feature (when the magnetometer survey took place the main fired parts of the structure would have been at least a metre below the modern ground surface), could explain the failure to detect an appreciable magnetic anomaly from the oven.

When so many features without clearly contrasting magnetic properties are all superimposed or intercut as was the case in Area 3, it is asking a lot for a magnetometer to define individual features belonging to separate phases of activity. In most cases, the responses to discrete features are usually subsumed into the general jumbled mass of anomalous activity.

Mass specific topsoil magnetic susceptibility measurements from samples taken at 30 m intervals along a N–S transect through the middle of the northern two-thirds of the enclosure range from $45 – 59$ m^3/Kg x 10^{-8} across the enclosure ditches and $52 – 57$ m^3/Kg x 10^{-8} in the interior of the enclosure. The topsoil MS values from Suddern Farm are consistent with comparable readings obtained over enclosures A and B at New Buildings (Suddern Farm: Xlf ranges from $45 – 59$ m^3/Kg x 10^{-8}, mean 53.5, New Buildings: Xlf ranges from $37 – 65$ m^3/Kg x 10^{-8}, mean 48.77). Equivalent readings from Nettlebank Copse were around twice as high, and readings from Houghton Down were moderately higher (mean Xlf values of 120.56 and 62.17 m^3/Kg x 10^{-8} respectively).

Bibliography

ALBARELLA, U. 1995: Depressions on Sheep Horncores. *Journ. Archaeol. Sci.* 22, 699–704.

ARMITAGE, P.L. 1982: A system for ageing and sexing the horn cores of cattle from British post-medieval sites. In Wilson, B., Grigson, C. and Payne, S., *Ageing and Sexing Animal Bones from Archaeological Sites* (BAR 109: Oxford), 37–54.

ARMITAGE, P.L. and CLUTTON-BROCK, J. 1976: A system for classification and description of the horn cores of cattle from archaeological sites. *Journ. Archaeol. Sci.* 3, 329–48.

BAKER, J. and BROTHWELL, D. 1980: *Animal Diseases in Archaeology* (London).

BOURDILLON, J. and COY, J. 1980: The animal remains. In Holdsworth, P., *Excavations at Melbourne Street, Southampton, 1971–76* (CBA Res. Rep. 33: London), 79–121.

BROTHWELL, D., DOBNEY, K. and ERVYNCK, A. 1996: On the Causes of Perforations in Archaeological Domestic Cattle Skulls. *Int. Journ. Osteoarchaeology* 6, 471–87.

CLARK, A.J. and NICHOLS, J.F. 1960: Romano-British Farms south of the Hog's Back. *Surrey Archaeol. Collect.* 51, 29–56.

CLARKE, G. 1979: *Pre-Roman and Roman Winchester. Part II The Roman Cemetery at Lankhills* (Winchester Studies 3: Oxford).

CLUTTON-BROCK, J., DENNIS-BRYAN, K., ARMITAGE, P.L. and JEWELL, P.A. 1990: Osteology of the Soay sheep. *Bull. Brit. Mus. Nat. Hist. (Zoology)* 56, 1–56.

COY, J. 1984: The bird bones. In Cunliffe, B. 1984, 527–31.

CUNLIFFE, B. 1974: *Iron Age Communities in Britain* (1st edn.) (London).

CUNLIFFE, B. 1984: *Danebury. An Iron Age Hillfort in Hampshire. Vol. 1, The Excavations 1969–1978: The site; Vol. 2, The Excavations 1969–1978: The finds* (CBA Res. Rep. 52: London).

CUNLIFFE, B. 1990: Before Hillforts. *Oxford Journ. Archaeol.* 9, 323–36.

CUNLIFFE, B. 1995: *Danebury. An Iron Age Hillfort in Hampshire. Vol. 6, A hillfort community in perspective* (CBA Res. Rep. 102: York).

DOBNEY, K.M., JAQUES, S.D. and IRVING, B.G. 1996: *Of Butchers and Breeds* (Lincoln Archaeol. Stud. 5: Lincoln).

DRIESCH, A. VON DEN 1976: *A Guide to the Measurement of Animal Bones from Archaeological Sites* (Peabody Mus. Bull. 1: Harvard University).

DRIESCH, A. VON DEN and BOESSNECK, J.A. 1974: Kritische Anmerkungen zur Widerristhoheberech-nung aus Langemassen vor- und fruhgeschichtlicher Tierknochen. *Sauegetierkundliche Mitteilungen* 22, 325–48.

EWBANK, J.M., PHILLIPSON, D.E. and WHITEHOUSE, R.D., with HIGGS, E.S. 1964: Sheep in the Iron Age: a method of study. *Proc. Prehist. Soc.* 30, 423–6.

FULFORD, M.G. 1975: *New Forest Roman Pottery* (BAR 17: Oxford).

GODDARD, E.N., TRASK, P.D., DE FORD, R.K., ROVE, O.N., SINGEWALD, J.T. and OVERBECK, R.M. 1948: *Rock Color Chart* (Boulder, Colorado).

GODWIN, H. 1975: *The History of the British Flora* (2nd edn.) (Cambridge).

GRANT, A. 1975: The animal bones. In Cunliffe, B.W., *Excavations at Portchester Castle. Vol. I: Roman* (Soc. Antiq. Res. Rep. XXXII: London), 378–408.

GRANT, A. 1982: The use of tooth wear as a guide to the age of domestic animals. In Wilson, B., Grigson, C. and Payne, S., *Ageing and Sexing Animal Bones from Archaeological Sites* (BAR 109: Oxford), 91–108.

GRANT, A. 1984a: The animal husbandry. In Cunliffe, B. 1984, 496–548.

GRANT, A. 1991: Animal husbandry. In Cunliffe, B. and Poole, C., *Danebury. An Iron Age Hillfort in Hampshire. Vol. 5, The Excavations 1979–1988: The finds* (CBA Res. Rep. 73: London), 447–87.

HARCOURT, R.A. 1974: The dog in prehistoric and early historic Britain. *Journ. Archaeol. Sci.* 1.2, 151–76.

HAWKES, S.C., HOGARTH, A. and DENSTON, C. 1974: The Anglo-Saxon cemetery at Monkton, Thanet. *Arch. Cant.* 89, 49–89.

HILLMAN, G. 1984: Interpretation of archaeological plant remains: The application of ethnographic models from Turkey. In van Zeist, W. and Casparie, W.A. (eds.), *Plants and Ancient Man* (Rotterdam), 1–41.

INIZAN, M.-L., ROCHE, H. and TIXIER, J. 1992: *Technology of knapped stone* (CREP Meudon).

JONES, M. 1984: The plant remains. In Cunliffe, B. 1984, 483–95.

LEVINE, M.A. 1982: The use of crown height measure-ments and eruption-wear sequences to age horse teeth. In Wilson, B., Grigson, C. and Payne, S., *Ageing and Sexing Animal Bones from Archaeological Sites* (BAR 109: Oxford), 223–50.

LEVITAN, B. 1985: A methodology for recording the pathology and other anomalies of ungulate mandibles from archaeological sites. In Fieller, N.R.J., Gilbertson, D.D. and Ralph, N.G.A., *Palaeo-biological Investigations* (BAR Int. Ser. 266: Oxford), 41–54.

LYNE, M.A.B. and JEFFERIES, R.S. 1979: *The Alice Holt/Farnham Roman Pottery Industry* (CBA Res. Rep. 30).

PALMER, R. 1984: *Danebury: an Iron Age hillfort in Hampshire. An aerial photographic interpretation of its environs* (RCHM(E) Supp. Ser. 6: London).

PAYNE, S. 1973: Kill-off patterns in sheep and goats: the mandibles from Asvan Kale. *Anatolian Stud.* 23, 281–303.

PEACOCK, D.P.S. 1987: Iron Age and Roman quern production at Lodsworth, West Sussex. *Antiq. Journ.* 67, 61–85.

PEACOCK, D.P.S. and WILLIAMS, D.F. 1986: *Amphorae and the Roman Economy* (London).

PIGGOTT, S. 1949: Roman Burials at Middle Wallop. *Proc. Hants. Field Club and Archaeol. Soc.* 17, 60–3.

SERJEANTSON, D. 1991b: The bird bones. In Cunliffe, B. and Poole, C., *Danebury. An Iron Age Hillfort in Hampshire. Vol. 5, The Excavations 1979–1988: The finds* (CBA Res. Rep. 73: London), 479–81.

SPETH, J.D. 1983: *Bison kills and bone counts* (Chicago).

STEAD, I.M. 1991: *Iron Age Cemeteries in East Yorkshire* (Engl. Heritage Archaeol. Rep. 22: London).

TROTTER, M. and GLESER, G.C. 1952: Estimation of stature from long-bones of American Whites and Negroes. *American Journ. Physical Anthropol.* 10 (n.s.), 463–514.

TROTTER, M. and GLESER, G.C. 1958: A re-evaluation of estimation of stature based on measurements of stature taken during life and long-bones after death. *American Journ. Physical Anthropol.* 16 (n.s.), 79–123.

WEST, B. and ZHOU, B.-X. 1988: Did Chickens Go North? New Evidence for Domestication. *Journ. Archaeol. Sci.* 15, 515–33.